Closer Walk

Confessions of a U.S. Jesuit Yat

Donald L. Gelpi

Hamilton Books
A member of
The Rowman & Littlefield Publishing Group
Lanham • Boulder • New York • Toronto • Oxford

Copyright © 2006 by
Hamilton Books
4501 Forbes Boulevard
Suite 200
Lanham, Maryland 20706
Hamilton Books Acquisitions Department (301) 459-3366

PO Box 317
Oxford
OX2 9RU, UK

Library of Congress Control Number: 2006921363
ISBN-13: 978-0-7618-3404-5 (paperback : alk. paper)
ISBN-10: 0-7618-3404-4 (paperback : alk. paper)

Author's Preface

New Orleanians sometimes call themselves "yats." In *The Times Picayune* one commonly reads sports headlines which inform the world that several thousand yats attended some athletic event. The term "yat" derives from one of the many dialects of English which thrive in different neighborhoods of the Crescent City. The locals call the dialect in question the Ninth Ward (pronounced "Nint Wawd") Accent. A male Ninth Ward yat traditionally greets another member of the species with the question, "Where y'at, man?" Female Ninth Ward yats say, "Where y'at, dawlin'?"

Other aspects of he title and subtitle of this work may require clarification and contextualization. The title, "Closer Walk," comes from an old New Orleans spiritual, whose first two verses I cited at the conclusion of *The Firstborn of Many*, the foundational Christology I published with Marquette University Press in 2001. The spiritual enjoyed some popularity in the Catholic charismatic circles in which I moved. I here quote it in full:

> Just a closer walk with Thee,
> Grant it, Jesus, is my plea.
> Daily walking close to Thee,
> Let it be, dear Lord, let it be.
>
> I am weak, but Thou art strong.
> Jesus, keep me from all wrong.
> I'll be satisfied as long
> As I walk, let me walk, close to Thee.
>
> Through this world of toils and snares
> If I falter, Lord, who cares?
> Who with me my burden shares?
> None but Thee, dear Lord, none but Thee.

When my feeble life is o'er,
Times for me won't be no more.
Guide me gently, safely o'er
To Thy kingdom's shore, to Thy shore.

The chapters which follow offer an account of my closer walk with Jesus, insofar as I can honestly and fallibly reconstruct it. That walk would have never happened as it did unless I had decided, as a high school senior, to join the Society of Jesus. Becoming a Jesuit did not originally fit into my life plan. As the reader will see, I came from a medical family on my father's side and as a high-school senior had decided on a medical career and a family. I had a scholarship to enter Tulane University's pre-med program and had decided to my own satisfaction my vocational identity. I then began to have the horrible feeling that God was calling me to join the Jesuits. Having grown up in a predominantly Catholic city, I had imbibed a measure of the anti-clericalism that not uncommonly surfaces in clericalized Catholic environments. As a result, the prospect of becoming a religious priest held for me no personal allure whatsoever. I became a true Israelite, wrestled with God for several months, and finally gave up in sheer exhaustion. I yielded to the divine dinning, applied for the Jesuit novitiate, found myself accepted by the order. One cannot, of course, join a group of men who call themselves "The Society of Jesus" and mean it without experiencing a growing involvement with the person who gives Jesuits their name: namely, Jesus of Nazareth. So I began my novitiate in Grand Coteau, Louisiana in 1951 and embarked on my closer walk with Him.

My closer walk led me eventually to ambition a career as a theologian. As a consequence, I intend these reminiscences primarily but not exclusively as a theological autobiography. By that I mean that I hope to retell the story of my life with a focus on the kinds of experiences which have led me to develop the kind of theology I have to date formulated and published. Since my closer walk has prompted me to wander down some new and unfamiliar theological paths, I retell my story in the hope that it will assist those who find what I have written strange, puzzling, or just plain unintelligible, to understand how the system I have been creating evolved into the shape it currently exemplifies. I find the system sufficiently matured to warrant telling the story of its crafting. Observing the beast evolve may domesticate it more effectively in the minds of those who scratch their heads over my method, vocabulary, and overall approach to the question of theological inculturation.

The term "inculturation" derives from the term "culture." "Culture" entered civilized Western parlance in the nineteenth century and still remains one of the celebrated weasel words in almost any language. If "culture" qualifies as a weasel word, "inculturation," as the newcomer on the block, does so even more. A weasel word means so many things that one finds oneself hard put to pin down what exactly it *does* mean. In using a weasel word, one has, then, no other recourse, if, that is, one aspires to clarity, than to say what one chooses to mean by it. By culture, I mean anything in space and time conditioned by human communication.

One inculturates a religion by actualizing it in a particular context conditioned by human communication. Inculturated theology serves such an actualization. Inculturated theological thinking faces three fundamental challenges:

1) It needs to speak with an idiom commonly spoken in the culture it addresses. I have been attempting to develop an inculturated Catholic theology in and for the United States. Accordingly, I have tried to ground my theological system in classical and contemporary U.S. philosophy and theology. By reflecting on the dialectical development of the philosophical tradition in this country, I have attempted to derive from it a metaphysics of experience which undergirds a normative account of human and of Christian conversion.

2) A second challenge faces inculturated theological thinking. Since every human culture blends folly, wisdom, virtue, vice, sin, faith, and unbelief, the effective inculturation of a religion requires that it challenge the culture it addresses to renounce those aspects of its reality and tradition which contradict authentic conversion. I hold that conversion comes in five forms: affective, intellectual, personal moral, socio-political, and religious. I view Christian conversion as a species of religious conversion. Accordingly, a normative account of an integral, five-fold conversion needs to challenge personal and institutionalized neurosis and psychosis, personal and institutionalized mendacity and folly, personal and corporate vice and sin, and personal and institutionalized religious unbelief, apathy, and ideology.

3) In a religion of universal love which inserts one into a universal Church, inculturation can bring with it some sectarian risks. Narrow focus on a local culture can begin to function like a set of blinders. Accordingly, inculturated theological thinking in a universal Church needs to keep local cultures in effective dialogue with the Great Church, with its Great Tradition, and with other cultures than the particular culture one addresses most immediately. The accelerated internationalization of culture which marks the end of the twentieth century and the onset of the twenty-first makes responding to this third challenge particularly pressing. In what follows, then, I shall attempt to describe the experiences which led me to aspire to creating such a theology. I shall do so in the hope of helping others understand why I did what I did and of encouraging them, if they feel the inclination or call, to go and do likewise.

In this context, I should make it clear that, while I intend what follows as a theological autobiography, I shall present more than just the history of my mind, since that topic alone would, no doubt, leave most readers monumentally bored. I feel as though I have lived through an era of major changes in the Catholic Church and in this nation. I shall, therefore, in the narrative which follows include sufficient anecdotal detail to give the reader a feeling for the context of my life and for my own participation in some of the significant public events through which I have lived.

In the subtitle to this work, I call myself "a U.S. Jesuit Yat." "U.S." alerts the reader to the fact that as a theologian living in the United States, I have tried to come to terms with the impact of U.S. culture on myself and on others while pursuing theological inculturation in the three senses proposed above.

"US" has other connotations. My study of philosophy in the United States has alerted me to the fact that a significant prophetic strain in the U.S. tradition mounts a telling critique of American individualism and insists on the social, relational, communal character of human life and thought. This prophetic strain surfaced in the nineteenth and twentieth centuries in the Catholic Transcendentalism of Orestes Augustus Brownson, in the scientific theism of Francis Ellingwood Abbot, in the pragmatistic theism of Charles Sanders Peirce, in the absolute pragmatism of Josiah Royce, in John Dewey's political philosophy, and in Roberto Unger's rethinking of the philosophical presuppositions of the United States legal system, just to name some major contributors to this prophetic philosophical tradition.

The "US," then, in the subtitle of this autobiography has some of the connotations it had in a spoof of academic anthropology which appeared in the sixties entitled *The Weens*. The author described an imaginary anthropological excavation of the United States in, as I recall, the year 4,000. The report of the excavation explained why the people who lived in this country at the end of the twentieth century must have referred to themselves and "the Weens" because they always symbolized their nation with the pronoun "us." In calling myself "an US yat," I wish, therefore, to alert the reader to the fact that I endorse the prophetic strain in classical and contemporary American thought which subjects to radical critique the individualism which fragments culture in the United States in such destructive ways.

Community and communion within community rank high among the things I value and have significantly influenced the foundational theology of conversion I have developed. I began to learn about both sixty-nine years ago as a lad in New Orleans. In the pages which follow, I shall attempt to describe how that happened and how it fits in with the other pieces of my life and thought.

A colleague who read part of this manuscript urged me to alert the reader that the older I get the more inclined I feel to call some theological ideas true and others false. Theologians more politically correct than I as well as theologians who incline to fix their theological beliefs on the basis of subjective taste may find making such claims arrogant. If so, I beg to disagree. The historical and eschatological events which reveal the Christian God make theological theories true or false, not I. I stand ready to revise any claims of truth or falsity I make as soon as anyone can show me that the evidence I cite fails to prove or disprove my point. Besides, if theologians cannot verify some theological theories and falsify others, then theology is not worth studying, because, however interesting one finds a theological idea, if one lacks the means to verify it or falsify it, it remains speculatively trivial.

In calling the narrative which follows "confessions," I do not use the term in the same sense as *True Confessions Magazine*, which exposed salacious secrets of celebrities, but in an Augustinian sense. Augustine's *Confessions* bore witness to the victory of divine grace in his life. I recently celebrated my fiftieth jubilee as a Jesuit. Passing such a milestone in living invites one to take account of the course of one's life. In reflecting on the course of mine, I feel overwhelmed with its giftedness and with the abundance of graces which the Lord has granted me. I have not always used the gifts well or responded to the graces with the love and generosity they ought to have evoked. In what follows, I hope, however, to bear witness in some measure to more than half a century of divine gifts and graces finally too numerous to allow naming them all.

Moreover, as Augustine's *Confessions* unfold, they grow increasingly speculative and culminate in a prolonged meditation on the nature of time and memory. My own confessions follow a similar pattern and culminate in a summary statement of the theological system I have been constructing since I joined the faculty of the Jesuit School of Theology at Berkeley in 1973. The story which follows asserts, then, an intimate connection between my biography and my theology.

In the spirit of Augustine's *Confessions* and in the manner of the Ignatian meditation, I have composed for each of the following chapters a concluding prayer, or colloquy. Such a literary convention strikes me as appropriate in a work which meditates the gracing of my life. In the narrative which follows, I shall also call the third person of the Trinity the Holy Breath and shall imagine Her as the feminine face of God. I have explained why I indulge in this stylistic idiosyncracy elsewhere and will not repeat it here. Besides, the reader will find out why I employ such terminology in the narrative which follows.

Another circumstance helps explain why I have chosen to tell my story as I have. For many years both colleagues and students have been urging me to popularize the theological system I have been creating since 1973. I have attempted to respond to their exhortations. In *The Conversion Experience* I tried to reduce my theological anthropology and sacramental theology to a teachable popular text; and I am currently attempting to do the same thing with my Christology and trinitarian theology.

It occurred to me, however, that I could also popularize my theology by turning it into a story. This I seek to do in the pages which follow. Growing up in the New Orleans of the thirties and forties shaped in very significant ways my adult theological perceptions. So did my education as a Jesuit. In the chapters which deal with my years of graduate study at Fordham University and of teaching philosophy at Loyola University in New Orleans, I describe how my studies of the United States philosophical tradition transformed the way I look at the world and at God. My involvement in the Catholic Charismatic Renewal confronted me with a discombobulating and unexpected religious and theological agenda. In the early stages of trying to think theology in a systematic way, I found myself wrestling with methodological issues. My involvement with the John Courtney Murray Group, a post-doctoral research seminar in theological inculturation with whom I work every summer provided me with my closest dialogue partners and colleagues; but the many friends, students, and colleagues I claimed at the Jesuit School of Theology in Berkeley of necessity all contributed enormously to my ongoing theological re-education. Since, however, in Berkeley I lived increasingly in the world of ideas I was in process of creating, those ideas play an important role in the final three chapters of this work. To all the good and wonderful people who have graced my life and professional career and who people the pages which follow, I owe the deepest debt of gratitude. I owe a special debt of gratitude to Nate Hinerman for the time, care, and kindness he expended on formatting this text.

Colloquy:

Divine Breathing,
Holy Wisdom,
All-Creator and All-Encompasser,
Dream Catcher,
Memory Gatherer,
Sower and Harvester of Hearts,
> *enlighten my mind with keen eyes,,*
> *my memory with shrewd perception,*
> *my conscience with true vision,*
> *my heart with tender compassion*
>> *to see clearly the persons I have loved,*
>> *to retrace unflinchingly the paths*
>>> *down which you have led me*
>>>> *so gently,*
>>>> *so lovingly.*

Help me to discern and to describe
 Your Presence
   in all of its shifting forms and
   permutations.
May the gift of memory
 swell the gift of love,
    gratitude,
    and praise.

Donald L. Gelpi, S.J.

The Jesuit School of Theology at Berkeley

Chapter One

I Become A YAT

On May 30, 1934, as the morning angelus chimed in the steeples of New Orleans, I hung by my feet, naked and upside down, from the hand of my grand uncle Maurice Gelpi in a delivery room of Hotel Dieu. I was protesting vociferously the indignities he had just taken with my derriere. Like all the offspring of Adam and Eve, I drew my first breath in rage.

I did not know it at the time, but I had a brother, Albert Jr., about three years older than myself. Both my parents came from rather large families, with my father's family, the Gelpis, outnumbering the Delaups, my mother's clan. In both families, we called grandmothers "memere" and grandfathers "pepere." "Memere" derives from French, the language of the Creole families of New Orleans. "Memere" elided "ma mere (my mother)" into a single word; and "pepere" seems to have resulted from replacing the "m's" in "memere" with "p's." Pepere Gelpi, surnamed Paul, died before I saw the light. So I knew him mostly through family folklore. He and Memere Gelpi had nine children: Paul, Robley, Clarence, John, Albert (my father), Sidney, Marie, Paola, and Coco. Memere and Pepere Delaup had five. If the Gelpis tended to specialize in boys, the Delaups tended to specialize in girls: Delphine, Hilda, Alice (my mother), Lydia (whom we called Nookie), and Alfred.

Pepere Gelpi ranked among the top surgeons in New Orleans and had invented a surgical instrument still in use today and called a Gelpi, pronounced with a hard "g." The medical profession never did learn to pronounce the family name correctly. Many people suppose Gelpi an Italian name. In fact the family has its roots in Catalonia. Pepere Gelpi had maintained, against the skepticism of the rest of the family, the existence of a family seat, a castle or manor, not far from Barcelona. The family began to take the story seriously only in the early 1970s, when I was teaching philosophy at Loyola University

1

The Dr. Paul Gelpi clan on vacation.

in New Orleans. My Uncle Sidney had gone shopping on Canal Street and was waiting in line to pay for his purchase. The man in front of him spoke with a slight accent, charged his purchase, and signed the charge slip with the name "Gelpi." Sidney introduced himself and learned that the gentleman came from a little seaside town in Spain called Vilasar del Mar not far from Barcelona. "My father," Sidney said, "always claimed that a castle Gelpi stood not far from Barcelona, but we never believed him." "It's true," the foreign Gelpi replied. "I own it."

To date, I myself have never seen the family seat, nor has my brother. But my cousin Jimmy, one of Sidney's sons, has visited the place and claims that extensive records of the family genealogy survive in the local parish church. I have never interested myself in tracing genealogies; but, when I taught at Loyola University in the late sixties and early seventies, Hacker Fagot, S.J., who has one of the truly memorable names in the New Orleans Province of the Society of Jesus, did trace his family tree. He informed me at the time that the name Gelpi surfaced early in the colonial records, although I do not know exactly when the first Gelpi arrived in Louisiana.

Catalonian descent marked the Gelpi physiognomy. Once, when my brother taught American literature at Harvard University, he attended a cocktail party. He noticed a man across the room staring fixedly at him. After a while, the man noticed that my brother had noticed his rude stare and crossed the room to apologize. "Please forgive me," he said. "I have been staring rudely at you; but you must understand. It's those bumps on your forehead!

Those bumps! I'm an anthropologist; and we only find bumps like that on skulls dug up around Barcelona." Ever since then we refer to the family bumps. I have them; and my brother has bequeathed them to my nephew, Christopher and to my niece, Adrienne.

My mother's family decided to migrate to Louisiana somewhat more tardily than did the Gelpis. The first Delaup arrived in New Orleans in the latter half of the nineteenth century from the Carribean where he owned a plantation. It appears that a slave uprising persuaded him to find some other form of financial support. In New Orleans he supposedly began publishing a French newspaper. I say supposedly because I know these things only by family hearsay.

When my father was growing up, the Gelpi clan lived in a large, three-story house on Esplanade Avenue not far from where I grew up on Bayou Road in New Orleans. Mansions lined both sides of Esplanade Avenue. The fact that the Gelpi's house stood among the other imposing homes on that street put them in a economic and social bracket higher than the Delaups. I never saw the interior of the Gelpi house; but the Esplanade bus which took us from Bayou Road to Canal Street and back always passed it. When it did, I knew that our stop to get off came next.

This knowledge helped motivate a major gefluffel in my childhood. At about the age of six, I was attending the birthday party of one of the children in the neighborhood. The celebration, in addition to the traditional cake and ice cream, consisted in attending a movie at the Sanger Theater near Canal Street. The mother of the birthday child apparently had no interest in seeing the movie (I forget its title). She dropped us off at the theater, returned home, took a nap, and slept far beyond the time she was supposed to pick us children up. After the movie ended, we killed time in the vestibule of the theater. After an hour of twiddling my thumbs, I got more than bored. I knew where on Canal Street to catch the Esplanade bus that would get me home. My mother had given me a little money, more than enough for bus fare; and I knew that by recognizing the old Gelpi house, I could get off at the right stop. I astonished my mother by showing up all by myself at the front door. She found the entire incident less than amusing; and, I suspect, she let the delinquent mother know about it.

The Gelpis lost heavily in the stock market crash of the twenties. They sold the house on Esplanade in order to help pay their debts. As a result, by the time I came along Memere Gelpi had moved uptown. We visited Memere Gelpi a few times every year; but we had more frequent contact with Memere and Pepere Delaup, who lived at 1924 Bayou Road, catacorner from our own house. For some reason, my brother and I dreaded visiting Memere Gelpi. As soon as our car made the turn into her street, we both would set up a wail. Perhaps, as young children we found visiting the elderly boring. Memere Gelpi for her part never received us with anything but love, graciousness, and good humor. She had a trick knee which she kept always bound in an ace bandage. As a result, she did not move around a lot when we visited her. I remember her, however, as a woman who, like all the members of the Gelpi family, and indeed like most citizens of New Orleans, loved good food, family reunions, parties, and celebrations.

I knew Pepere Gelpi only through the Gelpi family oral tradition. The patriarch of an old, established, Creole family, he moved easily in the upper echelons of New Orleans society. My father told stories of chauffeuring him to the various clubs to which he belonged, where I gather he had the reputation for playing a mean game of pinochle. One year, five different Mardi Gras krewes elected him king of their parade and ball. As I have already indicated, Pepere Gelpi achieved eminence as a surgeon. Not only did he invent the Gelpi; but, according to the family oral tradition, he once sewed back together a male penis that had somehow got sliced in two. Moreover, he did so so expertly that the organ thereafter remained fully functional.

He seems to have ruled over his boisterous brood like a Victorian papa. My father told me that when one of the boys ignored paternal warnings about excessively obstreperous behavior at the dinner table, Pepere Gelpi would rise, pick up a pitcher of ice water, and dump it on the child. This of course had a dampening effect on an excess of animal spirits; but it also indicated that, for this particular scion of the Gelpi family, dinner had ended. Presumably, the servants cleaned up the mess.

One endearing story about Pepere Gelpi makes it clear that he had a genuine fondness for a liqueur called Cherry Bounce which the Gelpis brewed at home. I tried many times to get a detailed recipe for Cherry Bounce; but I never succeeded. So I guess that I will never taste it. I do know, however, that one began its fermentation by filling a jar with Maraschino cherries and then drowning them in bourbon. Family legend has it that the fermented result had a memorable kick and that the intoxicating consequences of eating one of the cherries resembled an earthquake. Shortly before Pepere Gelpi died, the physician attending him told Memere Gelpi that he had about three days to live (a fact that Pepere Gelpi, given his expertise as a doctor, surely already knew) and that she should give him anything he wanted. When she told him that he could have whatever he desired, he asked for a glass of Cherry Bounce. That kind of dying wish suggests that my father learned his exuberant love of life in no small measure from his own father.

I came to imagine the Gelpi side of the family as its liquor-drinking, food-eating branch, even though as good New Orleanians, the Delaups too enjoyed good food, parties, and celebrations. Moreover, as we shall see, when it came to family reunions the Delaups belonged in a class by themselves. In contrast to the boisterous Gelpis, however, Memere Delaup, Mother, Nanny, and Nookie all teatotaled, although Pepere Delaup allowed himself a glass of sherry every day just before supper in the evening. The rowdiness of the Gelpi boys of my father's generation also made the Delaup household seem by comparison primly Victorian.

I think, however, that my image of the Gelpi side of the family probably derives in no small measure from stories about the Gelpi family reunions which happened regularly twice a year. At the first reunion, the entire family attended, including the children and grandchildren. In those days no one acted as a designated driver. As a consequence, the adults celebrated with the expectation that they would remain sufficiently sober on the trip home not to slaughter the upcoming generation. Only adults attended the second reunion and felt free to party with more enthusiasm.

After one such adult reunion, my Aunt Marie, who at that time had attained notable girth, was feeling no pain as she made her way back to her car. She slipped on the walk in front of the house and, though unhurt, seemed unable to rise on her own power. My Uncle John, who probably weighed one hundred and twenty pounds dripping wet, noticed Marie's plight and went out to assist her. However manfully he tried, he lacked the strength to get her back on her feet. The rest of the family noticed his efforts through the window. They immediately rushed outside, not to help John get Marie upright, but in order to watch him fail and to enhance his efforts with ongoing laughter and commentary.

Memere and Pepere Delaup lived on Bayou Road in an historic, two-story house which stood on brick stilts. Bayou Road counted among the oldest streets in New Orleans because it linked the original colonial city, now the Vieux Carré, to Bayou St. John which rises from underground not far from Lake Pontchartrain. The street retraced an old Indian path.

In 1853, Aimé Gautier built the house in which the Delaup family lived. In the history of New Orleans architecture, it goes by the name Gautier Villa, although we just called in 1924 Bayou Road. The old residence had seen better days and in my childhood stood in a working class neighborhood of black and white families. The house had high ceilings and heavily shuttered windows as defense against the sizzling New Orleans summers. It had no air conditioning and no central heating. Instead, it had fireplaces in all the major rooms. Various types of stoves warmed the smaller rooms which needed heating in the winter. During the winter months, you could have kept vegetables in the frigid hallway. The brick stilts which elevated the house served two purposes. First, they raised the house above the dampness of the earth. (Much of New Orleans rests on drained swamps.) Second, the space under the house also provided a place to store the coal we burned in the fireplaces. As a child, on Sunday afternoons, I used to love sitting in front of the crackling fires reading books.

The Delaup house had a capacious back yard shaded by the branches of an enormous pecan tree which grew in the yard of the family next door. We would harvest all the nuts which fell into our yard every fall. We children also harvested the eggs from the chicken coop, an appendix to the main yard, where my Uncle Alfred kept chickens. The rooster who ruled the coop hated us children with a savage intensity and immediately attacked us every time we ventured into his territory to harvest the eggs. It did nothing to improve relations between us and the rooster that we always took a croquet mallet with us into the coop to protect ourselves from his depredations. A smart whack with the mallet always discouraged him sufficiently to allow us to collect the eggs. The whack did nothing to improve the rooster's temper and went far to explain the single-minded hatred for us which rankled in that roosterly breast.

Pepere Delaup worked as a traveling salesman. He sold goods wholesale in Louisiana and neighboring states. Since he, like me, never learned to drive, he had a chauffeur, a *café-au-lait*-colored Black man named Lionel. I re-

Memere Delaup on the porch of Gauthier Villa.

member Pepere Delaup most vividly as a quiet man who loved to while away the evenings playing solitaire or, in his later years, listening to religious preachers on the radio.

The Delaup residence had five bays and a wide front porch lined with rocking chairs for sitting, chatting, and visiting with the neighbors, who in pre-television days spent warm evenings on their houses' stoops and porches actually enjoying human conversation. Since the house stood on brick stilts, one ascended to the front porch via a wide stair. Greek medallions and a dentiled cornice ornamented the entrance, which led to a wide center hall. Memere and Pepere Delaup occupied the rooms on the left of the hallway. My aunt Lydia, whom we called "Nookie," her husband Leo Hare, and her two sons Kenny and Danny occupied the first large room to the right of the entrance. Pepere Delaup's spinster sister, whom we called "Nana," had a room next to theirs. Beyond Nana's room lay the dining room, which held a huge, expandable table with carved, clawed feet that at full capacity seemed to fill the room. Beyond the dining room an ample kitchen protruded from an otherwise square house and gave the back porch an L shape. My Aunt Delphine,

The author making mud pies in Memere Delaup's big back yard.

also a spinster whom we called "Nanny," had a second-floor room next to a large attic-like area. Nanny's room gave onto a cast-iron balcony and a dentiled overhang. During World War II, the Albert Gelpi family–my father and mother, my brother Albert and myself–for three years of hard times lived in the attic area where, somehow we made do. Nanny had her own bathroom, which no one else could use. The rest of the family took turns with the other remaining bathroom.

Housing that much extended family in one house brought with it its understandable human challenges and tensions. Nanny had deep love and great goodness within her. During World War II she worked as a nurse's aide, but eventually she settled into clerical work. She had a few flirtations, but they never eventuated in marriage. Deeply religious and with a propensity for scrupulosity, she had very particular and unrevisable opinions about many things and especially about what she could and could not eat. Memere Delaup prepared her dinners for her in a daily, loving attempt to please her; but Memere, despite her culinary wizardry, did not always succeed. We all sensed a tension between Nana and Memere Delaup. Nookie had a sweetness and evenness of temper that seemed to make her unflappable. Her steady love and sense of humor helped stabilize the household; but when Leo got drafted

The Delaups: from left to right: Pepere Delaup, Memere Delaup, Lydia (Nookie), Delphine (Nanny).

during World War II and shipped to Europe, she grieved. I remember her taking her son Kenny, my brother, and myself to see war movies through which she wept quietly in her seat. Leo, always a quiet man, returned from the war even more withdrawn than when he left. He spoke of his war experiences almost never; but, from a few hints at some of the horrors he had seen, I sensed that the war had scarred him psychically, though not physically. Pepere Delaup, until he retired, spent everything but the weekend drumming wholesale goods to rural clients. As a very small child, I had no sense of these human tensions; but I became more aware of them as I matured. As I look back on life in 1924 Bayou Road, it seems to me that one major force bound it together and kept it functioning: the formidable love, the will, and the determination of Memere Delaup.

Though physically small, Memere Delaup bequeathed to my mother her enormous strength of will; and Mother bequeathed it to me. Her matriarchal, single-minded love of her family gathered the Delaup clan around her every Sunday in a weekly family reunion. You could have rubricized those weekly gatherings. The same families arrived at the same time every Sunday. Since our family lived across Bayou Road from the Delaup House, we just crossed the street on returning from Sunday Mass, so that we always arrived first. My Uncle Alfred Delaup and his wife Alberta usually arrived next with their two children, Jeanne and Alfred Jr. (In his younger years the family called Alfred Jr. "Brother Boo" or just plain "Boo.") My Aunt Hilda had married Leonard Nelson. The Nelsons always arrived last with their two daughters, Loyce and Karen, and with their son, Lenny. I always looked forward to Aunt Hilda's stories of the hair-raising tragedies which seemed for some reason to erupt in her neighborhood on a weekly basis.

On arriving, the uncles and uncles-in-law gathered in the front room of the house to talk man talk, while the aunts and Memere descended on the kitchen to complete the preparation of the mammoth mid-day dinner which divided those reunions temporally. The adults and children old enough to earn a seat with the adults all sat around the enormous, expandable dining room table, while the children who had not come of gustatory age ate in the kitchen or at a card table in the corner of the dining room. The children who rated sitting at the big table always jockeyed for the seats in the middle on either side. There lay the moveable leaves which expanded the table. A sharp, covert blow to one of those leaves successfully spilled soup onto the cousin sitting opposite.

After the dinner clean up, we moved on to the second half of the reunion. The adults gathered on the back porch to watch the children play in the back yard. Often we made ice cream with a hand churn and salted ice. As a child I used to love to rove the old house. I joined my brother and my cousins playing Flash Gordon underneath the dining room table which obligingly transformed itself into a space ship. During quieter winter afternoons, I curled up with a book in front of one of the fireplaces. I reread the books I really liked. I read *The Yearling*, Marjorie Kinnan Rawlings's poignant tale of coming of age in a Florida scrub forest, at least five times.

As a result of these weekly Delaup family gatherings, I grew up not only with my brother but also with all my Delaup cousins. The Gelpis too had a very strong family ethos and powerful sense of the importance of extended family, which my father had also interiorized; but those weekly Delaup reunions endowed the extended family with something akin to a religious aura. Small children absorb as though by osmosis the attitudes and values of the communities that nurture them. The Delaup reunions and to some extent the Gelpi clan whom I knew more distantly inculcated a single and simple ethos: Family and Family and Family and not just Family but Extended Family. That ethos would shape in significant ways my sense of the Society of Jesus as my extended religious family. Imagining the Church as extended family came as though by second nature as did imagining the Trinity as a divine family. I am not suggesting that these childhood experiences either verified or validated theological positions I developed later; but they did help sensitize me to sometimes overlooked theological possibilities in the Scriptures and in Christian tradition.

Those early family experiences had other consequences for my evolution as a theologian. My brother Al married Barbara Charlesworth. They met in Cambridge when Al was studying American literature with Perry Miller, the father of American Studies, and Barbara was studying English literature with the distinguished Victorian scholar, Walter Jackson Bate. Al and Barbara's courtship lasted well beyond graduate school. I got ordained the year before they wed. As a result, their wedding proved the first one I witnessed after ordination.

At the time of the wedding, Al taught at Harvard; and Barbara had taught first at the University of California at Santa Barbara and then at Brandeis University, until the birth of their son, Christopher. In 1968, they moved to Stanford which alone had offered them something remotely akin to a joint academic appointment. Stanford offered Al full professorship with tenure and Barbara a lectureship. My father died young just before turning fifty-two. In 1973, my mother, who lived longer as a widow than as a wife, joined Al and Barbara, both now working full-time while scrambling to raise two children, Christopher and his sister, Adrienne. Imbued with the same passionate commitment to family as Memere Delaup, Mother abandoned her roots in New Orleans, which sank very deep indeed, and came to California in order to or-

Albert and Barbara Gelpi and their son Christopher
shortly after their arrival at Stanford University.

der to help two harried professors with keeping the house and with raising
their two small children; but , I feel certain, she also came to Stanford because
it would keep her immediate family together. As Mother hoped, about six
months after she came to live with my brother's family, I joined the Jesuit
School of Theology in Berkeley. When I arrived in Berkeley, then, the rest of
my immediate family all lived in the San Francisco Bay area.

While I am jumping ahead, I mention these things here because they concern the impact of early family experiences on the way in which my own
thought has developed. By different routes, both my brother Al and I had developed a passionate interest in understanding culture in the United States. Al
approached U.S. culture through American literature and especially through
American poetry. I did it through philosophy and theology. Over the years we
have taught one another much about our respective fields. We also both became fascinated with the parallels one finds in the development of American
poetry, philosophy, and art. Barbara, my sister-in-law, made feminists of
both of Al and me. Her fascination with ideas and her ability to see religious
realities with unflinching honesty has borne fruit both in endless discussions,

theological and otherwise, and in a deep personal and professional friendship. Her critical read of various manuscripts of mine I have found always constructive and on target.

While my mother lived with Al and Barbara, I tried to visit them every weekend and continue the practice since my mother's death. With time, even my mother and I became good friends, to the extent that a parental relationship can allow friendship. If my immediate and extended family had not bred into me a deep commitment to family as such, I wonder if I would have found within my own family the kind of formative intellectual friendships which color much of the way I think. I suspect not.

Initially, Memere Delaup did not approve of my mother's wedding with my father. That fact needs some explaining. The Gelpi boys ran in a pack. Memere Gelpi seemed to have had a high degree of tolerance for youthful high jinks. She seems to have understood instinctively Karl Menninger's principle of child rearing: namely, that in childhood, children should be bad and parents should be good. The Gelpi boys did not do anything malicious or mean spirited; but they would regularly construct what they called stink bombs, go watch a movie, light the stink bomb after the movie had ended, and then stand across the street and watch the movie house empty out as the noisome fumes from their bomb filled the theater. Once, they built a makeshift airplane and came within an ace of pushing it off the roof of their three-story house with my uncle John inside. They made a pact that they would all attend the same high school. Unfortunately, when they matriculated into a new high school, with the passage of time one of them would with moral inevitability commit an infraction of discipline serious enough to get him expelled. When that happened, the other Gelpi brothers would get themselves expelled too so that they could all go to the same school. Since they got themselves successfully expelled from most high schools in New Orleans and since the family fortune evaporated with the Crash, the medical tradition of the Gelpi family ended with my father's generation.

All this boisterous rowdiness offended a Delaup sense of the fitting and gave Memere Delaup initial reservations about the advisability of her daughter Alice marrying Albert Gelpi. Shortly thereafter my father did something which only made the situation worse. Memere Delaup threw a watermelon party in her ample back yard. It did not help my father's courtship chances when the Gelpi boys, shortly after their arrival at the festivities, turned the watermelon party into a watermelon fight. Memere Delaup would have none of that. Like a true steel magnolia, she waded into the melee to put an immediate end to it. Unintentionally, Albert hit her in the face with a piece of watermelon rind. I do not know how he overcame that and other handicaps; but eventually love won out, and he secured a Delaup blessing on his and Alice's union.

My brother and I called our father "Daddy." As children, he awed, perhaps even baffled us, for some reason neither of us has ever fully understood. He never laid a hand to us or acted in any way aggressively. He loved us, worked very hard to get the best for us, and always wanted us to feel free to make our own life choices. Indeed, he worked so hard for us just to keep us above the poverty line that we did not see him as much as he would have preferred. I suspect that his considerable animal spirits made him seem to us somehow bigger than life, the incarnation of a life force that exceeded our youthful coping mechanisms. My father loved life passionately, loved to celebrate life, and did so with manifest gusto and relish. He loved to play with small children and did so regularly at our Delaup family reunions; but my brother and I usually held back from his rough and tumble games. He laughed a lot and had a great booming laugh that exploded from deep within him.

Daddy retained his love of life to the end, even though life did not always treat him kindly. He came from a formerly well-to-do family but began creating his own family at the moment the family fortune evaporated and the Great Depression settled in. My brother still has a small bronze statue of Napoleon which used to stand in the old Gelpi home. Before the family sold off other possessions to meet financial obligations in the wake of the Crash, each of the children had the opportunity to select one thing from the old house to keep as a memento of happier days. Daddy claimed the miniature Napoleon.

Daddy had boundless admiration for FDR, whom he regarded as the nation's savior. He held a white collar job until the onset of World War II; but he spent the duration of the war in the New Orleans shipyards helping to construct the U.S. wartime navy. Insufficient wages during the war years brought hard times to him and to our family. It forced us to migrate from our house on Bayou Road to the attic of 1924 Bayou Road. After the war, we rented a different house, this one a smaller shot-gun[1] structure, about half a block from the Delaup residence on Barracks Street and behind a Black bar called *The House of Joy*.

In the wake of the war, Daddy and his brothers Sydney and Clarence pooled their financial resources and bought out Manuel's Hot Tamale Company, a failing street vending business which they established on a solid financial basis. Eventually, they expanded their business enterprise into the Fiesta Hot Tamale Company, which also canned tamales, chile, and hot dogs and chile. By the time I approached high school, Daddy and mother had prospered enough to build a modest, one-story home on Vermillion Boulevard, one block off Elysian Fields and about six blocks from Lake Pontchartrain.

Daddy died in his sleep on July 21, 1959 just before turning fifty-two. About six months before, he began coughing blood. The doctor told him he had a ruptured vein in his throat. The prescribed treatment made the blood disappear; but a few weeks later the bleeding began again. Daddy had Hodgkin's disease, an ultimately fatal illness, more common in men than in women. At the time, I lived and taught as a scholastic at Jesuit high school in New Orleans. In my visits home every weekend of Daddy's final illness, he grew gradually but palpably weaker. He knew he was dying; and, although he did not speak a lot, I had the sense that, in those final months, he was looking back over the life he had lived and was blessing it with a great "Yes."

Both Al and I have a vivid memory of the mournful celebration of Al's birthday a few days before Daddy died. We had a very modest party for Al at home and within the immediate family. Daddy, who had by then grown quite weak, insisted on leaving his bed and coming to the dining room table where we were having cake and ice cream. I can still see him vividly in my memory sitting at the head of the table and singing Happy Birthday in a rasping voice. The disease had begun to affect his vocal cords. He died as he lived, celebrating the life he so passionately loved and had so passionately lived. He slipped quietly away in his sleep, probably because of a heart attack. When my mother woke on the morning of July 21, he lay dead in the bed beside her.

She continued to love him for the rest of her life. When she died at the age of eighty-nine, she asked us as one of her last wishes to attach her wedding ring to the chain around her neck. Arthritis had swollen her knuckles to the point that she could no longer wear it on her fingers; but she wanted it on her when she died. She took it with her into her grave, which lies in New Orleans next to Daddy's in the St. Louis Cemetery # 2 across Bayou St. John from the entrance to City Park.

As a young woman, Mother went to normal school and got certified to teach. She taught until Al came. Then she took a break in her teaching career until both of us reached high-school age. Until she retired from teaching at the age of sixty-five, Mother taught second and third grades, first in our parish school, then in the public school system. She took early retirement when violence began to penetrate even the grammar schools of New Orleans.

Mother retired the first time in order to raise and teach her own children. Anything I studied at an early age remains a blur. I suspect that the elementary things one learns at the beginning of life become so seemingly second nature that one forgets how one learned them. I do, however, remember Mother teaching us the French alphabet. My great grandparents had punished Memere Delaup if she spoke English at home. They regarded English as a street language. One spoke only French in the home. My mother grew up bilingual. I finally had to go to Quebec in order to learn how to speak French before I went to Belgium for my theological studies. As children, Al and I never got beyond the French alphabet. It helped later, however, with pronunciation. I used to love to say the last three letters: "eeks, eegrek, zed."

I do, however, have first-hand evidence of how Mother must have taught us as small children. When she came to live with my brother and his wife at Stanford, Adrienne, my niece, had at that point celebrated her second birthday; but my mother came to Stanford prepared to teach her. She brought all the reading text books she had accumulated over the years and began, as soon as she could get Adrienne's attention, to teach her to read. As I recall, Adrienne was doing second-grade readers before she went to kindergarten. I have no doubt that Mother did the same with Al and me. I feel certain that I owed my early bookishness to her tutelage. I loved to read and did so at every opportunity.

Mother also taught us to interiorize high standards in whatever we did, but especially in whatever we did with our minds. I can remember her telling us over and over again, "If you do something, do it right." "Right" meant no sloughing off, no half-way effort. Nothing met her standards except the best that one could do.

Did Mother's constant insistence on high standards help account for my anxiety as a child? If it did, I feel sure she did not intend that result. Our precarious financial situation could have fed the anxiety, as could human tensions in the extended family. I did for some reason feel anxiety. I bit my nails and had a recurring anxiety dream. I dreamed that I was flying around Memere Delaup's back yard in endless circles pursued by a giant black bird who sought to devour me. I could keep ahead of the giant crow but could not escape it.

Anxiety remains my most deeply disordered passion; but it has, I suspect, also helped shape the way I think. In an account of conscience[2] to Frank Houdek, S.J., the then rector of the Jesuit community in Berkeley, he surprised me by asking if I felt a lot of anxiety. I told him that anxiety remained my perennial *bête noire* and then asked him why he wanted to know. "Oh," he said, "I just read an article which says that psychological studies tend to show that creative people experience anxiety and that high anxiety often accompanies seasons of creativity." If so, I fit the pattern.

Anxiety has it drawbacks too, however. In religious matters, it bred in me a Pelagian perfectionism which I have spent a lifetime trying to unlearn. That same perfectionism transformed me very early into a law-and-order Catholic. When I joined the Society of Jesus, I also became a law-and-order Jesuit. Relating to God on God's terms came hard. Anxiety made it hard for me to trust God fully. I wanted to nail my relationship to him down, to control it; and unlearning that folly would cost me an enormous amount of personal pain. In the end, however, I inflicted it all on myself. I do not blame God for it. Nor do I blame Mother's inculcation of high intellectual standards. I myself transformed "doing it right" into a form of religious folly which would shackle me for many years; but You, Lord, dealt with me with infinite, loving patience.

I do not remember my mother as an especially verbal person. She showed her love in deeds rather than in words. She always had to have what she called her "projects." Her projects meant doing some kindness for someone else: frequently for some member of the immediate or extended family but often too for the needy. In her old age, she was constantly knitting woolen caps for the homeless, caps which her parish in Palo Alto distributed to the street people. She had originally taught herself to knit, I suspect, as a money-saving device. During my childhood, we had to scrimp to get by; and sweaters knitted at home cost a lot less than those in the stores. For the same frugal reason, I believe, she used to cut the family's hair.

Mother loved to cook for other people. She had learned Memere Delaup's best recipes as an apprentice. I can never remember Memere Delaup using a cook book. As she got on in years, I asked her to write down her recipes so that I could use them when I cooked. She did; but I never used them. She listed clearly all the ingredients and told me what to do with them; but, when it came to quantities, she lapsed into vagueness. She recommended "a pinch

The Albert Gelpi family.

of this" or "enough of that." She assumed that I had her culinary instincts, alas, erroneously.

My mother did. Her cuisine reached legendary proportions even in a family of capable Creole chefs. When my nephew Christopher married, his wife, Janet, who knew Christopher loved Mother's cooking, asked her to write down her recipes. She did so and included the quantities. When Adrienne got engaged, Janet typed up Mother's recipes and gave Adrienne a little cookbooklet entitled *Alice's Creole Kitchen*. When my cousins in New Orleans got wind of its existence, *Alice's Creole Kitchen* went through multiple editions. My mother viewed her cooking as a labor of love and cooked hundreds of meals for the rest of us even after her own aging stomach kept her from eating them. She communicated to me and my brother a love of good food and a love of cooking. As my life became more and more focused on writing and research, I used to say that, of all the things I did, only cooking and needlepoint had any visible consequence.

My mother had a sense of humor and expressed it from time to time in the gifts she gave. Every Valentine's Day she gave the adult males of the family drawers covered with red hearts and festooned with a Cupid. When she decided that my nephew Christopher had come of age, she included him in her Valentine gift. I can still see Christopher holding for the first time the heart-bespeckled drawers in his hand, laughing, and shaking his head in mild disbelief.

I remember both my parents as people of deep faith. When Al and I were growing up, they took us every Sunday to mass. They scrimped to put both of us through Catholic schools. They did not, however, receive communion. The older I got the more this troubled me. I never pried into their motives for refraining from communion. I remember Daddy saying once, however, that their behavior had something to do with something a priest had said to him, something that he had found insulting and infuriating. Although I never heard anything further, I suspect that it probably had something to do with the economic difficulties of raising a family during the Depression and with using birth control in order to keep the size of our family from driving us into the poor house. If so, then clericalism, Catholic moral rigorism, and legalism all reared their ugly heads early in our immediate family circle.

In my teens, I can remember praying fervently that Mother and Daddy would return to the sacraments; and eventually they did. When they did return, they both did it with enthusiasm. My mother eventually became a daily communicant; and Daddy, like my uncle Robley and his sons, made regular retreats at Manresa, the Jesuit retreat house in Convent, Louisiana. Later, while I lived in the Jesuit novitiate at Grand Coteau, Louisiana, Daddy told me that my faith had eased his way back to the sacraments. That surprised me, because I did not see myself as especially pious or gifted with faith. In high school, I had studiously avoided joining the Sodality, which struck me as religiously goody-goody. In my junior year at Jesuit High School, I did go to daily mass and receive communion during lunch time; but I had a salient anti-clerical streak in me. I certainly did not plan on joining the Society of Jesus or even find the prospect attractive. At first I felt that God had dragooned me into joining the order.

My parents conscientiously saw to it that I grew up Catholic. I did like the smells and bells of Catholic liturgical worship and loved to belt out *Holy God We Praise Thy Name* and *Tantum ergo* in church; but extremely pious people of my own age gave me the willies. I did not cultivate them as my friends. And so, I come in these reminiscences to my first experience of Church and of the way that experience shaped me in my early years.

During my years of teaching at the Jesuit School of Theology in Berkeley, I had the great good fortune to work with John Markey, O.P., a Southern Dominican. A native of Texas, John did both his M. Div. and his doctorate in theology at the Graduate Theological Union to which both our Jesuit school and the Dominican School of Philosophy and Theology belong. In completing his M.Div. degree, John did CPE[3] training in New Orleans. He had never visited the Big Easy before. I regard John as one of the brightest, most articulate people I know; and, during his summer in New Orleans, I craved to learn what he thought of my place of birth. When he returned to Berkeley, I asked him straight off, "Well, John, what did you think of New Orleans?" His face broke into a half-mocking grin. "I think it's wonderful," he replied. "They don't even notice the contradictions."

He could not have described more accurately the Church I grew up in as a maturing, Catholic yat. I went to racially segregated Catholic schools and worshiped in racially segregated Catholic churches, yet no one seemed to find it strange that our racism contradicted what we said we stood for as Catholic Christians. In as clericalized a city as New Orleans, I absorbed a measure of anti-clericalism just by breathing.

We went to St. Ann's parish. I had negative feelings about our pastor, a truculent old Cajun; but I did like our assistant pastor, Fr. Screen, a young red-headed priest with a face like the map of Ireland. He loved working with young people and eventually became diocesan director of the CYO.[4] When I went to St. Ann's Grammar School, he regularly hobnobbed with the students during recreation; and I enjoyed being with him.

In our segregated parish church, lily white parishioners worshiped on the floor of the church. Black Catholics had to sit segregated in the choir loft. I remember that, one Sunday, some of the Black children did something that disturbed and distracted the pastor during his sermon. He interrupted his pious remarks to yell up to the choir loft, "If you Negro children can't behave, then go to your own church down the street." None of the people on the floor of the church seemed to bat an eye.

Once the Civil Rights Movement took hold in the sixties, one heard on occasion anti-racist Sunday sermons. I remember one such sermon in St. Raphael church where we worshiped once we had moved to Vermillion Boulevard. You could have cut with a knife the feelings of undiluted hatred that flowed from the congregation to the priest in the pulpit. Prior to that, however, I cannot remember hearing a single anti-racist comment from the pulpit.

Barbara, my sister-in-law, grew up in an oil camp in the jungles of Colombia where her father headed the accounting department. She told me that New Orleans always struck her as a complete anomaly among American cities until she thought of it as the northernmost Latin American city. French and Spanish culture shape New Orleans mores even to this day. Together they imbue the citizens of the Big Easy with a remarkably high tolerance for moral ambiguity. The Church in the Big Easy acquiesced all too easily in that same moral ambiguity.

St. Ann's Grammar School and liturgical worship mediated my most extensive childhood experience of Church. Like my early schooling at home, what I learned in grammar school remains an indescribable blur; but a few experiences stand out from those years with a measure of clarity.

When I was losing my baby teeth, I got into a fight with another boy during recess between classes. He punched me in the mouth and knocked out one of my baby teeth, which I promptly swallowed. The Sisters of St. Joseph of Carondelet ran and staffed the school with the assistance of a handful of lay teachers. After one of the sisters broke up the melee, I told her I had swallowed my tooth. She took me up to the Principal's office, where the nuns started feeding me white bread. I imagine they thought that something else in my alimentary canal would ease the passage of the tooth through it. When I had polished off over half a loaf of bread, however, the sisters began to fear that something with me had gone awry. They called my mother and explained what had happened. They then broke the news to her that I had devoured more than half a loaf of bread and raised the possibility that something had indeed gone wrong with me. My mother laughed and told them that I loved bread and would continue eating it as long as they kept giving it to me. Relieved, they promptly cut off my supply.

I remember that I skipped a grade. If my memory serves me correctly, in a single year I did the first half of fifth grade and the second half of sixth. The sisters informed my parents that I was spinning my wheels intellectually in the grade in which I found myself; and they advised moving me up a grade. They felt confident that I could handle the advanced work. I did.

At some point of my schooling, Mother Superior, who resided in France and spoke no English, visited both the sisters' community and the school. The sisters got the idea of having one of the students greet her in a short speech in French. They selected me to do it. I remember spending an entire day with one of the sisters memorizing Gallic nonsense syllables. She seemed to enjoy herself; and I remember having fun with her despite my terror at the prospect of confronting Mother Superior in public. I survived that ordeal; but it burned itself into my memory.

One memory especially from those years at St. Ann's I can still see with my mind's eye as vividly as though I were perceiving it for the first time. I refer to the time I discovered Betty Bendix just after she had fallen through the ceiling. Our school had two attic classrooms. I found more than daunting the prospect of descending the fire escapes that linked one of the windows of each attic classroom to alleged safety. I found the descent both life-threatening and terrifying. The perilous fire escapes endowed those attic classrooms with one safety hazard; the catwalk that linked them provided another. It consisted of two planks nailed to the bottom rafters of the central attic which linked the two rooms. The catwalk had no railings.

On the day Betty Bendix fell through the ceiling, she was crossing the catwalk after school had ended, somehow lost her footing, and fell from the walkway and through the flimsy ceiling of the school's main hallway. St. Ann's school had an L shape. Sister Eugenie, the Principal, had her office in the small part of the L. We all lived in holy terror of Sister Eugenie, who preserved a severe, business-like demeanor that, no doubt, served her well as principal. As Betty fell through the ceiling, I was walking past the Principal's office and turned the corner into the long arm of the L at whose far end lay the stairs that would return me to the school yard and set me off on my walk home from school. I raised my eyes and saw two legs sticking through the ceiling. They were moving slowly backward and forward as if the owner were still taking a leisurely stroll. Betty's rump had prevented the rest of her from crashing through the ceiling.

I contemplated the moving legs for a long, long moment with utter fascination. Then, despite my trepidation at coming into The Presence, I traced my steps back to Sister Eugenie's office and told her that two legs were sticking out of the ceiling of the main hallway. For about five minutes she would not believe me and gave me a hard time for talking nonsense and sounding like a smart Alec. Finally, like a young Galileo, I challenged her to come out into the main hallway and look for herself. She did. Sure enough Betty's legs stuck through the ceiling and continued their saunter through thin air. I suddenly found myself transformed from the goat into the hero. Betty got rescued and proved shaken but unharmed by her perilous experience.

Sister Eugenie and her distant austerity did not typify the Sisters of St. Joseph who taught me. In the sixties, many Catholics indulged in a spate of nun-bashing and told hair-raising stories about nuns who had one way or another terrified or maltreated them during their Catholic grammar school education. I had no such experiences. I remember the sisters as competent, dedicated women who loved small children, who selflessly taught young people the things they needed to know, and who helped us to grow up. After I began attending Jesuit High School in New Orleans, my mother taught at St. Ann's Grammar School for several years and formed a warm friendship with Sister Melanie, a wonderful woman whom we both subsequently found great joy in visiting. We children even felt free to tease the sisters. We called one particularly stocky nun, Sister Mildrid, "Bodyguard." When we did, she would only laugh good-humoredly. I cannot remember her ever punishing our impudence. Although at this remove of time I cannot tell you exactly what she taught me, I do remember Sister Joseph Daniel, my eighth grade teacher, as a competent and effective teacher.

Only one thing about the sisters troubled me: their convent. We saw them only in the school and on its grounds. After that, they disappeared into their convent as though into a black hole. The convent had fairly extensive grounds surrounded by a high, thick, stucco fence with sharp broken bottles cemented into its top. I perceived those bottles as ominous. They made two statements loud and clear: "Stay out!" and "I dare you to escape!" I often wondered what religious did behind such cloistered walls and why they could not in fact leave the cloister and do things that normal people did. We knew that they lived on a level of holiness far above lay people. The old *Baltimore Catechism* I had to memorize had as one of its illustrations a married couple with the caption "This is good" next to a habited religious with the caption, "This is better." That might satisfy the authors of the *Baltimore Catechism*; but the secrecy and anonymity of the sisters' lives I found strange, uncanny, and off-putting.

After I joined the Jesuits, I would get some answers to my childhood musings about the goings on behind convent walls. The answers helped explain the broken bottles; but they did not make their jagged edges any more appealing. I would eventually come to understand that the codification of Canon Law in 1917 had led to a rigid standardization of religious life on a monastic model and that the hierarchicalism, formalism, legalism, and ritualism of the Catholic tradition had endowed many aspects of religious life with a questionable elitism and with an unreflective rigorism. Given the law-and-order

Catholicism which I had with the Delaup will tenaciously interiorized, it would take me many years to see through these distortions; and that failure would take its toll both on my own religious development and on my relationship to God.

Among my experiences of sacramental worship, my confirmation marked me in ways that had nothing to do with the significance and purpose of that ritual. The morning of the day before Archbishop Rummel would come to confirm us, we had to attend early morning mass and receive holy communion. While brushing my teeth I thought I might have swallowed some water and broken my eucharistic fast. In those days, the fast before receiving communion had an absolute quality. After midnight, nothing ought to pass one's lips until Jesus did so under the appearances of bread. Before leaving for church, I told my mother that I feared that I had broken my eucharistic fast. She quite sensibly told me that, if I did not know for sure, not to worry about it and to go to communion. I obediently did so; but I did not feel easy in my conscience. I knew that, if I received communion after breaking my eucharistic fast, I would have committed a mortal sin and that, if a tree fell on me or a car rolled over me before I could go to confession, I would go straight to hell, where God would gleefully roast me forever in eternal flames of fire. I had a bout of scruples which I eventually outgrew.

I mention these experiences here because they dramatize yet another experience of religious ambivalence I had as a child. I felt, as I recall, tender feelings toward Jesus, especially in His eucharistic presence; but God I feared because He supposedly punished unrelentingly in the flames of purgatory or in the everlasting and unquenchable flames of hellfire all those who flouted his will. A God of vindictive justice left me petrified. I knew I could not escape Him; and my fear of Him caused me at some deep level to want to control him. I would not face those feelings until almost two decades after my confirmation; but eventually they did surface.

Beyond me and my small world of home, school, and Church stretched the city of New Orleans. The Crescent City looked in the 1930s and early 1940s very different from the city that tourists encounter today. Today downtown New Orleans has a skyline of skyscrapers. In those days it lay flat as a pancake; and in the summers it sizzled on the griddle of deep muck on which it floated. Until architects developed the art of floating tall buildings on the equivalent of cement islands, any tall or heavy building erected in the Crescent City would have sunk into the two thousand feet of ooze on which New Orleans floats, like a body into quicksand.

Today a circulatory system of interstate highways and of overpasses interlinks the city's different sections, neighborhoods, and suburbs. New Orleans did not get its first overpass until after World War II. During the war, my uncle Clarence Gelpi and Chep Morrison, both U.S. Army officers, had struck up a mutual friendship. After World War II, Morrison became the first truly progressive mayor the city had known. Morrison had a vision for bringing New Orleans into the modern era. He supervised the first overpass on Elysian Fields Avenue about a mile from our new family home on Vermillion Boulevard. He built others and headed a reform city government which contrasted refreshingly with the traditional corruption and graft. Prior to the construction of the overpasses in New Orleans, one waited endlessly at the many railroad crossings that blocked the city's roads as heavy freight trains rumbled slowly and tediously past.

Despite all its modernization, much of old New Orleans still survives. I think of the city I knew as a child as a collective embodiment of history and of tradition, as a city of fantasy and of imagination, and as a racist city. As I reflect now on each of these early perceptions, I find them also fraught with ambiguity.

We cannot avoid getting born into a place; and, once born, we cannot keep the place from getting born into us. The only city in the United States to have preserved its old colonial settlement more or less intact, New Orleans feels older and more historically rooted than most United States cities. Boston and other New England cities as well as many cities on the east coast have a sense of historical roots that go back to the English colonization of the New World. Much of tourism in New England consists of visiting old colonial houses. New Orleans, however, derives even earlier from French colonization; and it preserves more or less intact most of the original Vieux Carré.

In 1682, Robert Cavalier, Sieur de La Salle explored the length of the Mississippi River to its delta. There he erected a wooden cross and a column with a lead plate attached to it inscribed with the royal French coat of arms and with the message: "Louis the Great, King of France and of Navarre, reigns, the 9th of August 1682." The plate then announced that "in the name of His Majesty and of the successors of his crown, I have taken and do take possession of this country of Louisiana." De la Salle recognized the importance of the river he had explored and annexed it and its tributaries to the possessions of colonial France.

In 1699, a French-Canadian, Pierre Lemoyne, Sieur d'Iberville, sailed down the Mississippi with the intent of beginning French occupation of the river's mouth. He established Fort Maurepas on Biloxi Bay. He named lakes Pontchartrain and Maurepas in honor of the French minister of marine and of his son. He christened the slow flowing river which emerged from underground and emptied into Lake Pontchartrain, Bayou St. John in honor of his brother, Jean Baptiste Le Moyne, Sieur de Bienville.

Bienville founded New Orleans in 1718. He located the Vieux Carré where we find it because he found the graceful curve of the river in which the city stands appealing, because the land on which the old city rose protruded above water in the river's spring flood, and because an Indian trail, the future Bayou Road, linked the city to Bayou St. John. In addition to the Mississippi, the bayou provided a second water access to the Gulf of Mexico through lakes Pontchartrain, Maurepas, and Borne.

In 1721, Pierre Leblond de la Tour laid out the plan of the old city and began construction. Not until the fall of Quebec to the English in the French and Indian War did the inhabitants of New Orleans begin construction on the fortifications which give Rampart Street its name. In the treaty ending that war, Louis XV gave all his Louisiana province east of the Mississippi above Bayou Manchac to England and the rest of it, including New Orleans to Spain. The Spanish Governor, Luis Hector, Baron de Carondelet completed the fortifications the French had begun. Napoleon won back Louisiana from Spain in 1803 and in the same year sold it to the United States, whose third president, Thomas Jefferson, had dreams of an American empire stretching from the Atlantic to the Pacific coast.

All these layers of history find embodiment in the buildings and monuments of Jackson Square, surely one of the most graceful collections of old buildings in the United States surviving as an architectural ensemble. On the northern side of the Square stands St. Louis Cathedral, with its three spires, flanked on the west by the Cabildo, the seat of Spanish colonial rule in Louisiana, and on the east by the Presbytère, the Cathedral rectory. The Cabildo and the Presbytère have identical facades; but the roof of the Cabildo sports a small cupola surrounded by a widow's walk. Behind the cathedral lies a small cathedral garden called St. Anthony's Square in honor of a legendary pastor of the cathedral, Antonio de Sedella, who came to Louisiana in 1779 and served until his death in 1829. The alley between the cathedral and the Presbytère bears the name Père Antoine Alley in his honor. Pirate's Alley divides the Cathedral from the Cabildo. It derives its name from Jean Lafitte, the pirate who, with his cutthroat crew, joined Andrew Jackson to defeat the English in the Battle of New Orleans, which took place after the War of 1812 had officially ended. The statue of Andy Jackson astride his rearing horse in the center of Jackson Square, the old Place d'Armes, reminds knowledgeable tourists and locals that the Chalmette Battlefield lies just down river. There the battle unfolded, while the Ursuline nuns prayed the alliance of Americans and pirates to victory. The Spaniards completed the Cabildo in 1803, but the Presbytère did not reach completion until 1813. On the east and west sides of Jackson Square lie the red-brick Pontalba Apartments with their graceful, filigreed porches. Called apartments, the buildings actually contain a series of town houses erected in 1850 by the Baroness Micaela de Pontalba, daughter of Don Alemonester.

When I was growing up in New Orleans, Jackson Square and the entire French Quarter kept reminding me of the deep historical ties that bound New Orleans to the past. Many native New Orleanians cultivate an intelligent conservatism and seek to preserve the city's oldest monuments for the benefit of posterity. In my childhood, however, I also imbibed a darker kind of conservatism. We called it "Our Southern Way of Life" which we imagined as gracious, civilized, hospitable, cultivated, polite, and racist. Every year endless lines of yats stretched from movie house box-offices in anticipation of a ritual viewing of *Gone With the Wind*. Our Southern Way of Life evoked feelings of a vanished era of gracious plantation living and of the slavery on which it constructed itself. In the 1930s and 1940s Southerners were still fighting The War Between the States (we preferred not to call it by the Yankee name, "The Civil War"); and we still nurtured deep-felt antipathy toward all Yankees. States Rights and white racism thrived in the New Orleans of my childhood.

I do not remember my immediate or extended family as violently racist, but the pervasive racism did corrupt us, did corrupt me. Lionel, the coffee-colored Black man who chauffeured Pepere Delaup on his selling rounds, from time to time visited at 1924 Bayou Road. The family there always received him cordially in the parlor; but no one in Gautier Villa would have thought of inviting Lionel and his family to dinner. No one ever said as much. The racial lines remained invisible, but everyone knew where they lay. I grew up, then, believing in the essential superiority of the white race, believing that Black people themselves preferred to live segregated from whites, and viewing with something akin to horror the idea of miscegenation. For me as for other yats, preserving "Our Southern Way of Life" meant preserving intact Jim Crow and the strict segregation of the races.

The Mardi Gras also profoundly shapes New Orleans culture. Most people equate Mardi Gras, or Fat Tuesday, with the Tuesday before Ash Wednesday, which begins the Lenten fast. In the New Orleans of my youth, however, Mardi Gras began with the Epiphany. People celebrated the Epiphany season with King Cake Parties. King cakes typically have an oval shape and come festooned with purple, green, and gold sugars, the three colors of the Mardi Gras. Every king cake has either a tiny baby Jesus or a pecan baked into it. Whoever got the piece of cake with the baby Jesus or the pecan got crowned the king or queen of that particular party. That privilege brought with it, however, the noblesse oblige of providing a king cake for next week's party. This went on until yats got tired of eating king cake. Then the serious Mardi Gras partying began. Next the parades and balls started. The latter became more frequent and orgiastic, until on Mardi Gras day itself innumerable parades made driving around the city unthinkable. Mardi Gras day confronted locals with three choices: stay at home, join the revels, or leave town.

Without the Mardi Gras, New Orleans would never had earned the sobriquet "The Big Easy." Mardi Gras makes New Orleans the party city par excellence. It deeply shapes the ethos of the people. No doubt growing up in New Orleans inspired my oft repeated and always ignored plea in my years at Berkeley that the school in which I worked sponsor more parties and fewer committee meetings.

An anecdote may explain best what I mean. Joseph Tetlow, S.J. and I both joined the faculty of Loyola University in New Orleans in 1969. While I had counseled Catholic draft resisters and written letters for them attesting to the religious sincerity of their convictions and to their justification in the documents of Vatican II, I had not reached the pitch of anti-war fervor Joe had. A committed pacifist, while completing his doctorate in American Studies at Brown University, he had helped organize many anti-war demonstrations in and around Providence. No sooner had he arrived at Loyola than he persuaded Tulane University to join with Loyola in sponsoring an anti-Vietnam-War protest march, the first and last such demonstration the Big Easy witnessed.

The racist police kept rerouting the parade through Black neighborhoods in the hope of causing violent confrontations there. They hoped in vain. As we walked through one of those neighborhoods, a tall Black woman came striding onto her porch and called sympathetically to the marchers, "You tell them. They killed five of my boys." As for Joe, he had no apprehensions about hostility from the crowds. In Providence he had felt apprehensive, for there moral sentiments pro and con ran high. A yat, like me, Joe realized, however, that in New Orleans, if any group of people marches down the middle of the street for whatever reason, all the onlookers will move spontaneously into their Mardi Gras syndrome. They did precisely that. Our anti-war protest turned into a big street party.

I myself witnessed only one example of nastiness. When the marchers reached Canal Street, a man in one of the older office buildings opened a window and started yelling curses at the marchers. They, however, responded playfully by drowning him out with the chant, "Jump for peace! Jump for peace!" I watched the incident wondering if yats have a single morally earnest bone in their bodies.

For me as a child the Mardi Gras season, especially the parades, created a magical time every year for which I yearned. I loved it all: the floats, the bands, the crowds yelling, "Throw me something, Mista!" to the maskers on the floats and then diving for the assorted trinkets and junk that the sometimes drunken revelers on the floats tossed into the crowds. When I taught at Loyola University in New Orleans, I supervised the program for the Jesuit collegians, the scholastics engaged in humanistic and philosophical studies. We had people from all over the country in the program; and I particularly loved taking the New England scholastics to their first Mardi Gras parade. Every one of them began with his back to the nearest wall, with arms crossed over his chest, and with defensive, suspicious eyes. It warmed the cockles of my heart to see every one of them totally corrupted by the end of the parade. They jumped up and down in the midst of the crowd yelling, "Throw me something, Mister!" They stomped the hands of small children to get a doubloon, pushed people aside to claim a cheap plastic necklace. They behaved, in a word, like a normal yat at a Mardi Gras parade.

Mardi Gras day brings masking in the streets; and that meant that from one year to the next, I, as a child, could decide whom I would transform myself into on Fat Tuesday. I remember opting for the pedestrian persona of a cowboy and of a pirate; but I loved most my devil costume. Once in high school, I transformed myself into a leper. It required the cheapest of costumes. One mixed ordinary white flour with water and different disgusting watercolors and smeared the paste on one's exposed skin. As it dried, it flaked off. One completed the effect with blood and puss colored bandages, mussed one's hair, wrapped oneself in a bedspread, and–voila!–a leper from whom other maskers actually shrank in horror if you tried to touch them.

The Mardi Gras krewes sponsor the larger parades and balls; but a grass-roots Mardi Gras also flourishes among yats. One year, when I taught at Loyola, one of the men's fraternities walked from their frat house to a local bar named "Tucks." The next year they invited another men's fraternity to join them. The year after that the two fraternities had transformed themselves into the Krewe of Tucks, registered the date and route of their parade, and even received tongue-in-cheek reviews of their performance in the newspapers. One read headlines like: TUCKS SHAMBLES, STAGGERS TO THE END OF ITS ROUTE. The Tucks parade had only one marching band: ROTC students wearing military shirts and long-johns shambled down the street humming military marches on tissue-paper combs.

Mardi Gras combined with my passion for reading novels in order to teach me to live in my imagination; and that experience bore speculative fruit in my instinctive tendency to look with jaundiced eyes on all forms of philosophical and theological rationalism which would attempt to reduce any human grasp of reality to corpse-cold inferences. Anyone who appreciates the human imagination knows that it grasps reality as truly and as fallibly as human reason. Growing up in New Orleans taught me to honor and cultivate the imagination and its spontaneous, creative, public expression. I doubt that growing up anywhere else would have inculcated the same lesson with the same thoroughness as the Big Easy.

The Mardi Gras too had, however, its sinister, racist side. The old established krewes practiced strict racial segregation. The oldest krewes excluded both Blacks and undertakers. Indeed, I find it hard to imagine anything about the New Orleans of my childhood which did not bear the taint of racism. The pervasive presence of racism in the Big Easy taught me and every other little white child of my generation to grow up racist.

Eventually, however, that experience too bore speculative fruit. It helped me rethink the experience of original sin. Augustine of Hippo created the term "original sin" and endowed it with strong psycho-sexual and individualistic connotations. Growing up in a society tainted by racism taught me to take a perspectival view of original sin. Sin divides into personal sin and original sin. "Personal sin" means my own sins, the sins which I deliberately commit and for which I stand personally responsible before God. Original sin means the rest of sin: all the personal sins other people commit and the ways in which any given society chooses to institutionalize sin, to give the immoral or sinful behavior of social groups official public sanction. Southern racists institutionalized racial bigotry and segregation. In other times and cultures, original sin could take different institutional form.

One commits personal sin; one acquiesces in original sin, not by a process of imitation, but by a kind of more or less conscious social osmosis. Acquiescing in original sin differs from committing personal sin in the way that appropriating more or less consciously the racist ethos of one's culture differs from deliberately deciding to participate in a lynching, even though one knows that the group murder violates the will of God. The spontaneous egocentrism of all organic life, including human life, makes the corrupting power of a sinful environment all the more potent. I call such a view of original sin perspectival because each individual perceives his or her environment of sin from a different angle of vision. You experience my personal sins as part of your experience of original sin, and I experience your personal sins as part of my experience of original sin.

My brother went to Jesuit High School in New Orleans; and I in my turn followed him the year he went to Loyola University with an ROTC scholarship. Like him I made it into the honor class. In those days and when I later taught there as a regent,[5] the school clung to the home-room system. That meant that one teacher taught as many different subjects as possible to the same students. The multiple preparations turned one's first year of regency into hell; but the system enabled one to get to know one's home room students extremely well, to show them connections among the different things they studied, and to understand each one of them as a unique individual.

At Jesuit High School, the home-room system had an explicitly elitist caste. The students who tested out the smartest made it into the honor class, the A class of that year. Students particularly gifted in mathematics and science made it into the next echelon of intellectual acumen, the scientific track, or B class. The other classes contained the hoi polloi; but I learned years later, while teaching there as a Jesuit, that they, if challenged, could do work of very high quality. Too often, however, they did not get so challenged; and therein lay the chief educational evil of the home-room system.

My attendance at Jesuit High School changed my life profoundly in four ways. 1) It forced me to face and renounce the racism which original sin New Orleans style had bred into my bones and conscience. 2) In academic matters, it re-enforced my intellectual perfectionism. 3) It began my academic preparation for a life of theological scholarship. 4) Finally, it introduced me to the Jesuit Order; and, despite everything I did to resist a religious vocation, it provided the remote catalyst for transforming me into a Jesuit.

I respected most of my teachers at Jesuit High and became deeply fond of the Jesuit scholastic who taught me in my sophomore year: Mr. Edward Romagosa, S.J. Besides working with him in the classroom, I joined the Philelectic Society which he directed, the school drama society which put on three plays a year: two major productions and a one-act play which we entered into various drama competitions.

For two years, however, I deeply resented the fact that my Jesuit teachers especially declared all-out war on our Southern, Jim-Crow, racist way of life. What they said challenged and troubled me; and I would argue passionately against their arguments for the need to end Jim Crow and all forms of racial segregation.

That experience taught me in subsequent years to deal kindly with students who disagreed with me or argued passionately a position contrary to my own. Their very passion meant that at some level what I was saying was getting to them, challenging them, making them rethink pet personal prejudices. Certainly, the unexpected assault on racist attitudes and institutions I encountered at Jesuit High School got to me, challenged me, and, whether I liked it or not, forced me to rethink and revise my personal racist bigotry. After two years of flailing about for some kind of justification for racism and segregation, I gave in, not just out of exhaustion, but because I realized that my teachers had it right and I had it wrong.

Although I would not have said it at the time, I look upon that transformation as my first experience of conversion. I had not converted religiously, but

I had converted morally and had made an initial step toward political conversion. I regard my renunciation of my personal racism as a personal moral conversion because I have come to believe that any genuine conversion requires one to advance beyond the conventional wisdom of the society which nurtures one to maturity and shapes one in all kinds of conscious and unconscious ways.

Conversion means taking responsibility for one's subsequent growth and development in some identifiable realm of human experience. No one who simply acquiesces in the values of one's nurturing society can live a personally responsible life, for the simple reason that every humanly constructed society inculcates truth, lies and folly; virtue, vice, and sin; religious belief, unbelief, and apathy; institutions which seek to foster the common good and those which protect selfish, vested interests; the healthy appreciation of beauty and excellence, on the one hand, and banality, neurosis, psychosis, and crude bigotry, on the other.

In renouncing my racism I had revised my personal conscience. I had branded as evil, as sinful, as unjust, and as something I personally opposed an institution which my society cherished and promoted. I still had a long way to go before I dealt in any way adequately with the emotional roots of my racism. I had even further to go before I would commit myself to fight racism publicly; but, at least in my own conscience, I acknowledged the evil of my former ways and took a stand in my heart against institutionalized racial bigotry.

My presence in the honor class meant that I hobnobbed on a regular basis with the smartest boys in our school. I formed a warm friendship with Joe Berrigan, Whitney Engeron, Jeremy Adams, and Roland Lesseps. Joe and I began immediately to enter into friendly competition for the highest grades in the honor class. The Jesuit pedagogy I encountered played on the spontaneous competitiveness of smart adolescent males in order to induce them to study harder. Each semester teachers awarded honor cards to the brightest students in each subject taught. The boy with the highest grade average in the senior honor class automatically gave the valedictory address. In the end, I barely edged Joe out and gave the valedictory, a diatribe against Communism which my senior teacher, Fr. Francis Xavier Entz, S.J. had largely written and which I delivered with adolescent bombast. My parents made me record the speech; and I have never heard it without an almost unconquerable impulse to bolt from the room in the acutest embarrassment.

Another less pleasant inducement made me study all the harder. Neither my brother nor I have ever felt athletically inclined. I inherited my Mother's relative lack of coordination and found myself really unsuited for competitive sports. To my dismay, I found myself in a thoroughly jock school and had to endure the kind of hazing which smart, bookish, non-athletic adolescents encounter in a macho, jock environment. I hated the boys who gave me a hard time; and I decided to show them just how smart I was. They might make me look like a fool on the playing field; but I would make them look like fools in matters of the mind. I genuinely enjoyed most of the things I studied; but my ongoing battle with insecure, teen-age jocks endowed my passionate cultivation of my own mind with a measure of meanness and of one-up-man-ship.

The curriculum of the Honor Class preserved the most traditional, conservative aspects of Jesuit education. The Honors curriculum trained one to become a Renaissance humanist. We studied Latin for four years and Greek for two. We immersed ourselves in literature and in history. We also studied mathematics and science; and, although I got good grades in both, I faded out of mathematics after plane geometry and had little taste for science. The Honors Curriculum began, however, to give me the linguistic, interpretative, and historical skills I would need to do theological research; not that I had a theological career in mind.

As I moved toward senior year, I felt drawn to some kind of career that served other people. Even though none of my father's generation had pursued medicine, I knew that I came from a traditionally medical family; and I had heard of the surgical achievements of Pepere Gelpi. Toward the beginning of my senior year, I decided that I would become a doctor. Through my uncle Clarence's connections with Mayor Morrison, I finessed a scholarship to Tulane University's pre-med program. I had decided my vocational identity. I would become a doctor and have a family.

Then to my horror, I began having the sense that God was calling me to become a Jesuit. The idea appalled me. I used to pray regularly in the evenings. I prayed the psalms and read a concordance of the gospels before going to bed. I prayed for the people I loved. During my junior year at Jesuit high, my home-room teacher, Emmet Beinvenue, S.J., who had studied with the Christian Brothers, had adopted some of their pedagogical techniques in his own teaching style. He began each day's study with a little moral or religious exhortation, with what we as Jesuit scholastics called a ferverino. He introduced me to the Acts of the Apostles and taught me for the first time to reflect seriously on the Holy Spirit. He also persuaded me to attend mass and receive communion during the first part of my lunch hour. That year of daily communion deepened my devotion to my eucharistic Lord. I had no problem with any of that; but joining the Jesuits? I had decided what I would do with my life. I had even asked my uncle Clarence to persuade the Mayor of New Orleans to get me into Tulane University. If I backed out now, I felt as though I would look like a fool. I asked my mother what she thought I should do, and she said that she and Daddy both wanted me to do what would make me happy. The thought of being a Jesuit did not make me at all happy; but the sense of call would not go away. The more I fought the vocation, the more miserable I felt. Finally, after months of wrestling with God, I gave in. I said yes. I applied for acceptance in the Society of Jesus and made the best decision of my life.

Colloquy:

Father,
All-Giver,
Eternal Wellspring,
River of Life,
Only Source,
Only Rest,
　　　how You delight
　　　　　in loving the small,
　　　　　　　the fragile,
　　　　　　　the vulnerable
　　　　　　　　into the plentitude
　　　　　　　　　of their possible life.
　　　You swell the rings
　　　　　of living forest giants
　　　　　　　already ancient
　　　　　　　　when Mary birthed
　　　　　　　　　Your sweet Son.
Sky-painter,
Sculptor of flowers,
Sparrow Cherisher,
　　　I entered Your good world
　　　　　which we so scar
　　　　　　with sin.
You encompass me.
You knew that sin would mar,
　　grace would shape me.
You raised up prophets
　　to arm me against myself.
You swaddled me with entwining bands of love,
　　　mother love,
　　　father love,
　　　brother love,
　　　family love,
　　　prayer love,
　　　nun love,
　　　Church love.

To crown all,
> *You called me to the Company of your Son,*
>> *a gift I did not understand*
>> *and so did not desire.*

Wisdom beyond wisdom, You march before me,
> *follow behind me,*
>> *lie beneath me,*
>>> *above me,*
>>> *within me.*

How then
> *shall I not rest content?*

NOTES

1. In New Orleans, a "shot-gun" house has a hallway which runs the length of one side of the building and which connects all the rooms.

2. Jesuit obedience rests on personal government. It requires superiors to know their subjects individually and personally so that they can, with their subjects, discern correctly how God is calling each member of the community to serve. The annual colloquy one has with one's rector goes by the name "an account of conscience."

3, Clinical Pastoral Education (CPE) usually consists of supervised work as a hospital chaplain together with group reflection on one's approach to such pastoral work.

4. CYO means Catholic Youth Organization.

5. Regency designates a period of active apostolic work in Jesuit formation which normally comes between the systematic study of philosophy and theology.

Chapter Two

I Become A Jesuit

When I told my friends that I would be entering the Jesuit Novitiate at Grand Coteau, LA, to my surprise and delight I learned that two of my best friends, Roland Lesseps and Whitney Engeron, had also decided to join the Jesuits and would be entering the order on the same day as I. I learned too that Jack May, one of my brother's best friends, was also entering on that day; and I looked forward to counting him among my own close friends.

Although I did not know it at the time, on the morning of the day I left for Grand Coteau, Al, who had graduated that spring from Loyola University, received a letter calling him up for active duty in the army. The Korean War dragged on inconclusively; and his ROTC scholarship had come home to roost. While I did my novitiate training, he would go to boot camp and then spend two years in Korea as a lieutenant in the military police at a prisoner of war camp just south of the battle line. As soon as he opened the letter, Al told Daddy, who told him to say nothing about it, especially to Mother. Daddy said he would handle the matter. He did not want Mother suddenly faced with losing both her sons at once. For the moment, Daddy seems to have felt that losing one son, yours truly, sufficed. I do not know when or how he broke the news to Mother; but eventually, of course, he did.

Al hated life in the army. Although promotions came automatically to those on active duty in Korea, Al never got one. He proved too Christian for the army. Whenever he served as Officer of the Day in the prison camp, he ordered the cooks to serve three meals to the refugees who orbited the camp, instead of the one meal the refugees were supposed to get. Every time Al ordered the three meals, his colonel chewed him out; and every time he took over as Officer of the Day, he gave the same order to the cooks. To his credit, he left Korea a first lieutenant. He did, however, form part of the honor guard at the signing of the peace treaty which ended the war.

I would not learn of all of this until much later. Roland, Whitney, Jack, and I had a rollicking good train trip to Lafayette, Louisiana. In high spirits, we gorged ourselves on the cookies and other delights with which family and friends had loaded us at our departure from the train station in New Orleans. We found several cars waiting for us at the train station in Lafayette, the closest city to Grand Coteau, the small village where the novitiate, St. Charles College, stood and still stands. The Novice Master, Anthony Mangiaracina, S.J., and some second year novices greeted us and drove us to the College, where I would do my first four years of training as a Jesuit: two years of novitiate and two of juniorate. In the novitiate, we studied the rule of the Jesuit order, made the thirty-day Ignatian retreat, helped take care of the older Jesuit priests in the infirmary, did physical labor, and in our second year spent a month doing odd jobs at Manresa, our retreat house in Convent, Louisiana. After taking our first vows as Jesuits, we moved to the other side of the building for our juniorate studies. Juniorate consisted of two years of humanistic studies.

As we drove from the train station in Lafayette, I began to have an anxiety attack. After a short drive, our car, which Tony Mangiaracina was driving, turned a corner. I saw a big, ugly, yellow, stucco building squatting in the middle of a big, empty field. In those days St. Charles College had only a few oak trees in front of it. I remember thinking in dismay, "Oh, God, what have I gotten into?" I would soon find out.

The Jesuits eased you into the novitiate with two weeks of what they called postulancy. We had an entering class of twenty-four, as I recall. Each postulant had a "guardian angel," a second year novice who showed one around and tried to show one the ropes. Fr. Master, had assigned Primo Contreras as my guardian angel, a young Hispanic who, like myself, had done some acting in high school. Every day before the evening meal, the community gathered to pray litanies together in Latin. After dinner, we had a period of group recreation. At recreation on that first day, Primo asked me what I had thought of litanies. He looked a little dismayed when I told him that they had sounded like the Alka Seltzer locomotive. In those days, Alka Seltzer ran an ad on the radio which ended with a chorus of male voices repeating "Alka Seltzer" over and over in an attempt to sound like a chugging train.

We recited the litanies in Latin with varying degrees of dispatch, depending on who led them. Fr. Walter Furman, S.J., who came during the summers from Spring Hill College in order to teach math to the juniors held the all time record for dispatch. He did not even wait for the community's "Ora pro nobis" in order to speak the next invocation. He also led the litanies with a broad Georgia accent which had diphthongs but no pure vowels. The combination of the accent and of his relentless pace in leading the prayer invariably reduced a significant number of the novices and juniors to such a pitch of hilarity that they betook themselves from the chapel until they could regain their composure. My first experience of litanies did not race ahead that fast; but the "Ora pro nobis. Ora pro nobis. Ora pro nobis" sounded to me exactly like "Alka Seltzer, Alka Seltzer, Alka Seltzer."

After two weeks of postulancy, we all received cassocks and began our novitiate proper. I knew that, if I was going to become a Jesuit, I had to "do it right." I had just turned seventeen; and, in my adolescent naivete, doing it right meant for me to play things by the book and keep all the rules. I had no lack of rules to keep. We novices lived scripted lives. An order of the day went up on the bulletin board every morning and told you what to do and when. Besides the rules of the Jesuit order, one had to take into account the American Assistancy Custom Book as well as the customs of the local community to which one belonged.

On the evening before we got our cassocks, Fr. John Minville, S.J., the assistant Novice Master, gave us what the second year novices called "the dip conference." A "dip," we learned, meant a discipline, a little knotted whip with which we were expected to lash ourselves on designated evenings. We also received the chain, a metal garter with prongs on its inside which hurt like hell and which one was supposed to wear for a couple of hours on designated days. I believe that I abandoned using the chain after the novitiate had ended; but it gives some measure of my adolescent capacity to do something just because someone told me to that I continued using the discipline until my second year of philosophical studies, even though, as far as I could see, lashing myself with knotted strings never did me an ounce of good and did nothing to improve my relationship with God.

Besides the dip and the chain, we encountered other "mortifications." One could shower only three times a week; and, in the summers especially, we novices smelled pretty ripe. Cleaning toilets supposedly inculcated humility in us novices. I did not find it particularly humiliating, especially since we all took turns. I rathered that than dirty, smelly toilets. On occasion the manual labor proved pretty taxing to a person of as slight of frame as myself. I learned to hate the College's diary herd. Loading bales of hay onto slow moving trucks from where they lay in the hayfields after harvest I found back-breaking work. Once a year we harvested the beans and corn which the Jesuit brothers ground up into silage. I found stomping the silo the absolute pits. Two people stomped simultaneously. The inside of the silo felt like a blast furnace. The stompers walked around in the ground corn and beans in order to tamp them down and allow for the storing of as much cow food as possible.

Jesuit asceticism greets such repugnant tasks with the council: *Agere contra* (Go against yourself.) In other words, face difficult tasks unflinchingly no matter what they demand. Big Red, the giant Black workman at the College who had seen hundreds of novices pass through the purifying alembic of the novitiate, in the midst of supervising unpleasant work like the stomping of the silo would with a big grin exhort the novices, saying "Agere country, brothers, agere country."

As I recall, none of us thought to question the novitiate rules and customs, least of all myself. That would begin to happen in the sixties; but in the fifties I would have found such questioning unthinkable. I had grown up a law-and-order Catholic. Now I became a law-and-order Jesuit.

I remember the novitiate as a shared ordeal. Shared ordeals bring people together, of course; and I made life-long friends with the novices who survived. Not all of them did. Periodically, this or that novice would throw in the towel and call it quits. I made it to the juniorate, but perseverance took its toll. I entered in 1951; and well into the 1970s, whenever I returned to Grand Coteau, I had a nightmare about being trapped inside an Iron-Curtain country without a passport and without any means of getting across the border.

We novices used to call one another "Carissime." In Latin, "Carissime" means dearly beloved. Bob Watkins, a tall, pudgy, intellectually brilliant novice from Tennessee even less coordinated and less athletic than I, told me that he had finally succeeded in calling the other novices "Carissime" by simply blocking from his mind what the title meant.

We laughed a lot as novices; but my family noticed on their periodic visits that novice laughter often had a tinge of hysteria. We novices used to exhort one another "not to strain": to cool it, not to try too hard, just to go with the flow. An element of artificiality pervaded our novitiate, not entirely unlike the artificiality of boot camps, but more pious. We regularly read the exhortations of Fr. Morris, an English Jesuit Novice Master, to his novices. Fr. Morris had devised an ingenious scheme for staying "recollected" all day long. He urged each novice to divide the day into fifteen minute periods and to assign to each period a different patron saint and a different special intention. He felt that changing patrons and intentions every fifteen minutes would keep any novice recollected, focused on divine things. I do not know if Fr. Morris succeeded in producing a generation of thoroughly neurotic English Jesuits; but, if he did fail, no one could fault him for not trying.

At Grand Coteau, we devised other means for staying recollected. A little picture frame hung over the urinal in the common bathroom and toilet. It contained a little reflection or pious aspiration which some novice changed periodically. Reading it sought to keep one recollected while one peed. One day, I remember raising my eyes from the urinal to read: "Why am I here?"

One had the sense of living under constant surveillance. An incident which happened at the Missouri province theologate in St. Marys, Kansas, illustrates what I mean. When the United States declared war on Hitler and the Axis, two German Jesuits were pursuing their theological studies at St. Marys. Shortly after the United States entered World War II, two FBI agents visited the theologate and had a conference with the rector of the community. They told the rector that they realized that the German scholastics were studying for the priesthood and posed no real threat to United States security. On the other hand, the two Germans had suddenly become enemy aliens living in this country at a time of war. The agents did not want to incarcerate the two Jesuits in a prisoner of war camp. They therefore told the rector that the FBI would remain satisfied, if only the rector gave his word to keep a special eye on the two Germans.

The rector, who had a sense of humor, began describing what happened during an ordinary day at the theologate. He told the agents that the community all rose at the same time and that he would send someone around to make sure that the German scholastics had risen promptly. Actually, somebody checked on all the scholastics and made sure that no one had turned into a slug-a-bed. "After a half hour," the rector said, "the entire community makes a visit to the Blessed Sacrament. I will be there and can check up on the two Germans. After that the scholastics do an hour of private prayer. I will send someone around to make sure that they are in their rooms. I will be at breakfast and make sure that they show up there as well. After that, they will have class, and I will see to it that someone makes sure that they attend all their classes."

As the rector proceeded in this monologue, the FBI agents showed increasing signs of dismay. Finally, one of them said, "Wait a minute, Father. Let's get something clear. We just want you to keep an eye on these two men. You don't need to turn this place into a prisoner of war camp." The agents didn't realize that the rector had been describing what happened to every scholastic every day of the year he resided at St. Marys. Similar things happened in every Jesuit scholasticate. No wonder we felt watched.

Before the reform of religious life which followed Vatican II, we scholastics had to get permission for just about everything we needed, including carfare, if we lived in the city. The system of permissions was supposed to inculcate a sense of poverty and of common life. In fact, it tended to inculcate infantilism.

We conversed with one another at meals only by way of exception. Ordinarily, one of the scholastics read a book to the community as we ate. At Grand Coteau, one of the juniorate faculty functioned as Repetat Master. "Repetat" in Latin means "let him repeat." If the reader mispronounced a word, the Repetat Master said, "Repetat. That's pronounced so-and-so." Once while one of the juniors was reading a book on the Oxford movement, he read a sentence which alluded to Magdalene College and Saintjohn. The reader pronounced "Magdalene" as though reading Mary Magdalene and Saintjohn like the name of the evangelist. The Repetat Master said, "Repetat. That's pronounced 'Mawdlin' and 'Sinjun.'" The befuddled reader could not figure out which words to correct. We read a lot of books that way; but that particular monastic custom did nothing for our social skills. We called conversing at table "having Deo Gratias" because the Rector gave permission to the community to converse by saying "Deo Gratias" after our common grace.

At some point in my second year novitiate, it all came to seem too much to bear. I felt desperately homesick. I had had enough of the stinking bodies and cassocks, of the infernal silo, of the self-flagellation, of the artificial regimented piety. I wanted out. I wanted to leave, to go home. I went into the Novice Master's office and told him that I was thinking of checking out. I don't know what kind of response I expected; but the one I got took me completely aback. Tony Mangiaracina looked at me with a big smile and said, "Carissime, I'll buy you your bus ticket to New Orleans any time you want." Clearly, my Novice Master thought that the Society of Jesus could survive without me. I had not expected that. I stammered something about needing to think and pray about it more.

Later, I had reached such a pitch of misery that I needed desperately to talk to someone. I went into the Novice Master's office, began to speak, and broke down in self-pitying, adolescent tears. Tony let me cry myself out and then listened to what I had to say. When I finished, I felt better. I rose and went to the door. Before I could open it, Tony spoke. He had a warm, friendly smile. "You know, Carissime," he said, "you are as proud as Lucifer; but it's all right. It's all starting to break down." I didn't know why he called me "proud as Lucifer"; but I suspect he referred to my immature propensity for intellectual one-up-manship, a bad habit I had acquired in high school. His smile, however, said more than his words. It said, "I understand. I love you. I believe in you." I left his office humiliated, discombobulated, encouraged. I thought, "He thinks I can make it."

Very early in our first year, we novices did what we called our "first probation." We made the thirty-day Ignatian retreat. In those days we did a preached, not a directed retreat, although during the thirty days, one had a conference every few days with the Novice Master to keep him posted as to how the retreat was progressing. We did five hours of prayer a day, with the prayer periods preceded by "points" delivered to us by the Novice Master. The points told you what to pray about. I had never prayed that much in my life. I remember my first long retreat as a crash course in Ignatian forms of prayer. I remember no dramatic graces, no strong consolations. I do remember that, when we got to the third week of the Exercises, the contemplations on the passion of Jesus, more than once, when Tony gave us points, I saw tears streaming down his face. No ostentatious sobbing, just constant tears running down his cheeks as he talked of Jesus' sufferings. I wondered what the gift of tears felt like and found it unimaginable.

Jesuits make the thirty-day retreat twice: early in the first year of their formation as Jesuits and early in the final year, called tertianship, because it supposedly functions as a third year of novitiate. In addition, every year, Jesuits do an eight-day retreat. After Vatican II, we as an order rediscovered the directed retreat. In the directed retreat, one works one on one with a retreat director who leads one through the prayer experience and adapts it to the personal needs of each retreatant. Gradually, very gradually, I began to absorb the wisdom of the *Spiritual Exercises*. Besides teaching one to pray, they also offer a crash course in conversion which culminates in a sense of vocation or call.

Ideally, the Ignatian directed retreatant comes to the retreat with some important decision to make: a vocational decision, a decision how best to use an inheritance, or some other life decision with major consequences. The second week of the retreat culminates in the "Election," in the moment when one finally decides what one will do. Like other key Ignatian terms, the term "Election" puns. One elects, chooses, in function of having first been chosen, called by God. The first two weeks of prayer prepare one to make the decision, the second two weeks confirm one in the decision one has made. The Ignatian phrase "discernment of spirits" puns analogously on "spirits." "Spirits" could mean animal spirits (the term for human emotion common in Ignatius's day), the human spirit with its powers of intellect and will, angels, devils, or the Holy Spirit.

The preface to the *Exercises*, the *First Principle and Foundation*, sets the fundamental parameters for making a good decision by choosing what in prayer one discerns as God's call. The *First Principle* informs one that human beings live created for an identifiable end: their personal salvation. This they accomplish by praising, reverencing, and serving God. All other creatures must serve as means to attaining salvation. Hence, one must cultivate indifference to any created reality or good; and one must desire it only insofar as it enables one to live for the end for which God has created one. Indifference does not mean apathy. It means freedom of heart. It means the refusal to make an idol of any creature, the refusal to cling to it as if it were God.

I remember my two years of novitiate to a great extent as a living out of the *First Principle*. I had made an idol of a medical career and clung tenaciously to it even when I knew that God was calling me to the Society of Jesus; but God kept after me until I abandoned that particular Baal. I found that I had other idols I needed to abandon. I got so used to naming and letting go of one

Anthony Margiaracina, S.J., giving points in the Grand Coteau chapel.

after another that I eventually could pretty much predict what God would ask me to give up next. In the end, of course, God always got things right. My idols did not make me happy; and giving them up left me a freer person, freer to move where God was calling me.

During the First Week of the *Exercises*, one confronts any sinful attachments which would prevent one from discerning and following God's call. One meditates on the Triple Sin: 1) the sin of the angels which met with immediate retribution and expulsion from heaven, 2) the sin of Adam and Eve which merited immediate punishment and expulsion from the garden of Eden; and 3) the one mortal sin of someone roasting in hell who had died before he could repent. All of this spoke to my image of a vengeful God. Many years later, I would learn that that particular conception of God derives not from Christian revelation but from classical Protestant Christology and from Catholic Jansenistic variations on and distortions of twelfth-century medieval atonement Christology.

It took years and years of making and studying the *Exercises* for me to realize that the meditation on the Triple Sin concerns not divine vengeance but divine mercy. The key to the meditation comes in the colloquy in which it culminates. Ignatius wanted the retreatant to imagine and to get a gut sense of what it would feel like to deal with God on the basis of strict retributive justice; but in the colloquy in which the meditation culminates, one contemplates the way God has in fact dealt with one in His compassionate Son. In the colloquy at the end of the meditation, Ignatius places the retreatant at the foot of the cross as Jesus hangs upon it on Calvary. He then invites the retreatant to enter into conversation with Jesus as he dies in agony and in forgiveness. One must first ask the dying Savior, "Lord, how did you come to suffer this terrible death?" The *Exercises* leave it up to the retreatant to imagine Jesus' response; but then, on the basis of that response, one asks oneself three questions, "What have I done for Christ? What am I doing for Him? What ought I to do for Him?"

I interpret the Triple Sin as one of several distinctively Ignatian test meditations which punctuate the *Exercises*. The Triple Sin seeks to evoke two gut responses from the retreatant: 1) a deep sense of what it would mean to deal with God on the basis of vindictive justice alone and 2) a profound realization of the infinite mercy, compassion, and forgiveness of God revealed to us in Christ Jesus. Until that second grace comes, one ought not to proceed to the next exercise: a review of one's own personal sins.

After that review and in the light of the grace of the colloquy of the Triple Sin, one renounces any sinful attitudes which would deafen or blind one to how God might eventually call one in the Election. One does so by making a general confession and accepting the grace of divine forgiveness.

The Kingdom meditation begins the second week of the *Exercises* and tests one's readiness to proceed to the Election. Ignatius has the retreatant imagine the personal call of an earthly king or of any purely human, charismatic leader and the kind of response that such a personal call from such an individual ought to evoke in one's heart. He then has one contemplate the call of Jesus Christ and the kind of personal, human response it deserves. Here the retreat director has to look for the grace of generosity. If the retreatant cannot respond to the call of Jesus Christ with unalloyed generosity, then the individual in question does not have the dispositions needed to proceed to the Election; for, in the second week, one is dealing with a choice not between good and evil but between good and better.

Once the grace of generosity prepares one to begin the process of the Election, the retreatant begins contemplating the infancy gospels. Ignatian contemplation engages the human imagination actively. It counsels the retreatant to imagine oneself as an active participant in the events one contemplates, in this case events surrounding Jesus' birth. Moreover, after a day of such active imaginative prayer, the *Exercises* urge one the get sensibly and affectively involved in the scene one is contemplating: to smell imaginatively the odors of the stable in Bethlehem, to see the brilliant glory surrounding the angels, to pick up the baby Jesus in one's arms and to imagine the feelings that such sensory experiences conjure up in one's breast.

While engaging in the contemplation of Jesus' birth, the retreatant also makes remote preparation for the Election. One lines up the possible things to which God might be calling one, given one's concrete historical circumstances. Once the retreatant reaches clarity on the different possible directions God's call might take, one begins the contemplation of Jesus' public ministry and of the generosity, trust, and love with which He responded to His mission. Moreover, Ignatius wants the retreatant to contemplate the events of Jesus' public ministry with the same active, imaginative intensity, with the same sensory and emotional involvement as one contemplated the infancy gospels.

Ignatius also punctuates the contemplation of the gospels with three test meditations, which tell the director of the retreat whether the retreatant ought to pass to the Election or not. The first test meditation, The Two Standards, tests whether or not one understands the concrete demands of discipleship and the difference between the way of Christ and the way of Satan. In a word, the Two Standards requires the retreatant to face the fact that the following of Christ can make stringent personal demands and can even require serious sacrifice and suffering. The first test engages the human mind.

The second test meditation, the Three Classes of Men, tests the will. It forces the retreatant to answer the question, when, among the possible options you face, you finally understand to which God calls you, do you stand completely willing to do what God requires of you, or will you weasel out or try to replace God's call with something else?

Ignatius expected that, at this point in the Election process, as the retreatant confronts the concrete menu of options, or possible divine calls, which he or she has faced and clarified in the first part of the Second Week, some will seem more appealing and others more repugnant. In a note to the retreat director, Ignatius warns immediately after the meditation on the Three Classes of Men that the spontaneous attractiveness or repugnance of particular options, or calls, indicates that the retreatant has not reached the degree of indifference required to advance to the Election. Ignatius writes in the note in question:

> It should be noted that when we feel an attachment opposed to actual poverty or
> a repugnance to it, when in fact we are not indifferent to poverty and riches, it

may be very helpful, in order to overcome this disordered attachment, though it is against our corrupt nature, to ask in the colloquies that our Lord choose us to serve in actual poverty. We should insist that we desire it, beg for it, plead for it, provided only that it be for the service and praise of the divine goodness (*Exercises*, 157).

The meditation on the Three Degrees of Humility echos the language of this note. It seeks to inform the Election and provides a final test of one's readiness to hear God's call rather than to yield selfishly to one's own personal preferences. One reaches the third degree of humility and passes the readiness test, if, in facing the various things to which God might call one, one can pray the following prayer: *Lord, among the various choices I face, I do not know to which you will eventually call me; but, if it gives you greater honor and glory, please call me to the one thing I least want to do.* Such a prayer does not determine the Election. God may not in fact be calling one to the most difficult option one faces; but, until one can ask God to call one to that most repugnant choice and mean it, one does not have the emotional freedom to advance to the Election and to hear in graced prayer what God has in mind.

The retreat director during the first and second weeks, has also been preparing the retreatant for the Election by explaining the "Rules for the Discernment of Spirits." The first set of rules, appropriate for the first week, explains basic concepts, like the difference between consolation and desolation. It also offers principles which apply to the human choice between good and evil and identifies the wiles Satan uses in order to deceive us into choosing sin. The second set of rules offers principles for discerning the movements of God's Spirit when one faces a choice not between good and evil but between two goods.

Armed with these rules, the retreatant who has passed all the readiness tests of the second week, now proceeds to make the Election. As I have already indicated, in the Election one chooses finally only in function of God's having chosen, called one to this rather than that. The realization of God's call can happen suddenly, spontaneously, and clearly; or, one may, after a series of experiences of consolation and of desolation, begin to discern the way the Spirit, the Breath, of God is leading.

Here, Ignatius probably alludes to his own earliest experiences of discernment. As he lay at Loyola convalescing from a leg shattered by a French cannon ball, he read some devotional books, the only ones provided him. One recounted the lives of the saints. While not reading, he would imagine himself doing the kinds of things that the saints did and then see himself in his own mind doing the kinds of things that knights did in the chivalrous romances he would have preferred to read. When he imagined himself acting like the saints, he experienced consolation: a peace and inner satisfaction leading to God which contrasted with the desolation, with the feelings of shallowness and emptiness he experienced when he imagined himself as a bone-crushing knight. The more he reflected on these experiences, the clearer it became to him that God was calling him to do the former, not the latter: to renounce an army career for a life of genuine sanctity.

If the Election does not happen either spontaneously or gradually, then, the retreatant uses human deliberation in order, hopefully, to facilitate a clear sense of where God is calling one. One clarifies in one's own mind the advantages and disadvantages of each of the options one faces. Then one continues praying until God makes it clear to which the deity summons one. If no Election in either of the first two modes subsequently occurs, then one can only conclude that God is not calling one to make the decision at this time.

Once one has chosen in the light of God's call, the second week ends; and the retreatant proceeds to the third and fourth weeks. In the third week, one contemplates the passion of Jesus. One accompanies Him as He lives out ultimate fidelity to the call the Father gave Him. Then, in the fourth week, one contemplates the victory of the risen Christ and the glory to which ultimate fidelity to one's own call leads.

Needless to say, I had none of these insights into the dynamics of the *Exercises* when I made my "first probation." I would reach them gradually, incrementally after decades of making the *Exercises* and studying them. I record them here, however, because in my judgment nothing shapes the religious self-identity of a Jesuit more profoundly than immersion in the prayer process of the *Exercises*.

I did the first two years of my theological studies in Eegenhoven, a little Belgian village just outside of Louvain. During those years, we Jesuit scholastics practiced sporadically a form of faith sharing we called in French "*colations*." These "*colations*" consisted of a free-ranging discussion of topics relevant to Jesuit spirituality. We had a thoroughly international community with scholastics from Africa, Central America, South America, the United States, and a variety of European nations. In one of our discussions, I raised the question, "Given our international diversity, what, if anything, do we share in common as Jesuits?"

Our group took the question seriously, as I had intended it. We decided that one event united us as Jesuits most immediately and profoundly: namely, the fact that we had all made the *Spiritual Exercises*. None of us had made the *Exercises* in exactly the same way. We might have interpreted this or that aspect of the *Exercises* differently; but the wisdom incarnate in the *Exercises* gave us Jesuit eyes, Jesuit hearts, Jesuit perceptions. At Grand Coteau, as I groped my way through my first long retreat, I started down a prayer path that would over the years transform me most profoundly into a Jesuit.

With time the experience of the *Exercises* would also shape in fundamental and decisive ways the kind of theology I would write. I have attempted to develop what Bernard Lonergan calls "foundational theology." Foundational theology, as I conceive it, proposes a fallible, revisable, but normative account of the forms and dynamics of conversion. I came to believe that the *Exercises* offer a wise and effective strategy to invite people, without coercing them, into an ever deeper experience of ongoing conversion. By "ongoing conversion" I mean what a more traditional theology of conversion called "sanctification." By "ongoing conversion" I also mean ongoing charismatic empowerment by the Breath of the risen Jesus to serve others concretely in His name and image.

Moreover, the Ignatian test meditations which punctuate the *Exercises* alerted me to the complexity of the conversion process. Ignatius wisely saw that all conversion, but especially ongoing conversion, engages the entire human person. Ongoing conversion has, therefore, a cognitive dimension: it engages one's fundamental beliefs about ultimate realities. It has, in other words, a reasonable, intellectual component. Ongoing conversion also engages choice, decision. It therefore engages one ethically. Finally, ongoing conversion engages one imaginatively and affectively. Moreover, disorder in one's affective attachments leads to disordered judgments about the way God is working in one's life. In other words, one judges reality, not just abstractly and inferentially, but affectively and emotionally. All discernment engages affective judgment. If so, then, sound perception of religious realities means making sure that one's heart, one's head, and one's conscience say the same things about the same realities.

Eventually, I would distinguish five forms of conversion: affective, intellectual, moral, and religious. That sounds like only four forms of conversion, not five; but I hold that moral conversion comes in two distinct but interrelated forms: personal moral conversion which deals primarily with questions of rights and duties and socio-political conversion which deals primarily with questions of the common good. I do not claim that immersion in the *Exercises* alone influenced the final formulation of that theology; but that the *Exercises* and the kind of conversion they promote did contribute significantly to its formulation I have no doubt.

Moreover, in the second volume of *The Firstborn of Many* and in the first part of the third volume, I tried to reflect with some theological sophistication and depth on the kind of practical knowing of Jesus Christ which the second, third, and fourth weeks of the *Exercises* seek to promote. In the course of making the Ignatian retreat, one allows the story of Jesus to intersect with one's own story in a way which throws clarifying light on the kinds of choices one ought to make personally. In reflecting on narrative Christology in *The Firstborn of Many* I tried to show that the four evangelists had told the story of Jesus and told it each time somewhat differently. They did so in order to facilitate the intersection of His story and the story of the community for which each evangelist wrote. They wrote, then, in order to illumine the kinds of concrete choices each community needed to make if it hoped to advance corporately in the knowledge of Jesus which results from assimilation to Him in the power and anointing of His Breath.

Mention of the Breath of Christ brings me to the one shortcoming I find in the text of the *Spiritual Exercises*. Ignatius himself had a strongly Trinitarian spirituality. The guidance of the Spirit, or Breath, of Christ in the living of Jesuit life had, he believed, to play the final and decisive role. Nevertheless, one finds little mention of the Spirit, the Breath, in the text of the *Exercises*. The most plausible explanation for this lack lies, I suspect, in Ignatius's relationship with the Spanish Inquisition. Before he went to Paris in order to study theology, Ignatius found himself three times interrogated by the Spanish Inquisition on the suspicion that the kind piety and religious experiences he was promoting in the *Exercises* bore the taint of a popular enthusiastic and sectarian movement spreading at the time in Spain. Its proponents went by the name of *Alumbrados*. The *Alumbrados* claimed the special illumination of the Spirit but sometimes in ways which divided rather than built up the Christian community. I suspect that Ignatius's reticence in invoking the Spirit more explicitly in the text of the *Exercises* resulted from his concern lest he find himself identified as an *Alumbrado*. In fact, his piety and spirituality tapped very different sources from these enthusiasts. With time, the Catholic Charismatic Renewal would enable me to fill in the caesura in the *Exercises* left by the lack of Spirit talk. In the process I would rediscover my own Jesuit tradition more profoundly.

Besides the *Exercises*, the Jesuit rule and the three vows of religion also have profound influence on one's self-perceptions as a Jesuit. Our Novice Master, Tony Mangiaracina, gave us conferences on the Constitutions and on the meaning of the three vows of poverty, chastity, and obedience. We studied a tedious canonical commentary on the Constitutions entitled "*Miles Christi Jesu*." With Tony we marched dutifully through the entire commentary. As in most education, what Tony took for granted communicated much more than what he said; and he took for granted that in interpreting any rule or regulation, one needs to use common sense. In so approaching the rule of the order, Tony manifested that he had understood well the spirit in which

Ignatius had written it. The rule begins by reminding Jesuits that sensitivity to the movements of the Holy Spirit takes precedence over any written law or regulation, even though written rules have their legitimate uses. In setting down concrete directives, however, Ignatius, throughout the constitutions, habitually qualified the directive in question by saying something like, "unless some other way of proceeding appears better to the people on the spot."

Only on one issue did Tony give us a hard line: on obedience. Once a superior had made a hard and fast decision, only one response sufficed: unquestioning conformity. If a superior tells one to jump off a tall building, one should blindly obey and do so. Unfortunately, that interpretation of obedience only tended to re-enforce my own adolescent, law-and-order tendencies. Years later, I felt deeply moved when Tony, in a private conversation, apologized for the way he had presented the vow of obedience to us novices.

He had, after over fifteen years, ceased functioning as Novice Master and served as the Minister of the Jesuit community at Loyola University in New Orleans. The Minister of a community tends to the physical plant and to the personal and corporate needs of the community and its members. I was visiting New Orleans and took the time to visit with Tony. Vatican II had yet to happen. I was sitting with Tony in his office chatting, when the bell for litanies rang. I reverted immediately to my "good-novice syndrome" and said, "Well, I guess we had better go to litanies." As we headed down the hall, Tony stopped me and said, "Wait a minute. Do you really want to go to litanies?" "No," I replied. "That's what I thought," he said. "Let's go back to my office and finish our drinks." As we chatted about this and that, Tony looked up at me and said, "You know, I think I stayed on as Novice Master too long. I stayed so long that I lost touch with what was actually going on in the province. If I had known how bad some of the superiors in this province are, I would have given you a completely different line on obedience." I felt, as I just said, deeply touched and moved at his humility and candor and felt all the more confirmed in my perception of Tony as one of the saints of our province. Tony eventually retired to Grand Coteau with a serious heart condition. There, until he died, every evening he helped the novices do the dishes.

I should in these rambling reminiscences recall one final seed which Tony planted in us as novices. In my second year he made us read a pamphlet written by Alban Goodier, a Jesuit who had received episcopal consecration and who had written a popular, devotional life of Christ which we novices all read. The pamphlet Tony gave us bore the title *A More Excellent Way*. It argued that a deep personal friendship with Jesus Christ holds the real key to spiritual progress and not rule-ridden legalism. We responded to the pamphlet enthusiastically, although it would take me years to realize the depths of meaning concealed in the phrase "friendship with Jesus Christ." *A More Ex-*

cellent Way did, however, inflict some significant chinks in the armor of my legalism.

In my second year of novitiate, as I recall, an event of province-wide significance took place. John Baptist Jansens, S.J., the then General of the Jesuits, ordered the Provincial of the New Orleans province to summon a province assembly in order to formulate an official statement on the immorality of racism and to draw up province policies for counteracting the evil influences of racism in our province and in the deep South. Although the Jesuits who taught me at Jesuit High School had eloquently denounced the sinfulness of racism and of Jim Crowism, not every Jesuit in the New Orleans province would have agreed with them. A handful of Jesuits openly preached racism and encouraged others to do so as well. Fr. Jansens wanted to make it clear that these pious bigots did not speak for the Society of Jesus. He wanted the New Orleans province to take a public stand against the sinfulness of all forms of racism and bigotry. Moreover, any Jesuit in the New Orleans province who disagreed with that official province policy would thereafter have to do so in the silence of his heart or suffer the consequences.

The elected delegates assembled at the novitiate for a three-day meeting. One of the delegates told me that when the discussions began, every variety of opinion surfaced. When it came to a final vote, however, the condemnation of racism and the province policies all passed unanimously. That event nudged me a little closer to a political conversion. As a sophomore in high school, I had renounced racism and bigotry in my heart. The actions of the province assembly made me realize that I had joined an organization actively opposed to racism and bigotry and that I had a responsibility to join in that active opposition. I would have no real opportunity to do so, however, until six years later when I myself began teaching sophomores at Jesuit High in New Orleans.

At the end of my second year of novitiate and shortly before we took our first vows as Jesuits, Gus Coyle, S.J., the dean of our juniorate, gave us a conference which sought to orient us to the major transition which passage from the novitiate to the juniorate marked in our progress through Jesuit formation. I remember Gus as a man of deep humility; but he sometimes spoke with a grandiloquence which made him seem to some pompous, even though he was not.

A story may give a feeling for what I am trying to convey. Gus faithfully celebrated the Eucharist for the Religious of the Sacred Heart, who had a convent and ran a girls' school about a mile from St. Charles College. A junior accompanied Gus and served his mass for the nuns. One morning, the sister sacristan informed the junior that this morning they would begin the Eucharist with a formal procession. "A procession?" responded the puzzled junior. "How can we have a procession? I'm the only other person here." "Fr. Coyle," the sister sacristan reposted, "*is* the procession."

Whether or not that morning Gus thought of himself as a procession, I do not know; but, if any individual could have pulled off being a procession, Gus could have done it. Very tall, quite portly, he wore his hair parted in the middle and slicked down. In his deportment, he had something of the aura and grandeur attributed to John Courtney Murray, the great Jesuit theologian. In describing Murray, one of his classmates remarked that "he sailed into a room like an ocean liner." I remember Gus sailing into the novitiate conference room with something of the same presence. He looked at us second-year novices and said in clipped speech and with the authority of an oracle, "Gentlemen, in a few weeks you are going to move from this side of the house to the juniorate. There you will study with C.J. McNaspy; and *then* your education will begin."

Dear, dear C.J., everything Gus said about you proved true; and I met you at the precise moment in my life when I needed to meet a genius, an enthralling teacher, a linguist, a historian, a classicist, a liturgist, an art critic, and a polymath. People who knew you could not help thinking at some point in their interaction with you that, in an age of narrow specialization, they were confronting the last of the Renaissance men.

As a Jesuit scholastic, C.J. decided that he would master all of the Romance languages. He did, applying himself last of all to Rumanian. He spoke five or six Romance languages, including Russian. After he left teaching in the juniorate at Grand Coteau and during the years he served on *America* magazine, he read *Pravda* every day and kept the staff of the magazine updated on how the Russian official party line perceived contemporary events.

When I met C.J., he had just become fluent in Spanish. Once he learned a language, he immediately read all its major classics in the original and shared them with his students. In the second year of my juniorate, C.J. felt satisfied with what he had done with Spanish and began absorbing Portugese. He happened to mention that fact to Lee Phillips, S.J., the Jesuit brother who took care of the community dining room. Lee spoke constantly in malapropisms; and he could not wait for the juniors to come into the refectory for morning "haustus," the Latin, in-house term for what the British call "elevenses," a beverage and a snack. We, of course, drank very strong coffee at haustus, not British tea. At any rate, as soon as the juniors arrived for haustus, Lee came bustling up to astonish us with this most recent news about C.J.'s linguistic achievements. "That McNaspy," burbled Lee. "He's something else. He comes in here and you don't know if he will be speaking Hingdorian or

Porkacheese." Used to Lee's mangled prose, we realized that C.J. had embarked on another linguistic adventure.

A fine pianist and organist, C.J. had a doctorate in musicology and had done a year of post-doctoral studies in history at Oxford with the great English historian, Christopher Dawson. C.J. taught us world history and introduced us to the Greek and Roman classics in the original, but as literature, not just as a grammatical exercise. Whatever he talked about he endowed with an infectious enthusiasm.

A native of Lafayette, Louisiana, he never lost contact with his Cajun roots and genuinely loved all people, but especially the little people, like the country folk among whom he had grown up. His father had coached football at the University of Southern Louisiana in Lafayette in McNaspy Stadium, to which Coach McNaspy had given his name. C.J. had one athletic skill: in basketball

The author as a junior with Daddy at Grand Coteau.

he could out-shoot all the juniors at the free-throw line. His shots swished through the net with mechanical accuracy.

C.J. introduced us to the splendor of art, architecture, and music. Every Friday evening, he gave an optional class which all the juniors attended. He projected the score of a major piece of music onto a large screen; and, as the record played the piece, he led us through it with a pointer. I cannot imagine a more effective way to teach a group of musically ignorant young people to hear the complexity of a great composition.

I love Gus Coyle, God rest him, and admire and appreciate his considerable classroom abilities as well as all he contributed to Jesuit formation, including my own. Still, Gus knew whereof he spoke when he predicted in his conference to us second-year novices that, when we met C.J., our education would begin. It certainly began for me. As a pedagogue of the humanities, C.J. had no rival. He captured my heart as well as my mind. Once the two of us listened to all the Beethoven string quartets through a series of mellow afternoons, with C.J. leading me, note by note, through the score. By the time I left Grand Coteau, I had begun, but only begun, to come of age intellectually. I wanted to imitate C.J. and to become everything he had become. I did not succeed, of course; but such dreams do young people no harm. Growing up in New Orleans had taught me to love imagination. C.J. taught me to appreciate the human imagination's greatest achievements.

C.J. did me another favor. In, as I recall, my second year juniorate, John Courtney Murray visited Grand Coteau. I believe that he was supposed to give a talk in Lafayette, Louisiana. C.J. never talked about his own achievements but showed constant enthusiasm for the accomplishments of other people. During Murray's visit, C.J. took the time to explain to us the importance of Murray's efforts at inculturating theology by wrestling with what the latter called "the American proposition." Murray had, of course, written extensively on the relationship of Church and state. He had argued that the United States system of separation of Church and state had, despite the de facto fusion of the two in most of Europe, solid foundations in the Catholic tradition and that it offered an institutional arrangement finally more advantageous to the Church than a state-established religion. Prior to Vatican II, his open disagreement in this matter with Cardinal Ottaviani, the head of the Congregation for the Doctrine of the Faith in Rome, had gotten him silenced on the subject.

During the second and following sessions of Vatican II, Murray would function as a council *peritus* (theological authority) and would serve as one of the chief architects of *Dignitatis humanae*, the council's Declaration on Religious Freedom. One day at Vatican II, Murray's nemesis, Cardinal Ottaviani, wandered into a conference Murray was giving to some bishops. The Cardinal found what he was hearing disturbing. Almost completely blind, Ottaviani asked one of the bishops who was speaking. Aware of the history of Murray's relation to the Cardinal, the bishop replied "Peritus quidam (Some *peritus* or other)."

C.J. ended his impassioned eulogy of Murray and his work by saying, "Someone in the generation following Murray's will have to continue the work he began." I remember thinking at the time, "I think I would like to do that." Moreover, over the years, the idea kept recurring.

I had done so well in the juniorate and had hit it off so well with both C.J. and Gus that they propositioned me about the possibility of returning to the juniorate as a professor. That sounded just fine to me. Accordingly, the province Prefect of Studies assigned me to do my philosophy at St. Louis University where I could also acquire a master's degree in the ancient classics. Another scholastic from our province, Pat Phillips, S.J., Lee's brother, accompanied me and would also live and study philosophy in the building the scholastics there called "The Fuse Box." "The Fuse Box" designated Fusz Memorial, the philosophate of the Missouri Province of the Society of Jesus.

During the summer before I left for St. Louis, I took an introductory course in physics at Spring Hill College in Mobile, Alabama, the only course in which I ever got and deserved the grade of "C." My other classmates would do their philosophy at our house of studies on the Spring Hill College campus. Although "The Fuse Box" typified the dry wit of Jesuit scholastics, we of the New Orleans province claimed that we had the best named philosophate in the entire American Assistancy. At its main entrance, one encountered a painting of Mary's assumption into heaven. The painting symbolized that our philosophate bore the name "Assumption Hall"; but, in calling it the best named philosophate in the American Assistancy, scholastic wit alluded to other kinds of assumptions. There my Jesuit classmates would learn a more pluralistic approach to philosophical thinking than I would in St. Louis.

I cut my own philosophical teeth with a fine, even distinguished faculty. Pre-eminent among the publishing faculty stood George Klubertanz, S.J., whom we scholastics affectionately called "Klubie," though not to his face. Many of the Jesuits who taught us, including Klubie, had studied in Toronto with Étienne Gilson; and the faculty had decided to introduce us to philosophy by a double strategy: 1) they gave us a thorough grounding in the historical development of philosophical thinking; and 2) they required us to master one philosophical system thoroughly. Their popularization of Gilsonian Thomism through teaching and publication bore the name in the New Orleans Province of "Missouri Valley Thomism."

Once Pope Leo XIII virtually legislated Thomism as the official philosophy of the Catholic Church, most Catholic philosophers toed the line and taught some form of Thomism. Not all did. Assumption Hall boasted one Suarezian and one Scotist. Modern Thomists, however, tended to put Aquinas's thought into dialogue with some modern philosophy. Étienne Gilson had studied with Henri Bergson. Gilsonian Thomism, therefore, read Aquinas through the lens of Bergson's theory of intuition. Missouri Valley Thomism claimed for the human intellect the power to intuit self-evidently and objectively the real distinction between essence and existence.

As I look back on my years in the Fuse Box, three teachers stand out especially. Bill Wade, S.J., whom we scholastics affectionately called "Daddy Wade" behind his back, taught me how to think critically; Klubie taught me the importance of interdisciplinary thinking; and the great historian of modern philosophy, James Collins, who taught in the University's philosophy department, taught me what my mother's injunction, "If you do anything, do it right" meant when applied to scholarly work. I never called James Collins anything other than "Doctor Collins" or perceived my relationship to him as anything other than professional.

As a teacher, Daddy Wade had mastered and practiced Socratic method. He taught us rational psychology and announced to us on the first day of class that he did not believe that the American male would think unless stood on his feet in public and asked a question. He taught a standard text book in Thomistic psychology and supplemented it with Klubie's book on the same subject.

I remember Daddy Wade as a shortish man with a slightly stooped walk. He had a face which looked like a blend between a bulldog and a cherub with high blood pressure. When he taught, he normally stood leaning on the chair behind the desk on the teacher's podium with his watery, blue eyes focused somewhere on the back wall. In those days, we had oral examinations in Latin at the end of every year; and after our third year we faced the examination we called the "de u," or "*de universa*," an oral on the whole of philosophy. In these oral examinations we had to defend a series of philosophical propositions called theses. Daddy Wade explained thoroughly each of the theses in rational psychology we would have to defend. We spent three weeks on each thesis.

Typically, Daddy Wade would walk into class and write the thesis we were studying on the blackboard. During the first week devoted to that thesis, he would call on two people each day. Having written on the blackboard, "The human intellect is spiritual," he would name one of the scholastics and then say in his high, breathy voice and pronounced Oklahoma accent, "Mister So-and-so, you have been living a spiritual life all these years. Why don't you

William (Daddy) Wade, S.J. doing his thing in the classroom.

stand up and explain to the rest of the class what spiritual means." The doomed student would rise and hazard a definition of "spiritual." Daddy Wade would then reduce anything he said to sheer gibberish, until the unfortunate student began to show signs of panicking. Daddy Wade would then give him a rest and turn to the second student. If he called on you at the beginning of a class, you knew that for that day you were it. This went on for a week.

At the beginning of the second week, Daddy Wade would announce, "All right, now I am going to teach you what you have to memorize for the exam." He would then explain the key terms of the thesis clearly and lay out the arguments which supposedly proved it.

During the third week, he would demonstrate to us the complete indefensibility of the proof we had learned during the second week. Anyone who studied with Daddy Wade had to think, could not not think.

Rightly or wrongly, I suspected that his own position approached fideism. At one point he announced to the class, "You know, I have survived four different philosophical systems on this faculty and I will be around when the fifth system becomes all the rage. Do you know why? It's because I will teach any system, since I don't believe any of them. To get into the history of philosophy, you don't have to say something true. You just have to say something different."

Daddy Wade did not hesitate to poke fun at the other members of the faculty, who took it in good humor. Once he asked us to turn to a certain page in Klubie's philosophy of the human person. "Now, look at that page," he said, "and you will see twelve statements about the human intellect. Fr. Klubertanz copied them all from Maritain. Maritain had only six theses; but Fr. Klubertanz has simplified them down to twelve." On another occasion, he quipped, "Whenever I am in doubt, I always consult an infallible source. So I ask Fr. Henle." He was referring to Robert Henle, S.J. who taught us theory of knowledge.

Daddy Wade and Bob Henle loved one another and also loved to argue. They seem, moreover, to have agreed on practically nothing, if you believed Daddy Wade's account of their dialogue. Once they got into a prolonged argument as to whether or not one could convert someone to Christianity through rational argument. Henle claimed that one could; Daddy Wade insisted that one could not. After several months of inconclusive sparring, Daddy Wade proposed that they decide the issue by putting it to a practical test. Both men taught a Hindu woman from India. Daddy Wade challenged Bob Henle to convert her by rational argument. When he failed, then Daddy would try his own methods. Henle pounced on the poor woman and argued Christian philosophy and theology for months. He got nowhere and admitted defeat. Daddy Wade used to celebrate the Eucharist for a congregation of religious women he called "The Pink Sisters." He described them as religious women with a strong contemplative spirituality who lived and worked among the urban poor. They also practiced Christian hospitality and welcomed guests. Daddy Wade befriended the woman from India and persuaded her to spend a weekend with The Pink Sisters. After doing so, she wanted to talk more with Daddy Wade about the experience.

I do not know if she ever did embrace the Christian faith; but Daddy Wade's account of this particular debate with Bob Henle left a deep impression on me. It convinced me that one converts with the heart before one converts with one's head; and it gave me my first real insight into the esthetic character of justifying faith.

I remember Klubie as another great teacher, even though his pedagogy differed *toto caelo* from Daddy Wade's. Klubie mostly taught books that he had written, a practice I would try to imitate after I joined the faculty of the Jesuit School of Theology at Berkeley. He would assign a section of his book for us to study. Then he would simply sit in front of the class until we asked him a question about the material. Eventually, I would adapt, with significant modification, this aspect of his teaching style to my own ends. Sometimes the class would begin with a long period of silence. Klubie never broke it. Eventually, someone would ask a question, and the class conversation took off.

Klubie had a round head, twinkling blue eyes, thinning, wavy, grey-brown hair, prominent ears, and a slightly protruding lower lip. He used the blackboard when he taught; and, when not actually writing with a piece of chalk, he held it against his lower lip, which always in class bore a white chalk mark in the middle. He was beginning to develop a small pot; and we scholastics claimed that it resulted from an accumulating chalk deposit in his stomach.

Klubie had enormous philosophical erudition. I found myself particularly impressed at his concern to put Thomistic philosophy into dialogue with the positive sciences. When I finally attempted to do my own philosophical and theological thinking, I would also emulate this aspect of his thought.

The New Orleans province sent me to St. Louis University so that I could earn a Masters degree in the classics. Some of the men from the Missouri and Wisconsin provinces were doing the same. I decided to take Thucydides in my first semester from the professor whom the other Jesuits studying the Greek and Roman classics described as the best teacher in the department. As the course unfolded I found myself appalled. C.J. had taught the classics as literature. In the Thucydides class we talked about nothing except Greek grammar. I was perishing with boredom and wondered how the other professors in the department must teach, if I was taking the best.

George Klubertanz, S.J. at his dean's desk.

Besides, I had fallen in love with philosophy. By the end of the semester, I decided that I could not bear the tedium of getting a masters degree in Greek and Latin grammar. I contacted the New Orleans province prefect of studies and told him that I wanted to switch my M.A. from the classics to philosophy but that I would concentrate on Greek philosophy. In fact, I wrote my M.A. thesis on *Logos as a Cosmological Principle in Plotinus* and even turned it into an article for *The Modern Schoolman*.

We scholastics got a B.A. in philosophy and letters at the end of our second year of philosophy. I got the M.A. and the Ph.L, the papal licentiate in philosophy, at the end of my third year of philosophical studies. While Klubie functioned as Dean of the Philosophate, Daddy Wade headed the philosophy department in St. Louis University. Daddy Wade required all undergraduate majors in philosophy and all philosophy M.A. candidates to take James Collins's course on the history of modern philosophy and get at least a B. Those who failed to get a B had to do some other advanced degree than an M.A. in philosophy. So in my second semester, I enrolled in Dr. Collins's course.

Dr. Collins taught from a wheelchair. Paralyzed in both his legs, despite his brilliance, he found that his handicap made it difficult to find a teaching position. He interviewed with Daddy Wade who recognized genius when he saw it and saw to it that Dr. Collins joined the St. Louis University philosophy department. Daddy also badgered the school administration into installing an elevator in the philosophy department office building so that Dr. Collins could get to his office by wheelchair. Thereafter, Dr. Collins remained deeply dedicated to St. Louis University and to Daddy Wade. When Dr. Collins died, he left his enormous philosophical library to the University.

Dr. Collins had written a huge tome on the history of modern philosophy and used it and selected works by modern philosophers as texts for his course on modern philosophy. Every time Dr. Collins taught the course, he had to get the Archbishop of St. Louis's permission to allow his students to read most of their text books, since the works of the modern philosophers we read generally lay condemned in the Vatican's *Index of Forbidden Books*. Since he taught the course every year, he staved off the tedium of repeating himself by tracing a particular philosophical concept, like the notion of "substance," of "God," of "Being" through a series of modern thinkers beginning with Descartes. He did not lecture on all the figures he treated in his book. He would require us to read one major work of the figures on whom he did not lecture. When I took the course, for example, we had to read Spinoza's *Ethics*. In our written examination on this batch of matter, Dr. Collins wanted us to reproduce one of the syllogisms from the seemingly endless string of syllogisms which constitute the text of the *Ethics*.

Prof. James Collins.

I got my B; and I took as many other courses as I could from Dr. Collins. I had never met a scholar of his stature and thoroughness before. I took him as a role model for serious scholarly work. C.J. had filled me with enthusiasm for the life of the mind. Dr. Collins taught me what disciplined and meticulously thorough scholarship demanded. When he had Jesuit scholastics in his class, as he regularly did, every Wednesday he would call one of us up to his desk after class and ask us the following Friday to take out from the Fusz Memorial library, which he found difficult to negotiate from a wheel chair, all the books it had on a particular thinker, like Paschal, or Leibniz, or Hegel. The next Friday one or more of us would stagger to class under the pile of books. Dr. Collins always thanked us cordially and returned the stack the following Monday. I once asked him in his office how he approached a new philosophical thinker. "Well," he said, "first you have to read the *opera omnia*, then you need to go through all the commentary and secondary source material on his work, then you have to reread the *opera omnia* and decide what you think about it." I realized that I had learned what doing scholarship "right" meant.

I came to philosophy with a personal agenda. As I have already indicated, my neurotic anxiety made it difficult for me to trust God completely and unconditionally. I came to the study of philosophy determined to demonstrate to myself rationally the existence of God and the immortality of the human soul. Indeed, I made that my principal project during my first year of philosophical studies. If I was going to give my life to this religious thing, I wanted those two truths nailed down solid. What begins as neurosis frequently ends as sin. Although I did not realize it at the time, I was committing the sin that the Bible calls "testing God." One tests God in the Bible by attempting to set the conditions oneself for one's relationship to God instead of meeting God on God's terms. My experience of religious vocation and the spiritual stripping I had experienced in the novitiate should have taught me better; but my anxious desire to have control of my relationship with God would give me no peace.

The more I tried to prove decisively and rationally to myself God's existence and the soul's immortality, the more I realized that I could not do it honestly and to my own intellectual satisfaction. Moreover, during the entire year I made the attempt to do so, I experienced total, unrelenting darkness in prayer. I had never before experienced that kind of religious blankness and blackness. At times, the only sense I had that God might exist derived from the fact that *something*, I knew not what, was sustaining me. I certainly knew that I was not sustaining myself. I felt as though I were hanging from a cliff by my fingers and toes in the blackest of black nights. By the end of a year, the darkness of soul had become unendurable. The darkness ended much in the way my resistance to a religious vocation had. I remember sitting at my desk during prayer time, utterly isolated, alone, and unutterably miserable. Finally, I turned to God and said, "All right! I can't prove it! I will just believe."

And then it happened. I experienced for the first time in my life what Ignatius of Loyola calls "consolation without cause." The moment I said, "I will just believe," the darkness lifted, instantly and totally. I felt flooded with joy, with consolation, with love of God the like of which I had never before experienced. More than that, I felt myself loved, embraced, encompassed by God's love and experienced the incredible truth that God loves *me*, only a speck in the great universe, but *me*. I cannot begin to express in words all that I experienced at that incredibly graced moment; but I knew without the shadow of a doubt, as Ignatius insists in describing consolation without cause, that whatever I was experiencing God was working in me.

At the moment when I turned to God and said, "I will just believe," I felt as though I were throwing my mind, my reason, away. In the wake of the experience of consolation without cause, I gradually began to realize that God was not asking me to throw my mind away. He was only asking me to use it on His terms and not on my own. Moreover, He was requiring this of me because He loved me and because I could find no better way to reach the truth about Him. At the time, I did not ambition a career in theology. I don't know what I ambitioned at that point in my young life. I still found the idea of teaching in the juniorate attractive; but I also knew that in philosophy I had found my first real intellectual love. Still, nothing could have prepared me better to do theology than that year of darkness and the consolation which ended it. Together they taught me to use my intellectual gifts on God's terms, not on my own.

As I look back upon this season of darkness and of grace, I discern grace even in the darkness. My desire to prove the existence of God and the immortality of my own soul sprang from a neurotic desire to control my relationship with God. The Lord responded by reducing me to a state of total dependence on Him. In the midst of all the darkness, I knew that Something was sustaining me. I knew that I was not doing it. I spent a year of cliff-hanging faith; and my misery ended as soon as I had the sense to acknowledge my need to believe, to trust my Sustainer.

My studies in St. Louis also enabled me to deepen in my personal repudiation of racism. I became good friends with Ted Cunningham, an African-American Jesuit scholastic of the Missouri province. We philosophers all spent our summers at the province villa on the Chain of Lakes near Waupaca, Wisconsin. There the Missouri and Wisconsin province scholastics took courses on education they needed to qualify them to teach high school in the Midwestern school system. Other out-of -province scholastics, like myself, could do whatever they wanted. I, for example, read the entire *Iliad* and *Odyssey* in Greek and studied Plotinus.

One day, Ted and I paddled to a picnic on Marl Lake, the lake furthest from the one which our villa overlooked. A hotel stood near Marl Lake. It had a wharf from which Ted and I were swimming. A family came down from the hotel to the wharf. A little white boy about five years old came running out onto the wharf, saw Ted, froze, and stared at him for about a minute. Then, he ran back up the path, crying, "Mother, Father, come and see the chocolate man!" Ted just laughed; but I suddenly realized that this child had never seen a Black man. I found that scarcely imaginable.

In my third year of philosophical studies, I had another life-transforming experience. I was completing class work for my masters degree in philosophy and so was taking more specialized courses than the introductory courses which every Jesuit took. One day, I was listening to my professor explain his understanding of the reality of relationship. All of a sudden, I remember saying to myself, "This man is talking bullshit; and I don't believe a word he is saying." Until that moment I had approached philosophy in the way that Daddy Wade assumed most of the scholastics did: I memorized and regurgitated what my professors taught me. In passing judgment on my teacher's position, I had, however, had my first, personal, philosophical thought.

Although I did not realize it at the time, I had experienced an intellectual conversion. For the first time in my life, I had taken responsibility for my own beliefs and had passed judgment on the received speculative wisdom my professor was handing out. Thereafter, I began thinking more thoughts of my own. In Klubie's class on the virtues, I wrote a paper exploring the relationship between artistic and prudential judgment, which he told me I could publish if I revised it. I did so, and it appeared as an article in *The Modern Schoolman*. I began to see that I might have a future as a research scholar and thinker. I subsequently transformed my M.A. thesis into another article in *The Modern Schoolman*, "*Logos* as a Cosmological Principle in Plotinus." While teaching high school in New Orleans, one summer I returned to St. Louis and did a course on Communist philosophy with Dr. Collins. He too pronounced my term paper on Communist esthetics publishable. It became an article in *Thought*.

I chose to do my M.A. thesis on Plotinus for a variety of reasons. I had promised the Prefect of Studies that I would concentrate on Greek philosophy in completing my M.A. Linus Thro, S.J., who taught us the history of philosophy, loved Plotinus. Linus tended to speak in periodic sentences of such grandeur that sometimes, by the time he got to the verb, he would have forgotten the subject of the sentence. He would then say airily, "Well, I guess you will have to complete that sentence for yourselves" and then launch into another rambling periodic masterpiece.

Often his lectures would end with reflections on how Plotinus viewed this or that issue. We knew that Plotinus was coming when he would draw a perfect circle on the board. He would locate on the circle various stages in the emanation of being from the One and in the return of being to the One. Moreover, he drew the perfect circle uncannily without looking at the blackboard and while staring out at the class. The perfection of the blindly drawn circle never ceased to amaze me. Linus's geometrical skills aside, he got me interested in the thought of Plotinus. I knew, moreover, that Plotinus had influenced many of the fathers of the Church and that knowledge of his thought would probably help me understand the development of patristic theology. I focused on Plotinus's conception of the *logos* because I also knew that the Platonization of the Johannine *Logos* played an important role in patristic Christology.

After I had written the thesis, I needed to find someone who could type Greek accurately and who could put my work into the format the university library required. It took some searching, but I eventually found a professional typist who fit the bill. I would pick up and proof the chapters as she finished them. Toward the end of this process, she said to me one day, "You know, after typing your thesis all day long, I feel as though I have been walking around downtown blindfolded." I guess Plotinus did that to people.

Leo Sweeney, S.J. directed my M.A. thesis. He told me that he found the thesis of doctoral quality. He suggested that I apply for the doctoral program, complete the course work necessary for the doctorate, and submit the M.A. thesis as a doctoral dissertation. I had not been thinking in those terms; but I liked the idea. I relayed Leo's suggestion to my provincial. He responded that I could apply for doctoral studies after one year of high school teaching. I would teach sophomores the next year at Jesuit High School in New Orleans, the school I had myself attended.

Daddy Wade had taken great joy in "undressing St. Thomas in public." By "undressing St. Thomas" he meant pointing out the contradictions and inconsistencies in his thought. Despite this debunking, I emerged from philosophy a Missouri Valley Thomist. Moreover, when I returned to my province, to my surprise I found that none of my classmates would have anything to do with Missouri Valley Thomism. In contrast to the faculty in St. Louis, the faculty of Assumption Hall had reached no philosophical consensus; and none of them defended Gilsonian Thomism.

With time, Daddy Wade's skepticism about the plausibility of the Thomistic synthesis bore fruit in my perceptions of things. While I knew that I owed a great deal to my professors in St. Louis, I felt disappointed with only one dimension of my philosophical training. I was preparing for ministry in the United States of America; but, in the course of three years of philosophical study, I had read only one essay by an American philosopher, George Santayana. Moreover, I had read it in an elective course I had taken from Dr. Collins. I felt in retrospect that I should have received a more thorough introduction to my own philosophical tradition. I began in my free time to read William James, George Santayana, and other U.S. philosophers. Gradually, Missouri Valley Thomism lost its allure. Eventually, C.S. Peirce taught me to see through its intuitionist claims and to acknowledge the fallibility of any complex hypothesis, including and especially metaphysical hypotheses. Once that happened, not only did Daddy Wade's undressing of St. Thomas acquire new cogency; but Klubie's cross-disciplinary approach to philosophical thinking enabled me to say goodbye forever to Missouri Valley Thomism. Fallible metaphysical hypotheses need verification not only in lived social experience but also in close scientific studies of reality. When, imitating Klubie, I tried to verify Thomistic anthropology in the results of individual and social psychology, I could not do it. I therefore abandoned it and the rest of the Thomistic synthesis. I still take Aquinas as a model for creative philosophical and theological thinking. I have convinced myself, however, that, if he lived and wrote today, Thomas Aquinas would not endorse Thomism.

I look back on my encounter with C.J. as providential. I met him at the precise moment in my life when I needed to. He instilled in me, as he did in the other people he taught, a zest and enthusiasm for the things of the mind. I also look back on the decision of superiors to send me to St. Louis for my philosophical studies as providential. My teachers there combined with the experience of graduate studies in order to endow my mind with the kind of systematic rigor it needed if I hoped eventually to think creatively.

Unfortunately, while I was learning to feel at home in the world of philosophy, problems began to surface in the Fuse Box. In the year of its completion, the Fusz Memorial had won an architectural award as a religious building . We who lived in it gave it considerably lower marks. It did not offer a really congenial living space. It had long, narrow, dark corridors lined by identical, cell-like rooms. We scholastics used to call our recreation room "the bowling alley." About fifteen feet wide, it stretched the length of basement, had small windows, and cold, green, tile walls. It did not invite one to relax.

Moreover, even though we had reached the third stage of our Jesuit formation, we still did not find ourselves treated as adults. We could read no uncensored newspaper or journal. At Waupaca, when we bathed in the lake in front of our house, we had to wear T-shirts, supposedly for reasons of religious modesty. We still kept a quasi-monastic daily regimen even at Waupaca. Every day we rose early and meditated for an hour before daily Eucharist and breakfast. One morning as I was praying close to the shore in front of our villa house, I saw two fishermen paddle by in a canoe. One asked the other as he nodded toward the villa, if he knew who lived there. "Don't know," responded the other. "Why do you want to know?" "They're strange," the first replied. "Every morning they all get up real early, and then they all sit for an hour under the trees and go to sleep."

In St. Louis, our contact with non-Jesuit students ordinarily did not go beyond attending classes in the University. We remained subject to seemingly arbitrary taboos. We could attend the symphony but not movie houses or public sporting events. Although priests could use the elevator, scholastics could not. In my second year at St. Louis, discontent boiled over in a wave of departures from religious life.

Garry Wills numbered among those leaving. We recognized his brilliance even then; and he would go on to a distinguished scholarly career. I myself did not even consider leaving the order. I suspect, however, but cannot prove that, if the reforms of religious life which Vatican II mandated had already taken shape, the order would not at that time have lost so many good men.

As I have already indicated, after completing my philosophical studies, I found myself assigned to teach in the high school I had attended. I began my teaching career as the home room teacher to the sophomore honors class. One event which occurred about three weeks after instruction began transformed me into a successful high school teacher. My students had for three weeks exhibited angelic behavior. Then, one day, when I turned around to write something on the blackboard, the entire room broke into pandemonium. That kind of outburst could only have resulted from planning. I had, at that point, never yelled at my class. I have a loud voice, when I want to use it. I whipped around and yelled at the top of my voice, "QUIET!" Suddenly everything stopped; and I found myself confronted by a sea of adolescent faces with their eyes bulging and their jaws unhinging. They looked so silly, I started to laugh. The more I laughed the more bewildered and even frightened they looked. Soon, I was leaning against the blackboard screaming hysterically with laughter. After that, I had no more disciplinary problems.

Three years later, one of the students from that class alluded to the incident and remarked, "That was the smartest thing you ever did."

"Well," I replied. "It wasn't as though I planned it."

"I don't care if you planned it or not," he rejoined. "From then on we knew that we were dealing with a lunatic." As a matter of fact, after my laughing binge, if anything untoward occurred in the class, I only had to stop whatever I was doing and order returned instantly.

Once, when I was prefecting a bus full of Jesuit High Blue Jays and their dates traveling to an out-of-town football game, one of my own students came to me where I sat in the front of the bus and told me that he thought I had better come to the rear where some bullies had stripped the shirt off of one of our eighth-grade boys and stuffed him under a seat. As soon as I got there, all activity ceased, and a palpable, nervous, adolescent silence fell. I told the eighth-grader to get out from under the seat and to put his shirt back on. I stood there in silence as he did so. One of my students sat with his date in the seat next to where I stood. The silence began to get to the date. She whispered to my student, "Why doesn't he say something?" He whispered in reply, "He never says anything. He just looks at you." I had to repress a chuckle.

Besides beginning to give me a classroom style, the years of high-school teaching, prefecting, and play directing, changed me in three ways. First of all, I found myself holding a full-time job for the first time in my life. Taking on that kind of responsibility helped me mature personally and emotionally.

Second, in relationship to southern racism and Jim Crowism, the classroom transformed me into a teaching activist. In the process, it nudged me closer to what I would one day call socio-political conversion. I had no choice in the matter. I found myself confronted with a classroom half filled with adolescent racists. I could not fulfill my responsibilities to them unless I challenged them to face their racism and renounce it. I began to study the forms and motives of racist bigotry and learned in the process that the judgment of prejudice comes co-naturally to the human mind.

In some ways, the crudely overt character of southern racism made it easier to deal with. Later when doing my doctoral studies at Fordham University, I would bridle when New Yorkers would refer to racism as a southern problem. I found lots of racism in New York City. It took a subtler form than southern racism; but it not only existed. It thrived. In dealing with the racism of my high school students I found myself heartened by the fact that only half of them really endorsed segregation and Jim Crowism. When I had gone to Jesuit High, everyone in my high-school class, as I recall, embraced racism as "our southern way of life." That only half of my students did gave me hope that in the struggle against that particular evil we were making some progress at least.

Third, at the end of my second year of regency, I almost left the Society of Jesus. When at the end of philosophy, I had asked for doctoral studies instead of high school teaching, my provincial had promised me that I would go to doctoral studies after teaching at Jesuit High for a year. Toward the end of that year, I had my account of conscience with the provincial and again requested permission to complete the doctorate I was so close to completing at St. Louis. He replied that I had taught for just one year and that I might as well teach for two. I felt disappointed but acquiesced. At the end of my second year of teaching, in my account of conscience with the same provincial, I raised the question of doctoral studies for a third time. "Well," he replied, "you have taught for two years, you might as well teach for three."

I said nothing to him at the time, but I felt furious. I decided that the provincial had been playing games with me. He had never intended to give me permission to do the doctoral studies I had requested. From the beginning, I told myself, he had decided that I would teach for three years like all the other scholastics; but he had coddled me by pretending that he would agree to the studies, if . . . I felt used and manipulated. The more manipulated I felt, the angrier I got. I eventually got myself worked up into such a snit that I decided that, if religious obedience meant this kind of manipulation, I for one had had it with religious life. I decided that I would chuck the whole thing and leave the Society. I had all but begun to draft the letter informing the provincial that I intended to leave the order and that I officially requested dispensation from the vows of religion, when it occurred to me that, before I left, I really ought to discuss my decision with someone else.

I immediately thought of Jimmy Yamaouchi, S.J. Jimmy taught theology at Loyola University. The son of a Japanese father and an American mother, he

The author as a third-year regent.

loved to startle his racist students at Loyola by saying things like, "The trouble with you white people is. . . ." They thought of Jimmy as white, while he insisted that if one drop of Black blood makes one an African American, having an Asian father made him Asian, not Caucasian. I did not know Jimmy that well at the time; but I knew that my brother and everyone who did know him held him in the highest esteem. I also knew him well enough to seek his advice. I called him and made an appointment to see him.

When I walked into his room in Thomas Hall, the Jesuit residence at Loyola University, he greeted me in a friendly way, told me to sit down, and asked me how he could help me. I told him that I was thinking of leaving the Society. To my utter astonishment he burst into laughter. He had a round face, twinkling eyes, and an infectious chuckle. When he stopped laughing, he said, "Oh, yes! I remember the time I decided I was going to leave." He then told me the story of why he had decided to leave only to reverse his decision and stay. Then we chatted about this and that, all small talk. I got up to leave the room; and, when I had closed the door behind me, I knew that I would not leave the Society, would not write the provincial that letter. Paradoxically, having definitely decided that I would leave, I now felt freer to stay.

While I still think that the provincial did wrong in stringing me along, in his defense the record should show that, at that point in my growth, I probably needed the maturation of holding down a full-time job and of shouldering the responsibilities of active ministry more than I needed to bury myself deeper into books. I think that the provincial saw that, even though at the time I did not. His decision had, moreover, a providential character. Had I done my doctoral studies instead of teaching high school, I would have specialized in ancient philosophy. Had that happened, I might never have discovered in a systematic way the United States' philosophical tradition and developed the kind of inculturated theology I eventually did. I had already begun to explore the American philosophical tradition. Two years of studying theology in Belgium would transform an initial interest in mastering the United States philosophical tradition into an crying need.

I decided that, if I could not do graduate studies during regency, I would at least begin research toward a doctoral dissertation. I had decided that I would pursue a doctorate in philosophy and that I would specialize in United States philosophy. I decided to focus my dissertation on one major American thinker. If I was going to approach my dissertation using the Collins method, I had to begin my research by reading that thinker's *opera omnia*. I could, however, find the complete works of only one American philosopher in our high school community's library: Ralph Waldo Emerson. During my third year of high school teaching, I began to immerse myself in Emerson's writings.

A fluke landed me in Eegenhoven, Belgium for my first two years of theology. Toward the end of my third year of regency, the General of the order had sent our provincial as a special visitor to the Mexican province. As a result, Andrew Cannon Smith, S.J., the acting provincial, heard my account of conscience. Most people in the province had nicknamed Andy "Boom-Boom" because of his middle name. He surely ranks among the great men of our province. Besides holding a number of important administrative posts, as President of Spring Hill College, he made the decision to integrate it racially before any of our other institutions had integrated. Once at a province assembly which I attended as a delegate, someone asked Andy, "How much did it cost to integrate Spring Hill College?" Andy thought a moment and replied, "About three buildings." Shortly after the integration, the Ku Klux Klan tried to burn a cross on the campus, but students came pouring out of the dormitories and drove them away before they could light it. The cowards came back the next night and burned a cross at an entrance to the campus where no one could see them and drive them away.

Despite his many virtues, listening did not function among Andy Smith's top skills, at least if my own experience with him counts as typical. As I walked into the room for my account of conscience, Andy greeted me cordially and said, "Well, I guess you will be wanting to go to Europe for theology." He intended the remark as a complement. Since we had no theologate, most of the men in our province studied theology in the Missouri Province at St. Marys, Kansas. Usually, however, we sent one or two to Europe. Those singled out for European studies, moreover, usually went on for doctoral work. Doing theology in Europe gave one a head start on the languages one needed to complete a doctorate.

As I have already narrated, in the juniorate C.J. had given me the idea of ambitioning a theological career in the image of John Courtney Murray. That idea had never left me. As my interest in American philosophy and culture grew, the idea of studying theology with Murray and with Gus Weigel, one of the leading Jesuit ecumenists of his generation, looked more and more appealing. So, when Andy Smith suggested that I probably wanted to study theology in Europe, I replied, "Instead of going to Europe, I would really like to study with Murray and Weigel at Woodstock."

"Well," Andy retorted, "there should be no difficulty with your doing that."

After my interview with Andy, I assumed that I would, after finishing regency, begin my theological studies at Woodstock College in Maryland. When, however, the status, the list of the following year's assignments, appeared on the community bulletin board, I saw written on it "Gelpi–Louvain." I felt surprised but thought, "Well, I have never seen Europe. I might as well check it out."

Right after seeing my name on the status, I went for a cup of coffee in the haustus room, where I found François Jansens, S.J., an old Belgian priest who had volunteered for one year of service in the New Orleans mission and never returned to his homeland. "Well, François," I said. "I just got word that I will be studying theology in Belgium."

"Oh," he said, "dat is too bad."

"Why?" I responded, "What's the problem?"

He said, "De weather is terrible."

"It can't," said I, thinking of the roasting, humid summers and bitter, wet winters in New Orleans, "be worse than New Orleans."

"Oh, yes," said he, "much worse."

"What's it like?" I asked.

Shaking his head grimly, he responded, "It rains continually, and it is bitterly cold." François knew whereof he spoke. He exaggerated only one fact. What falls in Belgium does fall constantly, but it does not quite qualify as rain. It resembles fog more, except that it falls like rain. In my first year in

Eegenhoven, it fell for nine months straight with at most seven non-consecutive clear days during that entire period.

When I got to Eegenhoven, I wrote to Andy Smith and informed him of the fact. He replied promptly and told me that he felt pleased that I was settling down "in the theologate of my choice."

Before going to Belgium, I went to Quebec City where I studied French at Laval University in order to prepare myself to live in a French-speaking community in Belgium. For the first time, I saw the United States through the eyes of foreigners. I would experience much more of the same during my two years in Europe.

In Quebec, Jesuits wore the cassock in public, a practice which I loathed. I have never lost the anticlericalism I absorbed as a youth. In fact, with the years, I have come to recognize it as a genuine grace. Once I joined the faculty of The Jesuit School of Theology in Berkeley, I found myself frequently asked to evaluate a young Jesuit's readiness for ordination. I used to tell the scholastics I taught that I always asked myself a question not on the official evaluation form: namely, *Is this young man sufficiently anticlerical to risk ordination?* Without a healthy dose of anticlericalism, the institutionalized clericalism in the Church can all too easily corrupt the ordained. It gives me no little satisfaction that all the candidates I have evaluated for ordination have passed my personal anti-clerical test. At any rate, in Quebec I perceived the public wearing of cassocks as an expression of clericalism and donned it in public with great repugnance.

About the middle of that summer, I had a strange experience. Learning to speak a foreign language takes its psychic toll. One day, feeling exhausted, I decided to take a nap in the middle of the day. Despite genuine weariness, I could not get to sleep. Moreover, I had an uncanny feeling that I was supposed to take a walk wearing my cassock. I fought the feeling, but it would not go away. Finally, I gave in, put on the bloody cassock, and started walking. For some inexplicable reason, I felt strongly drawn to the Plains of Abraham. There I met a man who desperately needed to talk to a priest. Though not yet ordained, I, all becassocked, seemed to him a priest. I ministered to him for two solid hours. As I did so, I could not shake the feeling that I had felt impelled to walk to the Plains of Abraham *so that* I could minister to him.

In Quebec, I also made distant contact with the first Jesuit missionaries to Canada. I resided at the Petit Seminaire, the minor diocesan seminary. One evening, several of us Jesuit students were walking in our cassocks in the Basse Ville, the old city of Quebec built on the flatlands along the St. Lawrence River that lie at the foot of the high bluffs on which modern Quebec rises. An elderly gentleman introduced himself and, eyeing our cassocks, asked us if we were Jesuits. Unlike diocesan cassocks, Jesuit cassocks had no buttons. We said that we were. "Follow me," he said, "I have something to show you." He took us to an old, light blue, stuccoed building. The bottom floor contained a barber shop. It appeared that the barber and his family resided on the top floor. The old gentleman directed our eyes to a spot halfway up the stucco wall. There we saw the seal of the Society of Jesus. Our guide explained to us that the first Jesuit missionaries to Canada had used the building as a residence and that new missionaries stopped there until they could find transport to Indian country. In the novitiate, I had read the life and martyrdom of Jean de Brébeuf, Isaac Jogues, and René Goupil. I had felt moved at their incredible courage and horrified at the sufferings they had endured. Now I was looking at the place where they had resided when in Quebec. I felt a sense of my Jesuit roots and felt proud of them.

On another occasion, I nearly got killed. A group of us were trying to cross a very wide street that led down the hill to the Basse Ville. We had gotten trapped between two moving lines of traffic and could move neither forward nor backward. I turned to look down the hill and saw an automobile whose driver was gunning the motor to make it up the hill. The setting sun shone in his eyes, and he could not see us. He was coming fast and was headed right for us. I stood closest to the onrushing car; so it was headed right for *me*. Oddly, I felt no fear. I remember looking at the vehicle in a detached way and thinking, "I wonder if it will stop before it hits me." It finally did stop, about three inches from my leg. I turned then to look at my companions, whose eyes were bugging out of their heads. Only then did fear overwhelm me. It gripped me with such force that my legs turned to water. I could barely make it across the street when the traffic finally broke and allowed us to complete our crossing of the intersection.

I had nearly died of pneumonia at the age of two. I would have another brush with death during the first year I taught in Berkeley. These confrontations with the Grim Reaper taught me to trust that I would live this life as long as God wanted me to and long enough to accomplish whatever God wanted me to accomplish.

Living in Quebec prepared me for life in Belgium in more ways than giving me fluency in speaking French. I experienced at first hand the French separatist movement, which would have strong analogies to the Flemish separatist movement I would encounter in Belgium. Flemish, Dutch-speaking Belgians outnumbered the Waloons, the French speaking Belgians. Prior to World War II, the Flemish found themselves an oppressed majority in their own country. Though they outnumbered the Waloons, the latter occupied positions of economic power. Created artificially from a part of France and a part of Holland to serve as a buffer state between France and Germany,

Belgium contained two populations divided by a huge cultural gap. When Germany invaded Belgium, some of the Flemish found more cultural affinity with the Germans than with the Waloons. As a consequence, it would appear that more Flemish collaborated with the Germans than did their own French-speaking countrymen. After the war, a backlash against the Flemish for the collaboration of some widened the gulf between the two groups. By the time I got to Belgium, a backlash against the backlash had begun. The backlash against the backlash took shape in the Flemish separatist movement. Some separatists wanted to annex the largely rural Flemish lands to Holland. The separatists also wanted to transform Louvain University, which stood in Flanders, into a Flemish-speaking institution. Our theologate in Eegenhoven had, as far as I could see, nothing to do with the University; but, during the two years I studied there, I heard stories of French-speaking professors at the University harassed by obscene phone calls. Eventually, the French-speaking faculty would split off and found *Louvain La Neuve*, the French-speaking version of Louvain University. That would happen only after I left Belgium. While living there, I used to tell the Belgian Jesuits that I understood their problem because I had grown up in the racist Gulf South. They did not like to hear that, but I spoke the truth.

After summer school in Quebec, I rendezvoused in New York with Roy Shilling, S.J., who was traveling to Europe for tertianship, the final year of Jesuit formation. A roly-poly Jesuit from the New Orleans province in high school work, Roy proved a wonderful traveling companion except on board the *Flandre*, the sister ship of the *Liberté*, on which we were sailing to England. From the moment we left New York harbor, Roy's face went green with seasickness and remained that way until his feet again rested on solid ground. Needless to say, his misery made him somewhat less than companionable. On the deck, his chair lay to my right. On my left lay a Parisian family with a loathsome little girl of the sort who intuits what will most annoy an adult and does it over and over again. Her lumpish parents saw what was going on but did nothing to discipline the brat other than to repeat over and over, "Don't do that, dear" to no effect.

Meals raised other problems. Roy and I made the mistake of showing up in clerics to get our table assignment. We wound up eating with two very elderly couples from the Midwest who spoke no French and whose only conversation consisted in yelling louder and louder in English for whatever they wanted. Since we were sailing on a French boat, the food tasted delicious; but the waiters spoke no English. Periodically, then, as I was chewing and trying to digest my food, I would hear an elderly voice next to me saying louder and louder, "Salt, *salt*, *SALT*, SALT!" Otherwise, I heard only an occasional groan from Roy or the sound of chewing coming from our table. I could not wait for the voyage to end.

I found only three things interesting on that ocean trip. First of all, I had no money for gambling and hate it anyway; but I did find some relief in the daily afternoon movie. Roy and I had a devil of a time getting to the theater. Only on the last day of the trip did we learn that we had been crashing the first-class screening of the film. Second, in the course of the ocean transit, I read in its entirety *Mont Saint Michel and Chartres*. It introduced me to the con-voluted mind of Henry Adams. Finally, during the last three days of the voy-age we outran a storm. In the dining room during meals one would find one-self looking down through a porthole at the churning sea and then up to the heavens at lowering clouds. The high seas almost did Roy in. I served his mass every morning; but, during the last three days, he could barely make his way through the entire ceremony. Luckily, I experienced no *mal de mer*. I had never sailed on an ocean vessel ploughing through high seas and found the whole thing fascinating: the metal guards around the tables to keep one's plate from spilling into one's lap, pulling oneself around the ship with ropes to hang on. The challenge brought us passengers a bit closer together; and I made the acquaintance of a young American couple. I felt relieved, however, when the otherwise tedious voyage ended; and I swore I would never again cross the ocean by boat.

In the first half of the trip, before we began racing the storm, an incident occurred which prepared me for Louvain. Just before leaving the deck for our cabin, I spotted a whale: flukes and a spout. When I entered the cabin the French steward was tidying up. To make conversation, I told him I had just seen a whale. "No, you didn't," he replied. "They never come this far north." "I saw it," I insisted, "with my own eyes." "No, you did not," he retorted. "They never come this far north." In fact, whales do. In a flash, I understood René Descartes. I grasped how the Gallic mind could imagine that it had the power to deduce the nature of all being while puffing one's pipe in front of one's fireplace. As we shall see, I would encounter the same a priorism in Ee-genhoven. I would, however, find it the least of my problems.

C.J. had expressed his delight at my voyage to Europe. He loved to travel and on two occasions girdled the world. Before I left, he told me, "Take an apocalyptic approach! You don't know if you will ever go back, so see as much as you can." I did my best during the three weeks I had with Roy to see as much of England and of France as I could; but I found I had less stamina than C.J. After about two weeks of touring, I felt glutted. Roy returned to his usual cheerfulness as soon as he left the boat; and I enjoyed traveling with him. I have a vivid memory of seeing him tippy-toeing in all his portliness down some stones jutting from the side of the dome of St. Paul's in London.

We did the obligatory museums in both London and Paris and visited the obligatory monuments: La Sainte Chapelle, Notre Dame, the Tuilleries, the terrifying elevators of the Eiffel Tower. We split, however, when I announced that I wanted to tour as many French medieval cathedrals as I could. I shall never forget the wonder of Chartres.

On my final journey to Eegenhoven, I stopped in Paris where I watched *Ben Hur* in dubbed French. On my first evening in Eegenhoven, I mentioned to one of the Belgian scholastics that the trees in Paris were already changing color. He responded exactly as the French steward on the *Flandre* had. "No, they were not changing," he said. "It's too early." Descartes *redivivus*. From that moment on I knew that Eegenhoven would be different; but I could not have predicted how different.

Before embarking from New York, I had seen the movie *The Nun's Story*. I felt mild insult and outrage after viewing it. It seemed to me an anti-Catholic parody of religious life as I had lived it in the United States. American religious in those days suffered from the same woes as other American Catholics: religious authoritarianism, hierarchicalism, clericalism, legalism, a measure of formalism. Vowed religious live with these things more constantly than lay Catholics, who seem to find it relatively easy to tune out the clergy when they talk or insist on nonsense. I found the portrait of religious life in *The Nun's Story* a parody of what I had known: impersonal, guilt-ridden, emotionally repressed, barren, Jansenistic. *The Nun's Story* recounts the experience of a modern Belgian nun. After a few months of life in Eegenhoven, I looked back on the movie more as a documentary than a parody. Not by chance was the tower of Cornelius Otto Jansen crumbling in the town of Louvain.

A few stories may give a feel for what I mean. An elderly Jesuit functioned as spiritual director to the Jesuit theologians. He used to give us regular exhortations: pious reflections on the ideals of religious life. In almost every exhortation he extolled the importance of joy. I noticed, however, that when he said "la joie," he never smiled. On the contrary, his brow furrowed and his face grew even grimmer. I soon realized that when he said "la joie," he meant that purely spiritual joy which one experiences, preferably, in the midst of complete and utter human misery.

Or ponder the case of our professor of canon law. During World War II, he and a Belgian woman of some years found themselves surprised on a open road by an air raid. They both took shelter in a ditch. After the all clear, the woman scrambled out of the ditch first. She turned and offered the Jesuit her hand to assist him back to the road. He replied, "Prenez plutôt mon bréviaire." Then, lest his vowed, celibate flesh touch female flesh, he had her haul him out of the ditch by his berviary.

Another anecdote may convey something of the ascetical tone of religious life in the Belgium I knew. I left Eegenhoven after two years. The following year, a New England Jesuit, Paul Paradis, S.J., began his theological studies in Eegenhoven. Paul grew up speaking French and spoke both French and English like a first language. I had met Paul in Quebec. After I had been teaching for a few years in Berkeley, Paul too came to the San Francisco Bay area. He had a degree in phychology and taught it for a time at the University of San Francisco. Shortly after he arrived, we had dinner together and glummed about our years in Belgium. In Paul's first year of theology, as I recall, one of the regents teaching in the Belgian equivalent of a high school in Namur had suffered a nervous breakdown. Paul, who welcomed the opportunity to get out of Eegenhoven volunteered to teach the scholastic's classes, even though it meant he had to travel by train to another town twice a week. Since he had saved the situation in the school, he soon became the pet of the local rector.

One day he got a call from the minister in Namur, the Jesuit who supervised care of the physical plant. The minister told him that the rector had called an extraordinary meeting of the entire Jesuit community and wanted Paul to attend. Paul protested that it meant a certain amount of inconvenience since the meeting did not coincide with one of the days when he normally traveled to the school. The minister informed him that the rector insisted that he attend. He did.

This school kept boarders. The door of every student's room had a wire connecting it to a board of lights in the room of the Jesuit who prefected that corridor of the dormitory. If a student opened his door, a light went on in the room of the prefect. Every time two lights went on simultaneously, the prefect had to check and see what was going on. Paul claimed that prefects haunted every room and corridor in the building, including the rest rooms. Only the chapel had no prefect.

Paul arrived late for the meeting; but the rector had saved a seat for Paul next to his own. The community sat in a circle and were giving their opinion one after another. Paul's position next to the rector made him the last to speak. As he listened, he gradually realized that the community was discussing a student whom some prefect had found masturbating in the chapel. At first, he assumed that they were discussing how to deal with the student pastorally. Then it became clear to him that the school administration had expelled the boy and informed his parents that they had raised a degenerate. In fact, the rector had summoned the community and had made Paul travel to another city in order to discuss whether or not he as rector needed to reconsecrate the chapel before allowing eucharistic celebrations there. When Paul's turn to speak came, he said, "This school has prefects in every room and corridor except the chapel. If I were a teenage student here and wanted to masturbate, I could only do it in privacy in the chapel." The minister of the community looked at Paul with amused admiration; but the rector, after a long pause, turned to him and said, "Mon père, je suis déçu (Father, I am disappointed)." Paul learned a few days later that the school no longer needed his services.

In my first year in Eegenhoven, we almost never saw the sun. We only surmised that the sun was in fact shining by the fact that the heavy mist falling outside began to glow and then at some point stopped glowing. As the winter wore on, the periods of glow got shorter and shorter. I learned that Belgium shares the same latitude with Labrador. By January, the falling mist started glowing about nine thirty in the morning and stopped at about three o'clock in the afternoon. By that point, a depressed desperation settled upon me.

We had little to eat. When in Berkeley I informed Joseph Powers, S.J., another member of the faculty there, that I had studied for two years in Belgium, he chuckled and said, "Oh, yes, the Belgian potato cure." In fact we had boiled potatoes and rotten apples to eat every day twice a day. We had ripe apples in the basement; but we got fed the rotten ones first lest they go to waste. Wasting the rotten apples would have violated "religious poverty." While we ate the rotten apples, some of the ripe ones got rotten. As a result, we had an endless supply of rotten apples. Finally, one of the New England Jesuits left the refectory with a knife in his hand slicing all the rotten apples in two in order to prevent their getting served again as dessert. We then got them for breakfast as rotten applesauce. Since the building we lived in housed both philosophers and theologians we had a sizeable community. Shortly before I left, I passed through the kitchen and saw the meat the cook would use to make a stew for the entire community. It consisted of a single cow's head.

John Stacer, S.J., who entered the New Orleans province a year before I did, had preceded me to Eegenhoven. We had taught together at Jesuit High in New Orleans. Our shared Belgian ordeal made us even closer friends. Roberto (Bobo) Muysondt, S.J., from El Salvador, also became a very dear friend. Bobo had studied philosophy at Assumption Hall and so had warm feelings for the members of the New Orleans province. He needed all the warm feelings he could get. He had found Mobile, Alabama, cold. Now his superiors had sent him to study theology as far north as Labrador. We had radiators in our rooms; but they had water in them and their pipes. The boiler worked only for an hour in the morning and for an hour in the afternoon. As a result, just as a hint of warmth began to creep into the pipes which fed the radiator, the boiler shut down and the heat stopped coming. Bobo coped with the frigid rooms and halls by having an overcoat made for him. He wore it in the house as long as he could. He told me that the thickness of the cloth made it so heavy that, if he wore it for more than four hours, his shoulders started to ache unpleasantly. A helicoptor which shuttled people to different cities in Belgium regularly flew over the building where we lived. Periodically, Bobo, when he heard the sound of the rotors, would stick his head out of his window and yell up to it in English, "Take me with you!"

We had some distinguished theologians on our faculty; but some of the professors simply handed out notes and then read the same notes to the students in the class. When that happened, I, like many of the other theologians, brought a book to class and read it rather than waste time. The practice got me used to doing intellectual work with noise in the room. As a result, I can now read and study almost anywhere, including the New York subway. I also enjoy listening to classical music while I work and date my ability to do so to the classes in which I studied some book while the professor read us his notes. We had all our classes in the morning for four consecutive and exhausting hours every day, so that the faculty could have the afternoons for their own work. On Friday afternoon we had a fifth class.

Somehow I made it through the first year. We had the option of doing vacation at a province villa house; but the Belgian scholastics spoke of it as a chamber of horrors. As a result, we scholastics voted unanimously to spend our two weeks of vacation in Germany, where we helped iron-curtain refugees build homes for themselves. I learned very quickly that I have no vocation in construction work; but I enjoyed the opportunity to get to know some of the refugees.

Since I had mastered French before coming to Eegenhoven, I had spent my first year in Belgium beginning to acquire fluency in German. After vacation, Louis Pascoe, S.J., and I headed for Munich where we studied and spoke German in a summer-school program designed for non-Germans who taught German. As part of the program, we spent over a week traveling around Bavaria and seeing the sights. University faculty and students traveled with us to keep us talking German. Once we went into the foothills of the Alps to watch Baierntheater, traditional melodramas written during the nineteenth century by the Bavarian peasantry in imitation of Shakespeare and produced now with tongue in cheek during the summers. I also got to watch a performance of the uncut *Lohengrin*. It began at three o'clock in the afternoon and ended at nine o'clock in the evening, with forty-five minutes off for dinner. I promised myself after it finally came to an end that I would never suffer the like again. To this day, Wagner does not rank among my favorite composers.

One weekend, Lou and I took a bus to Dachau. When we got off at the old death camp, we saw a little German boy of about four years saying goodbye to a habited Christian Brother. In the German manner, the boy said goodbye with a single brisk handshake, a bow of his head, and a click of his heels. Lou and I toured the camp and noticed that poor families were living in some of the decaying barracks. We saw the ovens, the places where German "scientists" performed experiments on human beings. We read the grim statistics. Finally, we emerged from the tour shaken and deeply depressed.

The same little boy was waiting for us when we reached the bus stop. He recognized our Roman collars, came up, introduced himself, and launched into a strange monologue in which he told us that he wanted to become a priest but that his parents would not let him. He apparently belonged to one of the poor families living in the barracks. Suddenly, he pointed into the camp, where lovely bushes lined the paths. "Isn't it pretty in there," he asked, obviously unaware of the horrors perpetrated in that dreadful place. Not wanting to upset him, I replied, "Yes, its pretty in there." His older sister, who understood well what had happened at Dachau, gave me a withering look and said, "I don't think it's pretty in there." I had felt devastated by what I had just seen; but the girl's look and comment felt like a *coup de grace*. Lou and I rode the bus back to Munich in grim silence.

My brother Al, after serving two years in Korea, had returned to New Orleans, where he completed an M.A. in American literature at Tulane University. He had then begun doctoral studies with Perry Miller at Harvard. The summer after my first year in Belgium, he and a friend of his, Christopher Green, had come to Europe on a Harvard Tour, a cheap air fare to Europe and back to Cambridge. I had finagled permission to spend a week with him in Venice.

I knew from scholastic scuttlebutt that, if one simply asked the Belgian provincial permission for doing anything, he would almost certainly refuse it. One first asked him to do something one did not particularly want to do and then suggested what one really wanted to do as an alternative. So, on the advice of some of the other Americans at Eegenhoven, I wrote him asking to spend a week with my brother in Rome or, if that proved impossible, to spend a week with him in Venice. Sure enough, the Provincial denied my first request and granted my second.

As small children, Al and I had played together a lot; but, once he reached his teens, we had tended to move in different social circles. When he returned from Korea, I saw him when the family visited, always in a group; but our week together in Venice offered us our first opportunity as adults to spend quality time together. We spent very mellow days touring Venice, visiting Ravenna and Padua, reflecting together about growing up on Bayou Road and Vermillion Boulevard, about Daddy's early death, and about a host of other things. In the course of the week, we also found to our mutual delight that by different routes we had both quite independently grown fascinated with American culture. Al was approaching it through American literature, especially American poetry, whereas I was doing it through American philosophy. That week began our adult friendship and subsequent scholarly collaboration. We started writing one another regularly. We both look back with great fondness on our days in Venice, since we both count friendship between siblings a great blessing and recognize that it need not happen.

After the week with Al, I returned, not without trepidation, to Eegenhoven. I took the Orient Express up the Rhine. When we started passing the castles, everyone came from their cabins into the corridor in order to view them. A young man with dark, curly hair came from the cabin next to ours. He made no sign or gesture, said nothing to me; but, as we commented on the castles, I knew with an uncanny certainty that he wanted to talk to me, just as in Quebec I knew that I needed to take a walk to the Fields of Abraham. After everyone returned to their cabins, I left mine and stood in the corridor looking out of the window. Sure enough, the young man came immediately from his cabin and engaged me in conversation. We talked for several hours. Whenever anyone approached us, he immediately sealed his lips. I learned that he came from Rumania, was headed with his family to London, where his father had a diplomatic post. The young Rumanian ached to talk to an American. The whole incident had the same uncanny feel as my conversation on the plains of Abraham.

Back in Belgium, I wrote our new Provincial, Cecil Lang, S.J., informing him that things for me were going less than swimmingly. He had studied theology in Germany right after World War II in circumstances even more austere than those in Eegenhoven. He wrote back equivalently telling me that he would bring me back to the United States to complete theology any time I wanted to but that I would have to decide whether and when I wanted to do so. By the end of my second year, I felt so weak that I could work only about two hours a day outside of class. I went to a doctor. He examined me and told me that I had no physical illness but was suffering from undernourishment. When I informed our new rector of the doctor's verdict, he suggested that two glasses of milk a day would solve the problem. I thanked him, marched up to my room, and wrote my Provincial asking him to get me out of Eegenhoven.

As I look back on my life, it seems to me that often the times of greatest difficulty have also proven the times of greatest grace. I had grown up a law-and-order Catholic and, until I went to Belgium, had lived as a law-and-order Jesuit. In Eegenhoven, for the first time I found myself in a situation where none of the rules applied. I remember lying in my room one day and coming to the realization that I had been taught many of the things which my Belgian

cohorts had learned about religious life but that, in the United States, no one
had actually expected me to take them seriously. In teaching us about Jesuit
spirituality, Tony Mangiaracina had communicated to us above all the importance of common sense. I realized that without changing the theory of religious life, American religious had in fact, with American practicality,
changed the practice. When I saw the theory lived, I did not want to have anything to do with it. That realization did not come easy, because, by assenting
to it, I suddenly lost any rationale I had for being a Jesuit religious. I knew
that, when I got back to the States, I would have to pray my way to a new understanding of religious life, after, of course, I had dealt with the emotional
fallout of two years in Eegenhoven. I made the decision to do both. I date my
personal religious conversion to that moment. I had finally gotten beyond
conventional religion and had taken personal responsibility for my relationship with God. I had resisted religious conversion so massively, that God had
to squeeze me between a rock and a hard place before I would take adult responsibility in faith for my relationship to Him; but that divine strategy finally worked.

I had no doubt that God had called and still called me to be a Jesuit. I just
no longer understood what that meant. At the same time, I felt confident that
with time and prayer I would let God teach me to figure out for myself the
meaning of vowed, religious, Jesuit living. In that sense, all the craziness I encountered at Eegehoven actually proved a great grace for which I feel paradoxically grateful. I don't feel grateful for the craziness but for the religious
decision it finally made me take.

During my second year in Belgium, Jean Lebeau, S.J. joined the faculty
there. He had studied in the United States, with Murray and Weigel, as I had
wanted to do. At Woodstock, MD, where they taught, Jean had recognized
that one could watch television without betraying one's commitment to live a
life of the vows. He persuaded the rector to acquire a black-and-white TV set.
We could only watch religious programs like televised Eucharists or religious
dramas; and only the minister of the house could turn the set on and off or ad-
just it while we were watching. We did, however, watch the opening of the
second Vatican Council. As the camera panned over the bishops sitting in tiers
inside St. Peter's, all mitered and robed in white, Bobo, who sat next to me
leaned over and said in English, "They look like bunny rabbits."

In returning to the States, I saw as much as I could of the Europe I had yet
to see. I completed my theological studies at St. Marys, Kansas. By the time
I got to St. Marys, the winds of change which the council was fanning were
already starting to blow. My classmates, who had all studied philosophy in an
urban environment, had already begun agitating to move the entire theologate

to St. Louis University, which in fact granted our degrees. I found myself the only happy person studying at St. Marys College.

I could not understand the problem my peers had with the place. It wasn't raining. We had three square meals a day. We had heat in the house. We did not have to go to as many classes. I found the instruction actually better than I had found it in Eegenhoven. Finally, we had an excellent library and could actually take the books out. In Eegenhoven, we had to use them in the library and got frisked by the librarian every time we left the library, lest we sneak out some tome under our cassocks. To my delight I found a lot of American philosophy in the library at St. Marys and began devouring it.

I got ordained at the end of my third year of theological studies in the chapel of Spring Hill College in Mobile, Alabama. My mother had asked me what I wanted for an ordination present. I told her I wanted *The Collected Papers of Charles Sanders Peirce*. During my second year at St. Marys, I spent a lot of time in the music room, listening to classical music and outlining each of the eight volumes of *The Collected Papers*. I found myself awed by the depth and scope of Peirce's speculative project. He had felt a divine vocation to rethink the foundations of logic and metaphysics; and, as far as I could tell, he had succeeded. Not only had he revised inferential logic but he had helped found symbolic logic. Moreover, I would come to see that his metaphysical categories re-conceived reality in social, relational terms which avoid major fallacies of the past and which replace the Kantian turn to the subject with the Peircean turn to community.[1]

After analyzing the eight volumes of *The Collected Papers* I not only regarded Peirce as the most brilliant philosopher this nation had produced but came to perceive him as perhaps the greatest philosopher who had ever lived. He had, as far as I could see, successfully rethought the foundations of logic and had crafted a new set of categories for thinking metaphysically, categories which seemed to me to avoid major fallacies of the past: essentialism, dualism, extreme pessimism, extreme optimism, nominalism, rationalism.

As time went by at St. Marys, however, I began to have second thoughts about spending so much time on American philosophy. I kept up with all my courses; but I realized that I had only four years to learn theology well, since I intended doing a doctorate in American philosophy. My two years in Eegenhoven had forced me to realize just how totally American I am as well as to recognize how little I knew about my own intellectual tradition. That experience had transformed coming to terms with "the American proposition" from an aspiration to a passionate need. I wanted, needed to get a doctorate in American philosophy because I needed to appropriate my own cultural roots and because I wanted to use American philosophy in order to do theology.

I had by this time learned enough theology to realize that only those who bring to systematic theological thinking a new set of categories that no one has so far used theologically make a creative contribution to the Catholic tradition. Courtney Murray had seen that and had put the thought of the founding fathers of this nation into dialogue with Catholicism. I wanted to master the whole American philosophical tradition and use it to think theologically. I saw, however, that unless I really mastered the Catholic theological tradition, I would have nothing with which to dialogue. I had spent my second year in Eegenhoven basically surviving physically. I now saw that unless I got some kind of research project going in theology, I could finish four years of theological studies and end by learning more philosophy than theology.

At St. Marys College we scholastics did most of the work involved in editing *Theology Digest*. We scoured the theological journals in the library, discussed the articles we liked, decided which we wanted to digest, wrote the digest, and then sent it to the author for approval before publishing it in *Theology Digest*. My involvement in the editorial work gave me the idea of doing a digest of everything Karl Rahner had published up to that point. I made the proposal to Gerald Van Ackeren, S.J, our dean, who approved it enthusiastically and even gave me time off from classes in order to do the research. I had polished up my German during my first year in Belgium and during the summer which followed it. During my second year in Europe, I had gotten on top of Spanish. I did not have as much fluency in Spanish as in French and German; but I could read it and in a pinch get by in conversation. I had enough confidence in my German, however, to know that I could read Rahner in the original, despite his rambling, convoluted, German prose. In Munich, I met a German scholastic who told me that he had to diagram Rahner's more rambling sentences in order to understand them.

Gradually, the book, eventually published as *Life and Light: A Guide to the Theology of Karl Rahner* (1966), took shape. After finishing the writing, I sent it to Fr. Rahner for him to correct any errors or oversights in my text. He wrote back saying that I had reproduced accurately the things he had written. He expressed only one reservation about my manuscript. He said that I had systematized his thought even more than he had. He told me that he did not think of himself as a systematic theologian but as one who addressed important problems which arose in the Church as they arose.

His modesty impressed me. I recognized that indeed he did address pressing issues as they arose in the Church; and I decided that, if I ever succeeded in creating an inculturated, North American theology, I would try to do the same. Still, everything Rahner wrote cohered philosophically because he addressed everything from the standpoint of his version of Maréchalean Transcendental Thomism. In calling attention to the coherence in his thought, I did not feel that I had falsified it. I sent my unrevised manuscript to Philip Sharper at Sheed and Ward, who published it under the title *Life and Light* in 1966.

Getting a handle on Rahner's theology as a coherent unity had really taught me how to think theologically for the first time. Rahner's masterful use of Martin Heidegger's distinction between ontic and ontological thinking enabled him to take even official conciliar statements and bring them to creative reformulation. By "ontic" Heidegger meant objectifying forms of thought; by "ontological" he meant the deeper structures of meaning in which ontic meaning roots itself. Rahner, of course, by "ontological" meant Maréchalean Thomism; but his unerring theological instincts enabled him to do some remarkably creative things with the Catholic tradition.

One does not master the thought of Charles Sanders Peirce by just reading it. One must live with Peirce over the course of a lifetime in order to penetrate his complex and brilliant mind. The more I mastered Peirce, the more problems I would have with Rahner. I would find Rahner's Transcendental Kantian logic[2] invalid, his turn to the subject inadequate, and his claim to have reached a necessary and universal insight into Being logically inflated and unverifiable. Once I recognized with Peirce the logical necessity of verifying or falsifying Rahner's metaphysical anthropology in the results of close scientific studies of the human, I would also recognize that those results tend to falsify that metaphysical anthropology.

Still, I owe a great debt to Rahner and to my study of his work in my final years of theology. He, more than anyone else, taught me how to think creatively as a theologian. I had many fine professors both in Eegenhoven and in St. Marys; but, if asked whom I deemed best of all, I would have to answer, "Karl Rahner." In my own theological thinking, I would attempt to restate philosophically some of his key theological positions; and, in restating them, I would transform them. The seminal insights I would develop and reformulate, however, would come from Rahner's penetrating vision into the Catholic faith. I find particularly probing his theology of symbol and theology of mystery. I would invoke both in the Trinitarian theology and Christology I would develop; but I would reformulate his insights in the light of the metaphysics of experience which I was, with help from Peirce and other American philosophers, in process of developing. In sacramental theology, I would endorse and reformulate in experiential terms his notion of primordial sacramentality.

I do not, however, endorse everything Rahner ever wrote. As I have already indicated, Peirce taught me to reject his endorsement of Kantian logic in the doing of theology. I also find his Thomistic anthropology essentialistic, marred by an operational dualism, and finally unverifiable in close scientific studies of human behavior. I also deem that his theology of the supernatural existential and his theory of anonymous Christianity rest on demonstrably false presuppositions, and I reject both positions. Still, reading him always repays one for the effort required to dissect his arcane, undisciplined, and convoluted prose.

My work on Rahner partially explains why I never learned to drive. Most of the time, when I was growing up, we had no family car; and so I never learned how to drive one. In the Society of Jesus which I entered, if one did not already know how to drive, getting permission to learn came only with difficulty, since in those days superiors seemed more to fear what one might do to the community cars in the process of learning to drive than to recognize an apostolic advantage in one's actually driving, especially since any given community already had more than enough drivers. At St. Marys, Robert Donnelly, S.J., a classmate of mine at Jesuit High and in the New Orleans province, kindly offered to teach me how to drive. Unfortunately, he started me off on a stick shift. After a few lessons, I saw that, given my lack of physical coordination, learning how to drive would take me a lot of practice. At the same time, I wanted to finish the Rahner book before I left St. Marys because then I would have to concentrate full time on finishing a doctorate. The choice lay between learning how to drive and scholarship. I chose scholarship.

Another experience I had at St. Marys contributed to the theology I would eventually formulate. The town of St. Marys lay not far from Topeka, Kansas; and we theologians did workshops at the Menninger Clinic in Topeka. The staff there designed the workshop for seminarians. They went out of their way to convince us of the great good we could do just by listening to people. They claimed that many people who seek out psychologists and psychiatrists are really just looking for someone to talk to. They assured us that as a religious figure we had powerful emotional significance for the people who came to us for counseling. They also set out to convince us that like most clerics we needed to learn to listen to other people's feelings.

In the workshop I attended, the psychiatrist leading one session asked us to name the components that we would want to include in our understanding of the human personality. Every time we made a suggestion, the psychiatrist would write our suggestion on the board. After about forty-five minutes, we had almost filled the blackboard. At that point I suggested that a theory of personality ought to include something about human emotions. I had said the magic word. "It took you forty-five minutes to suggest that a theory of personality ought to include feelings," said the psychiatrist. "Any psychologist or psychiatrist would have begun there. Why did it take you so long?" He had made his point.

While I found the workshop pastorally very profitable, it had long-term influence on the way I think by introducing me to Karl Menninger's psychology. I began reading systematically through his writings and found compelling his insistence that the negative emotions–fear, anger, shame, and guilt–cause humans the greatest number of problems. His insights would eventually condition the way I came to understand affective conversion.

I had to complete tertianship, however, before I could begin graduate studies full time. I used the summers while at St. Marys and while doing tertianship in Auriesville, New York, to get a head start on the doctorate. I completed during the summers the equivalent of a year of required classwork, and I spent long hours in Harvard's Widener Library applying the Collins method to understanding Emerson's thought. Even before I began doctoral residency at Fordham University, therefore, not only had I read and outlined Emerson's *opera omnia*, but I had also mastered all the secondary source material concerning him that I could get my hands on.

I completed my formation as a Jesuit with John McMahon, S.J., the tertian director of the New York province, at the Shrine of the North American Martyrs near Auriesville, NY, where the New York Province tertianship building stood. There René Goupil had pronounced his vows as a Jesuit and suffered martyrdom. Isaac Jogues, his fellow prisoner in the Iroquois village, had buried Goupil in the ravine near the shrine. No one ever found Goupil's body. I found descending into the ravine and reading Jogues's account of the martyrdom and burial reproduced there on a series of metal plaques a moving experience every time I did it. Later, Jogues himself died of a tomahawk blow to the head while serving as a peace ambassador to the Iroquois in the same village where he had suffered torture and spent several years as a prisoner. The Iroquois called the village Osernenon.

Not far from the Shrine I met an old, retired Franciscan priest who celebrated the Eucharist in a private chapel for a small congregation of locals. He had an enormous library of books about Native Americans and was writing, he hoped, the definitive history of the Iroquois Indians. I do not know if it ever saw print. Behind his residence he showed us the remains of an Iroquois village he had excavated. Here Blessed Kateri Tekaquitha had received baptism. She had been born in Osernenon. The old Franciscan told me that the outline of a palisade presented at the shrine as the site of the original Indian village probably surrounded a farmhouse erected there after the Indians had abandoned the site. He believed that Osernenon had stood somewhere near the site of the shrine; but he suspected that the remains of the actual Indian village where Jogues and Goupil both died would have lain under the cafeteria that served the pilgrims who frequented the shrine in droves on the weekends.

Since workmen had bulldozed the area in preparation for the erection of the cafeteria, they would have obliterated any archeological evidence of the village. As a result, no one would ever know whether my Franciscan scholar had it right or not. Still, the connections of the Shrine and of its environs to the past deepened my sense of my Jesuit and Catholic roots.

The Shrine itself reflected the popular piety of the pre-Vatican II church. Statues of saints who had nothing to do with the North American martyrs peppered its grounds. On the day I arrived, an English Jesuit who would make tertianship with us was showing me around. After encountering saint after saint during our stroll, we rounded a bush and found ourselves face to face with the Curé of Ars. My guide turned to me and said, "The place is rather like a pious rubbish heap."

I thought the most effective ministry we did there the four solid hours of confessions many of us heard every Sunday morning. On the other hand, I found selling pilgrims Goupil water for twenty-five cents a bottle frankly embarrassing. One made Goupil water by dipping a medal of René Goupil into a tub of water and reciting a prayer over it. Those who ran the shrine instructed us to explain to those who paid the twenty-five cents that they were paying for the bottle but not for the water, lest, in selling something blessed, we commit the sin of simony.

Our tertian instructor, John McMahon, had served as the provincial of the New York province. He had taken over as tertian instructor after spending a year in Rome reading theology and spirituality. Normally, tertians study in depth the Constitutions of the Society of Jesus during their nine-month tertianship. The documents of Vatican II, however, had just appeared in English; and John suggested that, given the monumental importance of the council, we spend the year studying its documents instead. We did. As a consequence, I mastered the theology of Vatican II, not during my four years of theology, but during tertianship.

Insight into Vatican II confirmed me in the approach I had decided to take to the doing of theology. After the council, it seemed to me, one could develop theology in a responsible way *only* if one did it in an inculturated idiom. To develop a systematic theology in the United States in a post-Vatican-II context without rooting it in the United States philosophical tradition seemed to me professionally irresponsible.

I also used my year at Auriesville to begin to master the complex philosophy of Josiah Royce. All tertians did some form of pastoral work. I did supply work on the weekends in a local parish or at the Newman Center in Delhi; but I began to wonder whether I was spending too much time on books. John McMahon and I had become good friends. One day I asked him whether he thought I should spend less time studying and more time doing pastoral work.

He shook his head. "Do you know which of the men cause me the greatest worry?" he asked. When I replied in the negative, he responded, "The most pastorally zealous. As far as I can see, too many of them do pastoral work because they have no real intellectual interests. As provincial, I found that such people tend very quickly to turn rigid and reactionary."

Besides weekend supply work, I also did over two solid months of pastoral ministry. During Lent, I gave retreats at Manresa, our retreat house in Convent, Louisiana. Once named Jefferson College, the old building served before the Civil War as a school for the sons of the planters whose plantation houses still line both banks of the Mississippi River north of New Orleans. The retreat house had a long row of Doric columns stretching across its façade. It looked like an elegant plantation house, only about five times larger. In Auriesville, I had developed a Biblical approach to the *Spiritual Exercises* and had in the process learned an enormous amount of New Testament theology. I now gave those retreats at Manresa and enjoyed long theological conversations with Ed Sheridan, S.J., the then director of the retreat house. Ed had functioned as a counselor at Jesuit High when I attended it; and he actually sat in on some of the conferences I gave the retreatants in order to get a sense of what kind of theology I had studied.

Moreover, my brother Al and his wife Barbara had arranged for me to spend a month assisting the Newman chaplain at Harvard University, Fr. Joe Collins, the then pastor of St. Paul's Church in Cambridge, where I had witnessed Al and Barbara's wedding. The Newman Center adjoined the church. During that month, Al and Barbara introduced me to the poet Adrienne Rich, whom they regarded as a close personal friend. When she and the rest of my immediate family all wound up in California, Adrienne became a family friend as well. My niece, Adrienne, takes her name from the poet, whom we sometimes call "big Adrienne" to distinguish her from my niece.

Through Al and Barbara I also met I.A. Richards and Jack Kerouac on the same evening. I joined Al, Barbara, Ivor, and Dorothea, Ivor's wife, for drinks before dinner in Al and Barbara's apartment on Acacia Street. Just before I arrived, Ivor had in a grandfatherly way asked to hold my infant nephew, Christopher. He responded in a grandsonly way by vomiting on Ivor's shirtfront. Ivor had tidied himself up by the time I arrived. Since Ivor had known Alfred North Whitehead personally, I asked him to tell me something about the great philosopher. Ivor recounted that once the two of them had gotten stuck for two hours in a Harvard elevator. I asked him what they had done. "Well," he replied, "we did the obvious. We sat on the floor and talked Plato."

I could not stay for dinner because I had a counseling appointment at the Newman Center; but I promised to return later in the evening. Just before I left for my counseling appointment the telephone rang. I watched Al answer it and saw his face go gray. The voice on the other end of the line was saying, "Hello, this is Jaques[3] Louis Kerouac." The voice went on to inform Al that he and a friend would visit him that evening. Al tried to meet personally as many poets as he could. While a tutor at Lowell House, he had arranged for Jack and many other poets to do readings there for the resident students. Kerouac, however, found the academic establishment intimidating and had coped by going on a three day binge which Al helped shepherd him through. During the binge, Jack scribbled Pietás and crucifixions on paper napkins and table cloths while deploring the dearth of contemporary religious poetry. At one point in all of this, Al told Jack that as a contemporary poet he himself ought to write religious poetry. The challenge evoked Kerouac's poem, *A Pun for Al Gelpi*.

The three intense days had established something of a bond between Jack and Al. As a consequence, Kerouac would show up at Al's apartment from time to time. Once when Al and Barbara returned from a vacation, the elderly Unitarian lady who had an apartment in the same house as they told them that a strange man had come to visit them. She did not know his name. When Al asked her what he looked like, she replied, "Like a lumberjack." Al thought, "Ah, Kerouac."

Al's face had gone grey when he heard Jack's voice on the phone because he was imagining his parlor with the polite and proper Richardses in conversation with the mercurial Kerouac. After I left, Al told Ivor and Dorothea that Kerouac was on the way. They had dinner and beat a retreat. When I returned later in the evening I found Al, Barbara, Jack, and a friend of Jack's having drinks. I had a scotch. I remember Jack's conversation as largely a stream-of-consciousness monologue. Since I had come from counseling, I still wore a Roman collar. I saw Jack eyeing me from time to time, not quite sure how to relate to me; but he seemed finally to give me a vote of approval, because he strode across the room, touched his glass of scotch to mine, and said, "The transsubstantiation is complete." I took what he said as acceptance.

Over the years, through Al and Barbara, I also got to know William Everson and Denise Levertov. I mention these contacts because, in addition to my friendship and scholarly collaboration with both Barbara and Al, personal acquaintance with first-rate poets and literary critics kept me attuned both to the realism of poetic insight and to the precision with which poetic genius expresses that reality. Friendship and ongoing dialogue with the Jesuit poet, Francis Sullivan, S.J., would also yield many insights into intuitive modes of thinking.

During the rest of tertianship, I not only took advantage of John McMahon's blessing on my bookishness, but I also began in tertianship to rethink my vision of religious life and of what it meant for *me* to be a Jesuit. At St. Marys I had gradually put my experience in Eegenhoven into some kind of emotional perspective. I used the long retreat at the beginning of tertianship to begin the process of revisioning religious life. I began praying my way with a pencil to a religious self-understanding. The long retreat bore fruit in *Functional Asceticism: A Guideline for American Religious*. In it I argued that recognizing the functional character of ecclesiastical and religious authority provided an important key to the renewal of religious life in a post-Vatican-II American Church. Religious authority serves people, serves the spread of the gospel. Recognition of that fact would enable religious in the United States to do more systematically what they had already begun to do: namely, to transform the spiritual traditions which religious orders and congregations in this country had inherited from Europe into structures adapted to culture in the United States. The editors at Sheed and Ward accepted this book too and published it even with a measure of enthusiasm.

My argument reflected the fact that the religious conversion I had experienced in Eegenhoven had indeed brought me beyond my adolescent legalism. Now as I looked back on my religious formation, I realized that we had found ourselves required to do too many things simply because some rule somewhere said we should do it even though it served no functional or apostolic purpose. The pseudo-monasticization of the Society of Jesus in the wake of the publication of the first unified Code of Canon Law accounted in no small measure for things like dips, chains, reading at table, the regimented daily order, the constant surveillance, the needless multiplication of permissions. In *Functional Asceticism*, I argued that if religious communities would recognize that religious authority serves the growth needs of people and of communities as well as the advancement of the community's service to the Church and to the world, we could begin to distinguish between customs and practices which did the same and those which did not.

The book expressed my emerging personal vision of religious life. I had identified an important principle for sorting through my own religious formation and for deciding what in it I really owned and what I did not. I realized, however, that *Functional Asceticism* marked only the beginning of my newly found religious self-understanding. I still had to rethink my fundamental understanding of the vows of religion. I looked forward to doing that after tertianship. I found it paradoxical that I had at the end of my Jesuit training found myself back at the beginning, trying like a novice to understand the meaning of vowed living. I did not feel out of step with the rest of my brothers in the order, however, since, in the wake of Vatican II, every Jesuit and every religious in the world were wrestling with the analogous issues.

By the end of tertianship, I had for all practical purposes become a Jesuit. I had also begun to pray my way to a new vision of what that meant. I hoped that my revisioning of religious life might make some contribution to the renewal of my own and of other religious communities. I would eventually formulate my new understanding of vowed living while pursuing doctoral studies in American philosophy at Fordham University. There and in the four years I spent teaching philosophy at Loyola University in New Orleans, I would also complete a process I had initiated during regency. I would discover America.

Colloquy:

Peremptory discombobulator of lives,
       patient prophet,
   Peter and Andrew You called,
       called James and John.
   They came,
       left all,
              father,
              mother,
              friends,
         ships,
         nets,
          all,
             followed,
                        drank the very cup You drained.

Me you also called,
   and I, poor enough,
      with nothing much to leave,
      would yet have idolized my emptiness,
         worshiped it,
            had You not worn me down.

Twice I tried to veer away,
      break loose,
        spit out the hook,
   but You held me fast,
      netted in the trammels of your love.

You shape me—
> *and I marvel at your gracious, unearnable artistry–*
>> *mold me a heart with eyes and ears,*
>> *hone my mind to sharpness,*
>> *make supple my stiff and awkward yearnings,*
>> *keep me to the course,*
>> *bless me with world-wide brothers*
>>> *whose hearts embrace the world.*

Keep battering.
> *I would feign surrender.*

NOTES

1. The Kantian turn to the subject envisions philosophy as the *a priori*, deductive exploration of the structure of human subjectivity. The Peircean turn to community rejects Kant's *a priori* deductive logic and endorses shared systematic inquiry as the proper context for thinking about anything.

2. Kantian transcendental logic deduces *a priori* (i.e., without any factual evidence to support one's conclusions) the intentional structures of human subjectivity. Peirce's logic rules out *a priori* thinking as logically invalid.

3. A friendly reader of this book in manuscript kindly informed me that "Jean" correctly translates Jack Kerouak's given name in French. I concede the point; but, when Jack called Al that evening he said "Jacques," not "Jean." Jack had just published *Satori in Paris*. I suspect that when he called Al that evening he was having fun playing with sound across languages by Frenchifying his American nickname "Jack" as "Jacques."

Chapter Three

I Discover America

I chose to do my doctoral degree at Fordham University for four principal reasons. First of all, Fordham's philosophy department, while doctrinally pluralistic had a strong focus on American philosophical thought. Second, while completing my theological studies, I had come to recognize the impact of the thought of Martin Heidegger on contemporary theology. If I succeeded in using United States philosophy to do theology, I realized that I needed to get on top of the issues which Heidegger's existentialism raised for theological thinking. One of the leading authorities on Heidegger, William Richardson, S.J., taught at Fordham. I would work closely for an entire year with him. Third, I wanted to do my doctorate in philosophy at a Catholic university because I wanted as much as possible to keep tightening my grip on the development of the United States philosophical tradition in dialogue with religious and theological issues. Finally, I had never lived in megalopolis and wanted to experience its advantages, challenges, and drawbacks.

Except for my three years in St. Louis and for my three years of high-school teaching in New Orleans, I had spent my entire Jesuit formation in bucolic isolation. When I finally terminated that artificial (for Jesuits), quasi-monastic, pastoral quarantine, I did so with a bang. I went from Auriesville to the Big Apple. Moreover, I re-entered urban life in the chaotic years of the late sixties.

In my first year at St. Marys, I sat reading in the scholastic recreation room. Someone was listening to a radio; and I heard the news that someone had shot President Kennedy. Kennedy had incredible wit, vitality, and intelligence, and he had broken the national taboo against allowing Catholics into the White House. I had admired the political artistry of his campaign and had voted for him enthusiastically. When the news came that he had died of his head wound, I went up to our small community chapel and wept. Decades later, I learned the extent to which JFK felt obsessed with death. He would often wonder how he would die and hoped that death would take him swiftly. It did.

Those who have not lived through the sixties find them hard to understand and even harder to appreciate. The Free Speech Movement and the Vietnam War protest had spread from the campus of the University of California in Berkeley to virtually every major campus in the country. The Civil Rights Movement had begun with the non-violent, pacifist activism of Martin Luther King. With the willing collaboration of Lyndon Johnson, King had scored important legislative victories in Congress. Nevertheless, Stokely Charmichael persuaded the northern urban branch of the Civil Rights Movement to split with King's pacifist Southern Christian Leadership Conference and to espouse the cause of Black power and of violence. Riots which expressed the depth of resentment African Americans felt toward a racist culture erupted in Black ghettos. The tragic assassinations of Robert Kennedy and of Martin Luther King made one wonder how any nation which so brutalized its best leaders could long survive. The counter-cultural movement still had enormous vitality and was teaching young Americans to experiment with sex and drugs. The New Left spouted Emersonian slogans like "Do your own thing." Hippie communes popped up everywhere, just as American utopian communities had at the beginning of nineteenth century. Culture in the United States seemed, then as in the sixties, to unravel at most of its seams.

The Civil Rights Movement had captured the support of religious people from all the churches. It certainly had my support. I eventually came to stand as well with those who opposed the Vietnam War; but that took a while, because my enthusiasm for JFK had borne the negative effect of transforming me into something of a Cold Warrior. My mother opposed the Vietnam war long before me. I did, however, assist young Catholic men who applied as conscientious objectors to the war. With time, as the Johnson administration defended our military involvement in Southeast Asia with more and more propagandistic double-talk, I recognized the sinful folly of what we were doing in Vietnam and repudiated the war effort. Since the draft did not normally look on Catholics as conscientious objectors, clerical support for those who did have problems of conscience with the war and documentation in the proclamations of Vatican II of a Catholic's right to object conscientiously made a significant difference in getting Catholics CO status.

The fact that the initial implementation of Vatican II coincided with this period of national turmoil linked that epoch-making council with images of threatening chaos in the minds of a small but articulate group of right-wing U.S. Catholic Integralists. Vatican II had, of course, nothing to do with the unraveling of United States culture in the sixties and early seventies. If David Halberstam has it right in his study of the fifties (and I suspect that he does), decisions taken in that decade sowed the seeds that bore bitter fruit in the sixties.

In the sixties, centuries of organized racism, which this nation has still not exorcized from its institutional life, came home to roost in the Civil Rights Movement and in the Black Power movement; but the growth of lily white suburbs and of inner-city, racial ghettos in the fifties exacerbated racial tensions in the sixties.

The Cold War began in the late forties. The systematic militarization of American life which the Cold War catalyzed during the following decade fueled an active American militarism which found expression during the sixties in the war in Vietnam. In the fifties, the Dulles brothers gave initial shape to Cold War policies. They enunciated the principle that in order to save American democracy, one must subvert it. This contradictory precept allowed the United States to do anything it needed to do, no matter how immoral, in order to win the Cold War. We justified "doing anything we needed to do" under the rubric of "national security." National security supposedly sanctioned giving financial and military support to oppressive and despotic regimes who mouthed lip service to anti-Communism. It also rationalized the creation of the Imperial Presidency, which waged undeclared wars fairly constantly during the entire era of the Cold War. National security supposedly justified the creation of a government within a government largely unaccountable to Congress for its actions. That government within a government took institutional shape in the Central Intelligence Agency (CIA), the National Security Council (NSC), and the Atomic Energy Commission (AEC).

Power corrupts and absolute power corrupts absolutely. By the late sixties, an increasing number of Americans felt fed up with a government which pursued policies unsanctioned by either Congress or the American people and which lied to those it governed, while asking them to die for a cause in which a growing number of U.S. citizens had ceased to believe.

Another set of circumstances which had nothing to do with Vatican II colored its implementation in the United States: namely, the systematic intellectual isolation of the United States clergy which had occurred in the wake of the Modernist Crisis during the first half of this century. That sad and tragic story needs retelling.

The American Church of the nineteenth century had for several reasons lagged intellectually and culturally behind the Church in Europe. The explosion of the Catholic immigrant population up until 1929 caused Church leaders to spend much of their energies on what a later generation of Catholics condescendingly called "brick and mortar" Catholicism. That pejorative term censured Church leaders of earlier generations for spending an inordinate amount of time building churches, schools, and charitable institutions. In fact, an immigrant Catholic population needed those buildings, even though the buildings did little at first to foster serious Catholic intellectualism. Anti-Catholic bigotry also transformed the creation of a Catholic culture in the United States into an uphill struggle. Anti-Catholic harassment made many Catholics, both clergy and laity, suspicious and even hostile toward a secular intelligentsia which too often falsely caricatured all religion as irrational, subjective superstition. Finally, Catholic Jansenism, which some missionaries transplanted from Europe to the Church in the United States, fostered a spiritualized Catholic anti-intellectualism through its pessimistic, Augustinian portrayal of human nature. Janesenistic piety made it appear that a mind corrupted by sin could only mislead.

Still, by the end of the nineteenth century, the four major national groups which made up the American Catholic Church had produced some impressive pastoral, intellectual, and cultural leaders. Among Anglo-Americans, one thinks of Cardinal Gibbons and of the two bishops Spalding. One thinks too of Orestes Brownson and of Isaac Hecker. The French clergy in the United States had often received excellent training at French colleges in classical Latin and Greek, in grammar, in *belles lettres*, in science, in rhetoric, in mathematics, in philosophy, and in theology. St. Mary's College founded by the Sulpicians in 1799 gave such quality education that prominent families of Baltimore sent sons to study there. French missionary clergy sometimes collected large and impressive scholarly libraries. The German clergy gave evidence of better intellectual training than the Irish, who on the whole lagged behind other nationalities in theological sophistication. The German clergy found it difficult, however, to dialogue with United States culture, because they tended to regard the Americans to whom they ministered as a country but as not yet a nation. Condescending snobbery like that inhibited serious efforts on the part of the German clergy to "Americanize" themselves. They tended therefore to isolate themselves in ethnic ghettos.

After the Civil War, inspired in part by the intellectual and cultural openness of Leo XIII, which contrasted tardily but refreshingly with the reactionary closed-mindedness of Pius IX, Church leaders like John Lancaster Spalding and other forward-looking bishops began insisting on higher intellectual standards in priestly formation. Through Spalding's leadership, in 1889 the American episcopacy founded The Catholic University of America in Washington, DC. Archbishop John Ireland supported energetically Spalding's efforts.

As a result of these developments, the modest beginnings of an American Catholic intellectual renaissance began to take shape around the turn of the century. One found genuine quality in Catholic journals like *The American Catholic Quarterly Review*, the *New York Review*, *The Catholic University Bulletin* and the *American Ecclesiastical Review*. Other Catholic journals and periodicals appeared: *Catholic World*, *Ave Maria*, *Sacred Heart Review*, and *The Homiletic Monthly and Catechist*, which eventually transformed itself into *The Homiletic and Pastoral Review*. Catholic scholars had begun to attain some distinction in a variety of fields. Fr. William Kerby broke new ground in the social sciences. John A. Ryan's, *A Living Wage: Its Ethical and Economic Aspects* received national attention and influenced FDR's New Deal. Francis E. Gigot, S.S. achieved some distinction as a scripture scholar.

Then in 1907, the Holy Office issued on July 3, *Lamentabili sine exitu*, which listed sixty-five heretical propositions taken mostly from the writings of Alfred Loisy. The document caused no special stir in the United States, since the condemned doctrines did not excite widespread interest or support in the American church. Initially, perhaps three American priestly scholars seem to have flirted with some Modernist notions. As a result, Church leaders in this country at first viewed Modernism as a European problem; and the American church absorbed *Lamentabili* without initial trauma. As the hunt for Modernists heated up in Rome, however, the episcopacy in the United States felt more and more pressure from powers along the Tiber to take a proactive anti-Modernist stance. This eventually bred a widespread Catholic Philistinism, not unlike that of contemporary Integralist heresy hunters. A mindless anti-intellectualism on the part of both clergy and laity led to the systematic suppression of intellectual creativity in the United States church and in American seminaries.

A small group of intellectuals strove manfully to resist anti-Modernist witch hunts. As the liturgical movement gained impetus, a handful of American liturgists, C.J. among them, advanced the reform of ritual in this country. *Divino afflante Spiritu* allowed the first stirrings of the Biblical renewal to emerge in the Church as a whole and in the American church. Nevertheless, the impact of the anti-intellectualism which flourished in the wake of the Modernist crisis left the vast majority of the clergy in the United States ill prepared to deal with the theological "revolution" caused by the documents of Vatican II. Ignorance of Church history made the teachings of Vatican II seem more revolutionary than they deserved. Indeed, the bishops at the council saw themselves as traditionalists restoring to the contemporary Church important elements of the Catholic past which had gone too long forgotten. The intellectual isolation of large segments of the United States clergy, however, brought it about that the publication of the council's decrees found the vast majority of American priests ill prepared to implement them. American priests found themselves suddenly expected, without any training or preparation, to transform themselves overnight from the Tridentine mass priests their seminary training had made them, into liturgists, homilists, and scripture scholars.

In the mean time, deeply felt resentment had been building among American Catholic intellectuals at what they perceived as arbitrary and uncritical mind control on the part of the Catholic hierarchy. In point of fact, prior to the council virtually all the chief architects of the documents of Vatican II had suffered either scrutiny or censure by a reactionary Roman curia. Resentment against such acts of clerical oppression colored the way some Catholic liberals responded to the council's challenge to update the American Church. Inspired in part by Kennedy's election to the White House, the Catholic intelligentia longed to break out of the religious ghetto in which Catholic religious Philistinism had imprisoned them for decades. In some cases, resentment against the restraints of ghetto Catholicism produced aberrations in the popular attempt to implement Vatican II, aberrations which hindsight recognizes as sometimes hasty and unreflective. Those aberrations combined with a residual Catholic Philistinism in order to widen the gap between Catholic liberals and Catholic conservatives. From a human standpoint, I find such blunders to some extent understandable. Given, moreover, the extreme polarization of American society during the sixties and early seventies, most people, whether liberal or conservative, found it hard to keep a cool head and always to make balanced judgments.

All of these factors which on occasion skewed the implementation of Vatican II in directions which had nothing to do with the Council's agenda or intent created the cultural and intellectual context in which I did my doctoral studies. They also help explain contemporary polarization in the American Catholic Church. In my judgment, the vast majority of American Catholics supported and continue to support enthusiastically the reforms of Vatican II. Nevertheless, even today a small but vocal group of Integralists with a nostalgia for the knee-jerk, anti-intellectualism of a bygone era long for a return to Ultramontanism, to authoritarianism, and to the theological witch hunts of the anti-Modernist era.

A baby priest when I began my doctoral residency at Fordham University, I also wanted during my doctoral studies to discover for myself the meaning of priestly ministry. Besides celebrating a daily liturgy, I counseled students and collaborated with Elizabeth Meier, a graduate student in theology, in organizing weekend student retreats. I found myself dealing pastorally with many angry young people alienated from their government and from the institutional Church. Some of them flirted with the counter culture.

Creating the kind of eucharistic worship which both engaged and challenged the young went far to keep them members of the Christian community.

In an effort to do that, George Glanzman, S.J., who taught Old Testament in Fordham's theology department, began deviating from strict rubrical conformity in his on-campus liturgies. When I heard of his liturgical experiments, I began hazarding a few of my own. Eventually, our rubrical liberties came to the attention of the New York Chancellory. I, George, and the Fordham campus ministry, who strongly supported what George and I were trying to do liturgically and pastorally, met with representatives from the Archdiocese and seem to have convinced them that what seemed like deviations from rubrical propriety responded to serious pastoral needs among the students and that neither of us was doing anything liturgically irresponsible. In the end, neither of us got official approval from the Archdiocese; nor, however, did we get told to cease and desist.

I had left tertianship understanding clearly that I needed to rethink the meaning of the three vows of religion: poverty, chastity, and obedience. Writing *Functional Asceticism* during my second long retreat had taught me how to pray with a pencil. During my graduate studies, I did the same during my morning meditation. We traditionally called the vows of religion "evangelical counsels." "Well," thought I, "since we supposedly derive our understanding of religious vows from the gospel, if I want to rethink their meaning, I need to return to the source from which religious life supposedly sprang." I began examining the gospels, especially the synoptic gospels, for those elements in Jesus' teaching which eventually got institutionalized as the three vows of religion. I knew perfectly well that Jesus did not Himself require any of His disciples to take formal religious vows. Still, those Christians in the fourth century who created religious life as an institution claimed to have found its elements in the gospels. In my daily prayer, I set out to identify those elements for myself. The fruits of my praying with a pencil provided on any given day that day's homily with its fundamental content. In other words, I tested my reading of the gospels against a random sample of the faithful and trusted their *sensus fidei* to help keep me on the right track.

As I prayed the synoptic gospels and jotted down on paper the insights I gleaned there, I began to see that one could use the account of Jesus' temptations in the desert in both Matthew and Luke as a hermeneutical key for discerning the fundamental outlines of what He meant by "the reign of God." Jesus' responses to Satan's temptations, I decided, held the interpretative key to understanding the real nature of each temptation. In Matthew's gospel the theme of fulfillment plays a central role, but it also surfaces in Luke. Matthew's Jesus comes "to fulfill the Law and the prophets." In each of His responses to Satan, Jesus cites the Old Testament. Might those citations, I asked myself, hold a key to understanding which aspects of the Law His religious vision especially fulfills? I decided to use Peirce's pragmatic logic to test out my hypothesis by identifying the operational consequences in Jesus' teachings of the moral and religious commitments He makes in rejecting Satan's wiles.

In the first temptation, Satan tempts Jesus to break His fast by turning stones into bread and eating. Jesus replies that one does not live on bread alone but by every word which comes from the mouth of God. In other words, Jesus interprets breaking His fast, not as an act of gluttony, but as an act of sinful self-reliance because the temptation strikes at the symbolic significance of Jesus' act of denying Himself food. He fasts in a desert. Jewish fasting served as a way of remembering the desert sojourn of God's people when they depended from day to day for physical survival on the manna God rained down upon them from heaven.

In all the synoptics, Jesus receives His messianic commissioning from the Father just before He begins His desert fast. The Jesus of the synoptics eschews the ascetical austerity of John the Baptizer, but He undertakes the unusual act of a forty-day fast as a prelude to His ministry. The fast expresses symbolically His determination to fulfill His messianic mission in complete dependence on the Father who has just commissioned Him messiah. In the first temptation, Satan wants the messiah to abandon the fast and all it signifies, to trust in Himself and not in the Father as He goes about the work of saving Israel. Jesus rejects the temptation and puts His trust in the Father.

I began to examine how Jesus developed the theme of trust in God in the discourses and pronouncement stories one finds in the synoptic gospels. I saw that in proclaiming the reign of God Jesus associated trust in God with "bread," with the physical possessions which make human life possible. Humans have to have before they can live. Deprive them of the physical supports of life, and they die. In Jesus' teachings, sharing the physical supports of life with others and especially with those less advantaged than oneself as an expression of faith in the Father's providence means that no disciple of Jesus can make material possessions into an idol. One makes them into an idol by clinging to them as though they were God. Alienating them by sharing them with others expresses the fact that one puts one's ultimate hope and trust in the Father's providential care. In other words, really trusting the Father to take care of one frees one to share the physical supports of one's human life with others, and especially with those in greatest need.

As I traced the theme of trust through Matthew and through the other synoptic evangelists I saw that it had other implications. Jesus required His disciples to choose between God and riches. In other words, no one who really trusts in God can deliberately set out to become rich. Genuine trust in God, as Jesus understood it, redefines the purpose of human labor. One works in order to have enough to support one's own fragile life and enough to share the fruits of one's labor freely with those in need. Moreover, I also realized that by sharing, Jesus did not just mean almsgiving, handouts, although Christian sharing did not exclude such a form of assistance. The kind of sharing about which Jesus spoke most frequently happens around a table. It takes the form of hospitality. Moreover, Jesus' disciples must take as their preferred guests the destitute, the homeless, the marginal. In other words, in proclaiming the reign of God, Jesus sought to bring into existence a community of sharing which guaranteed that every member of the new Israel He was embodying and proclaiming would find themselves and their physical needs cared for.

As I pondered these evangelical truths, I realized that such sharing defines the deep evangelical meaning of the first vow of religion: poverty. Vowing poverty committed one to sharing the physical supports of life in community and with a special care for those in the wider human and ecclesial community who have the greatest needs. So understood, vowed poverty commits a religious community of faith and trust to reach out actively to those in society at large and especially to the neediest and most marginalized. Genuine religious poverty, I saw, means much more than getting the superior's permission for car fare. I named the chapter on religious poverty "Gratuitous Sharing."

As I considered Jesus' second temptation in Matthew, I saw that Satan's urging Him to throw Himself from the pinnacle of the temple had nothing to do with committing suicide. The second temptation built directly on the first, and Jesus' response to it deepened the meaning of the trust in the Father to which His rejection of the first temptation had committed Him. Equivalently, Matthew's Satan was saying in the second temptation, "All right, trust God if you will; but first make sure that you have God on your side. Make Him send angels from heaven to save you after you throw yourself from the pinnacle of the temple, and then you will really know that you can rely on Him, that He really does stand on your side."

Jesus' response to the second temptation again unmasks its real intent. To Satan's urging Him to throw himself from the pinnacle, Jesus replies, "You shall not put the Lord your God to the test." In other words, Jesus interpreted the second temptation as committing the Biblical sin of testing God, the very sin I had committed naively and unwittingly in resisting God's call to forget about marriage and medicine and join the Jesuits and in attempting in St. Louis to use my puny human reason to nail God down and control Him. If one really trusts in God, Jesus is saying, then that trust has to have an unconditioned character. One can only respond to God on God's terms. Those who really trust the Father trust Him unconditionally, absolutely.

As in the case of the first temptation, I began to examine how the theme of unconditioned trust surfaced in Jesus' teachings as we find them recorded in

Matthew and in the other two synoptic gospels. I realized that in Jesus' religious vision, unconditioned trust required unconditioned sharing at least in the sense that Jesus' disciples must not ask whether those with whom they share deserve to receive what they share with them but whether or not they need it. Jesus, in other words, will have nothing to do with the phony, self-serving distinction concocted in right-wing, American "think tanks" between "deserving" and "undeserving" poor.

Jesus also required all His disciples to acknowledge their sinfulness and their need for divine forgiveness. The acknowledgment of universal sinfulness combined with the unconditioned character of Christian sharing in order to endow the new Israel which Jesus was summoning into existence with a strongly egalitarian character. No one who assented to Jesus' religious vision could look down with condescending, Pharisaical contempt on those less holy than oneself. In God's family, as Jesus conceived it, all the children of the Father relate to one another on an equal footing as sisters and brothers. All in God's family relate to one another on the same footing, as repentant sinners. All enjoy the same dignity as God's children. Accordingly, Jesus, unlike other rabbis of His day had women disciples and even allowed women to travel around with him and to participate actively in the inner circle of disciples who assisted Him in proclaiming God's reign. He apparently treated them as He would have treated any other person.

I also saw that the unrestricted character of the sharing which Jesus demanded of His disciples had significant social consequences. It explained His table fellowship with sinners. Public sin ostracized one in first-century Palestine. Unrestricted sharing, by contrast, sought to create a community of sharing dedicated to breaking down all the sinful barriers which separate humans from one another. The unrestricted character of the sharing Jesus inculcated sought to make the last first and the first last. It required of His disciples that they both personally and collectively, as a community, look upon the dregs of society, the expendables, the outcasts as the most important people in the new Israel. It also required those more advantaged, especially the wealthy and the powerful, to transform themselves freely into the servants (in first century Palestine read "slaves" for "servants") of the meanest, the weakest, the most marginal members of the human community. Making the last first and the first last leveled out the injustices.

The unrestricted character of the sharing Jesus embodied and inculcated gave, then, a special character to the love command which He also inculcated. It required one to love unrestrictedly, promiscuously. It required one to love those most marginal and least loveable. It even required one to love one's enemies. One can make a plausible historical case for the fact that Jesus Himself chose celibacy "for the sake of the kingdom" so that he could dedicate

Himself single-mindedly to the mission to which the Father had consecrated Him. If so, then His option for celibacy also expressed the universal character of His love.

The more I reflected on the form of love we call "charity," the clearer I saw that it possesses four fundamental characteristics: concreteness, reciprocity, gratuity, and universality. Charity has concreteness because humans love, not abstractions, but other persons and living communities of persons. Charity has reciprocity because it happens in communities of people who both give and receive love. Charity has gratuity because like God's love it puts no conditions on the offer of love and forgiveness. Charity has universality in virtue of its unrestricted character. It excludes no one in principle.

Every authentic embodiment of Christian love has to exemplify all four characteristics; but, as I pondered the love commitment made in taking marriage vows and the love commitment made in taking the vow of celibacy, it seemed to me that marriage vows committed one to a form of love which enhanced the concreteness and reciprocity of Christian love whereas a vow of celibacy enhanced the gratuity and universality of Christian love. In other words, religious renounce genital sex so that they can love gratuitously and universally. I therefore entitled the chapter on the vow of celibacy "Unrestricted Love."

As I pondered the third temptation of Matthew's Jesus, I saw that it concerned the foundations of the new Israel Jesus would summon into existence during His mortal ministry and in the paschal mystery. In the third temptation, Matthew's Satan equivalently says, "All right, if you must trust the Father absolutely, then at least take the kingdoms of this world as the model for establishing the kingdom of God on earth. Root God's kingdom in law, coercion, and violence; and recognize that in so doing you will be worshiping not God but me." Jesus repudiates Satan's outrageous suggestion absolutely and utterly: "The Lord your God shall you adore and Him only shall you serve." In other words, one can ground the new Israel which Jesus summons into existence only on the authentic worship of the Father.

Once again I applied Peirce's pragmatic maxim and searched Jesus' teachings for the practical consequences of a commitment to authentic worship of the Father. I found that He insisted that mutual forgiveness must authenticate such worship. His disciples must forgive one another with the same gratuity as God has forgiven them. Moreover, if mutual forgiveness tests the authenticity of worship, then love of enemies tests the authenticity of mutual forgiveness. Hence, gratuitous and universal sharing also expresses the mutual forgiveness which authenticates the prayer which creates the new Israel.

Because Jesus refused to pattern God's reign on the violent and oppressive kingdoms of this world, He also forbade the Twelve ever to take pagan kings as their role model for leadership. Christian leaders can take only one person as their model: Jesus Himself, the messiah who had come not to be served but to serve and to lay down His life for the sinners He came to redeem. Here I discovered the evangelical key to religious obedience. Those in positions of authority in religious communities must view themselves as servants of the community, of its members' needs, and of the common apostolic work to which the community dedicates itself: namely, to embodying in an endless variety of historical contexts the Father's just reign on earth as in heaven. I accordingly entitled the chapter on the vow of obedience "Service."

I mentioned at the beginning of this chapter that I celebrated a daily Eucharist on the Fordham campus in the Bronx. I preached the fruits of my prayer that day; and my prayer that day consisted in my praying with a pencil about an understanding of religious life to which I could in conscience consent. In the process of sharing the fruits of my spiritual groping with my little eucharistic flock, I had my first vivid experience of sacramental efficacy. In my scribbling prayer I was groping my way experimentally to a new sense of my own personal identity as a vowed, Jesuit religious. Far from feeling in control of my vocational commitment, I felt at the time very vulnerable and tentative as I inched my way to what I really believed about all this. Yet, to my surprise, when I shared the fruit of my prayerful gropings with others, what I said moved them in ways I truly had not foreseen. Again and again, I had a vivid sense at the time that the kinds of responses my little homilies seemed to elicit from others went far beyond anything I anticipated or intended. Some other reality than I moved the people I led in worship; and in my heart I identified that reality with the Spirit of Jesus. This experience would help to shape my theological approach to the efficacy of the sacraments as would my experience of sacramental worship in the Catholic Charismatic Renewal.

My first experience of leading eucharistic worship confirmed me in another theological habit. Ever since, I have taken care to preach the theology I write as a way of testing its pneumatic inspiration. If God's people, when they gather around the table of the Lord in prayer, respond positively to my theological musings, I take that as a sign that I am at least moving theologically in the right direction.

The fact that I groped my way to a new understanding of vowed commitment while immersing myself in the classical American philosophical tradition enabled me to rethink the meaning of religious life in an inchoately inculturated manner. I had not yet developed a systematic way of pursuing inculturated theological thinking; but in my new theological interpretation of the vows, I invoked a Peircean logic of consequences in order to interpret

Jesus' desert temptations. I clarified the theoretical meaning of Jesus' responses to those temptations by naming their practical operational consequences in His teachings.

I did not believe that my application to Jesus' disciples of the consequences of His desert temptations did violence to Matthew's text. Matthew's Satan, by invoking the title "Son of God," addresses Jesus as the messiah, since, in Jesus' messianic commissioning, the Father has just addressed Him as His beloved Son and as messiah in the image of the suffering servant. Only Jesus functions as the messiah. Since, however, Jesus in the desert also embodies the new Israel He will soon begin, Satan also tempts Jesus as the beginning of that new Israel. Jesus incarnates the ideal of God's kingdom which He proclaims and to which He summons His disciples. His temptations, therefore, have significance for his followers who must embody the same religious ideals and values as Jesus Himself. Jesus' responses to Satan, therefore, model for His disciples how to respond to the most fundamental temptations with which the Archdemon will confront them.

By searching Jesus' teachings for the practical consequences of each of his responses to Satan's wiles, I consciously and deliberately invoked Peirce's pragmatic maxim in order to clarify the meaning of Christian discipleship. A pragmatically clarified insight into Christian discipleship enabled me to redefine for myself the significance of the religious vows I had taken but whose meaning I had ceased in Eegenhoven to understand clearly. Accordingly, I named my book on the vows *The Pragmatic Meaning of Religious Life*. Perhaps I should have made my Peircean presuppositions clearer in its text; for Sheed and Ward did not like my title, even though Phil Sharper strongly encouraged my aspirations to create an inculturated theology for the United States. The book appeared as *Discerning the Spirit: Foundations and Futures of Religious Life*. I acquiesced in the new title but preferred my own.

I published *Discerning the Spirit* in part as a personal religious manifesto. In writing it, I had prayed myself to a new self-understanding as a contemporary Jesuit religious. I wanted my brother Jesuits and my religious superiors to know where I stood in my new understanding of the vows and in my personal religious commitment. I had determined that if that commitment proved irreconcilable with the Society of Jesus's own self-understanding as a community, then I had the responsibility to petition for a release from religious vows to whose meaning I could not in conscience consent. To my relief, I found only positive responses to my reformulation of the theology of religious life, not only from my brother Jesuits but from religious who belonged to other religious communities. Those responses further confirmed me in the habit of testing any new theological formulas I would come up with against the *sensus ecclesiae*. I got into the habit of always preaching the theology I write.

I had derived my new vision of the vows of religion from the gospels because the tradition had called them "evangelical counsels." I believed my reformulation of the meaning of the vows evangelical, but I could no longer look upon them as mere counsels. I had derived my new understanding of their meaning from meditating on Jesus' vision of the reign of God. Jesus, however, had not regarded the vision of the kingdom as mere counsels but as fundamental conditions for discipleship and for membership in the new Israel He embodied and was summoning into existence.

In writing *Discerning the Spirit*, however, I failed to take into adequate account the fact that Jesus had two kinds of disciples: 1) ordinary disciples like Martha, Mary, and Lazarus who believed in Him and tried to live His teachings in their ordinary, daily lives, and 2) close disciples who traveled around with Him and collaborated with Him in proclaiming the divine reign. The Twelve belonged to this inner circle of close disciples, who lived with Jesus on a day-to-day basis and like Him fostered the work of evangelization. The Twelve belonged to that inner circle and had a special leadership role within it; but others belonged to the circle of close disciples as well. Luke tells us that the inner circle included women and that it also included men other than the Twelve. We know that Jesus prophetically called some of His disciples. That call seems to have invited them to join the inner circle of evangelizing disciples. Luke's Jesus in His journey discourse sends out seventy-two disciples to evangelize. That suggests that the inner circle numbered at least seventy-two, probably more.

Moreover, Jesus required more of the inner circle of disciples than He did of his ordinary disciples, because the work of evangelization made more demands upon them. He required the inner circle to sell their possessions, give the proceeds to the poor, and to join a vagabond messiah and his wandering co-workers in spreading the kingdom. Together they lived on alms and on the financial support of some of the rich women disciples among them, like Mary Magdalene and Susanna, the wife of Herod's steward, Chuza. In addition, Jesus required the inner core of disciples to put the proclamation of God's reign before the most sacred family relationships.

With time I began to realize that, while the vision of the kingdom did allow one to redefine the meaning of discipleship, as the three vows of religion took institutional shape, they really sought to give institutional expression in the post-resurrection Church to a life of close discipleship. Jesus' close disciples exchanged personal possessions for both life in common and dependence on the generosity of others, and they shared what possessions came their way with those in greatest need. So do religious who renounce their possessions, share what comes their way in community, and use their material resources to minister to the needs of others, especially to the most marginal members of society. Jesus' close disciples had to put dedication to evangelization before the most sacred family relationships. Religious feel called to imitate Jesus' commitment to celibacy for the sake of the kingdom. Finally, testimony to the kingdom in imitation of a servant messiah gave religious leadership and therefore the vow of obedience its fundamental teleology. Among the close disciples, Jesus Himself acted as the leader in service, as, if you will, something like their religious "superior." In calling the rich young man, Jesus was calling him, not just to discipleship, but to close discipleship. Not unwisely, then, had the Catholic tradition seen religious poverty foreshadowed in his call, even though the story does not refer to the vow of poverty as such. I would come to these last insights in the late 1990s while researching an as yet unpublished book on ecclesiology.

The insights into the practical demands of life in God's reign which I reached in the course of my first rethinking of the meaning of the three vows of religion would inform the theological system I would eventually create while teaching theology in Berkeley. The practical demands of discipleship would give pragmatic meaning to justifying faith and would define the conditions for Christian sanctification by growth in hope, faith, charity, and the Christian search for a just social order.

While graduate studies had given me an opportunity to pray my way to a new self understanding as a Jesuit religious, I chiefly came to the Big Apple to complete or at least to advance my philosophical discovery of America. I arrived at Fordham ahead of the game when it came to fulfilling the academic requirements for a doctoral degree. Not only did I have fifteen years of a rigorous Jesuit formation and education behind me, but I had in Europe acquired fluency in the modern languages required for doctoral studies. As soon as I could, I took and passed the language examinations in German and French. Since I had begun serious research in Emerson in the final year of my regency, I had already completed much of the research I needed in order to write a dissertation on Emerson's thought. I had outlined in detail the Riverside Edition of *Emerson's Complete Works* which Al gave me in 1961. I had also taken copious notes on the published journals and lectures as well as on all the secondary source material I could find in the Widener Library in Cambridge where I did summer research. I knew that, if I aspired to Collins-like thoroughness, I would have to read all the sermons and unpublished lectures as well; but I intended to do that when the time came to write the dissertation. Finally, after two summers of class work at Fordham, I had already completed half the course requirements for the doctorate.

I had already begun applying the same kinds of research techniques as I was applying to Emerson to the works of other major American thinkers. By the time I got to graduate school I had read and outlined the principal writings of William James, George Santayana, and Josiah Royce. In my final year of theology at St. Marys, I had read and done detailed outlines of all eight volumes of the *Collected Papers of Charles Sanders Peirce*. As a result of all this antecedent preparation, I completed my doctoral degree in three years. In the first year, I finished up course requirements. In the second, I studied for and passed the written comprehensive examination. In the third year, I migrated to Cambridge to write the dissertation.

In the advanced philosophy courses I had already taken during two summers at Fordham, I had tried to learn something about ordinary language analysis, since it seemed to be taking over most philosophy departments in the country. The more I studied ordinary language analysis, the more convinced I became that it had relatively little to offer systematic theological thinking. Emerson and Royce had convinced me that religious insight has a strong synthetic character. The salvation the Christian religion offers seeks to put one in a life-giving relation with God, oneself, other people, and the world. In other words, it requires a consistent, verifiable way of thinking about God, oneself, other persons, and the world. It requires a metaphysics, an inferential, though fallible, theory of the whole. The highly analytic method of language analysis seemed to me unsuited to the kind of synthetic thinking which any genuine religious insight requires. Moreover, many years later, through dialogue in the John Courtney Murray Group, the post-doctoral research seminar which I helped found and in which I still participate each summer, I came to realize with help from Michael Mahon, S.J. that one cannot understand the meaning of language if one dissociates it from the context of practices it seeks to interpret. That, much of ordinary language analysis as the academy practiced it seemed to me to do.

In my second course on ordinary language analysis, for example, I wrote a paper which studied the ordinary language analysis of the phrase "I dreamed that. . . ." Someone began the debate by writing an article hazarding an interpretation of the meaning of this phrase. That gave rise to a series of articles which analyzed the analysis of the analysis of the analysis, until finally someone finally wrote a book on the phrase "I dreamed that. . . ." The book argued that, if anyone puts after the phrase "I dreamed that. . . ." a clause which claims to report the content of a dream he or she has had, that person must be lying because in order to dream one must go to sleep and in order to go to sleep one must lose consciousness. Having completed my own analysis of the book's argument, I thought to myself, "Either this man has lost his mind, or he is putting me on." My professor, however, pronounced my term paper

publishable and urged me to send it off to a journal. I never did. I deemed
what I had written so silly and trivial that I did not want my name associated
with it. Nor had I any interest in promoting that species of philosophical
discourse.

Another summer school course at Fordham influenced the way I would
come to think philosophically and theologically. I signed up for a course by
John McNeill, S.J. on the sources of Maurice Blondel's *L'Action*. I learned
from John that Blondel had called himself a "pragmatist" for a time until
William James paid him an extended visit and explained to the Frenchman
what he, James, meant by "pragmatism." It would appear that Blondel rejected Jamesean pragmatism without ever knowing Peirce's.

In the course on Blondel, John basically taught us his dissertation. He told
us that when he first read *L'Action*, he thought it the most original philosophical work he had studied. When, however, he completed his analysis of
the philosophical sources on which Blondel drew, John wondered if the book
contained a single original idea. John's analysis of the sources of *L'Action*
gave me a sound insight into the way the human mind creates, and that insight
ultimately shaped my own approach to creative speculation. I did not deem
Blondel's dependence on other minds for basic insights unusual or excep-
tional. I rather suspected that most original thinkers remain significantly be-
holden to the thoughts of other minds. That fact, however, did not make them
any the less original; for human originality derives not so much from the nov-
elty of one's ideas individually and separately considered but from the novel
way in which one synthesizes previously unrelated insights. Blondel had
written a very creative philosophical work because, even though he derived
most of his basic insights from other thinkers, no one else had put those ideas
together in the precise manner in which he had. Thereafter, I took Blondel's
approach to creativity as my model.

With William Richardson, S.J., I plunged into Heidegger. In my first semester of doctoral residency I took his lecture course on Heidegger; and in
the second semester I took his advanced seminar on Heidegger. I found much
to commend in the work of Heidegger. I resonated with his concern to transcend objectifying modes of thought and perception and to replace them with
a thoroughly relational understanding of reality. I liked his sensitivity to non-
rational forms of human intentionality. I found his use of phenomenological
method creative and inventive. With time, however, Peirce and Dewey would
teach me to regard Heidegger's system as fatally flawed.

The more I got inside of Heidegger's philosophical project at Fordham and
afterwards, the more convinced I felt that he had committed a fatal methodological error in using phenomenological description in order to do meta-

William Richardson, S.J.

physics. Heidegger equated Being, the proper object of metaphysical think-ing, with the total pattern of meaning; and he invoked his appropriation of Husserl's phenomenology in order to understand Being. Peirce's division of the philosophical sciences had, however, made me realize that normative thinking has to mediate between phenomenology and metaphysics. Phenom-enology describes whatever appears in experience without attempting to dis-tinguish between reality and mere appearance. Metaphysics does attempt to make that distinction. Peirce argued, and I agreed, that in order to make such a distinction successfully, the metaphysician needs to draw upon the norma-tive insights of esthetics, ethics, and logic.

In Peirce, esthetics means more than the philosophy of art. It means norma-tive thinking about what makes life ultimately worth living. Peirce called es-thetics the science of the *summum bonum*.[1] Ethics ponders normatively the kinds of choices one ought to make if one wishes to attain supreme goodness. Logic thinks normatively about the laws of sound reasoning which will allow one to grasp reality truly so that one can make realistic choices that will lead one to the *summum bonum*. If Peirce had it right (and I think that he did), one would have difficulty telling the difference between reality and illusion until one had put order into one's psyche, into one's conscience, and into one's mind. Until one did so, one would remain all too prone to identify reality with banal-ity, or with one's neurotic or psychotic fantasies, or with one's narrow, selfish, vested interests, or with one's fallacious and addled thinking. Over the years, as I implemented these Peircean logical principles in the theological thinking I was doing, I decided that, on these issues, Peirce, the logician and metaphysi-cian, had got it right and Heidegger, the phenomenologist, had got it wrong.

At the same time that I immersed myself in Heidegger, I was studying and outlining the major works of John Dewey with Robert Roth, S.J., who had himself written a fine study of Dewey's understanding of self-realization. Bob's seminar on pragmatism as a movement, one of the finest I had at Fordham, also introduced me to lesser pragmatic lights. Each week we read and discussed three works by major and minor pragmatists.

My study of Dewey convinced me that he had made an important distinction, implicit in Peirce's logic, which Heidegger badly needed to make: namely, the distinction between meaning and significance. Events signify, interpretations mean. Events signify because they have an intelligible relational structure capable of interpretation by a mind. Interpretations mean because the attribution of sensed and perceived qualities to significant events makes us present to them and them to us. When events behave in the way our interpretations predict, then our interpretations prove true. When events do not behave in the way our interpretations predict they will, then our interpretations prove false. When we re-interpret events truly, we endow real significance with meaning.

Heidegger's failure to distinguish between meaning and significance deprives his philosophical system of any adequate measure of truth and falsity. This fatal deficiency accounts in no small measure for the intellectual relativism of theologians and other scholars who invoke Heidegger in thinking hermeneutically. If one can only know meanings of meanings of meanings, one can only interpret someone else's interpretation; but one can never get at the facts. One can know that the weather forecast predicted it would rain yesterday; but one can never know whether or not the rain fell.

Jean Paul Sartre, I concluded, saw clearly the logical consequences of Heidegger's definition of Being as the total pattern of meaning. If Being and meaning coincide, then, anything other than the intentional structure of the mind counts as non-Being and absurdity. Heidegger never endorsed Sartre's

Robert Roth, S.J.

deduction of this conclusion from his own definition of Being; but, if one invokes a Peircean logic of consequences, then Sartre's conclusion flows deductively and necessarily from Heidegger's definition. By the way, phenomenologists have no right to formulate any definition universally applicable in intent. If they think with methodological consistency, they can only describe what appears in experience. Universal definition belongs to abductive, hypothetical logic, not to phenomenology.

These logical and methodological deficiencies in Heidegger did not incline me to invoke his philosophy in doing theology. Moreover, those aspects of Heidegger's thought which appealed to me, I found better and more accurately expressed in the philosophy of Charles Sanders Peirce. Peirce transcended objectifying modes of thought by developing a phenomenology, logic, and metaphysics of relationship. Peirce exhibited sensitivity to non-rational forms of intentionality and interpreted them realistically instead of just descriptively. Peirce also used phenomenology even more creatively than Heidegger, because, unlike Heidegger he, with consistent logic, transformed his phenomenological categories into verifiable metaphysical categories. In other words, given a choice between Peirce's philosophical frame of reference and Heidegger's, I found Peirce's by far the more adequate. I do not mean to suggest that all these insights came to me as a graduate student; but the work I did in graduate school eventually bore them as their fruit.

Moreover, as I got deeper into the thought of John Dewey, I saw that one could use his philosophy of art as experience in order to expand Peirce's notion of common sense thinking with an understanding of artistic creativity and of art criticism consonant with Peirce's vision. Both thinkers invoked a transactional, interactive understanding of knowing. Dewey, however, described more accurately than Peirce had how cognitive transactions occur in artistic and literary modes of expression.

I would eventually come to realize that Dewey, in his *Logic: The Theory of Inquiry* had also developed the logic of deliberative thinking in greater detail than Peirce had. One could, moreover, use that logic in order to clarify the kind of thinking that goes on in Peirce's normative science of ethics.

Finally, when I contrasted Dewey's instrumentalism with Peirce's logical focus on theoretical understanding and on the interface between logic and metaphysics, I eventually came to realize as my theological system began to take shape in Berkeley that Dewey had in fact articulated a formal logic for what Peirce called practical science. A formal logic examines the norms for thinking in general. Applied logic studies the norms for thinking appropriate to a specific discipline. Dewey's pragmatic instrumentalism, which sought to reduce problematic situations to settled ones, manifested little of Pierce's passionate concern with theoretical truth and none of Peirce's concern with

metaphysics. Instrumentalism seeks to transform the world by making it better and so exemplifies practical science. The practical sciences investigate
systematically how to get something done. Mining, engineering, animal husbandry exemplify practical sciences. Such insights matured in me gradually
over the years, but their roots stretch back to my exploration of pragmatism
at Fordham.

I had the great and providential good fortune at Fordham to get introduced
to the complex thought of Alfred North Whitehead by Walter Stokes, S.J.
Wally knew thoroughly both process philosophy and substance philosophy;
and he clarified the implications of Whitehead's system by contrasting it with
Aristotelian substance philosophy. Since I had found myself in St. Louis required to master Gilsonian Thomism as a system, Wally's way of presenting
Whitehead made his arcane cosmology much more accessible to me than I
would have otherwise found it. Wally argued, correctly I believe, that substance philosophy and Whiteadean cosmology propose contradictory and finally irreconcilable ways of viewing the universe. Moreover, Wally found
strengths and limitations in both systems. That kind of critical introduction to
Whitehead's system facilitated my own perception of its strengths and limitations. Even so, I found *Process and Reality* the hardest treatise in philosophy I had ever read. I outlined the whole thing; but one cannot just read such
a book. One must live with it, over the long haul.

I found myself initially much taken by Whitehead's system and would
eventually incorporate many of his insights into the theological system I
would myself create. Substance philosophy and process philosophy define
"Being," "reality," in contradictory ways. Substance philosophy equates Being with the immutable. Something is to the extent that it does not change.
Process philosophy identifies Being with process, with change. Something is
to the extent that it is in process of becoming other than what it is. Whatever
does not change has died, has by decision transformed itself into an unchanging, objectively immortal fact existing in the memory of God.

In accordance with its definition of Being, substance philosophy perceives
reality as constituted by fixed and immutable principles of being. Whitehead
views reality as concrescent experience, as the growing together of feelings
toward concreteness.

Substance philosophy conceives the subject of change as underlying the
change. Whitehead views the subject of change as emerging from change.

Substance philosophy grasps the nature of things by essential definition, by
identifying its genus and specific difference. Whitehead mistrusts abstractions and their ability to disclose reality to us exhaustively. He therefore holds
that one can grasp exhaustively what a thing has transformed itself into only

by recapitulating its entire history. History makes us what we are, not some abstract essence.

Substance philosophy recognizes two kinds of relations: predicamental, or accidental, relations between two substances, on the one hand, and transcendental relations between act and potency, on the other. Whitehead rejected the notion of transcendental relations and regarded what substance philosophy called predicamental relations, not as accidents, but as the extensive continuum, as a cosmic grid of geometrical relationships which every concrescent drop of experience atomizes.

Substance philosophy requires substances to exist in themselves and not in anything else as in a subject of inhesion. Whitehead, not unlike some forms of Buddhism, sees every reality "objectified," either positively or negatively, in everything else.

In substance philosophy, the quantification of matter creates a finite individual. Whitehead viewed individuality in qualitative rather than in quantitative terms. In the world of process, qualitative uniqueness makes one individual.

I gleaned these fundamental contrasts between substance and process philosophy from studying with Wally and, on the whole, in what concerned these issues, I felt more sympathetic to Whitehead. Moreover, while studying

Walter Stokes, S.J.

Whitehead at Fordham, I could not help but feel struck by the impact on his thought of the later Santayana. Both thinkers had paradoxically fused nominalism with a form of Platonism. I say "paradoxically" because during the middle ages, nominalism originally came into existence in no small measure as a repudiation of twelfth century Platonism.

In denying the reality of universals, classical nominalists had rejected the reality of Plato's transcendent realm of ideas but without criticizing systematically the dualistic presuppositions of Plato's cosmology. Having eliminated the transcendent, ideal realm of Spirit, classical nominalists found themselves left with the concrete realm of matter. As a consequence, nominalism has strong affinities with materialism. Classical nominalists "explained" universals by reducing them to a concrete word, like "horse" repeated again and again over some concrete horse. Conceptual nominalism allowed that universals do exist, but it confined them to human subjectivity. As a consequence, in conceptual nominalism, when one predicates a subjectively derived universal idea of some concrete object, one attributes to that object a universality it does not in fact have. Kant, perhaps, brought conceptual nominalism to its most systematic formulation in modern times.

Both Whitehead and Santayana espoused a form of conceptual nominalism. Both recognized a conceptual realm corresponding to Plato's realm of forms, and both located that realm in subjectivity. Both recognized a concrete physical realm corresponding to Plato's realm of matter. Whitehead seems to have developed his notion of a "prehension" in part from meditating passages in *Skepticism and Animal Faith*, Santayana's prolegomenon to his final monumental work, *Realms of Being*. Santayana's realm of matter corresponded roughly to Whitehead's physical feelings, just as Santayana's realm of essence corresponded roughly to Whitehead's realm of eternal objects. Whitehead, of course, opted to develop his modified Platonism in a theistic direction, while Santayana rejected theism. As I slowly tightened my grasp of Whitehead's system over the years, I found myself, however, no more inclined to adopt Santayana's system as a system than I felt inclined to endorse Whitehead's theistic cosmology as a system. Indeed, of all the American thinkers I have studied, in my own thinking I have derived the least insight from Santayana. His realm of essence did help me view human evaluative responses as a continuum. I liked his sensitivity to aesthetic experience and found some suggestive hints in his critique of the genteel tradition in United States culture. He perhaps brought that critique to its wittiest expression in his novel *The Last Puritan*.

In addition, when I pondered Whitehead's critiques of substance philosophy in the light of the philosophy of Charles Sanders Peirce, I saw that one could integrate most of them into Peirce's metaphysical system. Peirce, like Whitehead, had developed a kind of process philosophy. Peirce saw finite realities as constantly in process of either transforming themselves or being transformed in some way. He, like Whitehead, realized that only in such a universe can one think the evolution of the world from cataclysm, to purpose, to living purpose, to self-conscious living purpose, to persons and communities who have religious experiences. For Peirce as for Whitehead, the subject of change emerges from change. It makes sense in Peirce's metaphysics to say that history defines the nature or "essence" of any spatio-temporal reality.

Peirce also saw reality as relational; but here his metaphysics offered an alternative to both substance and process thought. Peirce recognized three fundamental kinds of relations: conceptual relations which link human evaluative responses into an intentional continuum, factual relationships which create environmental and social continuity among developing things and persons, and real, habitual relations which relate any developing entity to its future. Peirce called his theory of relational continuity "synechism" from the Greek verb "*synechô* (I hold together).)" This understanding of social and environmental relations interpreted my experience. Whitehead's atomized extensive continuum did not. I dismissed it therefore as an unverified and unverifiable postulate.

Peirce defended the mutual penetrability of finite realities. In that sense, he endorsed Whitehead's suggestion that spatio-temporal realities condition one another and to a certain extent exist in one another. I decided that in both Peirce and Whitehead quality explains individuality better than the Aristotelian notion of quantified matter. With time, however, I would reconceive individuality in functional, relational terms as autonomous functioning, as the capacity to initiate one's own activity.

Moreover, Peirce's philosophy, I would also eventually come to see, overcomes some of the more obvious defects of Whitehead's system. Whitehead, as Charles Hartshorne never tired of insisting, conceived reality in di-polar terms. Whitehead found only two kinds of feelings in any concrescing entity: concrete, physical feelings and particular, abstract conceptual feelings. In other words, Whitehead endorsed the kind of conceptual nominalism which he discovered in John Locke, David Hume, Immanuel Kant, George Santayana, Henri Bergson, and William James. Conceptual nominalism allows the existence of universals but confines that existence to human subjectivity alone. Every object of knowledge exemplifies concrete physicality and by definition can have no real generality.

In Whitehead, novel, creative process occurs when some entity prehends in the mind of God some particular conceptual possibility it does not yet embody and then through decision transforms that particular conceptual possibility into a concrete physical feeling. In other words, Whitehead also defends an indefensible ontologism. Ontologism holds that the human mind has immediate cognitive access to the ideas in the mind of God. Since we have no immediate cognitive access to the ideas in other human minds, I find it all the more unlikely that we would have immediate cognitive access to ideas in the transcendent divine mind.

Moreover, in Whitehead, when a particular occasion of experience concretizes itself through decision, it immediately perishes and becomes only a memory in the mind of God. Wiser than Whitehead, Peirce conceived reality in triadic rather than in di-polar terms. Peirce's universe contains particular, qualitative possibilities, concrete actions and reactions, concrete immanent activities, and real, habitual generality. By conceiving process as the transformation of a particular conceptual possibility into a concrete, physical reality through decision, Whitehead fell, along with Plato and Aristotle, into the fatal fallacy of essentialism. Essentialism reifies ideas as metaphysical principles of being. In a Whiteheadean universe, when a particular idea in the mind of God becomes ingredient in a finite entity through decision, it functions as a metaphysical principle of being by changing that entity's constitution.

Peirce saw more clearly than Whitehead that qualitative conceptions belong to the how of the experience not to its what. Our qualitative, intentional, cognitive responses to things define the way in which we become present to the realities and actualities we know. They do not exemplify the objects of knowledge. The physical object of knowledge, what we know, exemplifies a more or less complex continuum of concrete factual decisions and of the tendencies which ground them.

In human communication, of course, we also perceive other minds; but we do not know their evaluative responses immediately and directly. We know them when that other mind shapes some physical medium in order to express how it views the world. In Peirce's world, then, an essence does not exemplify a metaphysical principle of being but a qualitative sensation or perception abstracted from what it senses or perceives and from the mind which does the sensing and perceiving. We do not discover essences in things; we create them through an act of abstraction. We do so when we prescind the way we sense or perceive something from what we sense or perceive and from our minds which do the sensing or perceiving. Having created essences, we then arrange them alphabetically in dictionaries.

Even on my first reading of *Process and Reality*, I realized that, by endorsing an atomic view of process, Whitehead makes it impossible to think real continuity. Whitehead imagined an individual as a society of overlapping drops of experience which perish in the fraction of a second. If Whiteheadeans want to speak of George Washington, for example, they must decide which George Washington they mean: the idea of George Washington in the mind of God, the society of overlapping occasions which constitutes the "individual" we call George Washington and whose occasions each perish in the fraction of a second, or one atomic occasion of George Washington. Only one thing remotely resembles real continuity in Whitehead's account of the "society" of actual occasions which constitutes an "individual." God assigns to the first occasion of George Washington a final aim which recurs thereafter in each overlapping occasion of George.

The reader may find here an adequate philosophical account of individual and personal continuity; but I do not. Moreover, the absence of continuity in Whitehead causes him to deny in principle the possibility of physical motion. Each finite occasion of George Washington atomizes a different part of the extensive continuum, the embodied geometrical grid which in Whitehead's cosmos causes everything to relate to everything else. George Washington may seem to move, to walk, to speak, to ride; but he really does not. The coming to be and instant perishing of overlapping occasions of George only create the illusion of his moving and walking, like the blinking lights on a theater marquee. I find the suggestion unverifiable and unbelievable.

In *Process and Reality*, Whitehead compares his formulation of a theistic cosmology to an imaginative airplane flight. Wally did not find amusing my smart-ass remark in my term paper for his course that in my judgment Whitehead had bailed out rather than landed his airplane; but an initial insight into unverifiable aspects of his system had motivated my jibe.

Peirce's thought, by replacing Whitehead's di-polar, conceptual nominalism with a triadic realism, does in my judgment offer a plausible explanation of continuity. Peirce, as I have already indicated, called his doctrine of real continuity "synechism" from the Greek verb "*synechô*, I hold together." In Peirce's thought, action and reaction create social and environmental continuity. Inferential and allusive relations among ideas create conceptual and perceptual continuity, and the growing complexity of evolving, habitual tendencies creates individual and personal continuity. In other words, I found in Peirce's doctrine of synechism a more satisfying account of real continuity than Whitehead's nominalistic, atomized universe offers.

Moreover, in Whitehead real social relationships cannot in principle exist, because while an occasion of experience is in process of creating itself, while it is deciding what kind of experience it will become so that it can instantly perish, it remains by definition impervious to all outside influence. One can experience another occasion of experience only as a perished fact, as a datum for one's own subjective processing, never as what Martin Buber called a "Thou." If so, then, Whitehead's system lacks the conceptual means of thinking as common a human experience as falling in love.

Finally, while Whitehead wants to present a philosophical account of reality as process, his option for a form of conceptual nominalism makes it impossible for him to give a causal account of one of the most fundamental assertions his system makes: namely, his interpretation of how process happens. Whitehead locates efficacy in the physical pole of experience and inefficacious possibility in the conceptual pole of experience. The conceptual pole of experience lures the physical but effects nothing decisively. That the physical pole does. As soon, however, as an occasion of experience achieves concreteness, it immediately perishes and achieves what Whitehead calls "objective immortality." The perished physical fact survives only as a memory in the mind of God but will remain everlastingly the concrete actuality it has chosen to become.

Process, creativity, supposedly occurs in Whitehead's cosmos when one juxtaposes within a single occasion of experience an immutable, objectively immortal, concrete physical feeling and an inefficacious conceptual feeling in the mind of God, which can lure physical realities but can effect nothing efficaciously. Why, however, should anything in fact happen when such a juxtaposition occurs? Why should an everlastingly fixed fact feel the lure of an inefficacious possibility to become anything other than what it is already? One can lure a living dog to eat but not a dead one.

In other words, not only does Whitehead's conceptual nominalism fail to explain adequately both real continuity and social relationships; but it also fails to explain process itself. Since, moreover, Whitehead equates process with reality, his conceptual nominalism cannot explain reality.

Were Daddy Wade alive today, I feel certain that he would take great glee in "undressing Whitehead in public." Since he now lives with God, I guess that I, in grateful homage, must at least try to do it for him and hope that it brings him joy to find one of his students following in his footsteps.

By insisting on the reality of continuity, Peirce's doctrine of "synechism" offers, in my judgment, a verifiable account of process. For Peirce, the growing complexification of general tendencies explains continuity within process, somewhat in the manner of Teilhard's law of complexity consciousness. The law of complexity consciousness asserts that as finite realities grow in complexity they also tend to grow in awareness. The same logically holds true in Peirce's universe.

Moreover, in Peirce's metaphysics, real generality, the tendency to act decisively or respond evaluatively, also gives a processing universe the motor which Whitehead's world lacks precisely because real generality exemplifies a dynamic tendency to act or to respond in specific ways and under specifiable conditions. In other words, the more I compared and contrasted Pierce and Whitehead, the more convinced I felt over time that Peirce's account of process succeeds where Whitehead's fails.

The more I pondered the philosophical oversights of other thinkers in the light of Peirce's thought, the more the immensity of his speculative achievement astonished me. At the same time, the more I studied Peirce's logic and metaphysics in the light of other American thinkers, the more I saw the possibility of developing his thought in creative directions precisely because Peirce chose deliberately to think at the highest level of abstraction possible. Peirce viewed abstractions not as airy impracticalities but as the most practical ideas of all because they have the greatest number of consequences. We imagine them impractical because we, with our peanut brains, either will not or cannot deduce those consequences. In other words, the more I studied the American philosophical tradition, the more I discovered the possibility in insights from other American thinkers of clarifying deductively and verifying inductively the consequences of Peirce's overarching system. I also saw that such a creative amplification of Peirce's synthetic philosophical vision would exemplify Blondelian creativity.

It would, however, take time before I could draw systematically on the philosophical tradition in the United States as a whole in order to develop by deductive clarification and inductive verification the implications of Peirce's logic and metaphysics. By the time I had finished my course work and had passed my comprehensive examination at Fordham, I had established a firm grip on the thought of Peirce, James, Royce, Dewey, and Whitehead. In writing my dissertation, I would consolidate my grasp of Emerson. I remained, however, ignorant of the historical roots of Pragmatism within the American tradition.

On finishing my doctorate I would assume a position in the philosophy department of Loyola University in New Orleans. By that time, in educating younger Jesuits, we had collapsed the juniorate with its two years of literary study and the three traditional years of philosophy into what we called "collegiate formation." Young Jesuit collegians now do three years of literary and philosophical studies, with the emphasis on philosophy, and they do so on a college campus instead of sequestered in a rural hamlet like Grand Coteau. More recently, because a growing number of young Jesuits enter the Society relatively ignorant of the Catholic tradition, we have transferred one of the four years of theological studies to collegiate formation; and we are currently assessing the results of that experiment.

In addition to teaching full time in the philosophy department, I would, between 1969 and 1973, organize and supervise the Jesuit collegians' academic program at Loyola. I lived in their small community on Freret Street; but I told them that, as far as I was concerned, they must have their nervous breakdowns on Monday, Wednesday, and Friday. Loyola University abuts Tulane University; and on Tuesday and Thursday, I would spend the entire day in

Tulane's fine graduate philosophical library doing research. There I would consolidate my grip on the American philosophical tradition which antedated Peirce. I anticipate myself, however, since in what concerns this narrative I have not yet arrived in New Orleans and am just getting ready in 1968 to migrate from the Bronx to Cambridge, MA, in order to complete researching and writing my dissertation.

When the time came for me decide on the topic of my dissertation, I felt strongly drawn to study Peirce rather than to complete my research on Emerson. I decided to stick with Emerson for two reasons. First, I regarded a doctorate and still so regard it as a certification process. One should do it as thoroughly and as expeditiously as possible so that one can get on with the living of one's life. I had done so much work on Emerson already that I felt almost as though I could begin writing the dissertation at once. In fact, I had to do a detailed analysis of the unpublished sermons before I could write the first chapter. That done, however, for the rest of my year in Cambridge I spent the mornings, when I felt really fresh, writing and the afternoons in the Houghton Library, reading and taking extensive notes on the unpublished lectures. The fact that I could complete a dissertation on Emerson quickly and efficiently motivated me, then, to choose him over Peirce. Once I had the degree, I could immerse myself in Peirce with greater leisure.

I had a second reason for choosing Emerson. As I reflected on United States culture in the late sixties, I realized that what the New Left regarded as novel and radical battle cries, like "Do your own thing," echoed clichés of Emersonian Transcendentalism. That convinced me that Emerson had exerted a profound impact on culture in this country because the New Left was in fact quoting him but did not even know it. I would eventually come to realize that Ralph Waldo Emerson first formulated the ideology of expressive individualism which so skews the consciences of contemporary Americans just as it skewed the consciences of the New Left of the sixties.

At the same time that I was completing my two years of residency at Fordham, Robert Neville had recently joined the philosophy faculty. I had not taken any courses with him, but I heard him highly praised by students who had. I also found his first book, *God the Creator*, an impressive piece of sustained metaphysical speculation and wanted to get to know him better. I explained to him the work I had already done on Emerson and sketched the dissertation I hoped to write. I wanted to study Emerson's understanding of religious experience. Bob agreed to direct me. He later told me that he took me on as his first directee in part because he liked the idea of working with a graduate student who had already published a book.

Prof. Robert Neville.

I spent the academic year of 1968-1969 living in La Farge House at 6 Sumner Road in Cambridge. The residence derived its name from John La Farge, S.J., the son of the nineteenth-century American artist and one of the great Jesuit apostles of social justice in the United States. In his final years, La Farge worked on the staff of *America* magazine. Then in his eighties, he had found Kennedy's assassination an appalling tragedy and died quietly of a heart attack a few days after it. C.J. was working at *America* during my two years of residency at Fordham. Having lived with La Farge, he referred affectionately to him as "Uncle John."

While studying in the Bronx, I had tried to visit with C.J. as often as I could in the Manhattan offices and residence of *America*. As the music and arts editor of the magazine, C.J. constantly received complementary tickets to concerts. He kept my musical imagination alive by inviting me frequently to accompany him to a concert when he had extra tickets. Once we heard Peter Serkin give a superb rendering of the devilishly difficult Diabelli Variations by Beethoven. Transported by the performance, we both bellowed "Bravo!" before any one else made a sound. As Serkin took his bows, his eyes searched our part of the audience; but I do not think that he ever identified us.

I had never lived in New England and was looking forward to learning that part of the country. In New Orleans Jackson Square incarnates the French and

Spanish roots of Louisiana and reminds one both of Jefferson's purchase of
Louisiana and of the War of 1812. In New England I found myself surrounded
by historical reminders of the British colonial roots of the United States. On
the days when I took a break from research and writing, I tried to immerse
myself in the relics of United States history surrounding me. I walked the
Freedom trail many times. I saw the site of the Boston Massacre. I toured Paul
Revere's house and saw the steeple where a light had informed him that the
British troops were coming to Lexington and Concord by land. That news had
launched him on his famous ride. I saw Lexington Common where the British
and colonials clashed, while the grandfather of Theodore Parker looked on.
Years later, in Berkeley, I would through our charismatic prayer group befriend Jane Hartman, a convert to Catholicism and one of the descendants of
the Parker family. I walked upon the rude bridge that arched the flood in Concord, where the shot heard round the world had rung out as Ralph Waldo
Emerson's grandfather watched the skirmish from the door of the Old Manse.
I toured the Manse and saw Nathaniel Hawthorne's romantic scratchings on
the windowpane. I viewed "The Prophet's Room," the room ordinarily reserved for visiting ministers, where Emerson somewhat pretentiously preferred to stay when he visited the old rectory. There he had completed the
writing of *Nature*. I also toured the Alcott residence and saw the building in
which Bronson Alcott had conducted what William James called "his absurd
school." I saw where Louisa Mae had written her novels. I visited Sleepy
Hollow Cemetery and felt moved by the simplicity of Henry David Thoreau's
grave and somewhat amused at the pretentiousness of Emerson's. I walked
around Walden Pond and located the probable site of Thoreau's cabin. I visited the house in Salem where alleged witches faced trial. I walked through
Old Ironsides and examined old whaling vessels in Mystic Seaport. I enjoyed
the re-creation of town life in Young America at Old Sturbridge Village. In a
word, I tried not just to study texts from the American past but to get a feel
for the places which had witnessed the making of United States history.

    I also got better acquainted with Harvard University. By the time I got to
Cambridge, Al and Barbara had decamped with my nephew Christopher, aged
two, to Stanford University; but I used that year to befriend Bob and Jana
Kiely, already close friends of Al and Barbara and old graduate-school pals of
theirs. Through Bob I got a better feel for the University and met some of the
faculty. Bob had organized a Scripture study group composed of other
Catholic faculty and graduate students. He invited me to participate. We read
and discussed our way through the gospel of Matthew a chapter at a time.
Kevin Starr, then a doctoral candidate, also participated and was completing
his doctoral dissertation, which became the first volume of his multi-volume
study of California culture.

At La Farge House, I made some life-long friends. As I buried myself in the Emerson archives at the Houghton Library, Frank Oppenheim, S.J. buried himself in the Josiah Royce papers which it also housed. Frank was doing his doctorate at St. Louis when I studied philosophy there; but we tended to move in different worlds at that time. The year in Cambridge began a wonderful, life-long personal and professional friendship between the two of us.

In St. Louis, Frank had asked Dr. Collins to direct his dissertation. When he told Dr. Collins that he wanted to write on Royce, the latter not untypically replied, "Which Royce?" By that he meant that Royce's complex thought had evolved considerably in the course of his lifetime and that Frank would do well to focus on a particular period in that development. Frank chose Royce's final period. He would eventually write definitive studies of this extraordinarily rich phase of Royce's development. He now ranks as one of the leading experts on California's gift to philosophy.

In Cambridge, sometimes Frank and I went for walks together. Only a few blocks from La Farge House, Julia Child, television's French chef, lived in a former Royce residence. The William James residence stood on the same block only a few doors away. Frank had contacted Julia and explained to her that he was doing research on Royce. He told her that he liked to visit the places where Royce had lived on the chance that he might discover something about the great philosopher. Julia graciously gave him a tour of the former Royce residence; but Frank learned from his visit only that Julia had refurbished the kitchen, as one would expect, with state-of-the-art culinary appointments. I did not accompany Frank on that visit; but he did show me the fencepost where James and Royce used to stand in the snow arguing philosophy. I always pointed it out to friends when I gave them my Harvard tour. I also showed them the plaque commemorating Quentin Compson on the Anderson Bridge that spans the Charles River not far from Harvard Square. In *The Sound and the Fury*, Quentin drowns himself in the Charles.

A dialectical comparison of Royce and James, moreover, gave me some insight into the kinds of issues they must have discussed while standing in the snow. James provided Royce with his principal adversary in his *Sources of Religious Insight*. Like Royce, I acknowledged James's role in creating psychology as a science. I found in his *Principles of Psychology* a suggestive phenomenology of human experience; and I continue to regard his *Varieties of Religious Experience* as a classic in the psychology of religion. As I assessed Royce's criticism of James's account of religious experience, however, I found myself siding with Royce rather than James. Royce correctly censured James for failing to deal in any adequate way with the communal and historical dimensions of human religious experience. Royce again had it right when he criticized James's attempt to locate human access to God in a privileged way in the individual, subjective unconscious.

Royce correctly took exception to James's irrationalism in describing human religious experience. Royce vindicated an important role for human reason in approaching God and stressed more than James the role of conscious insight in religion. Royce also resisted James's attempt to justify religious faith by its psychological good works. In *Varieties* James had argued that religious commitment improves people morally through the process of sanctification and, that despite the occurrence of psychological religious aberrations, religion also tends to make people more emotionally balanced. Royce correctly argued that if religion does not do more than that, then it scarcely deserves the name of religion.

Royce's philosophy of loyalty strongly informed his account of human religious insight. Religious commitment, Royce argued, consecrates one to a cause which makes demands upon one and which draws one into atoning for human betrayal and treachery. Indeed, for Royce, commitment to a lost cause exemplifies one of the highest expressions of human religious commitment. Commitment to a lost cause need not express defeatism. I and many others, for example, remain committed to the cause of eliminating world hunger even though the chances seem slim that world hunger will disappear in our lifetimes, if indeed we ever ultimately succeed in eliminating it altogether. One hopes, of course, to alleviate the poverty and hunger of some people; but the certainty of ultimate success does not make such a cause worth espousing. One commits oneself to such a cause, not because one expects to succeed ultimately but because the inherent worthiness of the cause makes it worth espousing whether one succeeds ultimately or not. On all of the preceding issues, I decided that Royce got it right and James got it wrong.

Peirce too, I realized, had several valid criticisms of James. Like Royce, Peirce rejected James's di-polar conceptual nominalism and argued that one cannot do justice to the complexity of human thought and interpretation if one seeks to explain human knowing, as James did, as the subjective interrelation of abstract concepts and concrete percepts. Both Peirce and Royce correctly insisted on the triadic structure of human knowledge and interpretation of reality.

In his 1903 lectures on Pragmatism, Peirce repudiated James's attempt to psychologize his pragmatic maxim and reclaimed the maxim as a principle of abductive, hypothetical logic and nothing more. Peirce deplored James's "Will to Believe" and restricted the fixation of belief on passional grounds only to hypothetical thinking. Peirce held that the attractiveness of an hypothesis offers a good reason to adopt it initially but that deductive clarification and inductive verification which both demand strict logical validity must decide the truth or falsity of hypotheses or at least endow them with a degree of probability.

Peirce also correctly deplored James's attempt to portray metaphysical thinking as the result of a subjective, personal, temperamental bias. In the end, Peirce, as we have seen, required the normative sciences of esthetics, ethics, and logic to mediate between phenomenological description and the formulation of an experientially and scientifically verifiable metaphysics. On all of these issues too, I decided, Peirce got it right and James got it wrong.

Although I had not accompanied Frank on his visit to the home of Julia Child, I did accompany him on a tour of another former Royce residence. During my time in Cambridge. Jana Kiely had another baby. One Sunday I announced to Frank that I was going to visit her and invited him to accompany me. Since the time of our visit lay outside of visiting hours, we both wore clerics in the hope that we could bluff our way into seeing Jana. The ruse failed. The nurses had just distributed the babies for feeding and allowed no visitors during the nursing period.

Since we had the afternoon to kill, Frank suggested that we try to find and visit another former Royce residence in the neighborhood. "You never know what you may find," Frank said. "Sometimes a trunk in the attic will contain old papers." We succeeded in locating the house, climbed the steps, and rang the bell. An elderly, very Cambridge-looking lady opened the door. Frank did not say, "I am Professor Oppenheim. I am studying the American philosopher Josiah Royce. He once lived here. If it's not too inconvenient, would you have the time to show us around? Sometimes I find out something interesting about him in that way." Instead, he said in his best Mid-Western accent, "Pardon me, ma'am, but do you have a few minutes?"

The woman took one look at our clerical collars, and an expression of panic spread across her face. She thought us door-to-door evangelists. "No," she replied, "I do not; and, besides I am not interested." She started to slam the door, but Frank lunged at it before it closed, protesting, "No, please. You don't understand." There ensued a brief tug of war between him and the panic-stricken resident. Eventually, Frank explained to her that we had no intention of evangelizing her and had come in the hope of advancing research into the history of American philosophy. Once she understood Frank's real intent, the woman relented and graciously gave us a tour of the entire house. We learned nothing important; but perhaps we got a hint of why Kate Royce hated to cook. The ancient kitchen stove proved an ugly squat affair scarcely raised from the floor. To stir a pot one would have had either to stoop or to use long-handled spoons.

During my year at La Farge House, I also befriended John L'Heureux, S.J., who was pursuing a doctorate in English at Harvard. So was George Brown, S.J., whom I had known in St. Louis. George was pursuing a doctorate in medieval English literature. Both would wind up in the Stanford English department with Al and Barbara. Once I got to California, I renewed our friendship; but by the time both had got to Stanford, they had left the Society and married. Since John and Joan L'Heureux became good friends of Al and Barbara, through family connections I saw them more frequently.

When I knew John in Cambridge, he was beginning to write short fiction. Eventually, he would decide that his heart really lay in creative writing and would abandon his doctorate in English. His novel *The Clangbirds* convinced the Stanford English department that he had indeed established himself as a significant novelist. John, with considerable fictionalization, had based this particular novel on our La Farge house community. It contained an endearing portrait of old Joe Kelly, S.J., the superior of our community, for whom John had great affection.

The Clangbirds satirized the Catholic left during the sixties. In it, a group of doctoral candidates who belong to the fictional Thomasite order, decide to leave the order's more traditional residence for special students in order to found a community of radical Christianity. In trying to figure out what they mean by radical Christianity, each character in the novel turns into a Clangbird.

One does not learn until the end of the novel what a "Clangbird" signifies. Like Ignatius Loyola, the founder of the Jesuits, the founder of the Thomasites had a doctrine of The Three Classes of Men. In the case of Ignatius, they get better and better as one moves from class to class. In the case of the founder of the Thomasites, they get worse and worse. Finally, toward the end of his life, the first Thomasite discerned a fourth class of man, whom he called a Clangbird. Clangbirds fly in concentric circles with greater and greater velocity and with ever diminishing circumference until with a loud clang they disappear by flying up their own ass. One by one, the characters of the novel do precisely that. I have always taken it as a proof of his friendship that John did not include me among that novel's cast of characters.

William Russell, S.J. also became a permanent friend. He and I came to the Jesuit School of Theology in 1973, I as a member of the faculty, Bill as rector of the community. Through Bill I made the acquaintance of Henri de Lubac during my year in Cambridge. Bill had done his theology in France, where he and de Lubac struck up a friendship. Whenever de Lubac came to lecture in the United States, Bill would accompany him as a translator, since de Lubac spoke no English. During my Cambridge year, de Lubac had scheduled a series of lectures in different American cities, among them Chicago. Proclaiming de Lubac's theology suspect, Cardinal Cody canceled his lecture at the diocesan seminary in Chicago.

The auxiliary bishops of Chicago felt so outraged at the Cardinal's action, that they gave a special dinner in de Lubac's honor. Since de Lubac had to give another lecture later in the evening the bishops shortened the cocktail hour before dinner and told the waiters to serve doubles. De Lubac never drank hard alcohol; but he told Bill that, since the bishops were going out of their way to honor him, he would on this occasion drink whatever they gave him. The bishop next to de Lubac ordered a double martini; and de Lubac, not realizing what he was doing, ordered the same. When the waiter put the drink in front of him, de Lubac saw pure poison and decided to get an unpleasant experience over with as quickly as possible. He drained his glass in one gulp. The bishop, somewhat bemused, motioned to the server, who brought de Lubac a second double martini which he again chug-a-lugged. Fortunately, Bill saw what was happening and explained to the bishop that de Lubac never drank such cocktails and was, by way of exception, doing so this evening out of courtesy. During the meal the bishops had provided three wines. After dinner all drank a liqueur. Then de Lubac gave his lecture. Bill deemed his performance inspired, by far the best lecture of the entire tour.

After that one encounter, I never saw de Lubac again; but one of my colleagues in Berkeley, David Stagaman, S.J., had lived with him in Paris, where David was completing his doctorate at *L'Institut Catholique*. David and de Lubac normally did not move in the same social circles. Then, suddenly the latter started acting chummily. David soon found out that de Lubac wanted his assistance. De Lubac asked David whether he thought that he could arrange for him to lecture at Loyola University. De Lubac apparently did not realize that the Jesuits in the United States run more than one Loyola University. David belongs to the Chicago province. He responded that he had several friends in the theology department at Loyola in Chicago and that he felt sure they would feel delighted to extend an invitation to him to lecture. David, however, urged de Lubac to take lots of warm clothes, if he went to Chicago in the winter.

"I do not want to go to Chicago," de Lubac responded. "I want to go to Los Angeles."

"Well," David said, "we do have a Loyola University in Los Angeles; but why do you have to lecture there?"

"Because," de Lubac told him, " I just got a letter from Karl Rahner who lectured there, and Rahner tells me that I must not die without seeing Disneyland." Great theologians have their human side.

As the year in Cambridge wore on, I read through box after box of Emerson's unpublished lectures. The librarian would remove the box I had finished reading and replace it with the next box. Finally, toward the end of the academic year, as she brought me yet another collection of Emerson's increasingly scattered lecture notes, she regarded me with an air of disbelief and asked, "How can you do this?" Actually, I found tracking the gradual evolution of Emerson's thought fascinating.

As I read my way through Emerson's unpublished sermons, I realized that they really provided the key to his thought. In the course of them, he formulated the method which would structure, with minor variations, everything he wrote. He called his method spiritual discernment. It advanced phenomenologically. Moreover, like Heidegger, Emerson had committed the logical and methodological blunder of thinking that one can use phenomenology in order to develop a metaphysics.

Already in his sermons, Emerson had decided to espouse a simplified Neoplatonism. He had collapsed Plotinus's One, Intelligence, and World Soul into a single hypostasis, which he would eventually call the Over Soul. The essentially spiritual Over Soul supposedly contained within itself all the eternal laws which rule the material universe. Emerson believed that by a description of material facts, he could lead his bemused congregation to an immediate, self-evident perception within subjectivity of the eternal, moral laws which ground and explain physical events.

In his sermons, Emerson undertook an ambitious demonstration of "the good of evil." The "good of evil" consists in the fact that evil schools us to live, not in the body, not in the physical universe, but in the transcendent realm of spiritual goodness, truth, reality, God. Emerson's discernment of physical evil led him to an allegedly self-evident, subjective grasp of the eternal moral laws that rule the universe and in which material realities participate. His discernment of error led him to identify those same laws with eternal truth. His discernment of the physical self led him to discover two other spiritual selves: the finite spiritual self and the impersonal "Self" which coincides with eternal moral truth. His discernment of religious skepticism and unbelief led him to identify the impersonal "Self" in which all things participate with God.

During his years as pastor of Second Church in Boston, Emerson conceived the knowledge of God as the fruit of practical assimilation to the deity through the plodding cultivation of virtue. During his Transcendental period, from 1836 to 1842, he came to conceive of practical assimilation to the Over Soul as the result of spontaneous creative ecstasy, as divine creative energy empowering individual geniuses to suffuse some dimension of the material universe, however briefly, with spiritual Beauty and Reality. Once created, Emerson believed, the work of genius reverted to valueless fact, although it could make one aware of the eternal beauty it represented.

After 1842, the mature Emerson came to regard his middle, Transcendental period as a "saturnalia of faith": in other words, as naively optimistic. The Transcendental Emerson believed every individual a universal genius, another potential Leonardo da Vinci or Michelangelo, since he assumed without proof that every individual has immediate access within personal subjectivity to the infinite creative power of the Over Soul. The mature Emerson knew better. He rediscovered human finitude and transformed the finite self of his first period into a finite bias toward a certain kind of creativity assigned one by an impersonal Nature without concern for one's own personal satisfaction, happiness, or fulfillment.

I experienced reading through the whole of Emerson's published and unpublished writings the equivalent of reliving his life. I found in that life an element of the tragic. Emerson first formulated an ethic of expressive individualism in which so many contemporary Americans acquiesce. He believed that one must protect one's creative bias from any human relationship or institutional encroachment that might thwart or compromise it. My researches turned up evidence that success in that moral enterprise left him lonely, frustrated, and self-isolated.

Peirce's turn to community, which Royce endorsed and deepened, required one to renounce any form of individualism, including expressive individualism. Individualism exemplifies social dualism because it so conceives of the individual as to make it impossible thereafter to understand adequately the individual's relationship to other persons and to society. Moreover, I would eventually come to see that Peirce's philosophy avoided not just individualism but also the other dualisms that vitiated Emerson's vision of reality: his dualistic opposition of matter to spirit as essentially different, his dualistic sundering of eternity and time. Peirce's synechism discovered in religious experience and especially in shared religious experience evidence of a kind of social continuity between God and humanity.

On only four points did I find some convergence between Emerson and Peirce. 1) Both men believed that affectively charged, imaginative forms of thinking grasp reality in their own right. 2) Both believed that an experience of ultimate beauty endows the conscience with its must fundamental teleology. 3) Both located human creativity in intuitive, imaginative thinking. Emerson's thought enriched Peirce's system by insisting on the importance of artistic and literary expression. Peirce's thought corrected Emerson's by refusing to make privileged cognitive claims for imaginative thinking over inferential reasoning, as Emerson had. 4) Finally, both men viewed religious insight in synthetic terms.

After I finished writing each chapter of the dissertation, I would fly down to New York in order to consult with my committee and get their suggestions for revisions. Every time I did so, I remember thinking as I flew back to Boston, "They did it again. They told me to shorten the chapter and to lengthen it." So I did. I cut out some things and added others. By the end of the year, I had completed the revisions and sent the entire committee the final draft.

I had no reason to remain in Cambridge, since I had finished my writing and research. I had corresponded with Thomas Culley, S.J., who had entered the Jesuits the year before I did. Both Tom and I found ourselves in a period of transition. An accomplished harpsichordist, Tom had a degree in musicology from Harvard. He had taught at Brown but would begin teaching music the following academic year at the College of the Holy Cross in Worchester, MA. In the same year, I would join the philosophy faculty at Loyola University in New Orleans. Tom and C.J. were working on a monograph about the fine arts in the early days of the Society of Jesus. Tom suggested that we rent a place for the summer and found a lovely, two-story summer cottage on the east bank of Narragansett Bay, not far from Newport. Two Jesuit scholastics also joined us. Teddy Welsh, S.J. from the New Orleans Province spent the summer creating silk screens; and George Murphy, S.J. from the New England Province wanted to spend the summer reading theology. Tom practiced his harpsichord in the garage, which he deemed the driest place to house that temperamental musical instrument whose wooden stops swell with moisture.

During the first weeks of that summer, I compulsively revised my dissertation. I lived in the naive expectation that dissertation committees actually read dissertations during the summer. I hoped to incorporate their final suggestions for revisions in the final text of the dissertation. I waited to hear from them in vain.

I remember vividly the day I finished working on the dissertation. One morning early in the summer, I reached for the stack of papers I had written in order to reread and revise it yet one more time. When my hand touched the top paper, a wave of nausea swept over me. I felt as though I were going to vomit. I thought to myself, "I am never going to work on this stack of papers again. Either the committee accepts the dissertation as it is, or I do not need to get a Ph.D."

Eventually the committee did approve the final draft of the dissertation; but I could not bring myself to look at it again for five years. In 1973, the year I joined the faculty of the Jesuit School of Theology at Berkeley, I finally edited the text down to publishable length; but I did not publish it until 1991 because I could not figure out how to make it into a book that addressed contemporary issues.

In the final chapter of the original dissertation, I had criticized Emerson for his lack of historical consciousness. After reading *Habits of the Heart* and its critique of individualism in United States culture, however, I saw a way of relating my research in Emerson to contemporary issues. Emerson, I realized, had originally formulated what the *Habits of the Heart* team called an ethics of "expressive individualism." Expressive individualism teaches people in the United States to protect their "core self" from the demands of other individuals and from institutional encroachment. Emerson had called the core self one's "bias" or "genius."

Habits of the Heart correctly presented Walt Whitman as a proponent of expressive individualism; but Whitman had learned that ethos from Emerson. I saw that one could treat Emerson as a test case in trying to live by an ethics of expressive individualism in a religious context. As I have already indicated, I deemed the results of his ethical experiment tragic in their consequences. Eventually, the dissertation appeared in 1991 under the title: *Endless Seeker: The Religious Quest of Ralph Waldo Emerson.*

During our Narragansett summer in 1969, I and the other members of our little community, except for C.J., learned how to cook. When we arrived for the summer, none of us had ever cooked before. Fortunately, the house we rented had lots of cook books. For my first recipe, I tried the simplest one I could find: chicken breasts almondine. It turned out fine. I realized then that,

C.J. McNaspy, S.J. having fun with Herve Racivitch, S.J.

if one can read, one can cook. Indeed, if one has a good cook book, then cooking may exemplify the one realm of human activity in which blind obedience works. C.J. gave us moral encouragement in the kitchen; but, when it came to practicing the culinary arts, he mostly just puffed his pipe and left pipe tobacco and burnt matches scattered in odd places.

The Clavius Group was meeting at Holy Cross that summer. A postdoctoral research seminar in theoretical mathematics, the Clavius Group consisted originally of several Jesuits and one Christian Brother. One of my classmates in the Society, Andrew Whitman, S.J. had helped get the Clavius Group started. The Group visited a number of times at our bayside cottage. Their visits bore much creative fruit. Joseph Tetlow, S.J., a high-school classmate of my brother, was finishing his doctorate in American Studies at Brown University in Providence. He also visited us with some frequency. Like me, Joe was headed for Loyola University in New Orleans, where he hoped to start an interdisciplinary degree program in American Studies.

Joe and I hit it off from the beginning. His interest in American studies and my interest in American philosophy clearly converged. Taking the Clavius Group as our model, we agreed to begin a post-doctoral, summer research seminar in American Studies. Our plans stimulated Tom and C.J. to found a Jesuit Artists Group which also met during the summers and which put aspiring young Jesuit artists into contact with older, practicing Jesuit artists.

Our cabin stood on the east bank of Narragansett Bay; and, almost every evening, we enjoyed a spectacular sunset. Once, when the Clavius Group was visiting us, we waxed eloquent about the quality of sunsets on the Bay. Andy Whitman remained unimpressed. "I doubt," he said, "if the sunset will be anything to ooh and aah about." We sat on the shore of the Bay and watched the sunset take breathtakingly beautiful shape. Spontaneously, all of us but Andy started saying over and over, "Ooh! Aaa! Ooh! Aah!" Andy endured this stoically for several minutes and then conceded that we had the right of it.

By the time I completed my dissertation, I had discovered American philosophy from Peirce through Whitehead. I knew Emerson's thought thoroughly; but, apart from Emerson, I knew nothing about the development of the Puritan tradition in the British colonies, the thought of the founding fathers of this nation, and the other Transcendentalists. I don't think that I had even heard the name of Francis Ellingwood Abbot. I decided that while teaching philosophy at Loyola University in New Orleans I would explore those figures in the American philosophical tradition whom I had yet to study.

Colloquy:

In Easter light
        we learn to name
                the twists and turns of folly's maze,
                        the wideness of its gate,
                                where many enter,
                                which bears the name of fad.

Where lies the truth?
        Beyond the narrow gate,
                but where?

I tried to turn
        the search for wisdom into folly,
                but You turned thought to night,
                                barren blackness.
                        You paralyzed my mind
                but held me fast,
                                        held me always up,
                        until I tired of midnight,
                        surrendered,
                        felt Your presence,
                        saw Your face.

You led me by a different way from Paul,
        into the thicket of thought
                and kept me to the path,
                        showed me one you called once
                                to think of thinking,
                        one scorned by folly's children,
                        who knew the ease of error
                                        but hankered after truth.

Like Virgil once,
        he took my hand
                and led me to the narrow gate.

NOTE

1. In speaking of the normative science of esthetics, Peirce dropped the "a" from "esthetics" as a way of calling attention to the fact the he did not reduce the science of esthetics to the philosophy of art.

Chapter Four

Exploring America: The Loyola Years

When Joe and I arrived at Loyola University in New Orleans, we found a campus and a province in a state of ferment. The Free Speech Movement had reached the Loyola Campus. A faculty cabal was plotting against the administration. Thomas Clancy, S.J., the Academic Vice President of the University and one of the great men of our province, claimed that faculty politics at Loyola made the Byzantine Court look like a kindergarten. I did not understand then and still do not understand how academicians can waste so much time and energy playing political games when they could be expending that same energy on teaching and research. The political situation at the University seemed to me to verify George Santayana's wry aphorism: "The reason academic politics are so vicious is that the stakes are so low." I refused to have anything to do with palace intrigues and buried myself in teaching, in creating and supervising the collegiate program, and in researching the development of American philosophy in the Tulane University library.

Whatever its stakes, the academic politics had its casualties. The Dean of Arts and Sciences, a layman, found its pressures too taxing. He experienced an emotional collapse and resigned. As a result, Joe Tetlow never did get an American Studies program organized. Instead, he found himself drafted as the new Dean of Arts and Sciences. A natural leader and creative administrator, within a year not only had Joe quelled the faculty revolt; but he had also put a revised arts and sciences curriculum through the faculty senate. In effect, he diverted the energies wasted by the faculty on political jockeying into a prolonged debate about the new curriculum. Before proposing his new curriculum to the faculty, Joe researched it well and thought it through thoroughly. The revised arts and sciences curriculum encouraged team teaching and cross-disciplinary courses. Both increased discourse among the faculty of the school of Arts and Sciences about substantive issues. Counter-proposals to Joe's emerged from the faculty; but none held a candle to his. When he figured that the faculty senate had talked itself out, he called for a vote. They passed the new curriculum.

In my last year at Loyola, Joseph Fichter, S.J., whose sociological study of a southern Catholic parish had justly earned national attention and debate, organized a cross-disciplinary course on the nature of the human in which I participated. Joe wanted to put four disciplines into dialogue: sociology, psychology, philosophy, and theology. All four professors attended all the classes. Each professor began by using the lecture time allotted to him to explain the method of his discipline. The lecturer then used that method in order to formulate a construct of the human. I do not know if the students enjoyed our course; but all four professors did. Every time we met we had thought-provoking discussions.

As Academic Vice President, Tom Clancy actively recruited Jesuits to Loyola. He created several University Professorships which attracted distinguished scholars like Joe Fichter. C.J. had also accepted a University Professorship. University Professors belonged to no department and answered directly to the Academic Vice President. That exempted them from departmental meetings and increased time for their own writing and research. One year C.J., the Jesuit poet and theologian, Francis Sullivan, S.J., and I taught a two semester course in the history of Western culture. I represented the voice of philosophy; Frank, the voice of theology; and C.J. the voice of the fine arts.

In the course of his many travels, C.J. had acquired an extensive slide collection of which he took advantage every time he lectured. After each of his lectures, when he returned to his room, he unscrewed the carousel on his slide projector and dumped the slides for that day's lecture in a corner of his room. As the semester wore on, the pile of slides grew to impressive proportions. Uncannily, however, C.J. seemed to know where each of the slides lay in the growing mountain. On more that one occasion, I saw him reach into the pile and retrieve the precise slide he was looking for.

I began to organize discussions about philosophy among the members of our department. I became good friends with Patrick Bourgeois, who specialized in phenomenology, and with Sandra Rosenthal, who achieved academic distinction as a commentator on the American philosophical tradition. Our department cultivated a healthy pluralism. Inspired in part by Joe Tetlow's cross-disciplinary curriculum, we in our discussions invited a member of some other department to explain to us a research project on which he or she was working. Then we together would probe the philosophical questions which the project raised. All this dialogue in the classroom and within our department made Loyola an extremely stimulating place to work.

On arriving at Loyola, Joe and I also found the province in a state of ferment. We had a new provincial, John Edwards, S.J. John had completed a
doctorate in theology; but he found himself on the completion of his degree
appointed master of novices at Grand Coteau. I credit John more than anyone
else with the renewal of religious life in our province. John began with the
novitiate. He got rid of the archaic practices which had made the novitiate
seem so artificial to me: dips, chains, unwashed bodies, the needless permissions, the constant surveillance. He treated his novices like adults, and they
responded like adults. Moreover, as they moved through the formation program, they began to demand similar reforms at the more advanced levels of
their training.

As Provincial John began a province-wide discussion about our apostolic
commitments. He began calling annual province assemblies to assess the
state of our works and to advise him on province policy. Our province assemblies outlasted those in all the other provinces of the American Assistancy. I attribute that success to three factors: the way John organized the
election of delegates, the fact that both John and his successor as provincial,
Tom Clancy, took the assemblies very seriously, and a special session held at
the first assembly which we in the province referred to as "The Blood Letting
Session."

Most of the other provinces elected delegates according to apostolates. As
a result, in the assemblies of other provinces, the delegates tended to view
themselves as spokesmen for the apostolate they represented. Wisely, John
Edwards from the beginning arranged the election of our delegates according
to age groups. In my judgment, election by age groups increased the impar-
tiality of our discussions. Our delegates as a group did not seem to feel any
need to defend this or that apostolate against all comers.

I attended several assemblies as a delegate. We in our discussions addressed substantive issues in province policy. It made a difference that both
John and Tom as provincials made it clear that they took the advice of the assembly very seriously. The assemblies had only an advisory capacity; but, if
John or Tom thought that they could not go along with the assembly's rec-
ommendation, they explained to the province why they could not. Had those
early assemblies degenerated into mere debating societies, they would, in my
judgment, have died much sooner than they did.

The Blood Letting Session needs contextualization and expansion. John
Edwards asked the first province assembly to begin to draw up a five-year
plan for the New Orleans Province. He hired the Arthur D. Little people to facilitate the discussions. One hired the Arthur D. Little people to observe a

group process and then to tell the group what it had done during the process.

My brother Al had introduced me to the *I Ching*, a Chinese book of oracles which, I have heard, the first Jesuits who came to China believed wandering Jews had written because of the book's similarity to Old Testament wisdom literature. The *I Ching* presupposes that life mingles freedom and fate and gives wise advice about how to distinguish the two. Every morning I would consult the *I Ching* about the best way to approach the work of the assembly. One consults the *I Ching* by throwing coins or sticks whose configuration creates a figure of six lines, some broken, others unbroken. This hexagram breaks down into two trigrams; and each trigram has an abstract concept and a concrete image associated with it. The wise men of China had commented extensively on the implications of each clustering of ideas and images.

On the first day of the first assembly, I asked the *I Ching* how I should approach the assembly as a whole. The figure I created by throwing the coins had associated with it two images: pigs and fish. The commentary warned me that I was dealing with a group of human beings as unteachable and as intractable as pigs or fish. It advised me that one can eventually mobilize such a group to act constructively, but only after one has listened long, long, long to what its members have to say. That sounded to me like a fair description of a province assembly.

As we addressed the issue of formulating a five-year plan, inevitably we found ourselves forced to face the limitations of our resources. We have the geographically largest province in the American Assistancy but have always ranked numerically one of the smallest. Facing limited resources raised the question whether we should continue running all the institutions we currently ran. A consensus began to emerge that we probably needed to withdraw from some of our high schools. Jesuits invest a great deal of time and energy in the institutions they create; and talk of closing some of our schools started to make some of the delegates very nervous.

We launched into an endless discussion which amounted to a mutual exhortation. One speaker after another insisted that in this period of change and turmoil we needed men committed to our existing institutions. We seemed to be getting nowhere; and Tom Clancy was getting bored. He pushed the button in front of him indicating that he wanted to speak. When his turn came, he said in his Arkansas drawl, "I just want to say that I regard this as a very important topic. I think that half the people in this province ought to be committed to an institution." His quip brought a laugh that relieved the mounting tension in the room and ended that particular discussion, as I feel sure Tom had intended.

The Blood Letting Session resulted from an intervention by Hervé Racivitch, S.J. I and other friends of Hervé noticed that he had said nothing during the opening days of the assembly. We who knew Hervé well regarded him as brilliant, sensitive, and insightful. We therefore urged him to take a more active role in the discussions. He explained that he had not spoken because he did not know if he could say what he wanted to say in such a way that the delegates could hear him. We urged him to try to say whatever he wanted to say.

The next day, he did ask to speak. When he had the floor, he said, "My brothers, we have gathered here to discuss a five-year plan for the province. We are talking about opening and closing institutions. I believe, however, that we need to face a more fundamental question. This is how I understand the question: Half the people in this room believe in excommunicating those who disagree with them, and the other half do not. Those who believe in excommunicating those with whom they disagree do so because they feel afraid; and, as one of those in danger of being excommunicated, let me say that I too feel afraid. Can we get together and talk about that?" To the credit of the delegates, we all agreed to a special night session which would address Hervé's question.

During the session, we shared the fears and anxieties we felt about the future of the Society, of the province, of the Church. Each person who spoke did so with remarkable candor. Delegate after delegate made himself vulnerable by confessing his human doubts, fears, hesitations. The name "The Blood Letting Session" does not convey accurately in my judgment what that remarkable meeting accomplished. The willingness of the delegates to lay bare their fears and anxieties in public had the effect of creating a basis for mutual trust and support among us. In my judgment, that foundation paid off in spades in our subsequent province assemblies. As we grew in the conviction that we all shared the same kind of humanity, the same kind of vulnerability, and the same human need for support, we also grew in mutual trust and commitment. In retrospect, Hervé probably made the most significant intervention of that first assembly.

Three Jesuit priests lived with the collegians at Loyola–myself, Hacker Fagot, S.J., a learning theorist who taught in the psychology department, and George Wiltz, S.J., the community's superior. I had known George since grammar school. In fact, he too had seen Betty Bendix after she had fallen through the ceiling. George presided as the superior of our collegian community. Hacker taught learning theory in the department of psychology. Hacker also knew, among many other things, an enormous amount about the traditions of the Society. The three of us had prepared a proposal for the first province assembly concerning Jesuit formation. As a superior, George fully supported the kinds of changes which John Edwards as novice master had introduced into the formation program. As we discussed together the need for changes in the education of our men, we identified what we regarded as two pressing concerns. 1) We needed to insure more adequate personal government for our men and 2) we needed to insure better continuity of policy within formation.

Hacker had researched the issue of personal government and documented the fact that Ignatius did not conceive of a province primarily in geographical terms. Instead, he had established provinces in the Society of Jesus primarily as a means of insuring the personal government of all the members of the Society. After he created the first province in Spain, one of the members of the order wrote him protesting that the appointment of provincials as major superiors of provinces derogated from the authority of the General of the order. He replied that he as General could not provide personal government for all the men and that as the Society grew in numbers only the appointment of provincials could do that.

Personal government in the Society means that a major superior needs to know each of those he governs personally and intimately, because only such knowledge can insure making sound decisions concerning our men and our apostolates. In our proposal to the province assembly, we argued that, given the size of our province and the number of people then in formation, we could best insure personal government for all the men in formation by appointing a Vice-Provincial for formation with the right to receive the account of conscience from all of our younger men in studies. Given my experiences during regency and during my first two years of theology, I supported the proposal enthusiastically.

We also argued for the need to stabilize province policy with regard to the men in formation. We therefore proposed the formation of a policy board on formation to advise the new Vice-Provincial. Both measures passed the assembly. I think that the appointment of a Vice-Provincial for formation accomplished on the whole what we wanted it to do. The policy board worked, in my judgment, less well. Later, as the numbers of younger men in formation dropped, the office of Vice-Provincial began to look a bit like overkill; and we eventually abandoned it. Initially, however, it met, in my judgment, genuine needs.

The Blood Letting Session had not, however, allayed all the anxieties of all the members of the assembly. In the final days of that first province meeting after Vatican II, some of the older members of the province began to fear that having a major superior especially for those still in training would have the effect of dividing the young from the old. Hacker and I did the best we could to explain that our proposal intended nothing of the sort and that the office of the Vice-Provincial had only one purpose: to insure more effective personal government for our younger men; but I do not know whether we succeeded in quelling all suspicions about our plan. With time, those who had objected saw that our proposal did not in fact have the consequences they feared. The revised formation program eventually enjoyed broad support in the province.

Shortly after I joined the philosophy department at Loyola, Al Holloway, S.J., the department chair told me to let him know if I needed anything in the professional line. I replied that I had a research project in American philosophy and would like to acquire the complete works of Jonathan Edwards. True to his word, Al got me the funds to purchase all ten volumes of *The Works of President Edwards*. The new critical edition of Edwards's works had begun to appear from Yale University Press; and I had the volumes already published; but I felt I could not wait for the completion of the new edition in order to assimilate Edwards's thought. I saw only one way to master the first half of the philosophical tradition in this country: namely, to begin at the beginning and to move systematically forward.

My brother Al had introduced me to Perry Miller's reading of American Puritanism. I had also perused other studies of colonial Puritanism. I now read and highlighted all ten volumes of Edwards' writings and realized that within the intellectual tradition in this country he has all the importance which Miller attributed to him. As I sketched on paper my perception of his intellectual achievement, I realized that he had introduced major intellectual themes which subsequent American thinkers would deepen. I also saw some important points of convergence between Edwards and Peirce which would allow me to develop Peirce's thought in a theological direction.

Edwards's defense of the First Great Awakening had led him to reflect in considerable depth on the experience of Christian conversion. Focus on conversion gave his theology a strong experiential flavor. I knew from my study of the second half of the development of classical American philosophy that experience would eventually take on greater and greater philosophical importance, until eventually Whitehead would transform it into a metaphysical term.

Concern with conversion had also given Edwards's theology a strong esthetic flavor. Edwards interpreted aesthetic experience in thoroughly realistic terms. I endorsed his distinction between "excellence" and "beauty." By "excellence" Edwards meant the reality which an experience of beauty perceives. I also resonated with his definition of beauty as the simultaneous perception of goodness and truth with the heart, with the affections and imagination.

I recognized that his *Treatise Concerning Religious Affections*, to this day a masterful study of religious discernment, accurately described the dynamic shape and complexity of an initial Christian conversion experience. His insistence on the affective, imaginative, and esthetic dimensions of that experience had, I saw, also allowed him to develop an esthetic Christology, in

Peirce's sense of the term "esthetic." As Daddy Wade had seen, the initial assent of faith engages the heart much more than it does the head. I call Edwards's Christology esthetic because he grounds Christological faith in heartfelt consent to the excellence embodied in Jesus Christ and in those whose lives resemble His. Edwards also saw that consent to that excellence beautifies those who make it, causes them to incarnate some measure of the same excellence as Jesus Himself did.

Moreover, as my insight into the implications of Edwards's thought advanced, I began to see ways of synthesizing in a Blondelian way his theology of conversion, his esthetic Christology, Peirce's normative science of esthetics, Royce's philosophy of loyalty, and my own insights into Jesus' vision of God's reign which I had gleaned from my rethinking the vows of religion. These different philosophical and theological positions enjoy an interesting complementarity.

In his division of the sciences, Peirce, as we have seen, distinguished three normative philosophical sciences: esthetics, ethics, and logic. For Peirce, esthetics does not mean the philosophy of artistic expression but normative reflection on the ideals and realities which make life ultimately worth living. Peirce described esthetics as the science of the *summum bonum*. In effect, Peirce's theory of the normative sciences gave logical precision to Emerson's more diffuse argument in *The Conduct of Life*. In that late work, Emerson argued for the need to reground ethics in aesthetics. In Peirce's logic, ethics reflects normatively on the kinds of choices one ought to make in order to live for supreme excellence and value. Logic reflects normatively on how one ought to think in order to grasp reality truly and so make realistic decisions about how to choose in order to live for supreme excellence and value. In other words, esthetics, the science of the *summum bonum*, rules normatively both ethics and logic.

When Josiah Royce wrote *The Philosophy of Loyalty*, he probably looked upon that work as a study in ethics; but, when one studies his argument in the light of Peirce's theory of the normative sciences, Royce was in fact wrestling with esthetic rather than with ethical issues in Peirce's understanding of those terms. Royce defined "loyalty" initially as "the willing and practical and thoroughgoing devotion of a person to a cause." Loyalty requires more than emotional involvement; it requires decisive commitment, self-discipline, and selflessness. Authentic loyalty creates the conscience and provides an individual with a personal will and a social plan for creative living. One stands ready to make sacrifices for one's cause. Indeed, for Royce, as we have seen, commitment to a lost cause exemplifies one of the highest forms of religious loyalty.

Not every commitment to a cause exemplifies true loyalty. Selfish, self-seeking causes do not motivate true loyalty. Authentic loyalty dedicates one to causes of universal human benefit. Since the clash of causes makes loyal commitment tragic, authentic loyalty includes a loyalty to loyalty, an acknowledgment of the legitimacy of all genuinely loyal causes, even those other than one's own. Loyalty to loyalty commits one to the community of the loyal; for all loyalty inserts one into the community of those who espouse the same cause.

When one ponders Royce's argument in the light of Peirce's normative sciences, it becomes apparent that in *The Philosophy of Loyalty*, Royce is not wrestling with concrete decisions of conscience in the manner of a Peircean ethicist but with the question of how one comes to commit oneself to the kinds of ideals and values which make life ultimately worth living. In other words, Royce, in writing *The Philosophy of Loyalty*, was in fact engaging in normative esthetic thinking in Peirce's sense of esthetic.

Edwards's esthetic Christology, like Peirce's normative science of esthetics, also had ethical consequences. Edwards saw clearly that one could not commit oneself to the divine excellence embodied in Jesus of Nazareth without simultaneously committing oneself to live in Jesus' image. For Edwards, Christian practice, the willingness to live the gospel, authenticates a genuine Christian conversion. In other words, one cannot commit oneself in faith to Jesus Christ without simultaneously committing oneself to the cause for which he lived and died. One must accept the practical demands of living in what Jesus called "the reign of God"; and one must collaborate with other believers in seeking to establish God's just reign on earth as in heaven. As a result, in converting as a Christian, one makes Jesus' cause one's own.

As I reflected on Edwards's normative theological esthetic in the light both of Peirce's normative science of esthetics and of Royce's philosophy of loyalty, I realized that in my reflections on the meaning of the vows of religion, I had articulated in greater detail than Edwards himself had the practical demands of living in the divine reign. Moreover, I had done so by invoking Peirce's pragmatic logic of consequences in order to clarify the meaning of the basic moral demands of Christian discipleship. I saw that Jesus' demand that His disciples trust in the Father as He had, required them to share the physical supports of life with others and especially with those in greatest need. Trust in God requires a choice between God and wealth; and it seeks to bring into existence a community of sharing in which no one goes in need. Unconditioned trust in God requires one to share with others on the basis of need and not just of merit. It commits one to table fellowship with sinners, to seeking to bring into existence a community of sharing which breaks down the sinful barriers which fragment the human community and suffuse it with violence. Only authentic worship of the Father has the capacity to ground

God's just kingdom. Moreover, in Jesus' teachings only mutual forgiveness in the image of God authenticates worship, just as love of enemies ultimately authenticates mutual forgiveness. In other words, the converted Christian finds the cause which gives Christian living ultimate meaning embodied in Jesus of Nazareth and in the cause which He lived and proclaimed and for which He died. Moreover, one assents to that cause for esthetic motives in Peirce's sense of esthetic. For the committed Christian, the kingdom of God exemplifies the *summum bonum*.

I concluded, therefore, that I could complete Edwards's normative theological esthetic in Peirce's sense of esthetics by discovering embodied in Jesus the cause which gives ultimate orientation to Christian living. In developing a theology of the vows of religion, I had invoked a Peircean logic of consequences in order to clarify deductively the operational consequences of commitment to Jesus' cause. As Royce himself insisted in *The Problem of Christianity*, Christianity, more than any other religion, exemplifies a religion of loyalty. In other words, when one used Royce's philosophy of loyalty to clarify the kind of normative thinking that goes on in Peirce's esthetics, then Peirce's esthetics, when implemented in the context of Christian faith, correctly names the "logic" of an initial conversion to Christ. In confessing the divine excellence incarnate in Jesus, one simultaneously confesses that His cause, the reign of God, claims one with moral absoluteness and ultimacy and defines for the converted Christian the meaning of the *summum bonum*. A cause claims one ultimately when one stands willing not only to live for it but, if necessary, to die for it. A cause claims one absolutely when it does so in all circumstances. Like Jesus, converted Christians must consecrate their lives to making the reign of God a lived reality. They must do so corporately, as a community, as a Church, but also personally and individually. As my own theology developed, I would use all of these insights in order to give practical meaning to what Paul the apostle calls justifying faith. Moreover, as we shall soon see, like Paul the apostle, Edwards attributed to the divine Breath the human empowerment to consent in faith to Jesus and to the excellence He embodies.

I found other aspects of Edwards's thought theologically attractive and suggestive. He had, it seemed to me, correctly claimed the middle ground between the extreme anthropological optimism of Transcendental Thomism and the extreme anthropological pessimism of Augustinianism. Thomas Aquinas discovered in the human intellect a natural openness to infinite Being, to God. He therefore described the human intellect as a natural desire for the beatific vision. Transcendental Thomism resurrected these forgotten Thomistic theses in the twentieth century and transformed the human agent intellect into a virtually infinite, spiritual craving for all truth and ultimately for perfect, graced union with God.

Peirce had taught me to regard all hypotheses, including philosophical ones, as fallible and in need of ongoing verification both in lived, social experience and in the results of the idioscopic sciences, i.e., of those sciences which engage in in-depth study of limited aspects of nature and of the human condition. The more I studied developmental psychology, the more convinced I became that their results tend to falsify a Thomistic belief in the virtual infinity of the human intellect. The human mind begins finite. Not until the age of two do infants develop imaginations. At the age of eight, they learn to reason concretely. In literate cultures, at about the age of eleven abstract reasoning develops; but far from exhibiting an infinite and insatiable desire for all truth, the human mind suffers more from ego inertia, from the tendency to resent and resist challenges to one's pet beliefs. Prejudice and ego inertia better characterize human thinking than an insatiable desire for all truth, which Transcendental Thomists naively eulogize. I can relate to an insatiable desire for all truth as an ideal but not as a universal tendency necessarily built *a priori* into the essential structure of the human spirit. The latter belief bristles with fallacies.

At the same time, Augustinianism, in its portrait of the human, errs in the opposite direction. Augustine believed that God had created human nature good but that the sin of Adam and Eve had so corrupted human nature that, left to itself, it could only commit mortal sins. Though formed in a Calvinistic, Augustinian tradition, Edwards too repudiated an Augustinian doctrine of total human depravity. At the same time, he regarded human nature as radically finite rather than as virtually infinite. He believed that left to its natural resources, humans could perform naturally good acts. Edwards questioned, however, whether human nature, left to its natural resources, either loves or can love with the universality to which the gospel of Christ calls us. Left to ourselves, we tend naturally to love our own: our family, friends, benefactors; but we do not tend to love spontaneously strangers, aliens, and enemies. We tend rather to fear and avoid strangers and aliens and to fear and hate our enemies. Edwards held that for humans to love with the universal love of charity requires the assistance of supernatural grace, requires the empowerment and illumination of the Breath of Christ. On this point, in my opinion, Edwards got things better than either the Transcendental Thomists or the Augustinians.

I do not, however, endorse every aspect of Edwards's thought. I reject his predestinationism, his attempt to reconcile freedom and determinism, and his Ramist[1] logic. I do, however, find genuine insight in his theology of initial Christian conversion, in his esthetic approach to Christology, and in his middle-of-the-road anthropology. I committed to paper my reflections on Edwards's philosophical and theological achievement; and those notes served as the basis for subsequent published articles and essays on his thought.

As I explored the development of the philosophical tradition in the United States in the Tulane library, I turned next to the founding fathers. It seemed to me that among them, Benjamin Franklin, Thomas Jefferson, the authors of *The Federalist Papers*, Thomas Paine, Ethan Allen, and Elihu Palmer had made the most notable contributions to colonial Enlightenment philosophy.

Enlightenment religious thought developed in three stages in the American colonies. Franklin and Jefferson both espoused a more tolerant form of Deism than Tom Paine, Ethan Allen, and Elihu Palmer. While Jefferson and Franklin looked upon Deism as rationally superior to revealed religion, they tolerated the main line churches. Paine, especially in his later writings, together with Allen and Palmer took a more aggressive approach to traditional creeds. Paine promoted a religion of reason and of subjective moral enlightenment, and he derided Biblically based religion. Allen declared war on the Calvinist evangelical scheme, while Palmer ridiculed all forms of revealed religion with revivalistic fervor and even sought to found a Deistic Church of Reason.

The American Revolution intervened between tolerant and militant Deism. Religious thought during the revolution proclaimed it a holy war and predicted that victory would usher in an American millennium of prosperity. Revolutionary thinking culminated, of course, in the Declaration of Independence, in the Constitution, and in *The Federalist Papers*.

The emergence of militant Deism allowed the Unitarian Church to claim a middle ground between tolerant and militant Deism. The first Unitarians preserved the trappings of Calvinistic worship–Calvinist hymns and the Lord's Supper–while preaching Deism from the pulpit. The colonial Enlightenment produced, then, two major institutions: the United States government and the Unitarian Church.

While the American colonial Enlightenment derived its initial inspiration from the British Enlightenment and influenced the French Enlightenment through its revolutionary ethos, Enlightenment rationalism in the colonies, I concluded, derived its distinctive character from the fact that it took the Calvinist evangelical scheme as its principal religious adversary. In the end, colonial Deism mounted many of the same criticisms of Calvinism as had the Council of Trent. The American Deists denounced the doctrines of total human depravity, of predestination, and of volitional determinism as Trent had; but colonial *philosophes* never dreamed of becoming Tridentine Catholics, for the simple reason that the colonial Enlightenment derived much of its character from the Protestant tradition against which it revolted. The philosophical architects of the American Enlightenment proclaimed the American Revolution and the creation of American democratic government as the culmination of the Protestant Reformation. John Adams struck this note most clearly when he announced that just as the Protestant Reformation had purified Christianity of popery, so the American Revolution would purify American society of the parallel institutional abuse of monarchy. In the process, it would fulfill the religious impulse initiated by the first Protestant reformers.

Because it partially rooted itself in the Calvinism against which it protested, the American Enlightenment retained and promoted what David Tracy has called the Protestant, dialectical imagination. The colonial Deists denounced some of the same errors as the council of Trent; but the American Deists thought in either-or terms. They replaced an Augustinian doctrine of total human depravity with the myth of total human integrity.

As a result, they promoted a naively optimistic view of human nature. They created the myths of American innocence and of the American Adam. By the myth of the American Adam, I mean that the Enlightenment taught Americans to believe naively that each generation in the United States comes into the world free of the corruption of history and of the past, free to create the world anew from whole cloth. It also replaced Calvinist supernaturalism with a species of Deistic naturalism.

The colonial Deists also forced a false option between religious faith and scientific reason. Moreover, their naive faith in natural human integrity and innocence led them to exaggerate the capacity of scientific reason and technology to solve all human problems.

The American Deists in rejecting a deterministic doctrine of predestination, again overreacted by excluding all divine activity from history. The God of colonial Deism rested content to dwell in eternity and legislate the moral law; but the Deistic God left humans to their own devices in the living of life, other than to reward virtue and punish vice in the life to come.

The American Enlightenment bequeathed other fallacies to the American intellectual tradition besides naive optimism about human nature, exaggerated rationalistic claims for scientific reasoning and technology, a Deistic understanding of divine activity, and a naive declaration of independence from history. They also popularized Locke's conceptual nominalism and epistemological subjectivism. Chauncey Wright, William James, and Alfred North Whitehead would bequeath a Lockean conceptual nominalism to the philosophical tradition in the United States and would develop it in unhelpful ways.

The roots of the colonial Enlightenment in the Augustinian tradition led its intellectual architects again and again to make exaggerated claims for the subjective self-evidence of moral truth. Augustinian Platonism discovered truth by retiring from the senses and by ascending within subjectivity to the spiritual realm of eternal and self-evident truth. That same moral subjectivism caused colonial moralists to oppose the internal workings of the human conscience to "external" social institutions. By pitting "moral" individuals against "alien" institutions, the colonial Enlightenment fostered a destructive moral individualism which makes social ethics finally unthinkable. If only individuals can act morally, then institutions would seem, in such a world, to have the right to do whatever they want.

On the positive side of the ledger, the colonial Enlightenment bequeathed to this nation a relatively stable republican democracy, a shared belief in natural human rights and duties, and religious disestablishment. On the negative side of the ledger, the distorting fallacies of Enlightenment thinking have both in the American academy and in popular culture fossilized into an Enlightenment fundamentalism which endows those fallacies with a lying self-evidence.

I realized from the work I had done in Emerson that American Transcendentalism had begun the philosophical attempt to get beyond, to "transcend" unacceptable aspects of Enlightenment thinking. Emerson offered a modified Neo-Platonic realism as an alternative to Enlightenment nominalism. Emerson found especially troubling David Hume's religiously skeptical reformulation of Locke's nominalism. Emerson transcended nominalism by exalting a Platonized version of creative, artistic, and poetic intuition over the "linear logic" of scientific thinking.

Theodore Parker developed a different Transcendental doctrine of intuition. In the end, his serious misreading of Kant only left him all the more enmeshed in Enlightenment modernism. By claiming to grasp intuitively within human subjectivity the objective truth of basic Deistic beliefs–belief in God, morality, and human immortality–he became in fact the first systematic American Enlightenment fundamentalist. Enlightenment fundamentalists propound the allegedly self-evident and "objective truth" of the worst fallacies of eighteenth-century philosophy.

I found the complete works of Orestes Augustus Brownson in the Loyola University library and outlined all of them. Brownson, like Parker, moved on the fringes of the Transcendental Club. A contentious man who loved truth more than the good opinion of others, Brownson reveled in a good fight. In *The Boston Quarterly Review* which he founded and then transformed into *Brownson's Quarterly Review*, he took on all comers, sometimes appalling even his friends with the excesses of his rhetoric. As a consequence, he never found social acceptance in waspish, genteel Boston. His eventual conversion to Catholicism transformed him into even more of a social pariah. At the invitation of Archbishop Hughes, he took his *Quarterly Review* to New York city.

The fact that Brownson did not formulate his Transcendental doctrine of intuition until after his conversion to Catholicism enabled him to succeed far better than Emerson and Parker had in transcending the most glaring fallacies of the Enlightenment. Like the other Transcendentalists, Brownson too looked to intuitive forms of thinking to liberate his mind from the baleful effects of Enlightenment nominalism and subjectivism; but before he articulated his account of intuitive forms of knowing, Brownson had traced in reverse the intellectual journey of those liberal Congregational ministers who had created American Unitarianism. Liberal Congregational divines began by replacing a Calvinist doctrine of depravity with an Enlightenment doctrine of total human innocence and integrity. They then decided that a completely integral human nature needed no redemption. Those who need no redemption need no redeemer. Denial of the need for the Incarnation led to the denial of the Trinity which the Incarnation reveals. The thought of William Ellery Channing brought this movement in colonial Congregationalism to its culmination. His defense of the Unitarian denial of the Incarnation and of the Trinity shocked both Protestant and Catholic religious sensibilities; but his staid and proper rhetoric sought to make Unitarianism socially acceptable to genteel America.

Brownson had converted briefly and unsuccessfully to Presbyterianism as a youth, but he began his reverse religious journey as a naive Jeffersonian humanitarian optimist. Ordained in the Universalist Church, he eventually abandoned his Universalist pulpit but continued to believe in complete human innocence and integrity, until the Hard Cider campaign of 1840 caused him to rediscover the fact of human fallenness. Brownson actively supported Martin van Buren in that election, even though his espousal in print of a doctrine of all power to the people may in fact have helped defeat van Buren. Disgusted at the election of Tippecanoe and Tyler too, Brownson decided that if people could allow political sloganism to dupe them into voting against their own best interests, then something had gone seriously wrong with the human race. Politics led him to rediscover a doctrine of original sin but in its more moderate Tridentine formulation which eschewed an Augustinian rhetoric of total human depravity. Reaffirmation of original sin caused Brownson to reaffirm as well the need for a redeemer. Since Jesus of Nazareth seemed to him the only likely candidate for the role of redeemer, Brownson also rediscovered incarnational faith as well as belief in a triune God. This spiritual journey led him eventually to equate religious intuition with a robust faith in the divine Word incarnate. Having tried Protestantism and found it seriously wanting, Brownson, not without initial apprehensions, realized that he had no other choice than to seek baptism in the Catholic Church.

Even before he converted to Catholicism and while hobnobbing with the Boston Transcendentalists, Brownson had repudiated all forms of dualistic thinking. His studies of the French philosopher Pierre Leroux enabled him to replace Enlightenment nominalism and subjectivism with a metaphysical vitalism. Brownson's vitalism caused him to conceive reality in radically relational terms. He replaced Locke's di-polar construct of knowing with a triadic, symbolic understanding of cognition. His espousal of Catholicism endowed his thinking with a healthy sense of the importance of history, of tradition, and of community. In a word, Brownson saw through most of the fallacies of the American Enlightenment: its conceptual nominalism, its reduction of human cognition to the subjective interrelation of concrete percepts and abstract concepts, its individualism, its artificial opposition between faith and reason, its naive and extreme optimism about human nature and the human prospect, its naive belief in unlimited human perfectability through science and technology.

The Civil War also caused Brownson to rethink the philosophical presuppositions of American government. In *The American Republic*, he not only rejected Locke's social contract theory of government; but he also argued that God's providential constitution of the United States precluded a states-rights interpretation of its written Constitution, even though he himself had advocated a states-rights position before the Civil War. In rethinking the historical foundations of the American Constitution, Brownson also re-appropriated a qualified, faith-based optimism for the future of the nation, an optimism rooted, not in a naive belief in human innocence, but in the saving power of divine, supernatural grace. In that context, he prophesied a special role for the Catholic Church in the healing of American culture and in its liberation from the destructive presuppositions of Enlightenment modernism.

For all of Brownson's genius, his thought, I saw, had its limitations. Like Emerson, he espoused a finally indefensible form of Platonism, but unlike Emerson he resisted ontologism and denied that the human mind has immediate access to the forms of things in the mind of God. Brownson's Platonism appeared in his equation of Reason with the objective, universal forms of things grasped by the human mind. Like Aristotle, however, Brownson located these forms in finite created realities. The Platonic essentialism implicit in his thought eventually prevented him from endorsing John Henry Newman's interpretation of the development of Christian doctrine. Brownson held for the immutability of revealed truths and believed that only the formulation of Christian doctrine changed, not the doctrine itself. He would, in my opinion, have done better to regard the events which reveal the Triune God as unchanging while the doctrinal interpretation of those events does in fact evolve. The historically fixed and unchanging events of revelation verify or falsify doctrinal theories about them. These flaws in Brownson's thought should not, however, detract from the immensity of his intellectual achievement. In matters of the mind, he stood head and shoulders above any of the other Transcendentalists and anticipated some of Peirce's best insights.

During my Loyola years, my researches into the origins of the American philosophical tradition yielded an unexpected discovery. In my reading in American philosophy, I had come across the name Francis Ellingwood Abbot. I knew that Peirce admired him as a thinker; and, indeed, I found, somewhat to my surprise, that he had significantly advanced the critique of Enlightenment modernism. A much neglected figure in the development of American philosophy, Abbot moved on the fringes of the first Metaphysical Club in much the way that Brownson and Parker had orbited the Transcendental Club. Abbot began his career as an Emersonian Transcendentalist who endorsed aspects of Theodore Parker's Absolute Religion and imitated aspects of Parker's social activism.

Abbot's correspondence with Chauncey Wright, the oldest member of the Metaphysical Club and a philosophical positivist, alerted him to the fact that he needed to reconcile his commitment to Transcendental religion and metaphysics with the claims of science. He did so in a preliminary way in *Scientific Theism*, his most successful book. It underwent several printings. He prefaced this work with an article which had already appeared in a scholarly journal. In it Abbot successfully dismantled the philosophy of Immanuel Kant as a species of indefensible conceptual nominalism. *Scientific Theism* powerfully affected the mature thought of Peirce. It led the latter to seek a wedding of religion and science through logic and convinced him that he needed to think more systematically about the interface between logic and metaphysics.

Abbot's own metaphysics he called "relationism." At its heart lay his doctrine of relations *inter res*. In his final formulation of his metaphysics, *The Syllogistic Philosophy*, he transformed relations *inter res* into what he called "unit universals." This doctrine had certain analogies to Brownson's Platonic Aristotelianism. Abbot believed that individual realities, "units," participated in the same essential universal laws as the other individual members of their species. These laws, then, formed a bond among those same individuals. They existed in the laws; and the laws, in them. The law, then, tied together all the individuals existing in it. Hence, laws exemplified relations *inter res* (among things). Like Brownson, therefore, Abbot located universal forms in concrete individual things; but like Emerson he also located them in the mind of God. Abbot, therefore, again like Emerson, conceived reality in pantheistic terms. Abbot called God the "All Thing." By that he meant that God constitutes the whole of which finite creatures form a part. *E pluribus unum.*

Although I defend the relational character of reality, in the end I found Abbot's relationism philosophically unacceptable. The things of this world enjoy relational existence, but they also enjoy an individuality of their own because they initiate their own activities. In Abbot's relationism, a single law must account for the decisions of all the individuals subsisting in it. Like Royce, who had a knock-down-drag-out debate with Abbot concerning the tenability of the latter's ideas, I found Abbot's theory of relations *inter res* indefensible. Moreover, like Royce, I found this world too riddled with evil to identify it pantheistically with God.

Moreover, I believed that the Transcendental critique of Enlightenment modernity reached its true culmination in the mature logic and metaphysics of Charles Sanders Peirce. While Abbot tried to reconcile Emersonian pantheism with the method of science, unlike Peirce he never practiced science. Peirce understood scientific thinking as a practicing and published scientist, and in logical matters Pierce had no peer in the United States.

Like Brownson, Peirce rejected all forms of philosophical dualism. Dualism conceives of two interrelated realities in such a way that their relationship to one another becomes subsequently unintelligible. Peirce avoided dualism by conceiving reality in developing, relational, functional terms rather than as fixed and unchanging essences. Essences exist in a Peircean universe but they belong to the how of experience not to its what. They consist of sensations or perceptions abstracted from the realities to which they make us present as well as from the minds which do the sensing and perceiving. Essentialism, by contrast, reifies ideas and treats them as principles of being.

Essentialism, moreover, breeds dualism. Ideas can contradict one another. When we reify mutually contradictory ideas, or essences, we make it difficult to understand how the interrelated realities they allegedly constitute can in fact relate to one another. Spirit-matter dualism illustrates what I am talking about. Platonism, for example, conceives of the soul as essentially spiritual and defines spiritual as essentially immaterial, as the negation of matter. Platonism also conceives the body as material. Since immaterial contradicts material, Platonism makes it difficult to grasp how the spiritual soul can have a positive relationship to the body. Peirce's philosophy managed to avoid not only essentialism and dualism but other fundamental fallacies of the Enlightenment as well.

Peirce saw the need to come up with new metaphysical categories which avoid past philosophical fallacies. His metaphysical category Firstness exemplifies a particular qualitative possibility. Sensations and perceptions, indeed, the whole spectrum of human evaluative responses, exemplify Firstness. Because Firstness makes us present to ourselves and to our world it has an intentional character. It defines how we experience the realities to which they make us present. Secondness consists of action and reaction understood as a single complex reality and event. When we bump our heads on a tree limb, it bumps back. Secondness exemplifies actuality and concreteness. Secondness also endows reality with social and environmental relationships. Thirdness consists of real generality. It exemplifies a relationship to the future because it consists of a dynamic tendency to react or respond either decisively or evaluatively under specifiable circumstances. All rational human communication exemplifies Thirdness because rational symbols mediate between Firstness and Secondness by endowing significant events with meaning through the act of interpretation.

Peirce derived his relational categories from his revision of the logic of inference. All inferences, he argued, interrelate a rule, a case, and a result. A case exemplifies Firstness because it conceives reality in a particular way. A result exemplifies Secondness because it consists of named facts in need of explanation. A rule exemplifies Thirdness because it names the laws, the real tendencies which explain events.

Peirce argued, correctly in my estimate, that inference comes in three irreducible forms which each interrelate a rule, a case, and a result differently. An abduction, or hypothesis, concludes to a case because it characterizes a result in a new way on the basis of a rule which it supposes to obtain in reality. Einstein's general theory of relativity exemplifies a complex abduction about the nature of the physical universe which replaced Newtonian physics. A deduction, or prediction, concludes to a result because it argues that, if the rule presupposed by one's abduction obtains in reality, then facts not currently in evidence will appear under specifiable circumstances. When, for example, the scientific community argued that, if Einstein's abductive theory of relativity holds true, then one ought to be able to observe the bending of light during a solar eclipse, they argued deductively.

An induction concludes to a rule because, when the predicted evidence appears, an induction concludes that the rule originally presupposed in one's abduction actually functions in reality, in nature, because it allowed one to predict what would happen and the conditions under which it would happen. When, for example, scientists subsequently observed the bending of light during solar eclipses, they concluded that Einstein's general theory of relativity probably obtained in nature.

Peirce's theory of inference grounded his doctrine of fallibilism. Fallibilism differs from philosophical relativism. Relativism portrays all human knowledge as subjective opinion. Peirce avoided relativism by arguing that reality will teach us what it is by the way it behaves but *if and only if* we take the time to clarify our thinking by predicting the operational consequences of our hypotheses and only if we test those predictions against the observed behavior of things. Peirce saw, however, that in investigating any complex problem, one has limited time to formulate one's abduction and so must do so before one knows for sure that one has taken all the relevant facts into account. Moreover, in complex questions, one must verify one's abduction inductively only in a representative sample of the phenomena one is trying to explain. Deduction deals only with predictable possibilities, not with reality or actuality as such. At the two moments when the inferential mind deals directly with reality–namely, in abduction and induction–it could err. Some fact not in one's representative sample which contradicts one's hypothesis could conceivably turn up in the future; or some other mind could devise a better frame of reference for dealing with the evidence which could force a revision of one's own abduction.

Both the relational character of reality and the doctrine of fallibilism caused Peirce to replace the Cartesian and Kantian turn to the subject with the turn to community. The turn to the subject reduces philosophy to the *a priori*, deductive exploration of subjective human intentionality. The turn to community grounds all thinking in critical realism and in shared systematic inquiry. The turn to community counteracts the individualism which the Enlightenment popularized. The search for truth succeeds better when human minds collaborate. Finite human minds need the corrective and stimulus of other experiences and of other ways of thinking in order to advance the shared human understanding of reality. In other words, genuine commitment to the truth requires commitment as well to the community of truth seekers. One values, of course, individuals in their uniqueness; but one recognizes the necessity for communities of collaboration in order to foster the human enterprise.

The Enlightenment popularized a form of conceptual nominalism. Locke's empiricism inspired in part the Enlightenment's inflated perception of what science and technology can accomplish; and Lockean empiricism reduced human knowing to the subjective interrelation of concrete sensations and abstract conceptions. Such an epistemology cannot explain the social dimensions of knowing, cannot explain scientific thinking, and makes religious experience unthinkable. Let us try to understand why.

Locke's conceptual nominalism cannot explain the social dimensions of knowing, since on Lockean presuppositions all cognition takes place between one's ears. Conceptual nominalism cannot even interpret as familiar an act as one person speaking to another about some third reality. Peirce's relational, triadic logic and metaphysics, which grounds his turn to community, does explain social and communal experience by fostering a logically defensible theory of interpretation.

Nor can conceptual nominalism explain scientific knowing. As Kant saw clearly, if the objects of knowing consist exclusively of concrete sensible things, when scientists make universal generalizations, they impose on reality a universality it does not possess. Peirce's logical realism makes it clear that Kant got things exactly backwards. No functioning, self-respecting scientist wants to impose on the realities under study an intelligibility they do not possess. Science seeks instead a true account of the laws in nature which make natural activity intelligible.

Conceptual nominalism also makes religious experience unthinkable; for, if the human mind can only know finite sensibles–this rock, this tree, this cat, this house–it cannot know God because God, if real, cannot exemplify a finite sensible reality. Peirce took human religious experience very seriously and argued for an experienceable social continuity between humans and God which his doctrine of synechism rendered intelligible.

Finally, Locke's conceptual nominalism promoted an atomistic theory of human cognition just as his social contract theory promoted an atomistic understanding of society. Locke explained knowing as the active interrelation of atomic concepts and sensations. His social contract theory portrayed all social relations as manufactured and artificial. Peirce's insistence on the relationality of the real and on the reality of continuity ruled out both forms of atomism in principle.

Moreover, Peirce the practicing scientist had more modest expectations of science and technology than the philosophers of the Enlightenment. He learned to understand the logic of science by thinking scientifically. As a result, he had a vivid sense of science's fallibility and limitations. Indeed, Peirce argued that anyone who would try to live life on the basis of abstract inferential reasoning alone would end by acting the part of either a lunatic or a fool. As his thought matured, he learned to value the role of instinct and imagination in human living and accorded such thinking the ability to grasp reality in its own right. While Peirce hoped that science would eventually come to understand nature better and better, his insight into the limitations of what science and technology can accomplish prevented him from expecting science to solve all human problems or to usher in the millennium. Moreover, his theory of the normative sciences insists that science ought to think for life-giving ends; but Peirce did not imagine that everyone who claims to do science necessarily does what scientists ought to do.

The American Enlightenment replaced a Calvinistic doctrine of total human depravity with a naively optimistic understanding of the total integrity of human nature. Peirce's insight into the human condition rules out both hypotheses as unverifiable.

In the American colonies, Deistic philosophers derided the scandal of the sectarian divisions in Christianity in order to claim the high moral ground for a religion of pure reason. Peirce saw through that fallacy as well. He held that the scandal of sectarianism required Christians who profess a religion of love to work within the churches to eliminate sectarianism. After reading James's *Varieties of Religious Experience*, Pierce wrote him urging him, if he really believed what he had written, to join a church. Ever the individualist, James never did.

In his final wedding of religion and science through logic, Peirce also saw through the Deistic attempt to exalt reason over faith. Peirce did not have a very high opinion of the intellectual acumen of many of the theologians and high churchmen of his day; but in his mature thought he saw through the attempt to create a false opposition between religion and science. In his Neglected Argument for the reality of God, Peirce argued that the same logic which validates scientific reason also validates philosophical reasoning about religious realities. Moreover, in the Neglected Argument, the beauty of the idea of God motivates initial philosophical belief in God. Peirce never, to the best of my knowledge attempted to think theologically; but he did convert from Unitarianism to Episcopalianism. He also believed that we cannot think of God without feeling enthralled by the divine reality. In the end Peirce equated the reality of God with the *summum bonum* to which esthetics aspires.

American Deists tended to imagine the workings of the human conscience on the pattern of Protestant inner-light piety. They claimed for moral insight both subjectivity and self-evidence. Peirce's absolute opposition to all forms of *a priori* thinking combined with his relational view of reality to rule out the possibility that one can know anything by taking an inner look into one's own subjectivity, and he denied the human ability to discover anything self-evident within a non-existent pure subjectivity.

I have argued all these things in greater detail in *Varieties of Transcendental Experience: A Study in Constructive Postmodernism*. Though I published that work in the year 2000, I did the basic research for it in New Orleans between 1969 and 1973. That research provided the dialectical foundations for the metaphysics of experience I would begin to develop when I joined the faculty of the Jesuit School of Theology at Berkeley. I did not, however, publish the results of my research right away because I could not at first think of a way to relate my gradual mastery of the development of religious philosophy in the United States to contemporary issues.

I reached that insight in an advanced seminar about the meaning of praxis which I gave at the Graduate Theological Union in Berkeley. In the seminar I was trying to put Latin American liberation theology with its emphasis on praxis into dialogue with Peircean pragmatism. When we had worked at Peirce systematically for about four weeks, one of the women students remarked, "Peirce is really dismantling the Enlightenment." That insight rang a bell in my head, because I realized, from the research I had done in Cambridge and in New Orleans, that the American critique of the Enlightenment did not begin with Peirce. It began with Emerson. Peirce finally succeeded in doing systematically what Emerson and Brownson had tried to do but with less success. I also realized that, if one understood "modernity" as roughly equivalent with the Enlightenment, then Peirce's critique of the Enlightenment offered postmoderns a constructive philosophical alternative to a deconstructionist postmodernism, which really serves up as "postmodern" a slightly rewarmed version of a thoroughly modern form of nominalism. Those insights eventually took published shape in they year 2000 as *Varieties of Transcendental Experience*.

While teaching philosophy in New Orleans, I every year attended the meetings of the Catholic Philosophical Association (CPA); but I actually benefitted much more from the meetings of the Jesuit Philosophical Association (JPA), which met the day before the CPA. In the JPA, we circulated ahead of time the papers we discussed; and we had outstanding discussions.

One year Frank Oppenheim submitted a remarkable paper on Royce's understanding of the conditions for the possibility of shared communal awareness. In other words, Frank explored Royce's understanding of the conditions which had to obtain for a community to come to shared self-awareness as a community. The paper deepened my insight into the later Royce. I have invoked its insights more than once in the theology I have developed.

As Frank showed, Royce distinguished between personal and shared consciousness. Individual persons come to consciousness primarily by making distinctions and seeing relationships. Communities come to shared consciousness as communities through a much more complex process of self-interpretation. First, a community needs to reach a consensus about the significance of the events which found it and about the history which links it to those events. Such a consensus creates a community's present sense of identity because its history defines a community's present character. Second, since the process of self-interpretation has a spatio-temporal structure, communities need to reach a consensus about the ultimate and proximate future to which they experience themselves called. Third, a community will not reach full consciousness as a community until it actively mobilizes the gifts of all of its members in achieving at least some of its proximate goals as a community. The retrieval of its historical roots gives a community shared memories. Agreement about ultimate and proximate goals gives it shared hopes. Self-mobilization to achieve at least some of their shared goals creates shared lives. In addition, Royce argued, a community needs to forgive in advance its morally inevitable betrayal by at least some of its members, if it hopes to keep such betrayals from constantly fragmenting it.

Royce articulated these insights in his monumental work, *The Problem of Christianity*. Frank's in-depth reading of the philosophy of the second half of *The Problem*, caused me to see it with new eyes. Before writing *The Problem*, Royce reached what he called his "Peircean insight." Royce had already studied and appropriated fundamental insights from Peirce's logic which he further developed in his *Principles of Logic*. When Royce reached his Peircean insight, however, he grasped the metaphysical implications of Peirce's logic. In *The Problem*, he argued that an examination of the religious experiences of the New Testament Pauline churches reveals Christianity as the religion of community *par excellence*. In the second half of *The Problem*, Royce also argued that Peirce's metaphysics and semiotic realism correctly interprets a Christian religious experience. With Frank's help I began to see more clearly how I might complete Peirce's philosophy with Royce's and use both thinkers in constructing philosophical foundations for an inculturated North American theology.

By the end of four years in New Orleans, I had pretty well completed the research project in the origins of American philosophical thought which I had set myself when I came to Loyola. Besides my research on Tuesdays and Thursdays during the school year, I spent most of the summer at work on the project. Joe Tetlow and I had begun a post-doctoral research seminar in American Studies. We spent our first summer at Yale University and our second at The Jesuit School of Theology at Berkeley. The group had four members. Besides Joe and myself, Johnny Stacer, who had completed a doctorate in American philosophy at Tulane University participated, as did James Torrens, S.J., a California Jesuit who taught American literature. The American Studies group functioned until 1973 when I left Loyola to teach at the Jesuit School of Theology in Berkeley and when Joe left Loyola to serve on the Project One team. Project One undertook a systematic study of Jesuit colleges and universities in order to advise the provincials of the American Assistancy as to the status and possible future of Jesuit higher education.

The American Studies Group served as the prototype for the John Courtney Murray Group which would take shape in 1979. The Murray Group would have a more focused goal than the American Studies Group had. The cross-disciplinary character of the American Studies Group made communication within the group difficult. Joe in completing his degree in American studies had focused on American literature and history. Johnny and I, with our

degrees in philosophy, did not find ourselves well positioned to give either
Joe or Jim really constructive feedback on their particular research projects.
Moreover, we failed to create the kind of structures needed in order to foster
effective dialogue within the group.

When the Murray Group took shape, we tried to learn from the experience
of the American Studies Group and avoid its mistakes. The Murray Group
would try to create community around research, surely the loneliest of all the
apostolates, and would promote the formation of an inculturated philosophical theology in dialogue both with the classical American philosophical tradition and with issues of importance in contemporary United States culture.

During my years at Loyola, I began to discover America in yet another
way. As I have indicated, I arrived in New Orleans just as John Edwards began his term as our new provincial. I shall, moreover, always feel profoundly
grateful to John not only for presiding over the first phase of our religious renewal as a province but also for one of his first official acts as our new major superior. Very shortly after he became provincial, John wrote the province
a letter ordering every Jesuit in it to take a two week vacation. John knew that
Jesuits have propensities for workaholism and wanted to do something to
counter that particular aberration. As St. Ignatius said so well in his letter on
Jesuit obedience, "It is easy to obey when you love that which is com-
manded." I have taken a two-week vacation annually ever since.

Shortly after John's letter appeared, I got a call from Joe Tetlow. He suggested that we do vacation together. The telephone in my room had the same
number as the girls' dormitory except for one digit. As a consequence, I used
to get phone calls at all hours of the day and night. I told Joe that I would
gladly do vacation with him but that I wanted to go to a place which had no
telephones. "Have you ever gone camping?" Joe asked. When I replied in the
negative, he said, "Well, let's go camping for two weeks."

Thus began the adventures of the Cheerful Charlies, as Joe called our
vacation group. We made our first vacation together in 1970. We spent the
first half in the villa of our parish in Albuquerque, New Mexico, in the Jemez Mountains near the town of Cuba. From there we drove to the Grand
Canyon. As a small boy, I had formed three life ambitions: I wanted to see
a bull fight, Niagra Falls, and the Grand Canyon. I saw the bull fight in
Barcelona on my return to the United States from Eegenhoven. No Ernest
Hemingway I, I nevertheless felt my Catalonian blood quicken to the pag-
eant of death defied and conquered. While studying at Fordham, I took a
trip to Niagara and found the falls astonishingly beautiful; but I had saved
the best for last.

No words can convey one's first impression of the Grand Canyon; but it

Joseph Tetlow, S.J. on the Cheerful Charlies' first descent into the Grand Canyon.

became and remains my geological symbol for God. One cannot see it all from any one place. I find the Canyon, like God, inconceivable, unimaginable, sublime, and dangerous. We would return to it again and again, descend into its bowels, explore both rims, camp alone in the Ottoman Amphitheater. If asked to name my favorite place in all the world, I always reply, "The Grand Canyon."

Over the years, we have explored many, many national parks and wilderness areas: Yosemite, the Sierras, the Grand Tetons, the Wind River Range, the American and Canadian Rockies, the White Mountains, Shining Rock Wilderness, the Carolina Blue Ridge, the John Muir Trail, Devil's Postpile, the Minarets, Sequoia National Park, Mount Lassen, Death Valley, the Appalachian Trail, Carlesbad Caverns, Gettysburg, Vicksburg, Mesa Verde, the Gila Wilderness, the Pecos Wilderness, Desolation Wilderness, Bryce Canyon, Capitol Reef National Park, Donner Lake, Zion National Park. Twice we climbed Mount Whitney, the tallest peak in the contiguous states.

Until I went to Berkeley our vacations consisted mostly of car camping and day hiking, although we did attempt an initial backpack into the Canyon. We knew nothing about backpacking and could not have made more mistakes. We carried, believe it or not, canned food for three days. I expect that no one else has ever eaten marinated artichoke hearts at the bottom of the Grand Canyon. Earl Muller, S.J., who joined us and would become a regular member of the Cheerful Charlies, descended the North Rim wearing tennis shoes and black silk socks and carrying on his back a huge plastic bag filled with water. By the time he got to Cottonwood Campground on the North Rim, Earl was literally walking on water. The ranger there lanced all his blisters and bandaged them; and somehow he managed to make the rest of the hike.

We learned from our mistakes; and, once in California, I quickly realized that one can finally see the splendor of nature only by putting a pack on one's back and exploring. Our vacations transformed themselves into two back-country loops with a two-day break in between to get cleaned up and ready for the second hike.

As I have said, I have never missed a vacation since 1970. The first two weeks of August remain sacred time, consecrated exclusively to backpacking. At first I did not associate excursions into the wilderness with creating an inculturated theology for the United States. Then Frank Sullivan, the Jesuit poet and theologian who also taught at Loyola when I did and who became a life-long friend, made a remark that showed me my mistake. "If you want to create an American theology," he said, "you are going about it correctly. You are beginning by getting a feel for the shape and immensity of the land." Frank had it right. One can learn much about this nation from books and libraries; but wrestling personally with the American landscape and allowing its sublime beauty to seep into one's soul forms an indispensable way of discovering America and understanding its history and its people.

In my last year at Loyola, I discovered the method I would subsequently use in creating an inculturated theology for the United States. Three of the Jesuit collegians, Simon Hendry, S.J., George Lundy, S.J., and Tom Kearney, S.J. asked me to give them a reading course in the philosophy of Bernard Lonergan. I had never really worked systematically in Lonergan. My metaphysics professor in St. Louis abhorred what he called Lonergan's Kantianism. I had read Lonergan's *Insight* and did not object to learning more about his thought. I agreed to do the seminar. We read our way systematically through both *Insight* and *Method in Theology*, which had just appeared in print.

Si assures me that to this day he, George, and Tom all refer to that course as "The Seminar." Si also likes to describe an incident which took place in our first working class. I had assigned a section of *Insight* for study and discussion. We were sitting in a circle, with George, as I recall, on my left. I turned to him and asked him if he had any questions about the assigned pages. He replied in the negative. I then turned to Tom and asked him if he had any questions. Tom said he did; but before he could come out with them, I turned to George and said, "Well, George, since you understand the material and have no questions, why don't you answer Tom's questions?" A silence ensued while the three of them looked at one another. Thereafter, they always met to discuss the assigned reading before we met as a seminar. As a result, they learned a lot. I, for my part, discovered *Method in Theology*.

To this day, I endorse three elements in Lonergan's account of method in theology. I endorse his conception of the fundamental task facing theology: it needs to mediate between a religion and the culture in which that religion roots itself. Of all the studies of theological method that I have read, no one puts the question of incluturating theological thinking more squarely at the heart of the theological enterprise than Lonergan does.

I also endorsed and continue to endorse Lonergan's definition of method as "a pattern of recurring and related operations yielding cumulative and progressive results." I liked Lonergan's focus on operations as well as his tacit and probably unconscious invocation of Peirce's pragmatic maxim in judging the success or failure of a method.

Finally, I endorsed and continue to endorse his theory of functional specialties. Lonergan argues, correctly in my estimate, that theological method as such does not exist because theologians ask at least eight different kinds of questions and therefore need to employ eight different methods appropriate to answer the eight kinds of question they raise. *Research* theologians provide the rest of the theological community with the data they need in order to think theologically. They engage in religious archeology, edit sacred texts, create and update dictionaries and grammars of sacred languages. The specialty called *interpretation* offers an account of what religious texts and artifacts originally meant to those who created them and what they might mean to people living today. *History* tells the story of religious communities and of the cultures in which they root themselves and suggests explanations of why both evolved as they did. History contextualizes interpretation. In living traditions, those who hand them on argue constantly about what those traditions mean. The specialty named *dialectic* explains the terms of those debates by comparing and contrasting different frames of reference and by identifying points of agreement and of disagreement as well as the motives for both. I discovered *Method in Theology* just as I was completing my analysis of the development of philosophy in the United States. On reading

Lonergan, I realized that I had chosen to approach that development, not as a historian, but as a dialectician.

Research, interpretation, history, and dialectic constitute what Lonergan calls "mediating theology." Mediating theology retrieves a tradition. The four specialties which constitute mediated theology reformulate that tradition. In other words, mediating theology mediates mediated theology since one cannot reformulate a tradition until one has retrieved it. *Foundations* formulates a normative account of conversion. Moreover, Lonergan revolutionized the theology of conversion by arguing that conversion comes in more than one form and need not occur in a religious context of faith. In *Method*, Lonergan spoke of three kinds of conversion: intellectual, moral, and religious. Moreover, he argued that a normative insight into conversion provides the criteria for discriminating between sound and unsound doctrines. The specialty called *doctrines* re-examines the results of dialectical theology and draws on foundational insights to endorse some doctrines from the past as authentic and to discard other doctrines as inauthentic. Authentic doctrines advance the conversion process, inauthentic doctrines do not.

I saw a convergence here between Peirce's logic and Lonergan's theory of method. Peirce, as we have seen, argues that the normative sciences provide the criteria for discriminating between reality and illusion and so mediate between phenomenology and metaphysics. I decided that I would invoke the normative sciences to explore the different forms of conversion. I would use logic to explore intellectual conversion and ethics to explore moral conversion.

My study of Lonergan convinced me, however, that his thought remains opaque to affective and imaginative forms of thinking and reduces them to the epistemological equivalent of Kant's sense manifold: they provide rational thought with its raw material. My work in Peirce, in Edwards, in Emerson, and in Dewey had taught me better. I knew that imagination and feeling perceive reality in their own right and provide a realistic cognitive frame of reference distinct from inferential thinking. I decided, therefore, that in developing a normative theology of conversion, I would have to add "affective" conversion to intellectual, moral, and religious conversion. I also decided to use esthetics in Peirce's sense of that term, in order to develop a normative insight into affective conversion. My private readings in psychology and psychiatric theory also made me realize that they too yield normative insights into affective conversion, especially into its pathology and healing.

Once doctrinal theology has discriminated between sound and unsound doctrine, the theological specialty called *systematics* explains how sound doctrines relate to one another. The final specialty, *communications*, not only makes the results of the other specialties available to non-theologians; but it also invokes the normative insights of foundational theology to deal with the breakdown of communications. Breakdown in communications always indicates an absence of conversion at some level. The communications theologian uses the results of foundations to diagnose why communications have broken down in a particular community and then designs a catechesis which will call the people involved to that level of conversion needed to re-establish communication among them.

My discovery of Lonergan's theory of method came providentially at just the right time. I had completed my dialectical retrieval of the philosophical tradition in this nation. By the end of our little seminar on Lonergan, I decided that I would test the ability of his method to develop an inculturated North American theology. I determined that I would invoke the insights of North American philosophy in order to develop a normative, foundational theology of conversion in which conversion takes four forms: affective conversion, intellectual conversion, moral conversion, and religious conversion, with Christian conversion exemplifying a species of religious conversion. Since theology mediates between a religion and a culture, I would use my dialectical examination of United States philosophy as a point of entry into U.S. culture.

My study of Edwards had convinced me that Christian conversion contributes an important dynamic to the total process of conversion: it mediates between affective and moral conversion. It begins in the heart, in repentant confrontation with emotional obstacles to the initial consent of faith. Aesthetic sensitivity to the divine excellence incarnate in Jesus and in communities whose lives resemble His largely motivates the consent of justifying faith. That consent, however, commits one to living a life of discipleship in His image. Christian conversion, therefore, mediates between affective and moral conversion by putting them into a new relationship with one another. Initial faith informs the conscience with divinely revealed ideals, the ideals of the reign of God. Those ideals bind the Christian conscience. Moreover, the commitment of faith transforms prudential judgments of feeling into judgments of discernment guided by the Breath of Jesus.

Another complex set of experiences informed this initial insight into the dynamics of Christian conversion: my experiences in the Catholic Charismatic Renewal. Those experiences I shall attempt to describe in the chapter which follows.

Colloquy:

Star lighter,
World crafter,
Father of footless serpents and of millipedes,
Deft weaver of sky tapestries,
Sculptor of the lifting earth,

> *why did You make a world so enthralling,*
> > *so prolix,*
> > *this teasing maze in which we wander?*

> *Why make this swarming life*
> > *but to gather us into safaris of thought*
> > > *wonder-smitten*
> > > > *even at the twining texture of our own vine-like minds?*

> *Why but to nourish us at Wisdom's feast*
> > *where fools famish?*

I sought you in the tangle of my mind
> *not knowing*
> *half guessing where the unwinding thread would lead.*

Lead, hexer of hearts,
> *seducer of minds, lead on.*
> *I have so much to learn.*

NOTE

1. Peter Ramus (1515-1574) formulated a dyadic logic and theory of rhetoric popular among Puritans but ultimately, in my judgment, inadequate.

Chapter Five

Pentecost

The events narrated in this chapter overlap chronologically with those described in the two preceding chapters and with other events in the chapters which follow. The experiences with which the present chapter deals have, however, enough of a thematic unity to deserve treatment in their own right. In what follows, I shall attempt to describe how my experience of charismatic prayer has influenced the development of my theological thinking and of the system of theology I have been elaborating.

During my final year of doctoral residency at Fordham University, I began reading in the Catholic press about strange goings on at Ann Arbor and Notre Dame. The press releases carried accounts of groups of Catholics speaking in tongues, prophesying, and practicing faith healing. In fact, the goings on began at Duquesne University in Pittsburgh. There a group of lay Catholic faculty had in the mid-sixties begun praying regularly together for their own personal renewal in the Spirit. In 1966, at the National Cursillo Convention, they discovered and later read David Wilkerson's *The Cross and the Switchblade*, an account of Wilkerson's ministry to street gangs and addicts in the Bedford-Styvesant section of New York City. A Pentecostal minister, Wilkerson described the healing power which Pentecostal forms of prayer brought to his ministry. The professors at Duquesne began exploring Pentecostal prayer personally.

They organized a weekend retreat for some Duquesne students which participants in the Catholic Charismatic Renewal subsequently dubbed "the Duquesne weekend." The students who attended the weekend had no knowledge of the professors' Pentecostal prayer experiences; but those attending had prepared for the retreat by reading *The Cross and the Switchblade* and the first four chapters of the Acts of the Apostles. In the course of the retreat, two of the students, a man and a woman, were walking together and discussing why, if "Jesus Christ is the same yesterday, today, and forever," the charisms of the Spirit which the first Christians routinely experienced did not occur in the contemporary Church. The woman, Patti Gallagher, I knew at Loyola in New Orleans, where she served on the campus ministry team. The two young people felt drawn to the chapel where both had striking, transforming religious experiences. The other students heard that something unusual was happening in the chapel. As they gathered there, some began speaking in tongues, and all seem to have experienced a profound religious renovation. Their experience of the Spirit during that retreat had began the Catholic Charismatic Renewal, although the movement would not adopt that name until 1969, at the behest of the American Catholic Bishops. Originally, its participants called themselves "Catholic Pentecostals."

From Duquesne, Catholic Pentecostalism spread to Notre Dame and Ann Arbor, which quickly became major centers for leadership and organization in the movement. As the prayer movement exploded numerically, it attracted press attention; and so it came to pass that I read about it in the Bronx. I reacted to what I read with a cautious openness, but initially with more caution than openness.

One morning in 1968 as the spring semester began to draw to a close, I overslept. I had forgotten to set my alarm. I felt vexed because I had a full but tedious day ahead of me. I was preparing to leave Fordham for La Farge House in order to write my dissertation; and, since I was terminating my academic residency at Fordham, I had to fill out endless forms for different offices in the University bureaucracy in order to make the termination official.

I found myself at breakfast with James Powers, S.J., a New England Jesuit, who, like me was completing a doctorate in philosophy but who, unlike me, found language analysis fascinating. Jim had flown back to New York on a late flight the night before after several days of absence. He too had arisen late, though by choice; and so we had late breakfast together. When I asked Jim where he had been, he replied that he had just come from a leadership meeting for the Catholic Pentecostal Movement. His reply left me dumbfounded. The thought of a language analyst speaking in tongues quite took my breath away. At the same time, I felt intrigued. I knew Jim and trusted him. I asked him to explain to me what this new movement was trying to accomplish.

Jim basically told me the story of how he had gotten involved in Pentecostal forms of prayer quite independently of the Catholic Pentecostal Movement. He had started praying with a group of Pentecostals, who had prayed over him for the gift of tongues. Nothing occurred at the time, but the Pentecostal minister who led the prayer urged Jim to remain open to the gift. He warned him that one cannot force the Spirit to act; but he advised Jim during his personal prayer, as a sign of openness to the Spirit's gift, that he might from time to time repeat a nonsense syllable, like "la, la, la." Jim followed his advice and gradually grew into the gift of tongues. Jim told me that he found it a powerful way to pray. During counseling sessions, he said, whenever he met with an impasse, instead of talking, he would pray silently in tongues for his counselee. Every time he did so, a breakthrough in the counseling process occurred. He described other experiences of charismatic prayer he had known. He described singing in tongues.

During our entire conversation, I felt deeply moved. After breakfast, Jim went up to his room. The door to the chapel in Murray-Weigel Hall lay just beyond the entrance to the dining room. I found myself powerfully drawn into the chapel to pray. While praying, I felt myself moved to do what Jim had done, to repeat the nonsense syllable, "La, la, la." There ensued a rapid movement of tongue and lips which I could stop at any time but which just happened if I let it. I experienced no vocalization; but along with the labial and lingual movement I felt the most overwhelming experience of the presence of God I had ever known, far more overwhelming than the consolation without cause I had experienced as a philosopher in St. Louis. The sense of Presence, of God, remained with me when I left the chapel. It stayed for the rest of the day, which proved the strangest day of my life. I spent most of it going through the motions of filling out tedious bureaucratic forms for the University administration, but I was living simultaneously at another level of God-consciousness the like of which I had never experienced before.

Toward the end of the day, anxiety, my old enemy, reared its ugly head. I began to wonder if I were losing my mind. At that thought, I panicked. I did not have time to go crazy. I had to finish up the semester, go to Cambridge, and write my dissertation. I should at that point have gone to Jim and explained to him what had happened to me; but, like a fool, I did not. I simply froze and blocked the whole experience out of consciousness; and You, dear Lord, gently withdrew. I had only weeks to finish the semester. Soon after I would make my eight-day retreat. "I can't deal with this now," I told myself, "I will deal with it during my retreat."

That summer I made my retreat at Round Hill in the New England Province. Ned Green, the son of Hetty Green, the Witch of Wall Street, had built Round Hill on Buzzards Bay. Later I would read *The Day They Shook the Plum Tree*, the tragic story of the Green family. The book chronicles the destructiveness of greed. Hetty Green made her fortune in oil; but her crazy, insatiable avarice destroyed not only her own life but the lives of both her children. Ned Green had lost one leg as a boy because his mother would not take him to the doctors whom she believed had conspired to take her money away from her. The boy would have died of gangrene had his estranged father not chanced by and rushed him to a hospital where a surgeon amputated the gangrenous limb. Ned grew up to become a rich philanderer. He owned the second largest pornographic movie collection in the world. When Hetty Green finally died, Ned had her portrait removed from Round Hill and replaced with a stuffed whale penis. After Ned's death, his sister, a spinster, spent the rest of her life trying to keep the family fortune intact. The day she died, they shook the plum tree as the Green fortune scattered to the winds. When the lawyers were sorting through the estate, they found what they took for an out-sized oriental crown. They all tried it on, but it fit no head. Then the lawyers realized that they were holding a jewel-encrusted chamber pot.

The Massachusetts Institute of Technology had acquired Round Hill for a time and had transformed it, as I recall, into a center for weather research. As a result, great satellite dishes lay scattered about the property. The New England Province bought Round Hill from MIT and transformed the place into a retreat house. The Jesuits called the retreat house, "Our Lady of Round Hill," to the amusement of the locals, who used to call Ned Green's mistress "the lady of Round Hill."

When I got to Round Hill I learned something of the history of the place; but I had more important things to think about than the Ned Green estate. As I had promised myself, I prayed for guidance in dealing with my extraordinary prayer experience during that spring day at Fordham. I remember one evening climbing to the deck of one of the abandoned satellite dishes and saying to the Lord, "If what happened is a grace, I do want to be open to it; but, if I am really losing my mind, I will get whatever psychological or psychiatric help I need." I resolved to place the whole thing before my spiritual director when I got to Cambridge and to do whatever he told me to do.

Once installed in La Farge House, I asked Dick Clifford, S.J. whether he would take me on as a spiritual directee. He agreed. I explained to him what had happened to me in the chapel at Fordham and the events of the day that followed. I then looked at him apprehensively and asked him what he thought I ought to do. He responded, "What's the problem?" I felt like an ass. My wretched, neurotic anxiety had closed me to the most overwhelming experience of consolation without cause that I had ever known.

In my prayer, I acknowledged my folly to the Lord and professed my desire to stay open to whatever grace He intended to give me. We used to concelebrate the Eucharist as a community at La Farge House. During the silent parts of the liturgy, I would feel myself sinking to a deeper center within the prayer experience; and my tongue would begin to move. I began taking long walks by myself in the evenings, praying and singing in tongues sometimes for three hours at a stretch. I did this the whole time I stayed at La Farge House without ever attending a charismatic prayer meeting. As the year wore on, I decided that I had to come to terms with the Pentecostal Movement as a movement. I resolved to attend the national meeting at Notre Dame University that spring.

At Notre Dame, I recognized immediately that, if I were losing my mind in becoming a Catholic Pentecostal, I might as well toss it away, because the thousands who had gathered for the conference struck me as the happiest group of Catholics I had ever seen. Moreover, at that meeting, the leaders announced to the great joy of the assembled faithful that the Catholic Bishops Conference had investigated the movement and given it a tentative blessing. The bishops, in endorsing the movement, cited the teachings of Vatican II concerning the perennial character of gifts of the Spirit in the Church. They also called attention to pastoral problems in the movement to which they wanted the leaders to attend. The bishops expressed perhaps their greatest reservations about the name of the movement. They urged that the name "The Charismatic Renewal of the Church" replace the title "Catholic Pentecostals." The term "Pentecostal" had, understandably, sectarian connotations in episcopal ears. The movement itself had no desire to turn sectarian; but the bishops feared that the term "Catholic Pentecostals" could lead to serious misunderstandings within the Catholic community concerning the movement's intent.

Everyone at the Notre Dame meeting greeted the bishops' statement with great rejoicing. No one, including the leaders, cared what we called the movement. They just wanted freedom as Catholics to continue praying in the Spirit; and so Catholic Pentecostalism became the Catholic Charismatic Renewal.

I find it significant that the bishops in approving of the Catholic Charismatic Renewal cited the authority of the documents of Vatican II. The Eastern Orthodox have never lost a sense of the charisms as a perennial gift to the Church just as they have never lost a sense of the collegial character of Church leadership and government. The Latin Church lost both. After the Dark Ages which followed the Carolingian renaissance, one finds relatively little concern with the gifts of the divine Breath; and the Gregorian reform of the Church, which sought to rectify the Church's corruption during the Dark Ages, began a process of institutional and canonical development which eventually created the monarchical papacy as an institution in the thirteenth century. With the rise of the papal monarchy, collegiality, as a value, largely died in the Latin Church. Augustine taught that God intended the charisms only for the first generation of Christians but that, after that, they had become superfluous and ceased. His thinking tended to dominate Latin theology. Aquinas had a theology of charisms, but charismatic theology did not preoccupy most Latin theologians. Even at Vatican II, curial Integralists sought to suppress the charismatic activity of Christ's Breath by citing the position and authority of Augustine.

A theological retrieval of belief in the Holy Spirit occurred in three waves in western Catholicism. The first wave began in the nineteenth century and culminated in Leo XIII's encyclical letter on the Holy Spirit, *Divinum Illud Munus* in 1897. The pope's letter did little more than summarize medieval teaching about the Holy Spirit; but it did treat of the role of the Holy Spirit in the Incarnation and in the lives of the faithful. The encyclical also spoke of the Spirit as the soul of the Church. A second wave of pneumatological research bore fruit in Pius XII's *Mystici corporis* in 1943. Pius's encyclical did effectively popularize belief in the Holy Spirit as the soul of the "mystical body of Christ," the Church. It also called for more theological reflection on the gifts of the Spirit.

In the decades which preceded Vatican II, Karl Rahner and Yves Congar both repudiated the Augustinian doctrine that God intended the charisms only for the apostolic Church. Rahner portrayed the charisms as perennial endowments of the Church, and Congar argued that the charisms provide the key to the spirituality of the lay apostolate.

Contention about the charisms erupted during the second session of Vatican II when the assembled bishops began debating the revised schema on the Church, the document which would eventually evolve into *Lumen gentium*, one of the architectonic documents of the council's ecclesiology. At the first session, the bishops had in effect rejected the schema on the Church which the Vatican curia had prepared as a working document. The curial schema propounded an authoritarian, highly centralized, hierarchical view of the Church. The bishops, however, wanted an updated theology of the Church and one with a more pastoral tone. The revised schema endorsed both Rahner's defense of the perennial character of the charisms and Congar's suggestion that the charisms lie at the basis of the lay apostolate.

During the second session, in the course of the debate on the revised schema, Cardinal Ruffini, a curial conservative, called for the council to delete from the document any reference to the charisms of the Spirit and to make it clear that lay Catholics had as their primary responsibility to obey the hierarchy. In one of the landmark speeches of the council, Léon Joseph Cardinal Suenens of Belgium refuted Ruffini's arguments and called for even greater insistence on the centrality of the charisms in the life of the Church, especially in lay spirituality and in the lay apostolate. The speech made a discernable impact on the assembled bishops, an impact which the Curial conservatives tried ineffectually to undo, especially after the eastern rite bishops seconded Suenens and expressed satisfaction at any indication that, after all, the Latin Church really does believe in the Holy Spirit. In the end, Vatican II discovered charismatic inspiration at the basis both of the lay apostolate and of ordained ministry in the Church.

In invoking Vatican II to give sanction to The Catholic Charismatic Renewal, the American bishops tacitly asserted that , in their preliminary judgment, at least some of the experiences Catholic charismatics were having counted as authentic gifts of the Holy Spirit. As the movement spread to Europe, Cardinal Suenens in blessing it with careful theological support helped give it initial credibility in the eyes of the European Catholic community. The Malines Document, a pastoral and theological assessment of the European Renewal, lent the movement further legitimacy, as did other pastoral letters and directives issued both by individual bishops and by bishops' conferences.

I had already decided to involve myself with the Catholic Charismatic Renewal before I learned of its tentative approval by the American Conference of Catholic Bishops. The bishops' document confirmed me in that commitment, and it alerted me to the need to approach the movement with an discerning eye.

At the Notre Dame conference, I met Harold Cohen, S.J., the head chaplain at Loyola University in New Orleans where I would soon teach. Among Jesuits, Harold suffered the nickname "Abie," a kidding embellishment of his last name. He had brought with him to Notre Dame several Loyola students who wanted to learn about the Renewal so that they could go back to Loyola and start a charismatic prayer group there. By the time I arrived at Loyola, they had indeed started with a bang. Over four hundred people, most of them students, gathered every Friday night for three or more solid hours of prayer.

For my part, I returned from Notre Dame to Cambridge and to the final stages of dissertation writing; but, as I did so, I committed myself to personal and pastoral involvement in the Renewal. As I have already indicated, however, before going to New Orleans, I spent a summer on Narragansett Bay. I have already narrated how my work on my dissertation ended there. My determination to abandon the folly of compulsively rewriting my dissertation happened early in the summer. Since I had time on my hands for the rest of the summer, I decided to begin to come to terms theologically with Pentecostal forms of prayer.

My loss in Eegenhoven of a personal rationale for being a religious had left me so personally discombobulated that I had found myself compelled to pray my way with a pencil to a new understanding of vowed living. The experience of charismatic prayer had rediscombobulated my life. I was entering, for me at least, uncharted spiritual waters; and I decided that I needed a map. In the Myers-Briggs personality profile I test out an off-the-chart introvert and judgmental type. That means that I like to figure things out in advance of any overt action and that I like closure in ambiguous situations. Typically, I set myself that summer to pray my way on paper to clarity about the terms under which I could responsibly involve myself in a movement like the Charismatic Renewal.

My summer scribblings took shape in the year 1971 as *Pentecostalism: A Theological Viewpoint*. I had brought a New Testament with me to our cottage on Narragansett Bay. I had studied enough American philosophy to know that "experience" offered the best rubric for trying to understand something like shared charismatic prayer. In the course of the summer, I tried to distill basic affirmations which the New Testament makes about the experience of the charisms and about their role in the Christian community. I tried to transform the relevant texts into something like theses. Then, at the end of the book, I arranged the theses in what seemed to me something like a logical order. In the course of writing *Pentecostalism*, I began to realize that the charisms gave one a lot to think about theologically.

Paul the apostle not only prayed in tongues but wished that all Christians did so as well. I join him in that pious wish. Not all Christians do, of course, not even all Pentecostal Christians. Catholics who have never experienced the gift of tongues find it odd. Apparently, the same problem surfaced in the apostolic Church, because Paul counseled the Christians at Corinth not to pray in tongues without an interpreter when outsiders attended their prayer services lest those same outsiders think Christians mad.

I have experienced the gift of tongues primarily as a gift of prayer. It remains one of the most basic and frequent ways in which I pray. I find the true purpose of the gift disclosed when groups of people sing together in tongues. I remember sitting in the Notre Dame stadium at my first charismatic conference and hearing thousands of people start spontaneously and simultaneously to sing in tongues. I found the harmony beautiful but even more beautiful the spectacle of several thousand joyful Catholic Christians lifting their hands and voices together in the heartfelt praise of God.

Prior to receiving the gift of tongues, I had remained faithful to daily prayer. After receiving the gift of tongues, I found myself needing prayer more. If, on a particularly busy day, I missed prayer time or postponed it, I felt the lack of it palpably. I found it increasingly easy to pray for long periods of time. On arriving at Loyola, I joined the charismatic group Abie had started. Often I would begin the prayer meeting exhausted and with a head splitting with fatigue from the pressures of the week. By the end of the prayer meeting, the headache had gone, and I felt completely relaxed.

I found too that the gift of tongues teaches one greater receptivity in prayer. Before receiving tongues, I had meditated on different themes or practiced *lectio divina*.[1] I tended, however, during prayer times to yammer at God. With the gift of tongues, I began to learn to listen more to the movement of the Divine Breath in prayer. I began with some regularity to receive word gifts both during prayer and outside of prayer time.

John of the Cross describes three kinds of word gifts: consecutive words, formal words, and substantial words. In experiencing consecutive words, as the word takes shape in one's mind and heart, one has the sense of partly contributing to its formation. When one receives a formal word, one experiences it more passively, as simply given. Once for example, when I was typing in my office at Loyola University, I received a clear formal word: "Go to the receptionist's desk at Thomas Hall." Thomas Hall abutted St. Charles Avenue and housed most of the Jesuits who lived and worked at Loyola. I stopped typing and did what I was told. When I got there, the receptionist said, "Oh, Father, I'm so glad you came by. There's a man here who wants to talk to a priest. I have been calling around, but no one seems available to talk to him. Can you do it?" I did for about two hours with a feeling of *deja vu*. I felt as I had on the Plains of Abraham and in the passenger car on the Orient Express, except that this time the impulse which had brought me to Thomas Hall had taken shape in a formal word. I would not experience what John of the Cross calls a substantial word until I went to Berkeley. When one receives a substantial word, the grace which the word signifies accompanies it. John warns one to scrutinize carefully both consecutive and formal words; but he allows one to desire substantial words because of their manifest divine origin and because of the good they do those who receive them.

I used to give teachings at our Loyola charismatic prayer meetings. I commented on the gospel of John or on one of the other gospels. After a semester of teaching, it occurred to me that, while I had chosen teaching as a profession, I had not prayed for the gift of teaching. I asked the community to pray over me for the gift of teaching. Two little girls always sat on the first row. As a consequence, when I knelt for others to pray over me, they imposed hands on me. I remember at the time feeling it appropriate that children should impose hands on a Ph.D. and pray that he receive the gift of teaching. One of the girls was so small that she had to raise her hands to get them on top of my head. Nothing dramatic happened at the time; but, by the end of the second semester, I found my whole approach to teaching had gradually changed. I was praying about the things I taught. I was praying for my students. Even though I taught philosophy, the classroom had become more of a place to proclaim the gospel. Finally, I was not flaunting my Ph.D. quite as much as I had. I decided that God had heard the community's prayer. Moreover, that experience made me realize that the charisms can and often do transform natural gifts by rendering them more docile to the movement and inspiration of God's Breath. The charisms can also take evocative form, when, for example, membership in a community of faith calls forth from one forms of Breath-inspired ministry one would never have otherwise dreamed of exercising.

I also began giving teachings at major charismatic gatherings. Once, at one of the national meetings, after my presentation I found myself confronted with a very intense young Jesuit scholastic who was staring at me through glasses that looked like the bottom of coke bottles. He came from the California Province and called himself William Spohn, S.J. He told me later that the talk I had given had made more sense to him than anything else he had heard since joining the Charismatic Renewal.

In 1973, the year I came to Berkeley, Bill was doing his final year of theological studies and took some courses with me. He liked the idea of drawing on the American philosophical tradition to think theologically in an inculturated manner. Slated to begin doctoral studies after leaving Berkeley, Bill resolved to orient his doctoral studies toward developing such a theology. I had begun to test Lonergan's theory of functional specialties by starting to articulate a foundational theology of conversion. Bill had a passionate interest in moral theology and felt called to rethink the workings of the Christian conscience.

In 1978, he would return to the Jesuit School of Theology at Berkeley and become a cherished friend and colleague. Over the years we have taught one another an enormous amount. Bill undertook a dialectical study of ethical thinking in the United States parallel to my own dialectical study of the development of American philosophy of religion. I find Bill's moral theology thoroughly compatible with my own understanding of the forms and dynamics of conversion. Accordingly, I have incorporated with grateful acknowledgment many of his best insights into my own thinking.

As I have already indicated, the American Studies Group spent its second summer at the Jesuit School of Theology in Berkeley (JSTB). The school had moved from Alma, a town south west of San Jose, to Berkeley in 1968. Harry Corcoran, S.J. presided over the move as dean; and Michael Buckley, S.J. did so as rector of the community. Michael still served as rector when the American Studies Group came to Berkeley. Mike and I hit it off from the beginning. We both shared a passion for philosophy and for systematic theology. We also had both immersed ourselves in the mystical theology of St. John of the Cross. Mike at the time was pushing the idea of having the Jesuit school sponsor a one-year theological renewal program which eventually took shape in the Institute for Spirituality and Worship (ISW). In the course of the summer, Mike invited me to participate in some brain-storming sessions about the possible shape that the program would take.

During the academic year 1972-1973, the New Orleans Province undertook an assessment of the two collegiate programs we were running in New Orleans and in Mobile. We were running two programs but probably had adequate staff for one. The province administration was considering consolidating the collegiate program either in New Orleans or in Mobile. I had taught a semester at Spring Hill College in our Mobile collegiate program in the spring of 1970. Spring Hill College offers fine undergraduate education; but I did not find in Mobile the equivalent of the Tulane research library. I therefore decided that, if the province consolidated the two programs in Mobile, I would be looking for a job elsewhere.

While the assessment went on, I got news that a good friend of mine from my philosophical studies in St. Louis, Andrew Dufner, S.J., had just become dean of the Jesuit School of Theology in Berkeley. I wrote Andy to congratulate him on his appointment. I also explained to him my situation. I told him that, if the province decided to consolidate the collegiate programs at Spring Hill, I would be looking for work. I also told him that I would find it interesting to help get something like the Institute for Spirituality and Worship going at the Jesuit School of Theology in Berkeley.

Andy wrote back immediately and urged me to forget about working with collegians and to come to Berkeley and help James (Jake) Empereur, S.J. organize the Institute for Spirituality and Worship. Jake and I had also done philosophy together in St. Louis. He, however, had indicated that he would not organize the ISW by himself. Andy said that the school had been searching for someone to assist Jake for over a year and to date had found no takers for the job.

I knew that I could not just forget about our in-province collegiate program. If I left New Orleans and went to Berkeley, I realized that I would leave the staffs of our two collegiate programs even shorter handed. I therefore consulted the staffs first. I told them about Andy's offer to come to Berkeley. I also explained that I had done a degree in philosophy in the hope of using it to create an inculturated North American theology. I explained that I had completed the research project in American philosophy which I had set myself on coming to Loyola. I asked the two staffs in New Orleans and Mobile what they thought I ought to do. Half replied that Berkeley offered an ideal place to create the kind of theology I ambitioned and that I should accept the offer. The other half told me that I should decide the matter with my major superior, the Vice-Provincial for formation, Charles O'Neil, S.J. I discussed the matter with Charlie, and he approved my going to Berkeley for three to five years or until the Institute for Spirituality and Worship had consolidated itself.

I accepted Andy's offer; but, having done so, I felt not a little daunted. JSTB at the time taught on the quarter system. I decided to teach at Berkeley one course I taught in New Orleans, a survey of American religious philosophy which I upgraded to a graduate level; but I would have to prepare five new courses. Moreover, not only would I be teaching in a completely new discipline, theology, but I would be shifting from undergraduate to graduate instruction. I spent the summer before I began to teach boning up on the courses I would offer the following year. Andy had asked me to teach three courses in the Master of Divinity program, which prepared students for ordination: one on the theology of the human person, one on sacramental theology, and one on the Trinity with a focus on the Holy Spirit. In addition, I would offer a seminar for the charismatic track in the ISW.

Once the school year began, I found that I had in fact over-prepared all the courses I would teach. Unfortunately, as a result of my frantic work during the summer before classes in Berkeley began, I started the academic year completely exhausted. My exhaustion combined with other circumstances to make my first year at JSTB the most difficult year of my life.

First of all, I felt lonely. The Jesuit community lived in a cluster of buildings atop Holy Hill, the hill to the north of the campus of the University of California at Berkeley (UCB) where most of the schools which comprise the Graduate Theological Union (GTU) reside. Had God not in the late sixties smitten the fraternities and sororities which had inhabited Holy Hill, I doubt that the Jesuit School of Theology could have made its move to Berkeley. Many of the buildings we acquired had housed Greeks, both male and female. Moreover, the year I arrived in Berkeley, JSTB had just become an Assistancy apostolate.

The ten provinces of the United States comprise the American Assistancy of the Society of Jesus; and all the provinces assume the responsibility of supporting with money and manpower all Assistancy apostolates. Before it became an Assistancy apostolate, JSTB had served as the theologate for the California and Oregon provinces. After becoming an Assistancy project, the school drew students from all ten of the provinces.

We had over 180 people in our community in 1973. The entire community ate dinner at Claver house. Meals provided the best opportunity to get to know people. When I arrived, I knew well only two people, Andy and Jake. Given the size of the community, one counted oneself lucky to sit next to the same person twice in a month. The anonymity of large community living made for a very lonely year. I began groping for ways to make friends. I turned to hiking and camping. I found the California landscape breathtakingly beautiful. I began sponsoring wilderness weekends, camping trips along the California seashore and in the national parks.

Through camping and hiking I became good friends with a tall, redheaded scholastic from the Missouri Province named Gerald McMahon, S.J. Jerry loved nature and, as a regent teaching in high school, had taken students on canoeing trips during the summer. Jerry found an inflatable raft in the community store room and suggested that during the spring break we go rafting on the American River, a fork of which flows past the California Province villa at Applegate, a little town at about two thousand feet in the foothills of the Sierras. I and Mike Taylor, S.J., an Oregon province Jesuit, agreed to do the trip.

Paul Comisky, S.J., one of our Jesuit graduates who was teaching at the University of San Francisco, warned me that we might find rafting on the American River during the spring flood dangerous. I had no experience in rafting and canoeing. I told Jerry about Paul's warning and suggested that we postpone the trip until after the spring flood had subsided. He replied that the Applegate villa had a map which indicated how swiftly the river descends. Since Jerry did have experience in water trips and I did not, I decided to trust his judgment. He checked the map and decided that we could do the trip safely. To make assurance double sure, however, he and I together spot checked the river visually for safety. We saw some minor turbulence but mostly just a few bumps and swirls. The three of us agreed that we would not only wear life jackets during the rafting trip but that we would tie our life jackets to the raft in order to make sure we could get back to it if we were thrown overboard.

Mike and I boarded the raft and sat in the front. We put on our life jackets and tied them to the seats. We entered the river at a smooth stretch; but, as soon as we rounded the first bend we found ourselves in white water, just a little at first. Then some heavier waves filled the raft. The weight of the freezing water slowed us down somewhat. I subsequently learned that it takes eight paddles to control an inflated raft like ours. We had only three. Jerry tried to steer in the rear of the raft but had no control over our direction.

The raft smashed into a very large boulder in the middle of the river, and a wave of water swept Jerry off the back of the raft. Mike and I did not realize what had happened until we looked back to see how Jerry was doing. He had disappeared. His life vest trailed on a rope behind the raft. He had never put it on. I remember yelling, "Oh, God, where's Jerry? What happened to Jerry?" Then we saw him swimming on his back near the bank of the river to the right of the raft. I remember thinking that Jerry was close enough to the river bank to grab hold of something; but the vee shape on the river valley often made the banks very steep. Then the water took us and we lost all contact with Jerry. I tried to pray for him.

We found ourselves swirled into a small eddy; but the rocks around it ran so steeply upward that we could not climb out. We had to return to the rushing stream. Soon I found myself swept from the raft and into the icy torrent. Using the rope I succeeded in regaining the side of the raft. Mike tried to help me back into it; but by that time we both felt so benumbed by the cold that he could not. I tied one of my arms to the raft thinking, "If the raft does not sink, I will be OK." At least, I hoped that I would be OK. With typical dry humor, Mike said, "Remind me never to do this again." He did his best to keep me anchored to the raft.

We found ourselves swept into another small cove, this time with enough of a beach for us to get our feet onto dry land. The freezing water had so benumbed our hands that we had difficulty securing the raft. Mike thought that he had lost his glasses; but, when we retrieved the raft later, we found them in the water on the bottom.

I could only think of Jerry. Neither of us thought of going back to look for him. The steepness of the valley walls made that impractical; and we thought ourselves several miles downstream from where Jerry fell out. We started climbing out of the canyon. We reached a flat place and stopped to pray for Jerry. We were hoping to find a road with people who could help us. We climbed to a point where we could see a bridge over the river with a road that ran up the sides of the valley. Since we seemed closer to the top, Mike and I kept climbing until the steepness of the cliffs made further ascent impossible. I suggested to Mike that we make a lateral descent to the bridge and the road in the hope of hailing some vehicle and going for help. When we reached the bridge we saw an elderly man who, however, proved of little help. A young man named Fred picked us up in a truck and took us to the police station.

There, we called the villa at Applegate and told them what had happened. At the police station, I gave an officer a full account of the accident. He took down my story and had me fill out other forms. Ernest Martinez, S.J., who then taught New Testament at JSTB, arrived in the community van with some of the other people who were spending spring break at Applegate. The police assured us that they would search for Jerry and help him in any way they could if they found him. As we went to the van to drive back to Applegate, I suddenly realized as I stood in the parking lot before the van's open door that, in describing the accident to the policeman, in speaking of Jerry, I had used the past tense. In a flash, I realized how much I had come to love him and to cherish his friendship and saw just as clearly what the past tense meant. As I began to enter the van, suddenly and violently I burst into tears. Carmichael Peters, a Black lay student from the GTU visiting at Applegate who had lost both legs in an accident, held me as I sobbed and sobbed. Two days later the police retrieved Jerry's body. He had struck his head on a rock and drowned.

The year I came to Berkeley I began keeping a prayer journal and have kept it ever since. During my first summer in the Bay area, I received again and again in prayer the same word: "You must accept your own death." I did not know what exactly it meant; but I prayed my way to the point that I could say to God, "I stand ready to die whenever you want me to." Thereafter, I received again and again another word, "You must be one with My Son in His suffering."

As I clung to the raft as it careened down the river, the first word sustained me. Jerry's funeral in Denver proved an ordeal in anticipation and in fact. In the aftermath of the accident, as I tried to face my responsibility in having occasioned, albeit unintentionally, the death of a dear friend, the second word sustained me. As in the case of other words I have received, these two words have recurred over and over in prayer and acquire new connotations in new circumstances.

I did not blame God for Jerry's death. Nor did I blame the natural forces which killed him. The accident showed me, however, a new face of nature. Hitherto, I had seen only the beauty and sublimity. Now I understood how natural forces work. They have no malice; but they work with supreme indifference to the survival of individual life. I did blame myself for not having recognized that fact more clearly. Jerry and I had both badly underestimated the force of a rushing, mountain river; and Jerry had paid a terrible price. After the accident, I almost stopped venturing into nature. For almost a year, I could not look at rushing water without a feeling of horror. On reflection I recognized abandoning hiking and backpacking as foolish. I did, however, determine in the future, whenever I had any doubt about the advisability of some action in nature, always to take the conservative decision.

The very next summer, for example, the Cheerful Charlies went to the Grand Tetons. We decided to do a loop that would give us spectacular views of the Tetons themselves, which remain invisible from Jackson Hole. The trail would take us over a pass called Paintbrush Divide. Before setting out on the loop, we checked out the trail with a backcountry ranger. We asked him if we could make it through Paintbrush Divide. He replied, "Aaaaah, yes. Yes, you can get through; and, if you take care, you probably will not need an ice axe." We did not know what that meant but decided to make the loop and find out. As we got closer and closer to Paintbrush Divide we kept meeting hikers coming from the opposite direction. That seemed to suggest that one could indeed make it across the Divide. We asked everyone who passed us about the trail conditions at the Divide and kept getting the same answer as the back-country ranger had given us, "Aaaaah, yes. Yes, you can get through; and, if you are careful, you probably won't need an ice axe." The last person we questioned, a ranger, also added, "And watch your first step, it's starting to melt out from the bottom."

When we reached Paintbrush Divide, we found it blocked by a massive snow shelf jutting out over a three-hundred foot drop onto large boulders. The snow rose at such a sheer angle, that one needed an ice axe just to keep oneself perpendicular and anchored to the snow as one walked across a primitive path at its base, really only a set of footsteps at the base of the protruding snow shelf. As the ranger had warned, the snow over which one was supposed to walk was melting out from the bottom. I took one look at the path across the snow mass; and, with the memory of Jerry's death vividly in my mind, I said, "I will not cross that." Some of the other Cheerful Charlies seemed willing to contemplate trying, but I remained adamant. We never did cross Paintbrush Divide, and I felt no regrets whatsoever. I have on other occasions taken similar conservative decisions when in doubt in the back-country.

After Joe Tetlow finished working on Project One, he became president of The Jesuit School of Theology at Berkeley (JSTB) but only held the position for two years. After two years, Tom Clancy, then the Provincial of the New Orleans Province, reassigned Joe to the staff of *America* magazine. By the time Joe came to JSTB, I had started doing backpack retreats.

In 1976, William Fulco, S.J., who taught Old Testament at JSTB and Near Eastern languages at the University of California at Berkeley, told me that he had access to a cabin in the coastal redwoods in northern California and suggested that we do retreat there together. A linguistic genius, Bill also knew an extraordinary amount about ancient coins. At Chardin House, one of the Jesuit residences in Berkeley, he kept a lovely aquarium for the community; but privately he owned the most loathsome collection of pets I had ever seen. He kept in his room a Cuban tree frog named Fidel. He also had a two-toed, green lizard with swiveling eyeballs on stalks as well as a large, very hairy tarantula named Beaver. On occasion, he would persuade people to let Beaver walk up their bare arm.

I told Bill that I would gladly do retreat with him in the redwood forests. Andy Dufner also joined us, as did Michael Flecky, S.J., then one of the Jesuit scholastics studying theology at Berkeley. We took turns cooking for one another and spent the day walking the redwood forests and praying. In the evening, we celebrated Eucharist together.

On the first day that Bill cooked, we found him in the evening minus his eyebrows. He had tried to light the oven only to discover that it had a gas leak. The explosion blew him across the kitchen and fortunately did him no more harm than burn off his eyebrows. Gas ovens aside, I found that prayer came easily in the wilderness and resolved to do all future retreats in the back country.

Joe came to JSTB the following year; and that summer he, Johnny Stacer, Luis Calero, S.J., and I made our retreat together in Lassen Volcanic National Park in the Cascade Mountains in northern California. Born in Cali, Colombia, Luis had joined the New Orleans province of the Society. I had taught him as a collegian in New Orleans and would enjoy his friendship in Berkeley for eleven years while he completed multiple degrees both at JSTB and the University of California at Berkeley (UCB). The four of us did the first half of the retreat in the north of the park near the cinder cone and the second half at a backcountry campground in a place called Corral Meadows. The final night of the retreat we spent in a campground at Summit Lake. On that final night of the retreat, as I walked around Summit Lake contemplating the resurrection narratives in the gospels, I experienced for the first time a substantial word. I recorded the experience as soon as it ended. I reproduce what I wrote in the citation which follows:

This evening was a special time of grace in prayer. I wish to record it while it is fresh. I went from the camp to Summit Lake with the intention of reading more in Küng's *On Being a Christian*. I never did. I began praying about the resurrection. I imagined the excitement in the community of disciples on discovering the empty tomb. I felt the wonder and mystery. I imagined what the encounter with the risen Christ was like, and I felt strong devotion. I had rounded the lake and passed the campfire talk which the ranger was giving when a word came in prayer, first gently, then with greater and greater power, but gentle power. It was, "Yes, know that I am risen and know the joy and power of My resurrection." And with that came an increasingly powerful impulse to praise God in tongues. I felt the two were connected, that the prayer in tongues was the way the Lord was using to introduce me into the knowledge of the power and joy of His resurrection. I felt moved to prolong the prayer. I walked the trail that leads into the woods praising God in tongues and thanking Him. The prayer intensified into a welling up of love which I still feel the residue of. There was a powerful sense of the risen Son as the source of the impulse of that love. But there was the sense too of the Father standing behind Him as the source of that love and of the Holy Spirit as the font of that same love. I felt Daddy and Mother as images present through whom the Father and Holy Spirit are concrete for me. I felt, despite the abstractness and awkwardness of what I write, the truth of the basic insights to which the Lord led me in the Holy Spirit Course. I felt that the Lord is indeed present in all of this and that, despite its limits, He is at work here. I felt the

Holy Spirit as the Divine Mother, as a matrix of life. I felt how the Father is content that things exist in Him naturally because He loves them and treasures them and finds them good; but I felt that He calls us to more. As love intensified, I found myself yearning for Christ and standing still saying, "Oh, my Love, Oh, my Beloved." I felt the love welling up in me, accomplished in me. I could not move. I stood still with my hands out, palms lifted, filled with love, yet sensing how I need to grow more in it. I longed to yield more completely to the Lord. I longed to deepen in this grace. I felt jealous of anything that would stand in its way. I felt as though I was beginning to glimpse what that yielding would mean. I felt as though tongues was important as the Lord's instrument to break down my ego control. I felt all of this as the substantial word spoken at the lake, "Yes, I am risen, and know the joy and power of my resurrection." I felt this word in continuity with a word spoken earlier in the retreat, "You have only begun to understand the words I have spoken to you." Oh, praise you, my Lord. Blessing, praise, praise, praise, praise.

I record this grace as accurately as I can, because in retrospect it proved a watershed from which other significant graces flowed. I realized at the time that Ignatius warns in his rules for the discernment of spirits that, in dealing with consolation without cause, one must distinguish clearly between the consolation itself and one's subsequent fallible reflections on it. In the substantial word I received at Summit Lake, I took the welling up of love for the person of the risen Jesus as the true consolation without cause. I treated the confirmation in prayer of the general movement of my theology more gingerly, although as I deepened in the practice of praying my way to new theological insights and of testing my conclusions both within prayer and in the pulpit, I increasingly felt both confirmation and leadings as my thought developed.

I recognized, of course, that one cannot base one's theology simply on one's personal prayer experiences. I understood well the need for rigorous method, for valid argumentation, and for verification of one's theories in the historical and eschatological events which reveal the Christian God. Still, I found it encouraging that on more than one occasion I felt confirmation in prayer concerning the general movement of my understanding of the revelation we have in fact received in Jesus and the sending of His Breath.

In 1986, I completed an analysis of the prayer journal I had been keeping since 1973. I wanted to lay the results of my analysis before my spiritual director for his discerning appraisal. The prayer experiences I recorded fell under five categories: words, calls, feelings, insights, and formal prayers. I found another pattern: often over the course of a year, I would assimilate more deeply graces given during my annual retreat.

In 1977, the year I received the substantial word while praying at Summit Lake, I began to hear a call in prayer which got repeated and clarified between 1977 and 1987. Again and again, I felt God calling me to develop a new kind of discipline. In 1977, I heard the call to affective healing, to deal with emotional problems one by one, to grow in self-knowledge, and to give unconscious feelings, including unpleasant ones, permission to surface consciously for healing. As the reader will recall, in reflecting on Lonergan's suggestion that conversion comes in three forms: intellectual conversion, moral conversion, and religious conversion, my study of Edwards, of Emerson, and of James had made it clear to me that I needed to add another kind of conversion to Lonergan's list: namely, affective conversion. Besides taking responsibility for one's mind, one's conscience, and one's relationship to God, one also needs to take responsibility for one's psyche, for its healing and for its cultivation of sound habits of appreciation. I had over the years tried through prayer, spiritual direction, study, and reflection to deal in an ongoing way with my conscious and unconscious feelings. With the call to a new discipline I began, however, to do so in a more systematic way. In other words, I began to experience the affective conversion about which I had written.

I found myself called to face repressed feelings of anger that had been festering inside me for decades. I recognized that, in dealing with my neurotic anxiety, I could not heal myself but needed to face my hangups with others and above all to place with expectant faith my healing in God's capable hands. I doubt that we ever completely get rid of our pet neuroses, but we can learn to befriend them and to minimize the damage that they cause. I found myself called beyond old feelings of self-preoccupation and self-hatred. I felt called to monitor my use of alcohol. As I tested my ability to create an inculturated North American theology, I recognized that my theological aspirations sprang in part from vanity and ego noise. I felt called, instead, to follow the path of smallness and humility and to bring disordered feelings to healing in faith. In my theological search for God, I felt myself called to seek wisdom rather than achievement. Responding to calls such as these spans a lifetime, of course; but I attempted to respond as best I could as I heard them and to return to them again and again in prayer. At a deep level, I knew I had to forgive the past, let it be, and move on. As the call to a new discipline deepened over the years, I realized that the Lord by these graces was leading me gently and with a healing hand through my mid-life crisis.

Besides deepening psychic healing, the new discipline had a positive focus. I had tended to measure my spiritual progress against that of others and found myself rebuked here as well. The Lord seemed to be calling me to follow my own spiritual path and in the process to reset my most fundamental priorities for living. I felt called to surrender more fully to the Lord, to cultivate greater submission and stillness within prayer, to deepen in the sense of God's presence. I began practicing a quiet centering prayer that made it easier in an Ignatian way to live present to God throughout the day. I began to experience the kind of recollection to which I had aspired as a novice, and I began to understand in a preliminary but practical way what Ignatius meant by "finding God in all things."

The new discipline also called me to scrutinize my motives for doing what I did. It called me to transform scholarship into a genuine exploration into God, with the focus on the Lord and not on myself or on my scholarly achievements. As I deepened in the new discipline, I felt myself coming to the end of one phase of my life and spiritual growth and sensed the need to move on to the next phase. I felt the Lords calling me to trust my future and its fruitfulness into Their capable hands. I had at least to try to let go of wanting to control the consequences of the apostolic works I undertook, including my writing and research. In the Myers-Briggs test, I had tested out as strongly judgmental. I felt the new discipline calling me to grow in greater perceptiveness, to abandon the neurotic desire always to keep tight control of the future.

The new discipline called me to grow old in an expectant faith that the Lord who had pursued me with a gentle relentlessness in the past would continue to do so as I looked forward to aging. I recognized that I would have to let the Lord teach me how to age in faith; and I faced the second half of my life with a sense of joy and anticipation. I recognized my need to try to temper my introverted egocentrism with love and to seek and to find God in the ordinary, where all true love gets perfected. I prayed to grow in a love for my students and for all those whom God sent to me. The new discipline also called me to let the divine Breath teach me how to grow in Her fruits. Finally, I recognized that the new discipline required me, initially at least, to focus more consciously on the person of Jesus and to let Him teach me how to age and mature.

In 1980 I made a wilderness retreat with Bill Spohn, who had also joined the faculty of the Jesuit School of Theology at Berkeley, and with Van Hutton, S.J., an Oregon Jesuit and one of the school's graduates. Bill and Van had helped begin the charismatic communities at the University of San Francisco and in Berkeley. A scholastic from the New Orleans province, Patrick Madigan, S.J, also made the retreat that year. We drove to the northern part of Lassen Volcanic National Park and hiked in past the cinder cone to Snag Lake, where we made our base camp.

In our wilderness retreats we had established a pattern for each day. After breakfast we would meet for a brief period of shared prayer. Then we would tell the group where we expected to spend the day. We tried to locate our base camp at a spot where several trails converged. Most of us spent the day walking one of those trails and praying. In the evening we would gather for the Eucharist and for supper. During the homily, we would share with each other the major graces of the day. In that way we wound up directing one another's retreat. Moreover, we noticed a cross-fertilization in our prayer. In almost every retreat, a grace given one of the retreatants would begin to inform the prayer of another.

On the second day of this retreat, I felt moved to try a prayer technique Van had suggested. I had tried unsuccessfully to contemplate different gospel scenes. Finally, I decided to imagine within prayer Jesus sitting opposite me waiting to engage me in conversation. In my imagination, we simply sat facing one another in silence for a while. Then, in my imagination I saw Jesus raise His eyes to mine and ask me, "What do you want of Me?"

I cannot remember everything I said in response. I told Him that I wanted to love Him more, to love other people. I told him that I wanted peace of heart, that I wanted to tell the truth about Him in what I write. I said I wanted my scholarship to praise Him. I felt deep devotion as I said all these things, but I also felt challenged by the question. I sensed that the Lord really did respect my freedom to choose my response. I also felt a bit put off by the question because I had not expected it. I told the Lord that deep down I did not want success or achievement. I felt love for the Lord and sincerely wanted to grow in that love.

When that particular prayer time came to an end, I jotted in my prayer journal the graces received but returned immediately to the same contemplation. I felt dissatisfied with what I had told the Lord. I realized that I had not really answered the question He had put to me. He had asked me what I want of Him and I had responded by telling Him what I wanted to do for Him, not what I wanted Him to do for me. As I asked myself what I really wanted of Jesus, I felt from deep within me the words come welling up, "Lord, I want to be with You"; and with that I started to weep. I wept, and wept, and wept. This answer seemed to suffice. I felt deep love of the Lord, profound sorrow for all that separated us, and an abiding sense of His love for me. As a novice during my long retreat, I had watched the tears streaming down Tony Mangiaracina's face as he spoke of Jesus' passion. I had wondered then what the gift of tears felt like. Now I knew. I was already thinking ahead to the Christology I ambitioned writing, and I hoped that it would provide me with a way of being with the Lord.

On the final day of the retreat, I experienced completely unexpectedly another substantial word. For some reason, we had decided to cut the retreat short by one day. I prefer the full eight-day retreat but went along with the decision. On the way back to Berkeley, we decided to visit Bumpass Hell, a large thermal area on the slope of Mount Lassen filled with boiling lakes and mud pots. The area gets its name from Mr. Bumpass who explored it, fell through the crust of a boiling mud pot, and lost his leg to gangrene.

As we hiked into Bumpass Hell, I had lagged a little bit behind Van, Pat, and Bill; and as I often do at the end of a retreat, I was praying for friends and family. Then came a clear substantial word: "Abide in Me. Abide in My love." With the word, I felt a powerful welling up of love of the Lord which I did not express in words. Instead, I simply felt a deep yearning of my heart toward the Lord Jesus as well as a sense that He was working the love and the yearning in me. I had a vivid sense of the unexpectedness of the grace. I felt a strong impulse to close my eyes but resisted doing it for long for danger of falling off the trail we were walking. The consolation without cause lasted for quite a while. Moreover, I felt that it came in part in response to the tears I had shed when I told the Lord, "I want to be with you." The others were just sightseeing. Under the circumstances I could not give myself to the gift of consolation as single-mindedly as I would have liked; but I decided that, since the Lord seemed to be in charge, I would simply leave matters in His hands.

I must confess that I feel a certain reluctance in recording prayer experiences such as these. I would deceive the reader sorely were I to give the impression that my prayer life consists of one consolation without cause after another. Most of my prayer journal reads very differently. In most of the entries I find myself wrestling with my standard neuroses. I regularly experience periods of dryness and darkness, as Ignatius warns in his rules for the discernment of spirits. When exhausted I tend to feel depressed. Regularly, at the end of every school term, I would pass through a period of darkness until I got rested and returned to normal. I grew to expect end-of-the-semester blues as routine. Despite the reluctance, I nevertheless share with the reader some of the powerful graces I have from time to time received as pure and unmerited gift because they do condition the way I tend to think theologically. They inform, for example, my account of Christological knowing in *The Firstborn of Many*.

In the wake of the first substantial word I received at Summit Lake on the slopes of Mt Lassen, I found myself deepening in the kind of affective friendship with Jesus about which I had prated as a novice without really experiencing it. In 1982, Johnny Stacer and I did a back-pack retreat in Shining Rock Wilderness in the Carolina Blue Ridge. We found the wild laurel, azalea, and rhododendron in full and glorious bloom and every afternoon looked down on trails littered with flightless bumblebees drunk with nectar.

During the fifth day of the retreat, I felt drawn to reflect on how my relationship with Jesus had evolved over the years. I pondered the deep human friendships I had known like that I had with Johnny and with Joe. I saw that all friends feel mutually attracted to one another because they experience a certain kinship, share similar enthusiasms and interests. Friends take pleasure in one another's presence. Friendship always involves give and take, mutual appreciation and esteem, and a mutual respect that creates in one the freedom to be oneself. Friends remain bonded despite absence and, because bonded, find great joy in meeting again, especially in surprise encounters. The likeness of mind which friends share makes it unnecessary to talk a lot after periods of long absence. They simply take up again where they left off during the last encounter. Separation never diminishes a sense of familiarity. Friends share similar visions of life and tend to share similar commitments. The deepest friendships I have known have always rooted themselves in shared religious faith.

As the retreat progressed, I found myself pondering the shape of my relationship to Jesus. As I did so, I recognized that that relationship did in fact reproduce many of the traits of a human friendship. I had come to trust with an expectant faith that, no matter what happened, Jesus would take care of me in the future as he had taken care of me in the past. I had come to trust our relationship itself as one of the rocks on which I stood. Years later, while doing a retreat in 1986 on the north rim of Yosemite Valley, I hiked onto the rounded dome which caps El Capitan, the awesome granite massif which guards the entry to the Valley. As I stood there I suddenly realized that El Capitan had come to symbolize Jesus for me. I had claimed him as my captain, as my leader, as the rock on which I stand, as a rock more massive and solid than the soaring granite beneath my feet. I celebrated that insight by doing a series of oil-pastel sketches of El Capitan from a variety of angles.

The experience on El Capitan happened many years after my retreat with Johnny in Shining Rock Wilderness; but the Shining Rock may have foreshadowed El Capitan. During that retreat, as I pondered my relationship to Jesus, I saw that I had been growing in felt love and fondness for Him. It seemed to me that I valued our friendship more than anything else in my life. I knew that He understood and comprehended me in all my folly and finitude and that I could trust His patient love. I trusted Him to continue healing me as He had in the past. When I felt separated from Him, I truly suffered. I had heard His call to become a Jesuit and had, however tardily and hesitantly, given my life to Him. I trusted Him to continue to strip away my hypocrisy and to wean me from the idols whose worship only caused me sadness and misery.

I saw how through His Breath He had led me in prayer to begin to put on His mind. I felt joy in His presence and enthusiasm about sharing my relationship to Him with others. I knew that, no matter how badly I would bungle in my attempts to serve Him, He would always respect my freedom to choose, even to choose badly. I had learned to cling to Him in moments of suffering in a pale imitation of His clinging to the Father in His passion. I saw that, even if I tried to lie to Him, He would not abide it. He would either personally or through someone else gently and lovingly rebuke me. I clung to Him as my healer and knew that I could trust Him to continue to heal me as He had done in the past. All these things came to me on the last day of my retreat and evoked from me heartfelt praise in tongues.

In 2001, I published *The Firstborn of Many: A Christology for Converting Christians*. It represented about twenty years of scholarly work and reflection. Before I began the project I prayed that working my way through the New Testament witness to Jesus and through the attempts of Christian thinkers to delve into the mystery of His person would prove a way of being present to the Lord even in the midst of often tedious scholarly research. Gradually that began to happen. Ignatius wanted Jesuits to find God in all things; and I have experienced over the years a gradually growing though imperfect ability to do that. Doing theology requires a sound method, strict discipline, and long hours of patient, meticulous, and sometimes boring scholarly work; but doing theology rather than just teaching what other people think theologically brings its deep and genuine joys as well. Over the years, I have found more and more joy in doing theology as the Lord has gradually, gently transformed it into a prayer of presence. The sense of presence comes and goes, of course, seems more vivid at some times than at others; but more and more, especially if I have the leisure to work at my own pace, I find writing and research a way of being present to all three divine persons.

In 1984, I received a series of words while doing retreat in Desolation Wilderness on the south-west side of Lake Tahoe. Desolation Wilderness sounds like an improbable place to do a retreat. The name, however, has geological rather than spiritual origins. Desolation Valley gives the wilderness area its name. An enormous glacier scraped the grey, granite valley so clean that practically nothing grows there. The starkness of the landscape, topped by Pyramid Peak, has an austere and striking beauty. Toward the middle of the retreat, on two different days, I received seven words in all. Some seemed to come from all three divine persons, others from a particular person.

In my prayer, I had expressed sorrow to the Lord for my hardness of heart and failure to respond to Him with greater affective freedom, when the first word came. It took the form of a mild rebuke and seemed to come from all three divine persons: "Do not be so hard on yourself. You love Us more than you may know. Know that We love you and find healing in that knowledge. Our love encompasses you. You will never understand or comprehend it. We are faithful in love. Trust Us and be at peace." I felt this word as a consecutive word but also felt it welling up from within me. It filled me with consolation and love of the Lords. I felt a yearning toward the divine persons and felt that in fact I had been growing in a kind of familiarity with all three of them. As I prayed quietly in tongues, a second consecutive word began to take shape. It seemed to come from the Lord Jesus: "I love you because you are trying to love Me. We love you because you are trying to love Us. Take comfort in Our love and be at peace. You cannot earn Our love."

That evening, as I reflected on the graces of the day, I did not know quite what to make of the two words. Their consecutive character told me that I should test them before I regarded them as genuine graces. At the same time, they seemed to build on other movements of the Breath which had come in earlier retreats.

The next day, during my first prayer period, as I was praying quietly in tongues, another word from Jesus began to take shape: "What more can I have done to prove my love for You? I have laid down my life for you and have given you My Breath." I let it sink in as I prayed quietly in tongues, when another word began to take shape, this one from the divine Breath: "I have conceived and guided you. I have known you when you had no knowledge of Me. I have nurtured you, called you, instructed you, healed you, led you. I have loved you as a mother loves her fumbling child. Rejoice in My love and be at peace." I felt in these words a call to look to the Lords for the human support and intimacy which I needed; and the word from the Breath gave me sensible consolation. Then another word came, seemingly from all three divine persons: "We have claimed your heart. We have claimed you for Our own. Yield to Our love." This word evoked a welling up of love for the Lords in Their love for me.

When that first prayer period of the day ended, I recorded its graces in my journal and had begun the next hour of prayer, when yet another word came, this time from the Father: "You have feared me needlessly. I have shaped you lovingly and have found joy in your growing. I, the source of all, am pure love and pure giving. Trust Me. Trust My guidance. Heed my call."

Because all these words, though apparently graced, lacked a clearly substantial character, I did not know finally how to evaluate them; but they seemed to bear fruit in my subsequent prayer. Having recorded the words in my prayer journal, I felt myself over the years again and again called back to them to ponder them, to let them slowly sink deeper and deeper into my heart.

In both *Experiencing God* (1978) and *The Divine Mother* (1984), I had argued for the legitimacy of imagining the third person of the Trinity as the feminine face of God. Just as I had begun to grow in an affective friendship with Jesus, I began now also to respond affectionately to the Father and the

Breath as well. These graces came gradually, cumulatively, until in 1989, I experienced a substantial word which dramatically changed my relationship to the Father. Andrew Christiansen, Johnny Stacer, and I were doing retreat together in the Rockies in the Wind River Range. The Wind River Mountains lie two ranges south east of the Grand Tetons. We camped by Big Sandy Lake from which we prayed while hiking in all directions. The Wind River Range looks like a smaller, younger version of the Sierra Nevadas. As in the Sierras, glaciers have scraped away virtually all sedimentary rock and have exposed the grey granite beneath. The young peaks in the Wind Rivers, however, have not yet rounded into domes as they have in Yosemite Valley. They rise like pointed granite spires.

To lighten our packs in hiking in to Big Sandy Lake, we had left behind in the trunk of our car some of the food we had brought for the retreat. On the third day, I was walking back to the car to retrieve the freeze-dried victuals. I felt drawn to contemplate Jesus' baptism. I wondered what Jesus must have felt when He heard the Father's words: "You are my beloved Son in whom I am well pleased." Then, I realized that I had heard an analogous word in my call to the Society and in all the assurances in prayer I had received over the years of the Father's love for me. I saw my vocation with new eyes as an expression of the Father's love for me personally; and in the same instant I recognized my slowness to perceive that love and respond to it in the way it deserved. At the same time, I saw my very slowness to respond encompassed in the Father's love for me.

Suddenly, I experienced powerful consolation without cause which lasted for about forty-five minutes. During most of that time, I wept and wept. I found in myself an ability to say "Father" with a love which exceeded anything I had ever experienced before. I had a sense of the Mother and of Jesus making this love possible, working it in me. I felt a longing to remain anchored in love of the Father. Profound feelings of gratitude mingled with love welled up within me. As I wept, I remembered the tears I had shed on saying to Jesus: "I want to be with You," and I knew that the tears I was now shedding would transform my relationship to the Father as those earlier tears had transformed my relationship to His Son. Incredibly, I seemed to hear the Father saying to me, "You are my beloved son, in whom I am pleased," not, of course, in the same way as He said those words to Jesus; but I felt nevertheless that they applied to me in however attenuated a sense and that despite my sinfulness and slowness to respond to Him the Father in some true sense claimed me as "son" and "beloved." I knew that my relationship to the Father had changed profoundly and that the Lords had freely, gratuitously, and lovingly worked this change in me.

As time passed, I began to wonder if I would ever experience the same kind of affective breakthrough in my relationship to the Mother as I had in my relationship to the Father and the Son. In my prayer journal I had begun referring to the Holy Breath as "the Mother" and to feel Her as the feminine face of God. Then one day, I returned to the word I had received from the Mother in Desolation Wilderness, in which She assured me that She had known, loved, and nurtured me like a Mother long before I recognized Her nurture and Her presence; and I realized that an affective breakthrough in my relationship to Her had already occurred long ago as I was praying alone in the chapel of Murray-Weigel Hall in the Rose Hill campus of Fordham University. At the time, I had only experienced the presence of God. Now I began to name that God "the Mother." Moreover, during my retreat in 1990, I experienced an unusual abundance of tears. I felt them in continuity with the tears which had deepened my relationship to the Father; and this time they included Jesus and the Mother as well.

As my affective relation with the Father deepened, it transformed the way I see nature. The word, "I, the source of all, am pure love and pure giving," took on a deepening affective resonance. I began to see in nature an expression of the Father's unadulterated love and giving. I saw Him in its immensity, in its grandeur, in the minute beauty of desert flowers, in the fanciful diversity of its creatures. I even began to see Bill Fulco's menagerie with new eyes. I now looked upon the two-toed, green lizard with eyeballs on swiveling stalks as an expression of the Father's playfulness.

Prayer experiences such as these both inform and confirm the theology I have written and suffuse it for me with a powerful, affective resonance. As I have already indicated, I recognize that prayer experiences alone cannot guarantee doctrinal orthodoxy. Only one thing can do that: a sound interpretation of the historical and eschatological events which reveal to us the Triune God. On the other hand, if I could not pray from the heart about the things I write, I would begin to wonder if as a theologian I had in fact interpreted the revelation correctly.

When I arrived in Berkeley in 1973, I found there a thriving charismatic community. Bill Spohn and Van Hutton had started it before I arrived. It began dramatically. One of the men who attended the first prayer meeting died during it. The group, however, survived that traumatic start. When I joined it in the fall of 1973, the community contained students who attended the Graduate Theological Union; but it derived its stability from the residents of the city of Berkeley who also attended. I celebrated the Eucharist and gave teachings at the meetings. I told the lay leaders of the community that I could realistically do no more than that. Given all my other responsibilities in the school and GTU, I simply did not have time to take over the pastoral leadership of a moderately sized charismatic community. The community lasted until the end of my third sabbatical at JSTB in 1994. I spent that academic year living at the Stanford Newman Center in Palo Alto. During sabbatical, I successfully completed an initial draft of *The Firstborn of Many*, which I would subsequently teach as a text and, in the process of teaching, revise in the light of students' questions and responses to what I had written.

When I returned to Berkeley, the charismatic prayer community had dissolved for lack of leadership. It had run out of people who were willing to take pastoral responsibility for guiding it. Students, however, asked me on my return what had happened to the charismatic group. I explained the situation but told them that, if they still wanted to get together and pray once a week, nothing prevented us from doing that. We did. As a result, the prayer group I had originally discovered on arriving in Berkeley in 1973 still survives in much diminished form even to this day. We gather to pray once a week in a much smaller chapel than the Shalom House chapel in which the original charismatic community gathered; and our prayer has tended to become quieter and more contemplative.

During the years of my association with the ISW, I ran a tract in charismatic spirituality. I wanted to train people for the Renewal with the theological competence to give it sound leadership. In my last year, the Rev. James O'Brien took the charismatic tract. If I accomplished nothing more than help to train Jim, it would have made eminently worth while all the sweat and effort I put into helping get the ISW started. After a year of study, Jim left Berkeley with his own vision for organizing at a national level the diocesan liaisons for the Charismatic Renewal.

As the movement grew in size, pastorally sensitive bishops recognized that they had a responsibility to provide it with sound supervision. Most dioceses in the end appointed someone to act as a liaison between the local charismatic community and the diocese. Jim not only left Berkeley with a plan for organizing the diocesan liaisons nationally, but he did so with outstanding professionalism.

In their annual meetings, the liaisons, to the best of my knowledge, still follow the guidelines which Jim set up. In the fall, the liaisons sponsor a seminar on some aspect of the Charismatic Renewal. Initially, these seminars focused on dimensions of the movement which seemed to the liaisons pastorally problematic and in need of theological clarification: issues like fundamentalism, deliverance ministry, the discernment of spirits, the nature of the charisms, etc. Technicians taped all the presentations made during the seminar as well as the discussions which followed them and made all of that material available to the liaisons when they gathered for their annual meeting in the spring. Moreover, the organizers of the spring meeting invited those speakers from the fall seminar whom they deemed would most interest the liaisons themselves to re-present their papers at the spring gathering. In organizing the liaisons, Jim wisely went out of his way to convince the National Service Committee, the lay leadership of the Renewal, that he in no way intended to stage a clerical takeover of the movement's leadership. The liaisons had no interest in power plays but did recognize that the dioceses have the pastoral responsibility to help give the Renewal sound guidance; and that responsibility they felt, correctly, unwilling to shirk. Over the years, both the National Service Committee and the diocesan liaisons have together played a major role in steering the Catholic Charismatic Renewal in the United States.

With time, moreover, a certain number of competent theologians did associate themselves with the Renewal and gave it sound theological guidance. Kilian McDonnell, O.S.B., a seasoned veteran of the Catholic-Pentecostal ecumenical dialogue, combined his considerable knowledge of patristic theology with his ecumenical experience to put the Catholic Charismatic Renewal in a sound historical and ecumenical perspective. George Montague, S.M., used his remarkable gifts as a historical-critical exegete to make the riches of contemporary Biblical exegesis available to both leaders and participants in charismatic prayer. His explanation of all the texts in both the Old and New Testaments which mention the Breath of God, *The Holy Spirit: Growth of a Biblical Tradition*, continues to provide the movement with a rich scholarly resource. Montague also entered into a lively dialogue with Protestant exegete James Dunn concerning the meaning of Spirit-baptism in the New Testament witness. My studies in classical American philosophy enabled me to formulate a normative theology of conversion in which I attempted to contextualize the Church's experience of the gifts. Predictably, in those studies I took the term "experience" as a central and unifying category. Heribert Mühlen, a distinguished German pneumatologist who blended insights from John Duns Scotus with the personalist philosophy of Martin Buber in order to rethink trinitarian theology in communitarian terms, became involved in the European branch of the Renewal. His involvement in charismatic forms of prayer helped focus his attention on the lived experience of the Spirit. I have incorporated insights from all of these theologians of the Renewal into my own thought.

Other scholars collaborated in giving theological direction to charismatic prayer communities. Several anthologies appeared which discussed in helpful ways different dimensions of charismatic prayer and ministry. While at Loyola University in New Orleans, I had encouraged Joe Fichter to do the first sociological study of the movement. Other such studies followed which yielded a helpful sense of the movement's social shape and demographics.

Despite episcopal sanction and pastoral direction of the Charismatic Renewal, some pastors reacted to the movement with suspicion and hostility.

Large numbers of religious, however, men and women, lay and ordained, participated enthusiastically in charismatic prayer communities. The latter especially brought the special wisdom of their community's ascetical and spiritual traditions to the experience of shared charismatic prayer. David Garaets, O.S.B. founded a charismatic Benedictine monastery in Pecos, NM, which for many years informed the Renewal with the rich wisdom of Benedictine spirituality. David once remarked to me at a national meeting of the Charismatic Renewal that he felt impressed by the fact that not just Benedictines, but religious of every possible stripe all attested to the fact that their experience of shared charismatic prayer had made their own spiritual and ascetical traditions come to life in a new way. My own experience of charismatic prayer certainly caused me to read *The Spiritual Exercises* with new eyes; but one heard Franciscans, Dominicans, Christian Brothers, and members of various religious congregations saying the same kind of thing. David argued from this phenomenon that charismatic prayer must provide Christian spirituality with a least common denominator because it enriches and enlivens the piety of the other more defined paths within the ecclesiastical tradition. Certainly the spiritual wisdom handed down in the different religious communities within the Catholic tradition informed the piety of charismatic Catholics in helpful and stabilizing ways and enabled the movement to accomplish something to which "Mr. Pentecost," the Rev. David Du Plessis, had exhorted it. A pioneer among Classical Pentecostals in ecumenical work, David had urged Catholic charismatics in 1969 not to mimic Classical Pentecostals but to inform their Pentecostal prayer with a Catholic spirit. In my judgment, the religious who joined the movement and enriched it with the spiritual wisdom enshrined in their communities did precisely that and contributed significantly to making the Renewal both Catholic and charismatic.

Even given the considerable resources of the Catholic tradition for providing sound theological and pastoral direction to the Catholic Charismatic Renewal, problems did surface within the movement and did so early. It took the scholarly community much longer to respond to the call from the Renewal's lay leaders to help them understand the kinds of prayer experiences, unusual for traditional Catholics, which they were encountering in charismatic prayer communities. It also took time to organize local and national leadership structures to provide sound doctrinal and pastoral guidance to the rapidly expanding Catholic charismatic population. In the absence of counsel from the Catholic community, the Renewal's lay leaders turned to anyone willing to teach them about Pentecostal prayer. They found several willing teachers among classical Pentecostals. Unfortunately, their teaching too often suffused Catholic charismatic piety with significant doses of Biblical fundamentalism, authoritarianism, and sexism.

At the same time, the very existence of a rapidly expanding international movement in charismatic prayer among Roman Catholics was challenging traditional classical Pentecostal perceptions of Catholicism. Invoking Luke's account of the arrival of the divine Breath on Pentecost day, Classical Pentecostal theology equated "Spirit-baptism" with praying in tongues. While that same theology assumed that "Spirit-baptism" would never happen in the Catholic Church, Classical Pentecostals could not deny the evidence of their senses. One Pentecostal theologian whom I heard at the first ecumenical meeting of the Society for Pentecostal Studies put it this way: "Here were all these Roman Catholics praying in tongues and carrying around their ten-pound Jerusalem Bibles." Forced by events to acknowledge the fact of "Spirit-baptized" Catholics as well as "Spirit-baptized" members of other main-line Protestant churches, Classical Pentecostals began to take ecumenical dialogue more seriously than their tradition had originally inclined them. Today, a growing number of Pentecostal theologians have advanced down that path.

In his standard study of the Classical Pentecostal tradition, Walter Hollenweger has correctly argued that it showed itself much richer in religious experience than in rigorous theological reflection. Other forces besides the Charismatic Renewal were, however, also transforming the Classical Pentecostal churches. Russell Spittler, the first Pentecostal minister to receive a doctorate in theology from the Harvard Divinity School, seconded the efforts of David Du Plessis and pushed for greater ecumenical openness among Pentecostals. Russell represented one of the first of a new breed of Pentecostal theologians. One finds in their writings a growing intellectual, philosophical, and theological sophistication which, in my judgment, bodes positively for any future Pentecostal-Catholic ecumenical dialogue.

Despite these developments among the Classical Pentecostal churches, the forces of Biblical fundamentalism and authoritarianism in their tradition did influence the Catholic Charismatic Renewal, especially in its early formative years. Pentecostals have, of course, no corner on fundamentalism and authoritarianism; but they tend to give these two aberrations a distinctive cultural spin. Catholic Charismatics, for example, began to adopt a classical Pentecostal interpretation of "Spirit-baptism." From the standpoint of Catholic theology, however, serious theological and pastoral difficulties result if one equates "baptism in the Spirit" with any single charismatic gift. That particular theological gambit remains fraught with divisive consequences by suggesting that those who do not possess this or that charism have not yet experienced Breath-baptism. One might as well argue, then, as the extremes of Catholic clericalistic rhetoric at times almost seem to do, that only those with the charisms of ordained leadership can lay claim to having privileged access to the Pentecostal Spirit. The Catholic tradition agrees with Paul the Apostle that no one can profess faith in Jesus as Lord without the empowerment of His Pentecostal Breath; and Catholic sacramental theology recognizes with Pauline theology that all those ritually baptized live baptized in the Breath of Christ.

The term "Breath baptism" derives, of course, not from Paul's epistles, but from the synoptic gospels which depict John the Baptizer prophesying that another, mightier than himself, would follow him and baptize, not just with water, but with a sanctifying Breath (Mk 1:8, Mt 3:11, Lk 3:16). The gospel of John speaks in an analogous strain (Jn 1:26, 31-33). Although Paul the apostle never uses the term "Breath-baptism" as such, he does speak about the reality. In my own judgment, if one reads the letters of the apostle Paul carefully, then baptism in the divine Breath encompasses the believer's life-long transformation in the Breath of Jesus whom ritual baptism confers. So understood, Breath-baptism includes one's initial justification by faith, one's ritual incorporation into a worshiping, eucharistic Christian community of faith, one's sanctification, one's charismatic empowerment to serve others in Jesus' name and image, and eventually one's total transformation in the Breath of the risen Jesus through bodily resurrection.

From the beginning, therefore, in speaking about Breath-baptism I resisted any tendency to equate it with speaking in tongues or with any particular gift of the Breath of Jesus. I also discountenanced prefacing the term "Breath-baptism" with the article "the," as did the Life-in-the-Spirit Seminar, which introduced thousands of Catholics to charismatic prayer. Talk about "the baptism in the Spirit" connoted for me the tacit identification of Breath-baptism with the reception of a particular gift or grace instead of recognizing its full and all-encompassing scope. In my judgment, the use of the article ran afoul of the Pauline claim that all those ritually baptized share in Christ's Breath (cf. 1 Cor 12:12-13).

Indeed, the more I observed the development of Catholic charismatic prayer, the more I recognized the theological soundness of Abie Cohen's pastoral instincts. Catholics who would heed David du Plessis and develop a distinctively Catholic brand of charismatic piety needed to understand the intimate connection between sacramental and charismatic prayer which our student prayer community in New Orleans had experienced so spontaneously. Hence, as I gradually transformed into published manuscripts the three M. Div. courses which Andy Dufner had asked me to teach in Berkeley, when it came to publication, I gave top priority to seeing my book on the sacraments into print first. Like Karl Rahner, I wanted any theology I wrote to address concrete pastoral needs in the Church. Concern to demonstrate the charismatic basis for sacramental worship therefore dominated my argument in *Charism and Sacrament*. I published it before *Experiencing God*, even though from the standpoint of the normative theology of conversion I was trying to create, *Experiencing God*, which made an initial stab at developing a theological anthropology, came logically first. I have never retreated from the basic insights into sacramental theology which I reached in writing *Charism and Sacrament*, even though for reasons I shall discuss in greater detail in the following chapters, by the time I had translated into books all three of the courses Andy had assigned me, I had recognized the need to amend and expand my argument in *Charism and Sacrament*.

I finally did so in a two-volume study, *Committed Worship: A Sacramental Theology for Converting Christians* (1993). I hoped that my updated sacramental theology would address pastoral needs in the Charismatic Renewal; but by the time I wrote *Committed Worship*, it seemed to me that the theological community had addressed most of the pressing theological issues raised by the Renewal. I therefore focused *Committed Worship* on the restored catechumenate, which I deemed in greater need at that point of theological input than the Charismatic Renewal.

I look upon the restored catechumenate as the reform instituted by Vatican II with the greatest promise for Church renewal, if those who conduct it understand what they are doing. Unfortunately, one finds stark contrasts in the quality of formation provided in different "restorations" of the catechumenate. To restore the catechumenate effectively we need to infuse into it a sound, normative, theology of the five forms of conversion and a discerning understanding of the seven dynamics and counterdynamics which give developmental shape to the total process of conversion.

We also need a parish-renewal program parallel to the catechumenate which insures that the eucharistic communities into which we welcome the new catechumens exhibit at least the same degree of conversion as one ought to expect of neophytes. Unfortunately, too many of the products of the restored catechumenate who have a positive experience of community within the catechumenate itself find themselves wondering at the end of the mystagogy where to find the living eucharistic community they were supposed to be joining. The attrition rate among the graduates of the RCIA gives evidence that our existing eucharistic communities need but often lack the level of conversion one ought to expect of neophytes.

Finally, any sound restoration of the catechumenate needs to begin by insuring the integral conversion of the team which initiates neophytes into the Church. One cannot invite others into a conversion experience that one has not had oneself. Since, moreover, conversion has considerable complexity and lasts a lifetime, those who run the catechumenate need to attend constantly and conscientiously to their own integral and ongoing five-fold conversion.

A story may concretize what I am talking about. As I was giving shape to *Committed Worship* and using it as a text book in my course on the sacraments, Jan Chappa, a member of the team who ran the catechumenate at Holy Spirit Parish, the Newman Center for Catholic students attending the University of California in Berkeley, did two courses with me, one of them my course on sacraments. Both courses developed in significant ways the foundational theology of conversion which I was in process of formulating. Jan began to feed to the other members of her catechumenate team the theology I was developing. She told me that it transformed the way in which they structured the catechumenate. The team began using my construct of conversion for diagnosing the particular conversion needs of each of the catechumens. They then tailored each catechumen's instruction in ways that fostered his or her immediate need for conversion. At the same time, they had all the catechumens share with one another the kinds of conversion they were experiencing. Not only did everyone show up for the mystagogy, but by the end of the mystagogy they wanted to continue it indefinitely. The catechumenate began, as a consequence, to generate an impulse in the parish for grass-roots communities of people interested in supporting one another in a permanent way in the life-long process of ongoing conversion. I do not know how that impulse played itself out.

How fares the Catholic Charismatic Renewal today? On the twenty-fifth anniversary of the "Duquesne Weekend," the diocesan liaisons invited me to participate in both their fall seminar and spring meeting. Appropriately, they had chosen as a topic for that year to assess the first twenty-five years of the Renewal and to project foreseeable needs and goals for the movement. As the discussions of the seminar advanced, it became apparent that the Catholic Charismatic Renewal remains an important international movement, primarily in lay spirituality. The statistics of the National Service Committee indicated that in the United States, the number of Anglo-Americans attending charismatic prayer meetings on a regular basis had declined and probably would continue to decline. At the same time, the most recent influx of Catholic immigrants was reshaping the movement's demographics. A growing number of Latino and of Asian Catholics were becoming actively involved in the Renewal. Since our Denver meeting, these trends have only strengthened.

Moreover, as our discussions evolved over the weekend the seminar met, I thought I heard a kind of consensus emerging. A significant number of the delegates had reached the conclusion that, despite their good intentions in replacing the name "Catholic Pentecostals" with "The Charismatic Renewal of the Church," the American bishops had unwittingly created unrealistic expectations of a movement which remains, after all, a popular movement in lay spirituality focused on shared charismatic prayer. A significant number of the delegates seemed to agree that "the charismatic renewal of the Church" has to include all the renewal movements at work in the contemporary Christian community. In other words, the movement we call "the Charismatic Renewal of the Church" only makes a contribution to the total charismatic renewal of the contemporary Church. It does not single-handedly embody its charismatic renewal.

No one questioned the bishops' good intentions in renaming the movement as they did. The new name sought to avert popular misunderstandings which the name "Catholic Pentecostals" might have conjured up. The bishops' new name for the movement , however, unintentionally created its own set of popular misunderstandings. As we have seen, Vatican II's retrieval of faith in the charisms of the Holy Breath as perennial endowments of the Church marked a significant doctrinal breakthrough in Roman Catholic theology and in the pneumatology of the official pastoral magisterium, a breakthrough which theologically ignorant and frightened Integralists have since been systematically trying to stifle and undo. In my judgment, every Christian conversion ought to mature into a Pentecostal moment in which a developing, adult Christian feels called and empowered by the Breath of Jesus to serve the Church and humanity in particular ways. Every Christian, therefore, has access to the charismatic illumination of the charism-dispensing, Pentecostal Breath. Unfortunately, calling one particular renewal movement in the Church "the Charismatic Renewal of the Church" created the false popular impression that only those Catholics who attended charismatic prayer meetings qualified as "charismatic," while those who abstained from attendance did not.

In fact, we face a much more complex situation than that. In my own assessment of the first twenty-five years of the Renewal, I argued in Denver that the movement had allowed itself to become the prisoner of the most significant institution it had created: namely, the prayer meeting. The institution of the prayer meeting had focused the attention of its participants primarily on the kinds of charisms which one can share within charismatic prayer. Even if one restricts oneself to the Pauline lists of the charisms (and one need not do so), it becomes quickly apparent that one cannot share in any adequate way in the context of prayer the majority of the charisms which functioned in the apostolic Pauline churches. I refer to charisms like administration, active concern for the poor, pastoring, discernment, evangelization, helping, etc. Nor can one restrict the gift of prophecy to ritualistic pronouncements uttered in King James English at a prayer meeting. The prophetic voice sounded loud and clear in the sermons of Martin Luther King, and it takes embodied shape in The Catholic Worker Movement, in various liberation theologies, and in contemporary, non-violent protests against abortion on demand and the death penalty.

In the early days of the Charismatic Renewal, its lay leaders predicted that it would follow the same trajectory as the liturgical renewal and that the day would come when all Catholics would belong to some charismatic prayer group. That has not happened to date and will probably never happen unless both the Renewal and the Church evolve into one another in constructive ways. In my Denver paper on the present status of the Charismatic Renewal, I argued that narrow focus on those charisms which one can only share in the context of prayer had prevented the Renewal from inculcating a balanced form of charismatic piety. As a result, a significant number of Catholics found in the Renewal an initial experience of prayer and conversion but failed subsequently to find within the institutions which the Renewal had created sufficient scope for the exercise of those charisms which the Breath of Christ had given them.

I came to this insight while giving a workshop to the Jesuit tertians in Austin, Texas. After leaving Berkeley, Joe Tetlow had served for several years on the staff of *America* magazine, where, among many other things, he wrote the column *The Word*, homiletic reflections on the following Sunday's liturgical readings. Shortly after Joe left the staff of *America*, the provincial of the New Orleans Province appointed him tertian instructor. Joe decided to locate his tertianship in Austin, where the local bishop made available a former convent in one of the poorer neighborhoods of the city. I was teaching in Berkeley during the years that Joe served as tertian instructor; and he regularly invited me to give workshops to his tertians.

The tertianship cultivated a simple life style and practiced a form of open hospitality. As a result, in the course of one of my workshops, I found myself sitting across the dining table from an affable young man who ran a soup kitchen for the homeless in Austin. Our conversation ranged over a variety of topics and finally focused on the Charismatic Renewal. My young interlocutor asked me if I had any involvement with the movement. When strangers ask me that question, I never know what they presuppose. I admitted my involvement but began hedging it with a variety of theological and pastoral qualifications. My young friend smiled and said, "Oh, you don't have to apologize. I also came by the charismatic way." As I heard his words, I suddenly saw sitting before me hundreds of other Catholics I had known who had also come "by the charismatic way," had failed to find adequate scope for the exercise of their particular charisms within the Charismatic Renewal, and had moved on to other forms of Breath-inspired charismatic ministry within the

Church. Through their participation in charismatic prayer, they had experienced an initial Christian conversion as well as the Breath's empowering call to practical ministry. Both experiences led them to discover gifts within themselves which required exercise outside the context of shared charismatic prayer.

Here, I saw, lay one explanation for the decline in Anglo-American participants in charismatic prayer groups. The Renewal had not persuaded all Catholics to belong to some charismatic prayer community, but the movement was functioning as a leaven within the Church by inspiring a variety of other kinds of charismatic ministry which flourished outside of a prayer context. Those ministries in fact build up the body of Christ in important and necessary ways.

The history of the Shalom prayer community which I joined on arriving in Berkeley in 1973 offered another possible paradigm for understanding declining Anglo-American Catholic participation in charismatic prayer. That particular prayer community had flourished for over twenty years but had finally foundered on the lack of competent, pastoral lay leadership. I have since learned that many of the former members of the Shalom charismatic community continue to meet regularly for prayer but in smaller groups which do not make the same demands on community leaders that a relatively large charismatic community does. These small communities sustain their members but do not attract new ones as larger, more visible communities tend to do.

In the years to come, the Charismatic Renewal promises to continue to enrich the shared life of the Catholic Church. If so, then we can anticipate that it will continue to supply the great Church with a steady stream of Breath-filled, converted lay ministers. If the Charismatic Renewal did no more than that it would provide a signal service to the Catholic community and to the Church as a whole. I for one, however, for reasons I shall explain in greater detail below, would feel disappointed if the leaders of the Renewal only settled for that minimal pastoral outcome. In my judgment, every Catholic would benefit from the regular experience of shared charismatic prayer. It has the power to inspire the kind of Christian conversion which Vatican II says must ground and animate genuine liturgical renewal and for which liturgical committees provide an inadequate second best.

In my opinion, the restored catechumenate, which itself needs much bolstering and deepening, offers the leaders of the Catholic Charismatic Renewal in this country their best opportunity for institutionalizing a balanced, Catholic, charismatic piety that would gradually permeate the Catholic community as a whole. We need to build into every RCIA program an updated version of the Life-in-the-Spirit Seminars which served the Renewal well as a catechetical program for introducing people to shared charismatic prayer. We also need to build Life-in-the-Spirit Seminars into the parish renewal programs which seek to bring sacramentalized but unevangelized Catholics to at least the same level of conversion we expect of neophytes. At the same time, the Renewal itself needs to change and to develop institutional structures which foster a genuinely balanced charismatic piety and not one focused narrowly on prayer gifts. Finally, the demise of charismatic communities for lack of lay leaders suggests the need for a more systematic leadership training.

In addition, at our Denver meeting, as we assessed the future of the Charismatic Renewal, we seemed to agree that, if the Renewal does not embody the total charismatic renewal of the Church but only contributes to that total renewal, then the Catholic Charismatic Renewal needs to get into dialogue with the other renewal movements in the Church in order to share with them how charismatic prayer can contribute to the charismatic renewal of the Church as a whole. At the same time, the Charismatic Renewal also needs to absorb and assimilate from those other movements their best insights into how to foster comprehensive Church renewal.

I sensed among several delegates at the Denver meeting a kindling interest in the restored catechumenate. I encouraged that interest and continue to do so. In my judgment, the restored catechumenate offers the most promising instrument for introducing more and more Catholics to the benefits of shared charismatic prayer and to a living faith in the charismatic empowerment of the Pentecostal Breath. When run properly, the restored catechumenate gives institutional structure to the fundamental dynamics of initial Christian conversion. The pre-catechumenate must consist in more than a getting-to-know-you period prior to election into the catechumenate proper. The official Vatican instruction on the correct implementation of the catechumenate insists, and rightly so, that no one who has not already experienced an initial Christian conversion should enter the catechumenate proper.

What does such an initial conversion demand? As we have seen, when one interprets initial conversion in the light of a sound normative insight into the total process of conversion, then it embodies justifying faith; and justifying faith requires one to stand committed to living in obedience to the ideals of God's just reign. Those ideals, which I discovered while praying with a pencil in the Bronx, free one from the idolatry of personal possessions and require one to share one's physical resources with others and especially with those in greatest need. They require one to renounce both riches and the very desire for riches. They also commit one to collaborate with others in order to create a community of sharing dedicated to breaking down all the sinful barriers which divide humans from one another. Such communities replace corrupting environments of sin with nurturing, life-giving, charismatic environments of graced, mutual service. Justifying faith requires one to ground the Christian community, not in law, violence, or coercion, but in authentic worship of the Father. Mutual forgiveness in Jesus' image tests the authenticity of that worship, just as love of enemies tests the authenticity of mutual forgiveness. Finally, commitment to growing in sanctification by living the ideals of the kingdom also commits one to discerning the charisms of service which one brings to the total charismatic ministry of the Church.

Until those experiencing the pre-catechumenate have both clearly understood these practical demands of life in God's just reign and committed themselves to living them, they should not proceed to the catechumenate proper. Moreover, one cannot set *a priori* time limits on how long the catechumenate itself will last. The directors of the catechumenate and each of the elected catechumens ought to agree that the catechumenate will take as long as he or she needs in order to learn how to participate in the shared life of the Church as a fully converted adult. Achieving fully converted adult maturity could take some longer than others. In the course of the catechumenate, the elect should, as Jan Chappa saw, attend to their own specific needs for ongoing conversion; and they should share their conversion experiences with one another. One should not require heroic holiness of neophytes; but one ought to require of them a sound insight into the five forms and seven dynamics of conversion and an initial growth in all five areas of conversion. One should also require of them a sound insight into the practical demands of life-long, ongoing conversion. I confess that I regretfully wonder how many of those currently running the RCIA have themselves reached that level of insight and commitment.

If the precatechumenate needs to certify the presence in converts of a commitment of justifying faith and if the catechumenate needs to insure an initial, sanctifying advancement on the road to ongoing conversion, both the catechumenate itself and especially the mystagogy have to deal with the second dynamic which structures sanctification through ongoing conversion. That dynamic requires that growth in holiness mature into some form of charismatic ministry in the Church and to the human community which the Church serves. During the catechumenate, the elect need to recognize in the rite of confirmation a life-long commitment to respond to whatever charismatic call to ministry within the Church the Breath of Christ may impart. They need to understand the diversity of charisms and how they work; and they need to begin the process of discerning even during the catechumenate how the Breath is calling and empowering them to a charismatic ministry of service.

This process of discernment needs to intensify during the mystagogy and indeed provides the mystagogy with its primary agenda. Every well-run catechumenate ought, as a consequence, to introduce Christian neophytes to the experience of shared charismatic prayer as an appropriate context for discerning one's charismatic call to ministry within the Church. To such an introduction those who have already come "by the charismatic way" have an enormous amount to contribute to the full restoration of the catechumenate. Judged by the norms of a sound foundational theology of conversion, that restoration lies somewhere in the future. I wrote *The Conversion Experience* in part as a text for teaching in the RCIA. Its systematic use in the restored catechumenate could begin to educate both the RCIA teams and the catechumens to the practical demands of an initial and ongoing, integral, five-fold conversion.

Kilian McDonnell has demonstrated that in the catechumenate's heyday, i.e., during its first four centuries, in three different ritual traditions and in four different places in the Roman empire, those conducting the elect through the process of conversion expected the charisms to manifest themselves in the neophytes during the rite of initiation itself, either during baptism or in the Eucharist which followed it. If the restored catechumenate could ever successfully introduce not only new converts but existing Eucharistic communities to the full demands of Christian conversion, including its fulfillment in a Pentecostal moment when one knows and responds to the Breath's empowering charismatic call to service, then the restored catechumenate might begin to fulfill the dream which its early lay leaders had for the Catholic Charismatic Renewal. They, as we have seen, dreamed of a Church in which all the baptized experience, value, and share the fruits of their Pentecostal empowerment with one another.

I reached the preceding insights into the forms and dynamics of conversion in the course of trying to develop a foundational theology of conversion while teaching at the Jesuit School of Theology in Berkeley. In the chapters which follow I will try to share with the reader exactly how that theology evolved and why it took the shape it did.

Colloquy:

Wind ambush,
Arsonist of tongues,
Dove terrorist,
Encompassing Wisdom,
Gentle Mother,

> *You suckled and fondled me*
> > *but I could not see Your face,*
> *steadied my halting steps*
> > *with an invisible hand.*

I heard Your gentle voice,
> *coaxing,*
> *prodding,*
> *teaching,*
but still knew not your name.

Then, when you showed Yourself
> *clear,*
> *un-shrouded,*
> *unmistakable,*
Your star-burst of light still blinded me.

You did not care.
You did not come to flaunt Yourself,
> *but to bind me to your twin Beloved,*
> *from whom you came*
>> *and One conceived.*

They skinned my eyes,
> *and finally I saw.*

NOTE

1. *Lectio divina*, a standard form of monastic prayer, consists in the devout reading of some sacred text.

Chapter Six

Searching For A Method In
The People's Republic

I shall attempt to describe in this chapter and in those which follow how the theological system I have been creating gradually took shape during the years that I have been teaching at the Jesuit School of Theology at Berkeley (JSTB). Since in Berkeley, the attempt to create an inculturated North American theology caused me to live increasingly in the world of ideas, the story of my life increasingly coincided with how I was shaped by those ideas and tried to give shape to them.

I did not try to think systematically until I got to Berkeley because I had not begun to discover the kind of method I needed in order to do so until my last semester at Loyola University in New Orleans. As the reader will recall, in the special seminar I taught to Si Hendry, Tom Kearney, and George Lundy during that semester, I discovered for the first time Lonergan's theory of method in theology. Once the province decided to reassign me to JSTB, I resolved to test Lonergan's theory by using it.

I had adopted from Dewey the principle than any good method corrects itself as one uses it. I arrived in Berkeley wanting to see if Lonergan's method for doing theology would prove critically self-corrective. I felt attracted to exploring what Lonergan called "foundational theology," a normative theology of conversion in which conversion comes in more than one form, with only one form of conversion qualifying as religious. I sensed intuitively that the classical American philosophical tradition, with its double focus on experience and on religious experience, offered rich resources for developing such a theology. How to derive from the classical American philosophical tradition a consistent, normative language for talking about different forms of conversion in itself posed a formidable speculative challenge.

Moreover, as the reader shall see, when I actually tried to use Lonergan's method in order to do foundational thinking, I found that he had left the operational procedures of foundations and of other key functional theological specialties extremely vague. As a result, I found myself in many ways forced to create my method for thinking theologically as I went along, as the present chapter will narrate.

I also felt in an unspecified but real way genuine affinities between Peirce's logic and Lonergan's method. As far as I was concerned, Lonergan's *Method in Theology* exemplified what Royce called "applied logic," or normative reflection on the kind of operational procedures proper to different sciences and speculative disciplines. Peirce focused on formal logic, on a normative examination of inferential forms of thought, and on semiotic. Still, on several points, both Peirce and Lonergan developed analogous insights. Both held the logic of science in high respect. The later Lonergan had learned to approach God initially through religious experience, while Peirce had a strong respect for human religious experience, and especially for shared religious experience. Both valued shared systematic inquiry as the proper social context for seeking the truth. Both invoked normative thinking for discriminating between reality and illusion. I had already begun to realize that, if one added affective conversion to Lonergan's list of intellectual, moral, and religious conversion, then Peirce's normative sciences promised to throw light on the normative operational structure of those conversions which can occur outside of a religious context. Peirce's science of esthetics could yield a normative insight into affective conversion. His normative science of ethics cast light on moral conversion. His normative science of logic provided sound criteria for exploring intellectual conversion.

As I turned my face toward the Berkeley hills, all these initial insights amounted to little more than vague, abductive hunches. I felt, however, a kindling kind of excitement at the prospect of trying to clarify and verify them through philosophically rigorous theological thinking.

Where one chooses to think conditions how one finally does think. We settle into places, and then the places settle into us. If, then, one settles into a unique academic environment like the Graduate Theological Union, it will with moral inevitably condition how one goes about the doing of theology. In order, then, to understand how my theological system gradually evolved in the People's Republic of Berkeley, one needs to understand something about Berkeley itself and about the Graduate Theological Union (GTU) which took shape there.

Moreover, as the reader shall also see, Berkeley and the GTU provided the intellectually fertile ground from which the John Courtney Murray Group sprang. I have alluded before in this narrative to the Murray Group. I shall, however, postpone until the following chapter the story of how the Group came to exist, why it evolved the way it did, how I helped shape it at the same time that it shaped me, and why it played a decisive role in both stimulating and refining the theological vision I now find myself espousing.

In 1934, the same year I first saw the light, the California Province of the Society of Jesus decided to open a theologate near Alma, California, a little town in the coastal mountains south west of San Jose. West-coast Jesuit tradition has it that the super-pious provincial who presided over its founding rejoiced in a letter to Rome at the prospect of creating a center for the theological training of California Jesuits near a town named for Our Lady. If the oral-aural tradition deserves credence in this matter, then I imagine that the provincial in question was thinking of the old Latin hymn to Mary, *Alma redemptoris mater*. Unfortunately for super-piety, however, it appears that local tradition traced the name of the town to a memorable madam. Given the early history of California, the latter tradition would seem to enjoy a certain verisimilitude.

The California Jesuits constructed their theologate on a ridge of the coastal mountains in the midst of redwood forests. California boasts two species of native redwood: *sequoia sempervirens*, which populates the coastal mountains, and the *sequoia gigantea*, the giant sequoia which grows naturally only on the western slopes of the Sierra Nevadas at about six thousand feet, the normal Sierra snow line. The name "sequoia" derives from the Indian chief who created the Cherokee alphabet. I suspect that the term "*sequoia sempervirens*," or "the always-thriving sequoia," alludes to the fact that if you cut down the coastal redwoods, they simply grow back, while the fallen giants must repopulate from seeds. The coastal redwoods, which stand over 250 feet tall, top the giants in height, but the giants double the coastal redwoods in girth. The full grown coastal redwood grows to some fourteen feet in diameter at their base, while the fully grown giants reach a base diameter of over thirty feet.

I never saw Alma College in its heyday; but on one of our weekend JSTB faculty retreats which assembled at the California provincial residence and former novitiate in Los Gatos, Richard Hill, S.J., who had twice served as school president and who, in his first term, had presided over the move from Alma to Berkeley, took some of us faculty on a tour of the old place. None of the Jesuit houses of study I had seen could have matched its setting of rolling ridges and soaring redwoods. The old buildings did not seem to have any special architectural merit; but Alma college had one trait in common with almost all the other American Jesuit houses of study I had visited: its rustic setting.

Alma College served as the theologate for both the California and Oregon provinces of the American Assistancy. The California mission of the Society began with a group of Jesuits from the Turin province in Italy laboring for Christ at the end of the Oregon trail. When the California gold rush began in 1849, the Italian Jesuits quickly perceived the importance of one of the greatest human migrations in recorded history. Jesuits always feel more at home in large population centers. The Turin Jesuits in Oregon fit the pattern. They wrote Rome for permission to move their mission from Oregon to California. They posted the letter and then promptly took the next boat for San Francisco. West coast oral tradition has it that the Roman response did not reach them until two years later. It forbade them categorically from moving their mission to California and instructed them to stay put in Oregon. The Italians wrote back that they had already moved the mission and had in an incredibly short time founded two colleges. Rome responded that, under the circumstances, they could remain in California. The story perhaps best illustrates the principle enshrined in the Constitutions of the Jesuit order, that the people on the spot find themselves best situated to take the right decisions. The story also calls into question whether the development of instant planetary communication with imperial Rome has especially benefitted the Church. Finally, the tale of the founding of the California province suggests that Italian serendipity found the free-wheeling spirit of the California gold rush congenial.

Of all the Jesuit theologates, the Alma faculty, in the wake of Vatican II's call to update the Church and the Society, first conceived of moving Jesuit theological education from the silvan splendor of rolling mountains and teeming redwood forests to an urban, ecumenical theological center next to one of the greatest Universities in the United States. At the same time that the California Jesuits were contemplating decamping to a more stimulating theological environment, John Dillenberger was in the process of organizing The Graduate Theological Union in Berkeley. One of the Protestant observers at Vatican II, John returned from the council convinced that the time had come to do something about getting the churches back together.

John found on Holy Hill, to the north of the University of California at Berkeley (UCB) campus, three theological faculties. The Pacific School of Religion (PSR) outranked the others in age and had no specific denominational affiliation. It boasted an ecumenical, Protestant faculty. The episcopal faculty, The Church Divinity School of the Pacific (CDSP), stood east of PSR on Le Conte Ave., the street which ascends from the south-west the steepest slope of Holy Hill. The Starr King School for the Ministry (SKSM), a Unitarian faculty, faced CDSP on the northern side of Le Conte.

As he coaxed The Graduate Theological Union into existence, John cast his nets wider than Holy Hill. The American Baptist Seminary of the West (ABSW) lay on the south side of the UCB campus. The Pacific Lutheran Theological Seminary (PLTS) rose on the top of the Berkeley hills and terminated Marin Ave., one of the most abrupt streets in hilly Berkeley. The Lutheran school has a spectacular view of Tilden Regional Park, one of the many public parks which protect large stretches of the East Bay hills from urban sprawl. The Presbyterian faculty, San Francisco Theological Seminary (SFTS), stands on a smaller hilltop in the town of San Anselmo, in Marin County, north of the Golden Gate Bridge. These faculties too John persuaded to join the emerging Graduate Theological Union.

As the Graduate Theological Union took shape, John successfully cajoled the University of California at Berkeley into collaborating in the venture. As the GTU took shape, it would award both masters degrees and doctorates in theology. The graduate programs in theology include standard programs like Biblical exegesis, Church history, and systematic theology; but the Union also awards several "religion-and" degrees: religion and psychology, religion and society, art and religion. On the committees of students taking "religion-and" degrees, a member of the UCB faculty from the relevant secular discipline would ordinarily serve on both comprehensive and dissertation committees and would thus supply the needed "and." UCB also agreed to share library facilities with the GTU. The combined libraries of UCB and GTU provide an incredibly rich and accessible research resource for creative theological thinking. Eventually, for a fee, the University opened its athletic facilities to GTU students.

Daniel O'Hanlon, S.J., a member of the Alma faculty, made the first contacts with the faculties atop Holy Hill. While at Alma and again in Berkeley, Dan persistently pushed at the margins of Catholic theology in order to broaden them and make them both more flexible and more inclusive. He had done his dissertation on the theology of Paul Tillich and used it as a talking point with the Protestant faculties in Berkeley, to which he commuted regularly as long as the Jesuit campus remained in its silvan setting in the coastal range. Ecumenically involved more than any other member of the Alma faculty, after the Jesuit school moved to Berkeley, Dan also showed the first active interest in dialogue among world religions.

From the time that John Dillenberger learned about the possibility of the Jesuit faculty moving its operation from Alma to Berkeley, he welcomed the move and did everything he could to encourage it. John dreamed of a truly ecumenical theological center; and he wanted a strong Jesuit presence within the GTU in order to keep it from degenerating into a liberal Protestant enclave.

Harry Corcoran, S.J., the then dean of Alma College, presided over the nuts and bolts of the Jesuit move. I lived for eleven years in the same community with Harry at 2536 Virginia Street in Berkeley where I learned to love, admire, and revere him. Without his leadership and candor, the move to the Berkeley hills might never have happened; but I never once heard him take personal credit for JSTB's presence in the GTU. Instead, he insisted that he could have never brought the move off without the support of the entire Alma faculty.

Not everyone on the Alma faculty did initially support the hejira to Berkeley. The faculty did, however, agree to discuss the move. Harry hired the Arthur D. Little people to facilitate the discussion. In their summary report of what they heard the Alma faculty saying, the Little facilitators concluded that the Alma faculty as a whole would support the move if it involved the equivalent of transporting the Alma campus bodily into Berkeley. That would have required buying several blocks of the city of Berkeley, razing them to the ground, and constructing upon the vacant space an elaborate seminary complex complete with gymnasium and swimming pool. One may find an architect's sketch of this grandiose and utopian facility in the archives of the Jesuit School. When Pedro Arrupe, S.J., the General of the order, got wind of the Arthur D. Little plan, it turned him temporarily against the move to Berkeley, even though he had originally favored it. The construction of a huge seminary complex in the midst of the People's Republic never amounted to anything more than a pipe dream; but Harry claimed that the meeting which generated that particular fantasy played an important role in consolidating the Alma faculty's support behind the move to Berkeley. It only took abandoning the Little plan for more realistic urban housing in order to recommit Fr. Arrupe to the move.

Harry, however, had other obstacles to overcome before the move could actually take place. The provincial of the California province wanted the Alma faculty to move the theologate to the University of San Francisco, not to the GTU. Bishop Begin, the first bishop of Oakland, also balked initially at welcoming hoards of Jesuits into his diocese. The Alma faculty, however, had a warm and supportive friend in the Chancellor of the Oakland Diocese, John Cummins. John had attended UCB, felt at home and unthreatened in things academic, and from the beginning supported enthusiastically the idea of developing a major ecumenical center in the Oakland diocese. As the second bishop of Oakland, he has continued to endorse with the same enthusiasm a strong Catholic presence in the GTU. Once both Bishop Begin, with help from John, and Pedro Arrupe agreed to Jesuit participation in the GTU, Harry did a successful end run around the California provincial, who, of course, bowed to the General's decision.

Prior to the move, Harry had never hobnobbed with Protestants in any kind of systematic way, although he threw himself into ecumenism with great gusto once he wet his feet. The foot-wetting took place at an initial dinner meeting with the Dillenbergers, John and his then wife, Jane. As Harry drove the San Francisco peninsula in order to make that initial contact, he felt a certain anxiety. Harry had particular feelings about a good belt before dinner, and he faced with gloom the prospect of having to dine with tea-totaling Protestants. Harry had his first lesson in Protestant diversity when, to his immense relief, he found the Dillenbergers already seated at their restaurant table sipping martinis. To Harry, the sight augured well for future collaboration with the GTU.

All the negotiating took time. As a result, by the time Alma College migrated to Berkeley, two other Catholic faculties has joined the GTU before it. The Dominicans had both a philosophical and theological faculty at St. Albert's College in Oakland just south of the Berkeley city limit. There the former Beat poet William Everson/Brother Antoninus lived and wrote for fifteen years. Bill Everson also became a friend of the Albert Gelpi family; and through them I too made his acquaintance. Once the Dominicans joined the GTU, their faculty became The Dominican School of Philosophy and Theology (DSPT). DSPT at first remained in Oakland, until Patrick Labelle, O.P., became its president and moved the Dominican theological facility to the very top of Holy Hill across Le Conte Ave. from PSR and from the GTU library. The Franciscan faculty occupied a building at the intersection of Le Conte and Euclid and took the name The Franciscan School of Theology (FST). When the Alma faculty moved to Berkeley, they transformed themselves into The Jesuit School of Theology at Berkeley (JSTB). The arrival of the Jesuits brought the total number of theological faculties comprising the GTU to nine.

As the reader may have already surmised, given all the alphabetical acronyms popularly used in the GTU–UCB, PSR, DSPT, ABSW, FST, SKSM, PLTS, SFTS, CDSP, JSTB–working or studying on Holy Hill feels a bit like swimming in alphabet soup. When I joined the JSTB faculty I was working for the ISW of JSTB of the GTU.

Although, among the theologates of the American Assistancy, the Alma faculty had first conceived the idea of joining a major ecumenical center, the time it took to negotiate permission to abandon Alma for Berkeley made it the last of the United States theologates actually to make the change. The delay also meant that the Alma faculty became part of the GTU in the late sixties, at the height of the on-campus protest against the Vietnam War. The Jesuits arrived in Berkeley in time for Gov. Ronald Reagan's tear-gas bombing of the University students.

These circumstances, however, proved providential. Anti-war protest centered in Sproul Plaza, on the south side of the UCB campus. The fraternities and sororities which had settled on the north side of campus atop Holy Hill either were disintegrating for lack of funds and interest or were moving to the south side of campus for a bigger slice of the action. As the Greeks, both male and female, abandoned their residences, the Jesuit community acquired them together with the apartment buildings which now comprise JSTB. Moreover, the Jesuits did so for a fraction of what the construction of a giant seminary complex in the middle of a major urban center would have cost.

The JSTB buildings cluster within a few blocks of each other along four streets on Holy Hill: Virginia Street, LeConte Ave., Ridge Road, and Le Roy Ave. Le Conte Ave. took its name from one of the original professors at UCB, when the University consisted of two Victorian piles rising starkly from the middle of a treeless cow pasture. One of these original buildings, Old South Hall, still survives and houses the Education Department. It stands to the south-west of the University campanile and looks for all the world like something out of a Charles Addams cartoon. Old North Hall has long since perished. In those very buildings, Le Conte had taught Josiah Royce, one of the United States' greatest philosophers. Le Conte had also sided with John Muir in his public debate with Josiah Whitney concerning the geological cause of Yosemite Valley. Both Le Conte and Whitney taught geology. Whitney attributed Yosemite's massive, three-thousand-foot cliffs to faulting. Muir, the self-made naturalist and college dropout, insisted that only glaciers could have sculpted such U-shaped valleys and cliffs. LeConte supported the college dropout against his university colleague and proved right. Muir won the argument with Whitney by going to Alaska, studying glaciers, and returning to the Sierras, where he found his first glacier on Merced peak in the Clark range. A native of Georgia, LeConte loved Yosemite as passionately as Muir; and, after retiring from UCB, he, like Muir, lived there. He also died there, while leading a hike through the splendor of the "Mountains of Light."[1] One could find a worse way to go. A memorial to him stands in Yosemite Valley.

Due east of the Golden Gate, stretching upward into the hills of the coastal range and westward through the flatlands toward the Bay, lies the People's Republic of Berkeley. Most Americans still imagine Berkeley as a seething caldron of political radicalism and ferment; but the Berkeley of the sixties has long since ceased to exist. When I came to JSTB in the early seventies, a shallow rhetorical remnant of sixties political radicalism survived. Sproul Plaza still hosted a variety of political orators, several evangelical street preachers, guerilla theater, professional street people, and an assortment of odd balls. With the abolition of the draft, however, the heart of the protest movement of the sixties had died. Only the empty rhetoric survived. The adoration of the Golden Calf, a mocking response to the fundamentalism of the street preachers, still unfolded from time to time on Telegraph Avenue. Bearers would carry down Telegraph a papier-maché effigy of a calf painted gold, while mock worshipers cow-towed before it. Today all remnants of the political radicalism of the sixties have vanished. Hints of that radicalism did, however, begin to surface with George W. Bush's second Gulf War.

The city of Berkeley remains, however, the most tolerant and informal community in which I have ever lived. Formal dress looks odd in Berkeley and marks one as someone from out of town. Once in the mid-seventies, when I lived in a temporary, rented Jesuit residence on the south side of the UCB campus around the block from the Holy Spirit Newman Center, I was returning home on the College bus, when an elderly couple dressed completely in white boarded and took the two empty seats in front of me. When I say that they had dressed in white, I mean that absolutely everything visible that they wore had the color white: white shoes, white hats, white dress, white suit, white vest, white tie, white socks and stockings. I suspect that they were on their way to a wedding. Their apparel alone would have marked them as out-of-towners. So did the fact that the two sat bolt upright. Neither back touched the seat. Their heads kept swivelling back and forth as their eyes scanned the bus suspiciously. One could see written on their faces the terror that they felt; and I knew that they were saying to themselves: "We are actually sitting on a public vehicle in Berkeley."

Just before I got off the bus, it stopped at a playing field which belonged to the University. That particular playing field has since been converted into an ugly parking lot. There men and women students were playing baseball. In those days, the men all wore long hair. The white-clad woman looked out of the window, poked her husband in the ribs with her elbow, and pointed surreptitiously with her thumb to the students at their game. The husband looked out of the window, gazed at his wife in disbelief, and said, "What, what are they doing?"

She replied, "I, I think they're playing baseball."

The husband snorted, "Well, I guess you just don't know what you are going to see next." That Berkeley students would do anything as all-American as play baseball clearly did not fit this couple's stereotype of the way UCB students behave. Presumably, they should have been taking dope, having sex, and plotting the overthrow of the United States government. Such stereotypes die hard; but not for decades have I seen any activity in Berkeley which smacks of sixties activism.

The People's Republic today seems to these tired old eyes largely indistinguishable from any other American university city, except, of course, for its spectacular setting as it nestles in the stream-washed Berkeley hills directly across from the Golden Gate. As in other university towns, town-gown fracases flare up from time to time. The student population comes and goes, of course. The citizens of Berkeley give the population more stability and, apart from a veneer of liberalism, resemble most other middle-class Americans. When on occasion Berkeley politicians spout radical rhetoric, their behavior belies their words. In the eighties, for example, the Radical Party finally captured control of the Berkeley city government. The evening news televised their swearing in at City Hall. When the new incumbents reached the part of the oath which committed them to upholding the United States Constitution, the room burst into laughter. Once ensconced in power, however, the Radicals did–precisely nothing. As far as I could tell, business in Berkeley remained very much as usual.

The remarkable tolerance of the Berkeley citizenry does, however, make them unflappable. An anecdote may illustrate what I mean. One year the Jesuit community gave a costume party on Halloween night. Not everyone dressed in a costume; but some members of the community did. Hal Ellis, S.J., one of three wonderful Jesuit brothers in our community, decided that he would come as Little Bo Peep. He rented a wig with long golden curls and somehow procured a flouncy blue dress and a shepherd's crook. Thus appareled, he walked the two blocks from Claver House, where he lived, to Chardin House, where we were celebrating the party. At the corner of Le Roy Ave. and Ridge Road, a car pulled up to ask for directions. Confronted with an aged Little Bo Peep in drag, this Berkeley driver never even batted an eye. "Pardon me," he said matter-of-factly to Little Bo Peep, "can you tell me how to get to such and such a place?" Little Bo Peep gave him directions, and he drove off as though close encounters with an elderly Little Bo Peep in drag happened every day.

Like Lee Phillips at Grand Coteau, Hal used to talk in Malapropisms. Lee regularly mangled the English language; but Hal's eloquence made him a veritable poet of Malaprop. The JSTB secretaries called his *mots* "Halapropisms" and kept lists of them. Whenever Hal came out with a new one, the secretaries would add it to the most recent list and post them on the school bulletin board as soon as Hal had filled a page. This he did about once a week. He said things like, "So-and-so really gets under my goat." Asked about changing clocks for daylight-saving time, Hal replied, "That's easy to remember. It's 'Spring forward and fall down.'" Outraged at a movie poster on Euclid Ave. which he regarded as pornographic, Hal denounced it censoriously, saying, "It was worse than those centerfolds in Lifeboy."

On the Halloween evening when he dressed as Little Bo Peep, Halaprop poetry soared to new heights of eloquence. After giving directions to the unflappable Berkeley driver, Hal proceeded to the costume party at Chardin House, where his entrance caused a major sensation. The scholastics crowded around him complimenting him on his get up and asking him whom he represented. Confounding Little Boy Blue and Little Bo Peep, Hal replied, "Oh, I'm Little Boy Peep go blow your sheep." But I digress. I was using the encounter between a citizen of Berkeley with Little Bo Peep in drag as an example of the attitude of tolerance which still pervades the People's Republic.

The University of California no doubt contributes to the tolerance of Berkeleyites. I experience Berkeley as a place where ideas are always happening. On any given night, one can attend any number of presentations on a wide spectrum of topics. At the GTU and JSTB I found the same willingness to look at any theological question or issue. I also discovered to my satisfaction that our school administration encouraged writing and publication.

Moreover, I soon established a classroom pattern that allowed me to combine teaching and research. I offered seminars in areas of theology about which I knew nothing but which I desired to master. I began, for example, doing research in Christology by reading through several contemporary Christologies and then discussing them the following year in an advanced Christology seminar. When I had read my way through a field of theology like Christology, I would then transform my research into a lecture course and the lecture course into a manuscript which I would then teach and refine for several years before sending it off to a publisher. In what follows, I shall describe how the application of this strategy to one related area of theology after another slowly, incrementally molded a theological method and system that speaks with a Yankee idiom.

While the city of Berkeley provided the immediate environment for my professional work, I became quickly enthralled with the natural beauty of the state of California. The San Francisco Bay area abounds with national, state, and regional parks which I explored every Saturday with any friends and students interested in enjoying their incredible beauty and sublime prospects. I also began sponsoring excursions into California's many National Parks. The sublimity of the California landscape worked its way into my very bones. Like John Muir, I fell in love with the Sierra Nevadas at first sight. So often did I frequent Yosemite, Kings Canyon, Sequoia National Park, Death Valley, Lassen Volcanic National Park, and the Pinnacles Wilderness that, whenever I returned to them, they felt like second homes. Indeed, I finally reached the point of feeling as much at home in the wilderness as in civilization.

I also immersed myself in California history. I explored the Gold Rush country, saw the site of Sutter's Mill and where James Marshall discovered the first nugget of gold that set off the greatest human migration in history. I

The Cheerful Charlies on the summit of Mt. Whitney: from left to right: front row: James Lambert, S.J., the author, George Menke, S.J., John Stacer, S.J.; back row: Earl Muller, S.J., Louis Lambert, S.J., Patrick Madigan, S.J., Joseph Tetlow, S.J.

visited and studied the history of the California missions. I read Josiah Royce's history of early California and followed with fascination the unfolding of Kevin Starr's cultural history of the Golden State. For all practical purposes I became a Californian.

No doubt the California landscape itself influenced the way I think. The Golden State teems with broad, sweeping vistas which inspired in me as they had in Josiah Royce a fascination with the big picture and with the interconnectedness of all things created. Metaphysics comes easy to one who has stood on Cloud's Rest and on the summit of Mt. Whitney. As the philosophical and theological system which I crafted in California took shape, I attempted to endow it with a breadth of vision reminiscent of the sublime vistas in which the Golden State abounds and which daily dazzled my eyes and expanded my heart.

In my initial attempts to develop an inculturated North American foundational theology of conversion I faced three interrelated challenges. First of all, I had to develop a practical method for constructing a normative account of the forms and dynamics of conversion. I found both interesting and worth exploring Lonergan's attempt to ground the reconstruction of a theological tradition in a normative account of the conversion which founds that tradition.

Lonergan also presupposed that conversion comes in more than one form. I deemed these two methodological suggestions the most creative aspect of his theory of method in theology.

When, however, I studied what Lonergan had to say about the operations which constitute such foundational theological thinking, I found him laconic in the extreme. Lonergan instructed prospective foundational theologians to use transcendental philosophical notions, categories derived from secular sciences which study human religious experience, and theological categories. All well and good; but how does one go about transforming categories derived from such diverse speculative disciplines into a unified, logically consistent account of how conversion ought to happen? After all, philosophy, the positive sciences, and theology have very different presuppositions and different methodologies.

Clearly, if I expected to develop a foundational theology as Lonergan envisaged it, I needed to specify operational procedures for doing cross-disciplinary theological thinking. I agreed with Lonergan that contemporary theologians needed to engage in such thinking in their speculative approach to as complex an experience as conversion; but I found no hint in the text of *Method in Theology* concerning the operations which allow one to combine the results of different disciplines into a logical, coherent, applicable, and adequate theory of conversion.

I faced a two other speculative challenges if I expected to succeed in doing *inculturated*, foundational, theological thinking. I needed to derive from the philosophical tradition in this country a consistent way of talking about experience, about religious experience, and about the normative shape of different kinds of conversion. Finally, having laid a normative foundation for thinking theologically, I needed to construct upon it a theological system.

At the same time, I knew perfectly well that not all American philosophers adopted the same method, viewed reality from the same angle, or agreed in their philosophical accounts of reality. Clearly, in dealing with the American philosophical tradition, I would have to start making choices about which insights I endorsed and which I rejected. I felt less daunted here because, in my dialectical argument with that tradition, I had already begun taking personal stands on debated issues.

My dialectical analysis of the development of the philosophical tradition in the United States had also convinced me of the fact that the classical American philosophical tradition wrestled with recurring issues which endowed it with a certain coherence. That fact suggested that the tradition as a whole ought to provide resources for constructing a consistent philosophy of experience, of religious experience, and of conversion.

For example, even though multiple dualisms marred both colonial Enlightenment philosophy and the Transcendental visions of Emerson and Parker, after Brownson one finds a growing consensus that sound philosophy needs to avoid all forms of dualistic thinking. Dualism conceives interrelated realities in such a way that their relationship to one another remains subsequently unintelligible. Moreover, I also sensed an emerging consensus in the American tradition about how to avoid dualistic thinking. One needed to conceive reality from the beginning in relational, functional terms which included both positive and negative relationships.

Consensus on the need to avoid dualism and on the strategy for doing so led to a third emerging consensus among U.S. philosophers: one needed to abandon substance philosophy and replace its essentialistic understanding of reality with a relational, functional metaphysics. Philosophical essentialism confuses the "how" of experience and of cognition with its "what." The "how"of experience consists in the whole spectrum of human evaluative responses: sensations, emotions, memories, images, abstract concepts, ideals. The "what" of experience and cognition consists of interacting persons and things. One creates an "essence" when one abstracts how one senses or perceives some object of knowledge from the reality one knows and from the mind which does the knowing. Dictionaries catalogue such essences alphabetically. Essentialism errs by transforming evaluative responses, the way we become present to reality, into the metaphysical principles which constitute the objects of knowledge themselves. Of all the American thinkers I had studied, it seemed to me that Peirce had succeeded best in avoiding the two major philosophical fallacies which dogged classical and medieval philosophy: namely, essentialism and dualism.

Jonathan Edwards in his *Treatise Concerning Religious Affections* had enunciated another theme to which major U.S. philosophers returned again and again: namely, a philosophical focus on experience with the result that the term "experience" itself functioned as a central and integrating philosophical category. Think of the Transcendental fascination with imaginative, intuitive forms of experience and of William James's *Principles of Psychology* and *Varieties of Religious Experience*. John Dewey wrote two "experience-and" books: *Experience and Nature* and *Art as Experience*. In those books, he broadened the philosophical term "experience" to include every possible human evaluative response. Whitehead, however, extended the meaning of "experience" even further by transforming it into a metaphysical term. He did so by including the object of experience within experience. Accordingly, his revised subjectivist principle asserted that "apart from the experiencing of subjects, there is nothing, nothing, nothing, bare nothingness." I have already reflected on these issues in an earlier chapter.

I had already decided to replace Whitehead's nominalistic, dipolar construct of experience with a triadic, realistic, relational metaphysics of experience derived from Peirce's philosophy. At the same time, I knew that I could not just parrot Peirce. The metaphysics I needed to develop would have to go beyond anything Peirce himself had said; but I thought that I could develop basic Peircean insights while remaining faithful to their fundamental thrust. I saw that a synechistic[2] metaphysics of human experience would have to replace classical "faculty" psychology.[3] Peirce's synechism seemed to me to offer a developmental account of the human which better accorded with the results of contemporary psychology.

Jonathan Edwards introduced yet another theme which a variety of Americans developed in different but convergent or complementary ways: namely, in his *Treatise Concerning Religious Affections*, Edwards had assimilated religious and esthetic experience. He did not equate the two; but he did find a significant esthetic component in the initial consent of faith and in much of human religious experience. Emerson, Brownson, Peirce, and Dewey had all played variations on this theme. Moreover, as I indicated in chapter III, I had already grasped the possibility of using Peirce's normative science of esthetics in order to describe the logic of justifying faith by amplifying Peirce's esthetics with insights from Royce's philosophy of loyalty, by invoking Edwards's incarnational esthetic in order to contextualize these philosophical insights theologically, and by blending in my own insights into Jesus' vision of the kingdom in order to explain in greater detail than Edwards had the practical demands of justifying faith.[4]

I recognized as well that major U.S. thinkers replaced the virtual infinity of the human intellect which Transcendental Thomism naively celebrates with a more modest and, in my judgment, more accurate account of how the human mind actually works. The philosophical tradition in this country, beginning with the post-Transcendental Emerson, preferred to portray the human mind as radically finite, not as virtually infinite. The finitude of the human mind means that in the search for truth we need to rely on the experience and insights of other minds than our own in order to correct our oversights. That transforms the search for truth into a search for consensus grounded in evidence.

Portraying the human mind as finite and human thought as social and dialogic made good experiential and scientific sense to me. Having taught all my professional life, I can honestly say that I have never encountered a human mind imbued with the virtually infinite thirst for truth which Transcendental Thomism describes. On the contrary, in my experience, ego inertia better typifies human thought processes than a virtually infinite thirst for Truth. Humans do not thank you for asking them to revise pet beliefs. They tend rather to resent it when you suggest that they need to rethink cherished assertions and prejudices.

I used, for example, to attend the seminar on Dialectic in The American Academy of Religion. It mostly contained devotees of Bernard Lonergan, one of the most eloquent proponents of the virtual infinity of the human intellect and of its insatiable desire for more and more Truth and Being. I remember suggesting in the last meeting of the seminar I attended that, far from having provided an unrevisable starting place for thinking, Lonergan's own epistemology needed significant revision, including his normative account of how the mind works. I felt he had too narrow an understanding of experience, a woefully inadequate appreciation of esthetic experience, and too logically vague an understanding of what he called understanding and judgment. My remarks produced what I like to call the turd in the punchbowl effect. An embarrassed silence greeted my lack of Lonerganian philosophical orthodoxy. Finally, one of the group, who apparently spoke for the rest, said, "Oh please don't say that. We have all of that nailed down."

I felt silently amused that these staunch defenders of the mind's insatiable thirst for more and more Truth seemed unwilling to practice what they preached. No infinite questioning for them, only the dogged refusal to revise pet philosophical fallacies. They preferred to quote chapter and verse from the Master rather than question what seemed to me clear inadequacies in his epistemology and metaphysics. Their response sounded in my ears more like ego inertia than Lonergan's celebrated "unrestricted desire to know."

My study of the American philosophical tradition had, then, given me important clues about the shape an inculturated metaphysics of experience might take. Formulating such a metaphysics according to the principles of Peirce's logic still posed, however, a formidable speculative challenge. Peirce's theory of inference forbids one to claim any *a priori* necessity for a fallible metaphysical hypothesis. I had no doubt that I could, as Peirce himself had done in his final lecture on pragmatism in 1903, verify, in a preliminary way, a triadic, realistic, relational construct of experience in an analysis of the human act of perception; but Peirce's logic also required the ongoing verification of any fallible metaphysical abduction in the results of the idioscopic sciences. As the reader will recall, in Peirce's logic, philosophy exemplifies coenoscopic thinking because it reflects on lived social experience as lived, while the idioscopic sciences–like physics, chemistry, biology, astronomy–focus on limited realms of experience and often use both mathematical measurement and special instruments which expand the frontiers of human sensation and perception.

I also recognized the need to expand Peirce's division of the idioscopic sciences to include what Lonergan called "scholarship." Scholarship thinks in an organized way about reality and invokes different methods; but it eschews mathematical measurement and specialized instrumentation in formulating its theories. History exemplifies scholarship. Historians face two speculative challenges. They must on the basis of the surviving evidence formulate as accurate a chronology as possible of the historical events they are studying. Then historians must verify or falsify in that chronology their theories about why history went this way rather than that.

Theological scholarship in retrieving a religious tradition tries to give as accurate an account as possible of the chronological events which shape a religious tradition. Then it must verify or falsify in those revelatory events its theories about what that religion signifies. If one includes theology in scholarship, as one must, then my fallible metaphysics of experience had not only to interpret the results of the natural sciences but also the historical and eschatological events which reveal the Christian God. That meant that it would have to interpret complex and mysterious realities like the Incarnation and the Trinity. No small speculative challenge, that.

Besides completing Lonergan's account of method in theology as well as formulating and verifying a metaphysics of experience, I also faced formidable theological challenges. I had to derive from my account of experience a verifiable, normative insight into the forms and dynamics of conversion. I decided that, if I intended to take experience as my integrating metaphysical category, I needed to start exploring theologically those religious realities which we experience most immediately. That meant that I needed to begin to lay new theological foundations by reflecting on personal religious experience, since, as self-conscious, we humans experience ourselves most immediately, even though we do so in a transactional relationship with sense objects and with other persons. Because we experience ourselves in faith as having a graced transaction with a self-revealing, self-communicating God, any account of the self-conscious, transactional human person must deal with the issues raised by the debate over the relation between human nature and supernatural grace. In 1978, I had dealt with these issues in a preliminary and inadequate way in *Experiencing God*.

Since in a religious context, we next experience most immediately shared worship, my theological understanding of nature and grace had to account as well for shared Christian prayer: both devotional, charismatic prayer and sacramental worship. This I attempted in a preliminary but inadequate way in *Charism and Sacrament*, which I published in 1976.

Next, I saw, I would have to begin to give an account of the God we encounter in worship. In *Charism and Sacrament* I linked the real presence of Christ in the Eucharist and in all forms of sacramental worship to the action of the divine Breath. I still defend that position. No one has ever seen the Father, and Jesus now lives with the Father in heaven. Christians experience

God most immediately through faith and prayer in the empowering enlightenment of God's Breath; but one cannot talk about the reality of God's Breath without giving an account of the Trinity. In *The Divine Mother*, I attempted in 1984 to do precisely that.

By the time I had completed *The Divine Mother*, however, I had already realized that I needed to revise both my account of the human person and my sacramental theology. With Charles Peirce I regard all human thought as fallible. I also endorse the wisdom of William Ernest Hocking, who argued that in constructing a fallible metaphysical hypothesis, one needs to alternate between close investigations of particular problems and one's metaphysical account of reality in general. I invoked this principle in writing my first three essays in foundational theology. Since each study caused me to revise my metaphysics of experience, by the time I had completed *The Divine Mother*, both my account of experience and my construct of conversion had evolved considerably. That alone would have forced a rethinking of the relationship between nature and grace.

In addition, however, as the reader shall soon see, in writing *Experiencing God* and *Charism and Sacrament*, I felt preoccupied with methodological issues. In order to rethink trinitarian theology, I found myself forced to deal both with Biblical pneumatology and with the dialectical development of twenty centuries of trinitarian speculation. As a result, in writing *The Divine Mother* I invoked for the first time in a systematic way the insights of the functional specialties of interpretation, of history, and of dialectic in order to develop a systematic foundational position. I had not done the same in writing either *Experiencing God* or *Charism and Sacrament*. In both books I had dealt almost exclusively with contemporary issues. That meant that in both studies I had failed to deal in a systematic way with the relevant dialectical issues raised by the Christian tradition. That omission forced me to rethink my theological anthropology and account of the Christian sacraments with greater exegetical, historical, and dialectical thoroughness.

Before I attempted to do either, however, Hocking's principle of alternation required me to stand back from all three studies and explore the relationship among the conclusions I had reached in writing them. As a methodological principle, Hocking's principle of alternation requires the speculative mind to alternate between close study of a particular problem or complex of problems and one's metaphysical theory of the whole. I did the latter in 1988 in a number of essays which appeared in *Grace as Transmuted Experience and Social Process*.

The first methodological principle I had derived from Lonergan–namely, that theology mediates between a religion and the culture in which that religion roots itself–required me to explore the relationship between Christianity and the cultural tradition in the United States. That tradition, however, had forced me to call into question the logical, anthropological, and metaphysical presuppositions which grounded Lonergan's theory of method in theology.

Frank Oppenheim had wisely urged me to situate my emerging position with respect to both Rahner and Lonergan. I had published my critique of Rahner in two articles in *Spirituality Today* (1983) and had republished them in *Grace as Transmuted Experience and Social Process*. I saw that before I could do any revision of my emerging foundational scheme, I needed to indicate in a preliminary but systematic way how my understanding of theological method differed from Lonergan's. This I did in *Inculturating North American Theology* in 1988. New clarity about how to go about the task of foundational thinking bore fruit in *Committed Worship*, my updated sacramental theology, which appeared in 1993.

In writing *The Divine Mother*, I had found myself forced to concede that one cannot do Trinitarian theology without coordinating it with Christology. In that same work, I had sketched in a preliminary way the construct of the hypostatic union I wanted to defend. I realized, however, that I could not justify that construct without dealing systematically with the issues raised by the complex historical development of Christology. That meant that in formulating a foundational Christology I needed to deal not only with New Testament Christology but with two thousand years of post-Biblical Christological speculation. The very prospect of attempting that Herculean labor left me daunted. One cannot deal adequately with New Testament Christology without dealing with virtually all of the New Testament. Moreover, I would have to figure out how to do that specifically as a foundational theologian, not as an exegete or interpretative theologian. Moreover, the sheer bulk of Christological speculation made dealing with the whole of post-Biblical trinitarian theology seem like child's play. As things turned out, formulating a foundational Christology took me over twenty years of research and reflection. Even though I had grown acutely aware by this time of the many flaws in my argument in *Experiencing God*, I did not want to revise it until I had formulated a systematic foundational Christology, because I anticipated that finding a verifiable way of thinking the hypostatic union would yield new insights into my understanding of human nature and therefore of the relation between human nature and supernatural grace. That hunch proved true.

All this refining and qualification of my emerging foundational system led to the fluke of my publishing five volumes in the year 2001. First of all, to the dismay of those who read my theology, I could not deal adequately with the whole of New Testament Christology and with the issues raised by two thousand years of post-Biblical Christology in less than three volumes.

Secondly, in the year 2000, I had brushed up some of the results of the dialectical study of the American philosophical tradition I had done in New Orleans between 1969 and 1973 and had published it as *Varieties of Transcendental Experience*. In the conclusion of that work, I called for the creation of a fallibilistic metaphysics of experience. In some class notes, I had already drafted a dialectical analysis of the issues raised by traditional speculation concerning nature and grace. Once revised, it formed the first part of my updated theological anthropology. It took a while to find a publisher who would undertake a three-volume work in Christology; and it took more time to proofread all three volumes. While doing that, I had successfully revised my theological anthropology in *The Gracing of Human Experience*, which appeared in 2001. That work also did something I had called for in the conclusion of *Varieties of Transcendental Experience*. In it, with considerable help from Peirce, I had formulated a logically and philosophically defensible metaphysics which avoided the objections to metaphysical thinking raised by deconstructionist post-modernism. The Liturgical Press had produced an elegant edition of *Varieties*. Since *The Gracing* developed themes in that earlier work, I also sent it to The Liturgical Press. Since the editors in Collegeville had found a book club willing to market both books as a set, they rushed the production of *The Gracing of Human Experience* and brought it out in 2001, the same year in which *The Firstborn of Many: A Christology for Converting Christians* appeared.

Moreover, it took little effort to update my understanding of theological method on the basis of what I had learned in writing *The Firstborn*. My study in method took the form of a slim little volume called *Peirce and Theology: Essays in the Authentication of Doctrine* (2001). As the title of that work indicates, formulating a Christology, a trinitarian theology, a sacramental theology, and a revised theological anthropology verifiable in the historical and eschatological events which reveal the Christian God had forced me in my reflections on theological method to come to terms with the relationship between foundations and doctrines. Since Lonergan had left shrouded in vagueness the operational procedures for doing foundational theology and since doctrines depends on foundations for the norms it employs for authenticating some doctrines and for rejecting others, Lonergan had also left obscure the operational procedures for doing doctrinal theology. *Peirce and Theology* sought to dispel some of that obscurity. It also amplified my attempt in *The Turn to Experience in Contemporary Theology* (1994) to situate my own understanding of theological method with respect to that of other major contemporary theologians.

Amos Yong, one of the bright and rising lights among the new breed of Pentecostal theologians, kindly published in *The Journal of Pentecostal Studies* a review article of all five volumes, with a special focus on the Christology. In it he argued that charismatic prayer had formed and informed the system I was creating. In my response to his article, I thanked him and told him that he had gotten it right.

As the preceding sketch of my major publications to date indicate, my theological position has evolved over the years; but, as a position which takes experience as its root metaphor for reality requires, my philosophical, theological, and methodological position has evolved organically. The qualifications of my earlier thought which my later research and writing produced on the whole corrected and amplified it instead of negating it. In what follows, I shall try to explain first how my understanding of theological method developed. Then, in the next chapter, I shall describe how my metaphysics of experience and normative theology of conversion evolved; and, in the final chapter, I shall try to indicate the broad lines of how my theological system took shape. I begin with the question of method.

As I have already indicated, even though Lonergan grounds creative theological thinking in the functional specialty he calls "foundations," he remains laconic to a fault when it comes to naming the operations which structure normative theological thinking about conversion. He requires foundational theologians to use metaphysical, theological, scientific, and scholarly categories; but he fails to indicate how one derives an integrated account of conversion from speculative disciplines which invoke very different kinds of method and evidence. In other words, how does one get metaphysics, theology, science, and scholarship to agree about the way conversion ought to evolve?

The dialectical work I had done in the development of American philosophy had already convinced me that one could not confine oneself to invoking the transcendental notions of Being, Beauty, Truth, Goodness, and Unity in normative thinking about conversion, as Lonergan's account of foundational method apparently requires. If I as a foundational theologian drew in a systematic way on the American philosophical and theological tradition in order to develop a defensible metaphysics of experience, as I intended to do, I would have to deal with a host of complex methodological issues as well. This I began to do in the first foundational study I published: namely, *Charism and Sacrament*; and here I made my first serious methodological blunder.

Toward the end of the sixties, as I recall, *The New York Times Magazine*, published a controversial essay on the death of classical American philosophy. In it the author argued, correctly in my opinion, that language analysis was transforming itself into a narrow dogmatism in the philosophy departments in this country. First the proponents of linguistic analysis as a philosophical method saw to it that they constituted a majority in any given department of philosophy. Then they saw to it that the department hired only language analysts. Since universities in the United States had imported language analysis from Great Britain, its domination of more and more philosophy departments was having the negative effect of drowning out the kind of public philosophical discourse which had characterized classical American philosophy. The more philosophers in the United States expended all their intellectual energies on such earth-shaking issues as how to analyze "The cat is on the mat," the more irrelevant philosophy in this country made itself to the actual living of life in an increasingly complex, democratic, technocratic, capitalistic society. In my judgment, the author of the article had put his finger on a very serious problem in contemporary American education.

I disagreed with him on one point. The classical American philosophical tradition had not expired. It had simply migrated from philosophy departments to theology departments. Classical American philosophical discourse still lived in the many generations of process theologians. I decided that, if I wanted to develop a theology in dialogue with the kind of philosophical issues debated by the classical American philosophical tradition, I needed to develop my own metaphysics of experience in dialogue with contemporary process theology.

Joseph Bracken, S.J. had quite independently come to the same conclusion. He, however, conceded to Whitehead's philosophical system more than I felt willing to do. Joe has made a manful effort to move Whiteheadean process speculation away from the Unitarianism which most Protestant process theologians espouse to an orthodox trinitarian theology. In my judgment, Whitehead's philosophy needed much more radical philosophical criticism than Joe seemed willing to give it. My study of Peirce had led me to recognize that Whitehead had in fact paradoxically espoused a Platonized version of conceptual nominalism, a philosophical position which, in my opinion, Peirce's triadic realism had decisively refuted.

I decided therefore to rethink Whitehead's metaphysics of experience in the light of Peirce's logic, metaphysics, and theory of knowledge. Accordingly, I attempted to redefine the technical metaphysical language which Whitehead had developed in *Process and Reality* for talking about experience. I tried to do so in terms compatible with Peirce's triadic metaphysics. In my first two studies in foundational theology, therefore, I used technical Whiteheadean terms like "conformal feelings," "dative feelings," "physical purposes," and "conceptual feelings" but conceived the realities they designated as triadic instead of di-polar in structure.

By "conformal feelings," I meant what Peirce meant by "Secondness," the brute physical impact of one's environment upon a developing experience. By "dative feelings" I meant sensations, one's initial evaluative perception of complete or degenerate Secondness. Complete Secondness in Peirce consists of a concrete physical action and its corresponding reaction viewed, not as two distinct things, but as a single, complex, relational event. Degenerate Secondness finds exemplification in the immanent activity of living things on their own bodies. In immanent activity, action fails to evoke from another a corresponding reaction, even though it enjoys the factual concreteness of Secondness. By "dative feelings" I meant both external sensation and propriosensation. By "physical purposes" I meant the whole spectrum of positive and negative emotions as well as imaginative, intuitive thinking. By "conceptual feelings" I meant Peirce's three elemental forms of inference: abduction, deduction, and induction.

I now regard as a serious methodological blunder this early attempt on my part to adapt Whitehead's technical philosophical language in order to talk about Peirce's triadic, realistic metaphysics. I do so for two reasons. A scholarly lifetime of close study of the American philosophical tradition had made me thoroughly familiar with the technical language of both Peirce and Whitehead. I realized too late that I could not expect a similar familiarity in those who read what I wrote. Most speculative Catholic theologians in this country languish in deplorable ignorance of their own intellectual tradition. As a consequence, they found my philosophical language jargon.

I should have anticipated that response. By the time Whitehead completed the Gifford Lectures which eventually became *Process and Reality*, his arcane philosophical terminology had driven, I am told, all but two or three of his audience from the lecture hall. Moreover, I had chosen to write philosophical jargon in the ineffectual hope of opening process philosophy and theology to Peirce's subtle rethinking of metaphysics. I quickly found out that process theologians had little interest in responding to a triadic rethinking of Whiteheadean philosophy.

Process theology in the United States developed largely in response to the "death-of-God" theology of the sixties. "Death-of-God" theology had declared publicly the demise of a classical metaphysical account of God. Liberal Protestant theologians who became Whiteheadeans cheerfully buried the old metaphysical God but replaced him instead with the nominalistic, di-polar God of Alfred North Whitehead. Moreover, they endorsed Whitehead's fatal fallacy of claiming that philosophy supplies theology with its conceptual content. In other words, they embraced the traditional Liberal Protestant fallacy of rationalism. Rationalistic theology uses this or that philosophical system as a Procrustean bed into which Christian revelation must fit. In fact, the application of Peirce's logic to theological issues correctly requires one to verify or falsify one's philosophical God-talk in the historical and eschatological events which reveal the Christian God.

As a foundational theologian, I had no intention of endorsing the fallacy of rationalism. That fallacy invalidated most of the Protestant process theology

I had read. I perceived that process theologians tended to relate to Whitehead in the same way in which devotees of Lonergan tended to relate to him. The Protestant process theologians I studied on the whole refused adamantly to question the methodological and metaphysical inadequacies of Whitehead's thought and rested content for the most part to cite chapter and verse from his writings with, at best, only minor qualifications.

By the time I wrote *The Divine Mother*, I had recognized the folly of sacrificing communicability to an ineffectual attempt to dialogue with process theology. I abandoned Whiteheadean language and began the not inconsiderable task of translating Peirce's own philosophical jargon into ordinary language. As we shall see, the switch to ordinary language also led me to develop and nuance my construct of experience in ways which made it more philosophically and metaphysically rigorous.

In *Charism and Sacrament* I had made an initial and finally inadequate attempt to develop a metaphysics of experience. In *Experiencing God*, I decided to face head-on the most formidable challenge confronting any foundational theologian: namely, deriving a consistent theological account of conversion from the results of different disciplines with different vocabularies and different methodologies which nevertheless all study aspects of religious experience. This second foundational study put my emerging philosophy of experience into an initial dialogue with both theology and developmental psychology in order to develop a cross-disciplinary portrait of human nature in its relationship to divine grace. Moreover, in the final chapter of *Inculturating North American Theology* (1988), I summarized the methodology for cross-disciplinary thinking which I had created in writing *Experiencing God*.

Cross-disciplinary thinking faces two interrelated challenges. In *Inculturating North American Theology*, I called them the coordination and the interplay of categories. In formulating my cross-disciplinary account of human nature, I had in fact coordinated the categories derived from philosophy, psychology, and theology. That effort at coordination forced me to ponder how each set of categories relates to reality. The interplay of categories, on the other hand, studies how the categories from different disciplines interpret one another. Study of the interplay of categories forced me to specify the precise contribution which metaphysics, secular scientific and scholarly research, and theology make to developing a normative construct of conversion. The operations which effect the coordination and the interplay of categories provide a useable method for formulating a cross-disciplinary foundational theology. I begin by considering the coordination of categories.

The coordination of categories ponders critically their relationship to reality. In Peirce's logic, real events make categories true or false by the way they behave. I discerned four fundamental techniques for coordinating categories supplied by the different disciplines which shape foundational thinking: namely, agreement, complementarity, convergence, and dialectical reversal. The categories derived from different disciplines agree, both within the discipline which originates them and with categories from other disciplines, when they assert fundamentally the same thing about the same reality.

My philosophical construct of experience, for example, distinguishes intuitive from inferential thinking. Jean Piaget speaks of transductive thinking and contrasts it with operational thinking. Piaget, however, means by transductive thinking largely the same thing that I do when I speak of intuitive thinking. By fully operational thinking, he means what I mean by inferential thinking. Both he and I recognize a realm of non-rational, imaginative thinking distinct from inferential reason. We both assert that both forms of thinking grasp reality in its own right. On these points, we agree.

Similarly, as my own reflection on the evaluative shape of experience developed, I came to distinguish deliberation from both intuitive and inferential forms of thought. I shall explore the nature and implications of this distinction in the following chapter. Here it suffices to note that we deliberate about mutually exclusive decisions by weighing the pros and cons, the advantages and disadvantages of choosing this rather than that. Deliberation functions within intuitive thinking when, for example, a painter weighs the advantages and disadvantages of positioning the realities in a painting here rather than there, of coloring them this way rather than that. Scientists deliberate about which hypothesis to adopt and test. Deliberation, however, especially characterizes both ethical thinking and practical thinking. I derive the distinction between ethical and practical thinking from the medievals, who correctly distinguished *recta ratio factiblium* (the right way to get something done) from *recta ratio agibilium* (making ethical choices for the right prudential motive). During my philosophical studies in St. Louis, I had wrestled with these issues in a preliminary way in the first article I published in *The Modern Schoolman* (1959).

Developmental psychology also discovers a difference between deliberation, on the one hand, and intuition and inference, on the other, when it studies stages of moral cognitive development distinct from the stages of transductive (intuitive) thinking and of operational (inferential) thinking. The fact that Jean Piaget, Lawrence Kohlberg, and William Damon all offer different interpretations of how humans develop morally requires one to coordinate, if possible, their different theories within the discipline of developmental psychology itself. If one cannot get them to agree, then one must apply some other method of category coordination: convergence, complementarity, or dialectical reversal.

Categories converge when they assert different but non-contradictory things about the same reality. Piaget, for example, interprets the first stage of human moral development as infantile authoritarianism, while Kohlberg interprets it as a kind of infantile hedonism. By that I mean that Piaget characterizes the infantile conscience as assenting blindly to parental authority, while Kohlberg characterizes the infantile conscience as a guileless desire for what the child finds pleasant and as a guileless rejection of what the child finds unpleasant. These contrasting psychological interpretations of infantile moral development could conceivably offer convergent rather than contradictory accounts of the first stage of moral development. When confronted with parental authority, little hedonists could, for example, tend to obey blindly in order to avoid the unpleasantness of punishment. Similarly, infantile authoritarians could, in the absence of parental interference tend spontaneously to seek what pleases them most.

Philosophical categories can also converge with those derived from the personality sciences. For example, the philosophy of experience which I have developed out of the classical American philosophical tradition recognizes intuitive, or imaginative, thinking as one realm of human cognitive response and interprets it realistically. That philosophy converges with Jungian archetypal theory. Archetypal theory also takes intuitive thinking very seriously and insists that it grapples with reality. In addition, however, archetypal theory discovers patterns in the otherwise chance chaos of the human imagination. The same archetypal images recur in different individuals, cultures, and epochs. They have powerful affective resonance. The archetypes of the masculine, of the feminine, of the persona, of the shadow, and of the self have generic meanings which the one who imagines archetypally must specify. Jungian archetypal theory converges therefore with the philosophy I have developed by offering a clinical insight into predictable patterns in imaginative thinking which goes beyond what philosophical reflection on lived, social experience as lived can discern. In other words, besides agreeing about the realistic character of intuitive perceptions, my philosophy and Jungian theory make true but different statements about the same reality and therefore converge.

Categories can converge, but they can also complement one another.[5] They can also contradict one another and so invite dialectical reversal. I have reflected on the convergence of categories. When do categories complement one another? Categories complement one another when they interpret accurately two different but interrelated realities. Thus Piaget's theory of moral development complements his theory of cognitive development because the two theories make true statements about different but interrelated realities. In philosophy, John Dewey's philosophy of artistic creativity complements Peirce's theory of inference by providing a plausible account of an important and sophisticated realm of common sense thinking which Peirce's logic and semiotic largely ignores.

Besides agreeing, converging, and complementing one another both within disciplines and across disciplines, the same categories can also contradict one another. When that occurs, then one needs to coordinate them through dialectical reversal. Even in a philosophical world which denies essentialism, as mine does, strictly contradictory accounts of one and the same reality cannot both assert the truth. When faced with strict categorical contradictions, one may do one of three things:

1) One may endorse the truth of one set of categories and discard their contradictory counterparts as false.

2) One may also decide that both sets of categories could offer plausible or even probable accounts of reality but endorse one set of categories as more adequate and discard their contradictory counterparts as less adequate. The endorsement of one set of categories as more adequate and the rejection of another set as inadequate or as less adequate leaves the question of their final interpretation unresolved.

The final interpretant of any disputed question offers that account of reality to which any mind must assent which decides questions of truth and falsity on the basis of evidence. Judgments of adequacy target, not particular propositions, which enjoy truth and falsity, but the frames of reference in which one thinks. Since one never asserts or denies frames of reference as such, they require other norms than truth or falsity in assessing them: namely, adequacy or inadequacy. An adequate frame of reference allows one to ask and answer all relevant questions about the reality one is trying to understand. An inadequate frame of reference does not.

3) When categories contradict one another because of the inadequacy of the frames of reference in which they occur, it seems likely that the frames of reference, in virtue of their inadequacy, are blinding the mind to relevant evidence which could conceivably resolve the contradiction. When that happens, the creation of a new and adequate frame of reference which takes into account all the evidence as well as the best insights of inadequate frames of reference could conceivably require one to reject one, several, or all of the contradictory accounts of the real. In what follows, I shall try to concretize these abstractions with some examples.

1) Endorsing one set of categories as true and rejecting another as false.
We commonly employ the first method for reversing dialectically contradic-

tory assertions about the same reality or realities in legal processes. At the start of the Watergate investigations, for example, the investigating Congressional committee found itself confronted with a variety of contradictory accounts of what had happened during the Watergate break-in. As the investigators amassed more and more evidence, however, they found themselves increasingly able to certify some of those accounts as true and reject others as lies.

Something similar happens in both philosophy and theology when philosophers or theologians debate over centuries the implications of different philosophical and theological hypotheses. Augustine of Hippo, for example, in his debate with Pelagius over the relationship between nature and grace, argued that original sin has so corrupted human nature that, left to its own devices, it can only commit mortal sins. Over the centuries, different theologians have urged the truth of Augustine's overly pessimistic anthropology with a variety of arguments and for a variety of motives. Generation after generation, the Christian community has found itself faced with the destructive consequences of such an understanding of the human; and it has gradually amassed more and more evidence which supports the position that, despite the fact that sin wounds and debases human nature, human beings can still desire some naturally good things. In other words, we have, in my judgment, reached a point in the debate about the relationship between nature and grace which allows us to assert that the evidence falsifies Augustinian pessimism and justifies consigning it to the dustbin of failed theories.

2) Choosing the more probable explanation and rejecting the less probable. Paradigm shifts in the development of scientific thinking illustrate how a going interpretation loses probability and even plausibility as the evidence mounts against it. The scientific community shifted from a geocentric, Ptolemaic astronomy to a heliocentric, Copernican astronomy because observations of the movements of heavenly bodies kept bringing up more and more facts which Ptolemaic theory could not explain but which a heliocentric Copernican theory did explain.

Something analogous happens in theological thinking. For centuries, for example, the Catholic Church has promoted what some theologians today call an "ecclesiology from above." Ecclesiology from above argues *a priori* about the divine constitution of different Church institutions usually in an effort either to consolidate clerical power over others or to rationalize the ecclesiastical *status quo*.

The attempt to invoke Mt 16:18 in order to justify the existence of a papal monarchy which did not take institutional shape until centuries after Matthew wrote his gospel illustrates the thought processes of ecclesiology from above. The papal monarchy conceives the pope as the equivalent of the emperor of the Church. Instead of sanctioning the papal monarchy, which did not exist when Matthew wrote, the evangelist's text probably presents Petrine Christianity as the best way to institutionalize the Church in the eighth decade of the Christian era.

The argument that one cannot ordain women because Jesus did not ordain women also exemplifies ecclesiology from above. The more we learn to distinguish between the historical Jesus and subsequent theological interpretations of what Jesus said and did, the clearer it becomes that Jesus never ordained anyone. If, then, His failure to ordain women prevents us from ordaining them, then his failure to ordain men bars males from ordination to Christian leadership as well. In other words, the more we learn about the history of the Church, the clearer it becomes that any Christian interested in the truth needs to abandon ecclesiology from above and replace it with an "ecclesiology from below": namely, with an ecclesiology which argues *a posteriori* and on the basis of factual, historical evidence.

3) Preferring adequate to inadequate frames of reference. The third technique for effecting the dialectical reversal of contradictory accounts of the same reality has the greatest complexity. The debate over the relationship between population control and world hunger illustrates how this particular method works. In the early stages of the debate, one found three causal explanations of world hunger vying with one another. Those who attributed the persistence of world hunger to poverty pushed for a redistribution of the earth's collective wealth in such a way that present and future generations had their need for food met. Others attributed the persistence of world hunger to unjust economic structures and argued that only their elimination could finally alleviate world hunger. Still others argued that the explosion of the world's population explained why half the people on the planet lack adequate food. This third group pushed for birth control as the correct solution to the problem of world hunger.

As the technical study of the causes of world hunger advanced, it became apparent that none of the preceding analyses had sufficiently taken into account the complexity of the forces which combine to keep half the human race starving. Each of the preceding theories had grasped a piece of the puzzle, but none of them had all the pieces. Clearly, ending world hunger required a more complex analysis of its multiple causes before we could begin to devise practical strategies for eliminating it. In the year 2000, the Bread for the World Institute for the study of world hunger claimed that it had in fact come up with the needed analysis and with the corresponding strategies.[6]

Within the scholarly discipline of theology, the relationship between the functional specialties of dialectic and foundations also illustrates this third technique for effecting dialectical reversal. The functional theological specialty of dialectic studies, as we have seen, different philosophical and theological frames of reference which different thinkers have espoused over the centuries. As one comes to clarity about the kinds of issues which have divided Christian thinkers in the past, one grows in the capacity to name the fallacies which have heretofore skewed theological perceptions of the events which reveal to us the Triune God. I would, for example, include among those fallacies the essentialistic reification of ideas, all forms of dualism, extreme pessimism about the human condition, extreme optimism about the human condition, nominalism, rationalism, and all forms of *a priori* reasoning. As one comes to greater and greater clarity about the presuppositions which motivate past errors, one begins to glimpse the possibility of creating a new, more comprehensive way of thinking theologically which can incorporate the best that the Christian tradition has to offer while avoiding its manifest blunders.

Foundational thinking undertakes the creation of just such new and comprehensive frames of reference for thinking both philosophically and theologically. In writing *The Gracing of Human Experience*, for example, I argued that Peirce's attempt to rethink the foundations of logic and of metaphysics had created a novel philosophical frame of reference which avoids all of the traditional fallacies listed above and which therefore offers a more comprehensive frame of reference for thinking the relationship between nature and grace than any other frame of reference which Christian thinkers have to date employed.

In the course of writing *Experiencing God*, I came to realize that not only does interdisciplinary thinking require the coordination of categories within disciplines and across disciplines; but it also requires one to take account of the interplay of categories. The coordination of categories engages their relationship to reality and invokes norms of truth and falsity, of adequacy and inadequacy, of validity and invalidity.[7] The interplay of categories examines critically how categories derived from different disciplines interact interpretatively in constructing a unified account of conversion and of the realities encountered within conversion. One understands the interplay of categories by coming to clarity concerning the precise contribution which different disciplines make to one's understanding of the total process of conversion.

In this context, I found Peirce's division of the sciences particularly illuminating. In the course of this narrative, I have already alluded more than once to Peirce's division of the sciences. In what follows, I shall first recall briefly those aspects of his architectonic ordering of scientific thought which throw light on the cross-disciplinary character of foundational thinking. Then

I shall explain how I built on Peirce's insights in order to name the operations which give structure to cross-disciplinary foundational thinking.

In 1885, Francis Ellingwood Abbot, an acquaintance and former classmate of Peirce, published his most successful work, *Scientific Theism*. In it he sought to reconcile religious faith with the method of positive science. When Peirce read this work, it convinced him that the logic of relations and of consequences which he had himself been developing had both metaphysical and religious implications which he needed to articulate. He therefore set about formulating his triadic, realistic metaphysics. Peirce believed, however, that no one ought to undertake metaphysical thinking without first surveying the present state of human knowledge. His survey of the state of scientific thinking at the end of the nineteenth century led him to formulate what he called a "natural classification of the sciences."

By a "natural classification of the sciences" Peirce meant a kind of genealogy of knowing. In his division of the sciences he argued that the more general sciences ground and make possible the more specialized sciences. Peirce's division of the sciences exemplifies his passion for "architectonic thinking." Architectonic thinking aspires to systematic comprehensiveness. His genealogy of knowledge confirmed him in the belief that the most abstract ideas count as the most practical because they have the greatest number of predictable operational consequences. We think abstract ideas impractical because our lethargic minds rarely take the trouble to clarify those operational consequences deductively so that we can verify them inductively.

Peirce divided science initially into sciences of discovery, sciences of review, and practical science. Sciences of discovery advance human knowing with speculative breakthroughs. Peirce divided the sciences of discovery into mathematics, philosophy (or the coenoscopic sciences, which reflect on lived social experience as lived), and the idioscopic sciences which focus on limited realms of reality and which often invoke both mathematical measurement for precision of thought and technological instrumentation in order to extend the scope of ordinary human experience and perception. Physics, chemistry, psychology, sociology all exemplify idioscopic sciences.

I shall consider the sciences of discovery in greater detail below. Here it suffices to distinguish them from sciences of review and from practical science. Sciences of review depend on sciences of discovery for their data. The study of evolution exemplifies a science of review. Evolutionary theory depends on the results of biology, geology, anthropology, and astronomy in order to construct a unified theory of how evolution happened. Sciences of review exemplify therefore cross-disciplinary thinking. Practical science studies how to get some job done most efficiently. The systematic study of mining, of agriculture, or of animal husbandry all exemplify practical sciences. As I pondered Peirce's division of the sciences, it seemed to me that his understanding of the relationship among the sciences of discovery offered some interesting suggestions about the interplay of philosophical thought with scientific, scholarly, idioscopic thinking.

Among the sciences of discovery, mathematics, the scientific study of pure possibility, prepares the ground for philosophical thinking by demonstrating the mathematical importance of the triad. The mathematics of the dyad, what Peirce called "the simplest mathematics" (i.e., the mathematics of two), can only generate a finite number of other numbers and mathematical relationships. The triad, however, manifests greater mathematical fecundity. With the triad, one can generate an infinity of other numbers and relationships. How, then, does this mathematical understanding of the triad clear the ground for philosophical thinking?

Peirce called philosophical thinking "coenoscopic" from the Greek term κοινος, common. He derived the odd term "coenoscopic" from Jeremy Bentham; but its application to philosophical modes of thinking in Peirce's logic reflected his replacement of the Cartesian and Kantian turn to the subject with the Peircean turn to community. Peirce's turn to community requires that shared systematic inquiry, not the solitary deduction *a priori* of the structures of human intentionality, provide the only adequate method for fixing human beliefs.

Philosophy divides into phenomenology, the three normative sciences of esthetics, ethics, and logic, and metaphysics. Phenomenology merely describes what appears in experience without attempting to distinguish between reality and illusion. The mathematical importance of the triad in the world of pure possibility, however, alerts the phenomenologist to the possible triadic structure of shared, social experience. Peirce realized that the logical exploration of phenomenological thinking does not require exhaustive descriptions of all experiences. Instead, the logic of phenomenology seeks to identify the most generic descriptive categories. In Peirce's phenomenology those generic categories reduce to a triad: quality, fact, and law.

Quality, Peirce defined as "an instance of particular suchness." Qualities belong to the how of experience because they make us present to what we experience: namely, to ourselves and to our world. The realm of quality begins with sensations but extends to feelings, memories, images, concepts, ideals. Qualities enjoy particularity and endow experience with a sense of possibility and therefore with spontaneity.

Facts consist of brute, physical action and its corresponding brute physical reaction. If in groping my way around a dark room I bump into a desk, it bumps back. Train wrecks, automobile collisions, earthquakes all exemplify facts. If qualities endow experience with particularity and presence, facts, which have a dynamic dyadic structure, endow experience with actuality and concreteness. Facts make experience this rather than that.

Laws exemplify real generality. One can think of Peirce's law as an Aristotelian habit deprived of its accidental status and functioning more like an Aristotelian substance, although in Peirce's relational, functional universe neither "accident" nor "substance" occur or can occur as categories since both presuppose the fallacy of essentialism. Laws endow experience with a conditioned, dynamic orientation to the future. The conditioned character of a law entails that, when I understand a law correctly, I can predict "what will happen if. . . ." If qualities endow experience with particularity and presence, if facts endow experience with actuality and concreteness, laws endow experience with reality and generality, with a dynamic orientation to the future, and with intelligibility. By telling us what will happen together with the conditions under which events will transpire, correctly interpreted laws explain those events.

As we have seen, for Peirce the three normative sciences of esthetics, ethics, and logic all mediate between phenomenology and metaphysics. Esthetics, the normative science of the *summum bonum*, studies the kinds of habits of appreciation one needs to cultivate if one hopes to live for realities and ideals which make human life ultimately worth living. Ethics studies the kinds of habits of choice which I ought to cultivate in order to live habitually for the *summum bonum*. Logic studies the kinds of habits of thought I ought to cultivate in order to understand reality truly so that I can make realistic choices which lead me habitually to supreme goodness.

Phenomenology only describes what appears in experience without presuming to discriminate between reality and illusion. Metaphysics does attempt to discriminate between reality and illusion. The normative sciences mediate between phenomenology and metaphysics. How do the normative sciences effect that mediation? Each of the normative sciences invokes different criteria for discriminating between reality and illusion. Until one puts order into one's appreciative perceptions of the *summum bonum*, one will find oneself unable to discriminate between genuine beauty and banality, between ideals which enhance life and those which impoverish it. Similarly, until one has faced the emotional disorders which make it difficult to grasp the *summum bonum*, one will live inclined to confuse one's pet bigotry and one's neuroses and psychoses with reality. Think of the psychotic, anti-Semitic visions of Adolf Hitler. By the same token, until one has put right order into one's conscience, one will tend to confuse reality with one's narrowly selfish and unjust preferences. Think of the complacent CEOs of the tobacco industry denying under oath any connection between smoking and lung cancer despite massive evidence to the contrary. Finally, until one puts order into one's mind, one will remain inclined to mistake reality for one's own unexamined prejudices and confused thinking. Think, for example, of the confusion which fallacies like essentialism, dualism, nominalism, and rationalism have spawned in philosophical and theological speculation.

In the end, however, the normative science of logic transforms Peirce's three descriptive categories–quality, fact, and law–into the three metaphysical categories of Firstness, Secondness, and Thirdness. Peirce shifted the focus of logical analysis from the analysis of propositions to the analysis of acts of inference. He regarded grammatical propositions as linguistic shorthand for more complex inferential acts of reasoning. Moreover, as we have also already seen in chapter four, Peirce discerned three irreducible forms of inference: abduction which concludes to a case, deduction which concludes to a result, and induction which concludes to a law.

Peirce's logic took doubt seriously and rejected the Cartesian method of fictive, universal doubt. If, however, one takes doubt seriously, then one cannot really doubt the reality of quality, of those cognitive experiences which make one present to oneself and to one's world. Nor can one seriously doubt the actuality of facts, which force themselves on us whether we want them to or not. The child who accidentally thrusts a hand into a flame cannot doubt that the fire is searing its flesh. Peirce conceded, however, that in the history of philosophy many thinkers, all of them nominalists, had called into question the reality of law, of real generality. He therefore felt constrained to construct a logical demonstration of the reality of generality, of what he called Thirdness.

Peirce's argument for the reality of Thirdness invoked his theory of inference. Inductive inference concludes a process of continuous inferential reasoning and asserts the reality of a law. One cannot, however, grasp at the end of a continuous process of inferential argumentation something which that process did not perceive, albeit more vaguely, at its beginning. In other words, in formulating an hypothesis, the reasoning mind perceives, though more vaguely than at the end of an inferential argument, the laws whose implications deductive reasoning clarifies and which inductive reasoning verifies. Viewed as an act of cognition, however, abductive inference shades into every human judgment of perception. Peirce concluded, therefore, that the human mind perceives more than it senses. It senses the brute, factual impact of the world upon experience, but it perceives real generality, the general tendency to act in a predictable way under specifiable circumstances, and does so both imaginatively and inferentially. The inclusion of generality among things which enjoy reality transformed Peirce's descriptive category "law" into his metaphysical category of Thirdness.

The preliminary verification of Firstness, Secondness, and Thirdness in the ordinary human act of perception does not, however, terminate the work of metaphysics. It only begins it. The logic of inference requires one to look on every abduction about complex realities as fallible. Formulating a metaphysical hypothesis about the nature of reality in general raises the ultimately complex question. Peirce's logic of inference requires one, therefore, to test one's preliminary metaphysical abduction for its ability to interpret as defined not only whatever appears in lived, day-to-day, social experience but also the results of the idioscopic sciences which study in greater depth circumscribed dimensions of reality and which do so in greater detail and with greater precision than philosophy can. Moreover, the idioscopic sciences employ, when appropriate, technological instruments which expand the field of human sensations and perceptions beyond day-to-day, lived perceptions.

If, as I believe one must, one divides the idioscopic sciences into the hard sciences, like physics and chemistry, and scholarly forms of idioscopic thinking, like history or artistic and literary criticism, and if one simultaneously includes theology among the scholarly idioscopic sciences, then Peirce's logical division of the sciences becomes extremely suggestive for describing how philosophy, positive science, scholarship, and theology interplay with one another in the cross-disciplinary pursuit of foundational theological thinking.

According to Peirce's theory of inference, which I personally regard as logically sound, one understands the meaning of any abduction by predicting the sum total of its operational consequences. The consequences of any metaphysical hypothesis lie entirely in the realm of interpretation. When one formulates a theory about the nature of reality in general, one predicts that one's metaphysical hypothesis will successfully interpret any reality whatever. A working metaphysical hypothesis has to enjoy applicability and adequacy. It must apply to whatever appears in experience in the sense in which one had defined its key metaphysical terms philosophically, and that same working metaphysical hypothesis can encounter nothing in reality it cannot interpret. Those used to claiming for metaphysical thinking *a priori* universality and necessity will find settling for only a fallible, working, metaphysical hypothesis something second best; but think of it this way: a metaphysical hypothesis which works has it all over one which does not work. Moreover, the logical hypothesis that the human mind can grasp reality with *a priori* universality and necessity does not work.

These methodological clarifications derived from reflecting on Peirce's logical division of the sciences enabled me to identify the specific contributions which philosophy, science, secular scholarship, and theological scholarship make to the formulation of working foundational hypotheses about the forms and dynamics of conversion. Once I reached clarity on that point, I found myself in a position to clarify further how philosophy, science, secular scholarship, and theology interplay within foundational theological thinking.

One's metaphysical categories must have the capacity to *interpret* both lived, social human experience as lived and the results of close idioscopic investigations into more circumscribed realms of reality. Metaphysics will interpret both lived experience and the verified results of the idioscopic sciences if its categories apply to both in the sense in which one has defined those categories philosophically. A successful metaphysics, i.e., a working metaphysical abduction about the nature of reality in general, will in addition have the capacity to *contextualize* the results of the idioscopic sciences by assigning those results their proper place within the overall scheme of things. Finally, the insights of the normative philosophical sciences, which generate and verify one's preliminary metaphysical categories, provide one with criteria for *criticizing* indefensible esthetic, ethical, and logical assumptions which skew common sense thinking. Those same normative sciences have the capacity to critique the uncriticized assumptions of idioscopic thinkers, whether of a scientific or a scholarly bent. A working metaphysical hypothesis will, moreover, facilitate naming metaphysical assumptions about reality which do not work.

In sum, then, as one goes about formulating a foundational working hypothesis about the forms and dynamics of conversion, philosophical categories interplay with the categories of science and of secular scholarship, on the one hand, and of theological scholarship, on the other 1) by interpreting them philosophically, 2) by contextualizing in the overall scheme of things the results of those more focused investigations into reality, and 3) by criticizing the fallacies and indefensible assumptions of common sense and of idioscopic thought.

If, however, one's metaphysical categories have to interpret not only lived experience as lived but also the results of close idioscopic studies of limited realms of reality, then, within foundational theological thinking, idioscopic categories interplay with metaphysical categories in two ways. First, the idioscopic categories must *verify or falsify* one's philosophical, metaphysical categories. Moreover, because idioscopic thinking undertakes more detailed and focused explorations into the nature of the real than does coenoscopic, philosophical thinking, when idioscopic categories verify coenoscopic, philosophical categories, they simultaneously *amplify* them.

For example, the interplay between my philosophical account of human experience as lived interprets successfully Piaget's developmental theory of human cognitive development. Both my philosophical categories and Piaget's psychological categories discern three general realms of human interpretative response: intuitive-transductive, inferential-operational, and deliberative-ethical. In verifying this particular philosophical hypothesis, however, developmental psychology simultaneously amplifies it. Why? Because philosophy can only interpret lived, adult, social experience as lived. Developmental psychology anatomizes the kinds of growth processes through which the human mind needs to pass in order for it to think as an adult philosopher.

The secular sciences invoke human reason alone and therefore fail altogether to invoke revelatory events as evidence; for one must understand revelatory events in the same way in which one understands all events: namely, on the terms which those events impose. Revelatory events disclose sacramentally God's free and gratuitous intervention in history for saving ends, an intervention which goes beyond the divine creative act which summons the universe into being. In other words, the nature of revelatory events requires that one understand them in faith.

Because the secular sciences invoke reason alone, not faith, they as idioscopic sciences, investigate only events which transpire naturally. Events transpire naturally when they prescind from the gracious, historical self-revelation and self-communication of God. As a result, the secular sciences have the rational capacity either to falsify or to verify and amplify the metaphysical categories which structure foundational theological thinking only in events in the natural world. They have nothing to say about divine revelation. They have no capacity to verify, falsify, or amplify metaphysical God-talk.

Theological scholarship does investigate the gracious events which reveal God historically and eschatologically on the terms which those events require: namely, in faith. In other words, within the enterprise of foundational thinking, the categories supplied by theological scholarship do have the capacity to *verify, falsify,* or *amplify* metaphysical God-talk. Since many people, indeed many theologians, will find strange the claim that, in cross-disciplinary theological thinking, metaphysical categories as philosophically defined must interpret theological God-talk, perhaps I should give a few examples of what I mean.

I did not begin to reflect in any systematic way on the relation between metaphysics and God-talk until I wrote *The Divine Mother.* Indeed, I undertook that study in part as a test of the human mind's ability to engage in *a posteriori* theological thinking about the Trinity. *A posteriori* theological thinking requires that the events which reveal the Triune God verify or falsify any metaphysical or theological affirmations one makes about the divine reality. When those events verify one's theological categories, they yield an insight into how in fact a saving God has chosen to deal with a sinful world. When one's abstract metaphysical hypothesis successfully interprets verified theological accounts of religious events, the latter tend in turn to verify one's metaphysical conception of God.

Theology examines how in fact God has chosen to deal with us in our sinfulness. As a result, when one's metaphysical God-talk successfully interprets historically verified theological God-talk, the latter *concretizes* and *amplifies* the former. In the course of writing *The Divine Mother*, I began to understand in greater detail how this logical process of verification and amplification happens.

The abstractness of most Trinitarian speculation seemed to me to make it an apt test case for the possibility of engaging in *a posteriori* foundational theological thinking. Reflection on the triune God did not always have an abstract character. Indeed, New Testament thinking about the Trinity tends to take either a kerygmatic or a narrative form. The New Testament meditates on the mystery of the Trinity by testifying to the events which reveal the triune God concretely, historically, and eschatologically: namely, Jesus' birth, ministry, passion, resurrection, and mission of the divine Breath. The gospels narrate those events. The letters of Paul and of other New Testament writers proclaim those same events kerygmatically.

As I wrestled with the methodological challenge of verifying trinitarian God-talk *a posteriori*, I realized that the problem of verification engages seven nests of interrelated issues:

1) the need to bridge the gulf between the immanent and the economic Trinity;

2) the need for analogous predication in speaking of a self-revealing God;

3) the need for a sound experiential grounding for any analogous conception of God;

4) the inevitability of metaphysical language in speaking about the immanent Trinity;

5) the need for a defensible understanding of the relation of God and the world;

6) the need for a sound inferential logic in pursuing trinitarian theology;

7) the need to verify the immanent Trinity in the economic Trinity.

The paragraphs which follow explore how these different nests of issues interplay with one another in the formulation of a defensible foundational theology of the Triune God.

1) The Need to Bridge the Gulf between the Immanent and Economic Trinities. The events which culminated in the Arian controversy began the process of interpreting in abstract philosophical terms the divine reality revealed in the New Testament. Not all Christian thinkers in the fourth century felt easy about approaching the God of the New Testament in philosophical abstractions. Some blamed the philosophical Hellenization of Christian faith for pitting Arians against the Orthodox and for dividing the Church into bickering factions.

As a result, one finds in the wake of the Arian controversy, an impulse within patristic theology to replace philosophy with mysticism. Instead of trying to reduce to philosophical abstractions the mystery of the God revealed in Christianity, one ought to approach that mystery as a mystery and recognize that it eludes categorization in finite human images and concepts. The mystical impulse in patristic theology reached one climax in the thought of Gregory of Nyssa, who located the reality of the Trinity in an eternal realm of transcendence beyond being, beyond the intelligible, Platonic realm of forms, beyond all finite human conception. Eventually, the mystical turn found expression in the apophatic mysticism of Pseudo-Dionysus. Apophatic mysticism holds that creation can only tell us what God is *not*, not what God is.

Because this kind of thinking located the triune God in a transcendent realm of absolute mystery divorced not only from space and time but from all intelligibility, it opened a gap between the "economic Trinity" and the "immanent Trinity" which medieval scholasticism only widened. The "economic Trinity" refers to the theological attempt to describe as they occur the events which reveal to us the triune God. The "immanent Trinity" designates the attempt to formulate a language for talking about the reality of the Trinity in its transcendence of space and time. The language for talking about the economic Trinity has an experiential, historical, and eschatological character. The language for talking about the immanent Trinity has a metaphysical character.

The economic Trinity reveals the immanent Trinity. As we shall see in more detail below, the question of the relationship between the economic and the immanent Trinity does not, therefore, imply the reality of two distinct Trinities but the theological need to develop and to coordinate two different kinds of language for talking and thinking about the triune God.

The medieval dissociation of the economic from the immanent Trinity resulted from the attempt of theologians to think about the reality of the triune God in its transcendence of space and time without any attempt to verify or even to ground that language in the events which reveal the Christian God within space and time. That dissociation reflected in turn a theological propensity for *a priori* thinking. *A priori* reasoning vindicates for the human mind a fallacious ability to make assertions about the nature of reality without corroborating factual and perceptual evidence. Accordingly medieval trinitarian theology proposed conceptual constructs of the triune God in its transcendence without any overt reference to the events which reveal that God in space and time, and without any attempt to verify or falsify the revelation of the immanent Trinity in those events. At St. Marys we used to joke that the medieval trinitarian theology we had to learn in class asserted one God, two processions, three persons, four relations, five notions, and no proof. Our mocking humor vaguely perceived important logical and methodological issues in textbook trinitarian theology.

2) The Need for an Analogous Resemblance between God and Creation. Among contemporary theologians, Karl Rahner first saw the need to heal the rift between the economic and immanent Trinities. He did so, however, by simply identifying the two. For Rahner, then, the economic Trinity is the immanent Trinity and vice versa.

During my early years in the People's Republic of Berkeley, the more I wrestled with the methodological issues raised by the development of trinitarian theology, the more convinced I felt that Rahner had done well in calling for a healing of the gap between the immanent and economic Trinity which patristic theology had opened and which medieval theology had only widened. I deemed, however, that by simply identifying the two "Trinities," Rahner had, from both a theological and a methodological standpoint, badly oversimplified their relationship to one another. Let us try to understand why.

Talking about a transcendent God who reveals God's self within history, within the limits of space and time, requires that God and creation have some kind of resemblance to one another; for, if, as the apophatic mystical tradition does, one absolutizes the mystery of God by conceiving of the deity as "wholly other" than created realities, then one ends by making God in principle unrevealable. Creation cannot reveal a God with whom it shares nothing in common. Paul Tillich saw this point clearly. Since Tillich could find no commonality between an infinite God and a finite creation, he denied the possibility that God could reveal God's self within space and time, within history. Tillich therefore ruled out the possibility of the Incarnation happening and denied the Trinity which the Incarnation reveals.

Belief in the revealability of God results necessarily from the fact that revelation has in fact happened. *Ab esse ad posse valet illatio* (One argues validly from actuality to possibility). If, however, a revealable God has to have some kind of resemblance to creation for creation to have the capacity to reveal God historically, then the historical self-revelation of God makes it necessary to conceive of a self-revealing God on some kind of analogy with the created universe. Why? Because an infinite God and a finite creation cannot share identically the same nature. In other words, though they enjoy some kind of resemblance, they also differ in the kind of reality they exemplify. If, then, one does assert some kind of similarity between God and creation, then one's metaphysical God-talk has to find a way of asserting similarity-in-difference between God and the world. This the language of analogy in fact asserts.

It also seemed to me that Aquinas had succeeded best in developing a method for thinking and speaking about God analogously. Apophatic, mystical theology follows exclusively the way of negation. It finds such a difference between creator and creature that creation lacks any ability to reveal positively to us God's reality. Creation can, therefore, only tell us what God is not. God is not this house, not this tree, not this plant, not this human being. Apophatic theology grasps a truth. No simple and unqualified identification between an infinite God and finite reality will serve. Aquinas conceded this point but correctly saw the need to move beyond the language of mere negation to a language of transcendence.

Jesus' designation of God as "*Abba* (Father)" illustrates how analogous predication works in God-talk. In calling God "Father," Jesus asserted some kind of resemblance between His relation to God and a human child's relation to his or her father. The language of analogy, however, demands that, having asserted some kind of resemblance between two realities, one immediately negate a relation of identity. Our relation to God as Father does not reproduce in every respect our relationship to our human fathers. God did not, for example, beget us physically, as our human fathers did. Similarly, our relation to God as Father does not reproduce the finitude and sinfulness of human parental relationships.

Having, however, denied any simple identity between our relationship to God and to our human fathers, the language of analogy asserts that the positive, life-giving aspects of our relationship to our human fathers finds exemplification in our relationship to God with supreme perfection. So, if we experience our human fathers as life-giving, we experience our heavenly Father as supremely and transcendently life-giving. If we find in our human fathers at their best the loving tendency to forgive us when we blunder or sin, then we experience our relationship to our heavenly Father as supremely and transcendently forgiving.

3) The Need for a Sound Grounding of Analogous God-Talk. To rule out the possibility in principle of God's historical self-revelation when in fact God has chosen to reveal God's self in space and time indulges fallaciously and irresponsibly in reductive, *a priori* reasoning. God-talk has a reductive character when it confines the transcendent reality of an infinite God to finite, fallible, human categories. It has an *a priori* character when it makes assertions about God without corroborating evidence. If, however, one of necessity invokes the language of analogy in speaking about the self-revealing God of the New Testament, then one cannot heal the gap of predication between the immanent Trinity and the economic Trinity by simply identifying the two, as Rahner did.

I found other difficulties with Rahner's position. It seemed to me that his insistence on the absolute mystery of the transcendent God led him finally to replace Aquinas's language of strict analogy with a language of paradox. The language of analogy discovers similarity-in-difference between creature and creator. The language of paradox asserts the apparent identity of two finally incompatible and irreconcilable realities. In Rahner's paradoxical universe, it seemed to me that logical consistency required one to assert that a God of absolute mystery finally makes the reality of God, despite Rahner's protests to the contrary, absolutely unrevealable. Rahner refused, for example, to find any analogy between divine and human persons and cited the absoluteness of the divine mystery as the reason for his denial.

In addition, Rahner's *a priori* Kantian logic betrayed him into endowing a Thomistic metaphysical conception of God as *actu infinitus* with *a priori* necessity. It seemed to me that Benedict Spinoza grasped the logical consequence of such a conception of God. He argued that, if God represents infinite being, then only God can exist. He reduced creation (*natura naturata*) to a modality of the divine nature (*natura naturans*).

Rather than replace analogy with paradox, as it seemed to me Rahner had, I groped for a better way of conceiving the transcendent reality of the triune God analogously. I found help in the thought of Anselm of Canterbury. Instead of conceiving of the deity in its transcendence as actual infinity, Anselm in his *Proslogion* understood the divine transcendence under the rubric of the divine supremacy. For Anselm, the supremacy of divine perfection transforms God into that reality than which none greater can be conceived. Supremacy like infinity can, I saw, also ground analogous God-talk and does so better than infinite actuality.

In his *Proslogion* Anselm invoked the divine supremacy as the basis for his ontological proof of God's existence. Anselm influenced in significant ways Charles Hartshorne's appropriation of Whitehead's di-polar theism. Students of Hartshorne know that he made a manful but inconclusive effort to rehabilitate the ontological argument. I joined Peirce and Aquinas in rejecting the ontological argument; and I also rejected, as we have seen, Whitehead's di-polar theism.

I realized, however, that the notion of the divine supremacy also served other, more experiential ends in the *Proslogion* than the ontological proof of the existence of God. Anselm developed his ontological argument early in that work, but the bulk of its chapters dealt with other issues than arguing fallaciously from the idea of God to the existence of God. Anselm preferred to understand the transcendence of God under the rubric of supremacy because such an understanding of the divine reality functions as a lure for religious experience, as a lure for contemplation. Anselm wrote his little treatise for monks interested in exploring the mystery of God through prayer. The notion of supremacy reminded them that no human insight into this or that divine perfection can exhaust the inexhaustible plentitude of the God's intelligibility. Conceiving God as supremely perfect, as perfect beyond the finite human mind's power to conceive, reminded Anselm's monks that God is always more, more than any finite, feeble, human head or heart can ever encompass. If with Anselm, one opts to conceive the reality of God under the rubric of supremacy, then one can never rest content with any limited image of God or limited insight into the divine perfection; but one does not therefore deny a limited insight's power to disclose to you an aspect of the supreme perfection of God. Instead, the notion of supremacy allows one to let the inexhaustible fruitfulness of divine intelligibility lure one ever deeper and deeper into the contemplation of its inexhaustible perfection.

The attempt to approach God as a foundational theologian forces one to think experientially. Foundational theology probes the way the perception of divine reality unfolds within the context of an integral experience of conversion. Anselm's language of supremacy seemed to me to account better for the unfolding of human religious experience than Aquinas's metaphysical language of actual infinity. *Deus semper major.* Never imagine, finite mortal, that your peanut brain can ever encompass the reality of God; but never let God's ultimate incomprehensibility discourage you from exploring the divine encounter in the rich fullness of its intelligibility.

I decided that Anselm's language of supremacy justified approaching divine revelation analogously and without falling into Rahner's fallacy of confusing analogy with paradox. Moreover, the Christian tradition offers another perfectly orthodox definition of the infinity of God than *actu infinitus.* Hilary of Poitiers defined "the infinite" as that which encompasses all things but is itself encompassed by nothing else. A supremely perfect God would do precisely that. Moreover, understanding God as all-encompassing logically implied panentheism.

4) The Need for a Defensible Understanding of the Relations of God and the World. Panentheism differs from pantheism. Pantheism identifies the reality of God and creation. Panentheism insists on the distinction between God and creation but asserts at the same time that creation exists in the all-encompassing reality of God.

Christian revelation excludes pantheism; but it finds panentheism positively congenial. This understanding of the relation of God and creation surfaces more than once in the New Testament and keeps surfacing in the Christian tradition. I myself found the idea of panentheism philosophically and theologically attractive. I rejected, however, the Whiteheadean panentheism popularized by Charles Hartshorne because I rejected the conceptual nominalism which his di-polar theism endorses. Moreover, as I worked my way through the historical development of Christian God-talk, I also realized that one could make sense of panentheism in a variety of metaphysical contexts. I shall return to this point later.

5) The Need for a Sound Inferential Logic in Pursuing Trinitarian Theology. Peirce's logic and metaphysics provided me with the final clue I needed for bridging the gap between the immanent and economic Trinity. Peirce replaced a propositional logic with an inferential one; and he adopted and developed a logic of relations. His inferential logic repudiated all forms of *a priori* reasoning and required that events make human perceptions of reality true or false. Events make a human abduction true when things in fact behave in the way in which one's deductively clarified hypothesis predicts that they will behave.

In Peirce's logic of consequences, one verifies or falsifies an hypothesis by clarifying its operational consequences and then by seeing whether or not events behave in the way one predicts that they will. Something analogous happens when we formulate hypotheses about the past. The events of the past remain everlastingly fixed. They will never exemplify anything other than the reality and actuality which they in fact decided to become. We have access to past events, however, only through the mediation of historical evidence. We must construct our understanding of the past on the basis of that evidence.

Historical thinking faces two interrelated tasks. On the basis of the surviving evidence, it must reconstruct a sound chronology of past events. It must decide what happened when and where. Then it must verify or falsify all historical hypotheses about the reason those events developed in the way in which they did by testing its hypotheses against the evidence it possesses concerning the way in which things in the past in fact behaved.

The events of Christian revelation reveal a transcendent God sacramentally. By that I mean that historical events both reveal and conceal the transcendent reality of God. They reveal God to the extent that those events manifest God's gratuitous, saving intervention in human history over and above the divine act of creation. The same revelatory events conceal the reality of God because no finite event can ever manifest a supremely perfect God exhaustively. One will, therefore, always need two kinds of language for talking about the God of Christian revelation. One will need a language which gives an accurate account of how the historical events which reveal God to us in fact transpired. That account will yield an insight into the economic

Trinity. Since, however, no finite historical event can reveal the transcendent reality of God exhaustively one will also need a metaphysical language for talking analogously about the divine reality in its transcendence.

The language of supremacy offers one legitimate way of approaching the transcendent reality of God analogously, a way which invites both the unfolding of human religious experience and imaginative, inferential, and contemplative exploration into the inexhaustible intelligibility and fecundity of God. Such a language offers a way of thinking the immanent Trinity without claiming to have comprehended it.

6) The Need to Verify the Immanent in the Economic Trinity. Sound logic requires that one close the gap between the immanent and economic Trinity, not by simply identifying the two kinds of God-talk, but by verifying or falsifying the immanent Trinity in the economic. One will do that successfully, if one can verify one's metaphysical account of the immanent Trinity in one's historical account of the economic Trinity. In other words, one's account of the immanent Trinity must successfully interpret the historical events which reveal to us the Triune God.

When I attempted this strategy in formulating my own experiential construct of the Trinity, I discovered that it did indeed allow one to falsify some traditional theological accounts of the immanent Trinity. In the second century, for example, Justin Martyr formulated a very influential abduction about the way the divine persons relate within the transcendent reality of the Godhead. Invoking an invalid *a priori* logic, Justin equated the *Logos* of the prologue to John's gospel with the *Logos* of Middle Platonism. Middle Platonism located the eternal forms in which all created reality participates in an eternal divine intelligence. In effect, then, Justin hypothesized that the Word who became flesh, the Son of God, the second person of the Trinity, functions within the transcendent, immanent, eternal life of God as the mind or intelligence of God.

This particular hypothesis about the immanent Trinity enjoyed considerable popularity in patristic and medieval thought. Clement of Alexandria, Origen, and Athanasius had all endorsed Justin's suggestion. So had Augustine of Hippo. Moreover, given Augustine's enormous speculative impact upon the Latin church, such an understanding of the transcendent reality of the Son of God dominated medieval trinitarian thinking.

Unfortunately, when theologians invoke *a priori* forms of reasoning, the mere repetition of an idea seems to endow it with authority and serves as a logically invalid substitute for proof. If, however, I had understood correctly the relationship between the economic and immanent Trinity, *a posteriori* reasoning about Christian revelation required one to show that such a conception of the second person of the Trinity actually interprets the events which reveal Him to us historically. As theologians continue to hone the criteria they invoke in deriving from the New Testament what we can say historically about Jesus, we can begin to characterize historical assertions about Jesus as certain or uncertain, as probable or improbable, as plausible or implausible, or as possible or impossible.

By invoking the criteria of the new quests for the historical Jesus, we can, in my judgment, take it as historically certain that Jesus perceived Himself as conducting His mortal ministry in the power and anointing of the divine Breath and that many of His contemporaries, who regarded Him as a prophet, did so as well. The divine Breath inspired His religious self-understanding and religious vision of the kingdom.

In conducting His mortal ministry, Jesus, moreover, through the divine Breath's illumination experienced Himself as sent to proclaim the divine reign. In proclaiming the divine reign, Jesus invited those who believed in Him to enter God's family by participating in His own filial relationship to God as *Abba*. In other words, the events which reveal to us how the divine persons relate to one another, the events of which the economic Trinity gives an account, tell us that Jesus came to His understanding both of His person and of His mission by the Father through the gracious illumination of the Breath of God. Since, the paschal mystery reveals the divinity of Jesus, it lends the sanction of divine authority to Jesus' human religious perceptions.

The historical and eschatological events which reveal to us the Christian God, also reveal how the divine persons relate to one another within the Trinity. Those events, however, make it clear that the divine Breath functions as the cognitive link between the Son and the Father. Hence, the Breath of God, not the Son of God functions as the divine mind. That means that the events of Christian revelation falsify Justin's theological interpretation of the Johannine *Logos* as the mind of God no matter who in the Christian tradition parroted his false abduction.

Even in writing *The Divine Mother*, I recognized that this conclusion had enormous implications for a sound understanding of theological method. First of all, it endowed theological thinking with potential respectability. One finds in the contemporary academy a tendency to deride any form of "onto-theology" either as lacking any evidence to support it or as the projection of irrational, human subjectivity. The contemporary deconstructionist assault on onto-theology derives its rhetorical plausibility from the fact that in the past theologians have too often acquiesced in the invalid presuppositions of classical metaphysical thinking and have as a consequence claimed, implausibly and fallaciously, that others must accept as true, positions which they espouse simply because they espouse them. In addition, one finds a widespread and disreputable tendency in the theological academy to invoke taste in the fixation of theological belief. One invokes taste in the fixation of theological belief when one fallaciously cites the personal appeal of an hypothesis, one's subjective preference for it, as certifying its inductive truth.

As Charles Peirce saw clearly, "taste," or the spontaneous attractiveness of an hypothesis, offers a good reason to prefer it for deductive clarification and inductive testing, for the simple reason that the history of science shows that the educated hunches of scientists often enough test out inductively as either true or probable. The mere personal attractiveness of an hypothesis can, however, never replace the strictly logical processes of deductive clarification and inductive verification.

The fact that Lonergan's method, when re-grounded in Peirce's logic, allowed me to falsify trinitarian hypotheses in the events which reveal the triune God pointed the way beyond the invalid fixing of theological belief through taste alone. Until, moreover, theology can in fact falsify some theological beliefs inductively in the evidence of history, then, it deserves all the derision which the contemporary opponents of "onto-theology" heap upon it. If, however, by invoking a sound *a posteriori* logic one can demonstrate the possibility of falsifying some theological hypotheses in historical events, then one can demonstrate the possibility of developing a sound onto-theology which avoids the very objections which make its pursuit currently seem to some intellectually ridiculous.

The historical falsifiability of theological hypotheses in the data of revelation does not transform theology into a hard science, since theology never qualifies as any more than scholarship. Theology does not employ mathematical measurement or special technological instruments for extending human perception in the manner of the hard sciences. If, however, Lonergan's theory of method in theology when re-grounded in Peirce's logic does enable one to falsify at least some theological hypotheses, then among all the fallible human attempts to understand a great and baffling world, theology enjoys as much respectability as a discipline like scholarly history. Indeed, the historical and eschatological character of divine revelation makes historical and theological scholarship analogous disciplines. They differ principally in the fact that history as a purely rational science prescinds from the eschatological data provided by the paschal mystery. As the culmination of God's self-revelation in space and time, the paschal mystery requires one to assent to it on the terms which the events in question demand, as Peirce's logic insists. Events make hypotheses true; and one can grasp the full truth and significance of an eschatological event like the paschal mystery only on God's terms, and therefore in faith.

This chapter has reflected on the kinds of methodological issues which preoccupied me in the first three books I wrote after joining the faculty as JSTB. When I wrote the third of those studies, *The Divine Mother*, I had only begun to grapple with the question of verifying and falsifying theological beliefs. The attempt to formulate a verifiable foundational Christology coordinate with the trinitarian theology I developed in *The Divine Mother* forced me to think in greater detail about the authentication and repudiation of theological doctrines. In the process, I found myself forced to grapple with the method of the theological specialty which Lonergan calls "doctrines" and its relationship to foundational method.

In order, however, to understand how my grasp of doctrinal method evolved, one needs first to grasp how my metaphysics of experience and my construct of conversion developed. To those intimately related conceptions I turn in the chapter which follows.

Colloquy:

Having seen
> *with vision unfathomable,*
having known with a Wisdom
>> *mobile beyond all motion,*
>> *vaster than the star-studded universe,*
>> *all-embracing,*
>> *all encompassing,*
> *how, gentle Lord,*
>> *could You suffer confinement*
>>> *in our straight-jacketed thoughts?*

My mind inches toward you like a slug.
> *I would feign love you with my mind*
>> *as with my heart,*
>>> *my soul,*
>>> *my feeble strength.*
> *Yet measured by your vastness,*
>> *my concepts snap.*

Cosmos bears but distant traces of its Sculptor,
> *speaks You darkly*
>> *like a blurred shape in distant mist.*

Had You not fitted Yourself flesh,
> *how would we know you truly*
>> *when even You conceal as you reveal?*

And yet, Your great and agonizing Yes
> *gives sight to sin-blinded eyes*
>> *which see,*
>>> *discern,*
>>> *perceive in Easter light*
>>>> *the human face of God.*

NOTES

1. John Muir lamented the Spanish name for this glorious range. In English Sierra Nevada means "Snow Saw." Muir suggested futilely renaming the range "The Mountains of Light."

2. Peirce's doctrine of synechism asserts real continuity in development. It grounds individual continuity in development in Thirdness: i.e., in real generality, in subsistent habit. It also acknowledges social and environmental relations, conceptual relations among human evaluative responses, and an experienced social continuity between God and human communities.

3. Faculty psychology explains human activity by grounding it in essentially different powers of activity that move one another to act. Besides committing the essence fallacy and endorsing operational dualism, Thomistic faculty psychology finds no verification in the results of contemporary psychology.

4. The reader will find these insights developed in more detail in chapter four toward the end of my discussion of Edwards's theology.

5. That I have, in what I have written, sometimes used the terms "convergence" and "complementarity" interchangeably testifies to the fallibility of my mind and to the imprudence of trusting memory in defining technical terms, even technical terms one has defined oneself. In this autobiography, I revert to the original definitions I gave these terms in *Inculturating North American Theology*, which offers the clearest account of them.

6. Bread for the World Institute, *A Program to End Hunger* (Silver Spring, MD: Bread for the World Institute, 2000).

7. The rejection of *a priori* modes of argumentation, for example, invokes the norm of invalidity because *a priori* thinking violates fundamental principles of sound reasoning. In order to verify an abduction, one needs to produce factual evidence which verifies or falsifies inductively its deductively clarified meaning.

Chapter Seven

The Murray Group And
The Search For Foundations

When I began systematic theological thinking in 1973, I faced three interrelated speculative challenges: 1) I had to clarify the operations proper to foundational thinking, 2) I had to derive from the philosophical tradition in the United States a logically valid, coherent, applicable, and adequate metaphysics of experience. I also had to formulate a normative, foundational account of the forms and dynamics of conversion coordinate with that metaphysics. 3) Finally, I had to construct a theological system on the foundations I had laid. The last chapter described how I responded to the first challenge in the first three studies in foundational theology which I published. This chapter gives an account of how I dealt with the second challenge. The final chapter will describe system building. In this chapter, I will describe first how my metaphysics of experience evolved; but, in order to contextualize historically how my thinking developed, I need first to describe the formation of that scholarly community of faith which most supported me in that creative enterprise. I refer, of course, to the John Courtney Murray Group.

The initial formation of the John Courtney Murray Group resulted from the convergence of its five founding members at the Jesuit School of Theology in Berkeley during the summer of 1979. At the beginning of the academic year 1978-79 Bill Spohn had joined the faculty of JSTB as an associate professor of moral theology. Bill had completed his doctorate at the University of Chicago, where he had studied with James Gustavsen. Like me, Bill had gut theological questions he needed to clarify for himself. He felt especially fascinated by the *de facto* functioning of the Christian conscience. He felt sure that neither Kantian, deontological ethics nor traditional, Catholic, natural-law ethics offered defensible models for Christian moral reasoning. Bill

wanted to explore the philosophical tradition in the United States for the light
it had to throw on this fundamental problem in theological ethics; and, under
Gustavson's direction, he had written his dissertation on the thought of
Jonathan Edwards. He eventually transformed the dissertation into several
scholarly theological articles which laid initial foundations for the theological ethics he would develop. As Bill's rethinking of the dynamics of the
Christian conscience evolved, it significantly influenced my own understanding of moral deliberation in faith.

In 1977, Johnny Stacer had enjoyed a sabbatical from teaching in the collegiate program of the New Orleans Province. He spent it writing a creative
statement of his own philosophy in a manuscript entitled *Pilgrim's Process*.
Johnny had done his doctorate in United States philosophy at Tulane University in New Orleans and had written his dissertation on the thought of William
Ernest Hocking, about whom he has taught me much over the years. Johnny
had spent the first semester of his sabbatical where the Cheerful Charlies had
spent the first half of their first vacation in 1970: namely, in the villa of our
parish in Albuquerque, in the Jemez Mountains, near the town of Cuba, New
Mexico. While working on his manuscript, Johnny had witnessed the glory of
an aspen fall in the Rocky Mountains. He came to JSTB during the second

William Spohn, S.J. at the upper Yosemite Falls overlook.

semester, where he completed work on his book. Since he and I had both participated in the American Studies Group which Joe and I had started at Loyola University in New Orleans, during that spring semester in Berkeley Johnny and I resumed our collaboration by sharing manuscripts with one another and by critiquing constructively one another's work.

In the spring of 1979, J.J. Mueller, S.J., of the Missouri Province, completed his doctorate at the Graduate Theological Union. J.J. had gotten interested in process theology and had written his dissertation on the theology of Bernard Meland. He subsequently published it in 1981 under the title: *Faith and Appreciative Awareness: The Cultural Theology of Bernard E. Meland.*

Finally, during the summer of 1979 Frank Oppenheim came to Berkeley in order to study the Royce manuscripts in the Bancroft Library. Hubert Howe Bancroft had possessed the historical prescience to begin collecting original documents relevant to the history of the American presence in early California after the Gold Rush of 1849. In writing his history of the early years of California, Josiah Royce had drawn on Bancroft's collection, which eventually evolved into the manuscript library of the University of California in Berkeley. Royce had taught at the University of California before William James secured him a temporary position on the Harvard faculty. As a consequence, the Bancroft Library contains a significant collection of Royce papers which Frank had come to study and peruse.

During the summer, the Jesuit community in Berkeley shrinks drastically in size as the scholastics depart for a variety of pastoral and academic projects during the summer months. While scattered among the different houses of the JSTB complex, the members of the summer community gather for lunch and dinner at Claver House, which has a cook. During the academic year, the scholastic communities cook for themselves. It therefore came to pass one day early in the summer of '79 that the five of us–myself, Johnny, Frank, J.J., and Bill–all had lunch together in the garden adjoining Claver House. In the course of lunch, Johnny and I described to the others how we had been reading and critiquing one another's writing projects. We both waxed eloquent about the advantages of scholarly collaboration. Since all five of us found ourselves engaged in different research projects, we agreed to read and critique one another's projects over the course of the summer.

During the summer of 1979, the Jesuit Community in Berkeley had undertaken extensive renovations of our buildings and had advertised for any Jesuit scholastics who felt willing to donate a summer in order to assist the JSTB maintenance crew in completing its many projects. Michael Mahon, S.J., of the Missouri Province, had volunteered. Mike had done his M.A. thesis at St. Louis University on the philosophy of Josiah Royce; and, when he got wind of what the five of us were doing, he asked if he could sit in on our working sessions, especially on those dealing with Royce. Mike had volunteered to assist the maintenance crew in part as a way of checking out JSTB as a place for him to do his own theological studies. In fact, he opted for theology in The People's Republic. That summer, we welcomed him into the Murray Group and urged him to participate in as many sessions as he could fit into his work schedule. Mike did join us for several sessions and eventually became a full member of the Murray Group.

In the course of that summer, the Murray Group took initial institutional shape. We set aside two hours for each working session during which we discussed each participant's project. We also agreed to set aside one day a week to recreate and have fun together. Since we all attended the summer community Eucharists, we prayed regularly together. In other words, during that first summer, in giving initial shape to the Murray Group we focused our energies primarily on the working sessions and on recreating regularly together. We took praying together for granted.

From the beginning we approached one another's work positively and constructively. We tried as much as we could to help one another improve each project. During that summer we experienced a truth which both Peirce and Royce had articulated theoretically: namely, that human thinking advances best in a community of discourse whose members stand corporately committed to the truth. In the course of our discussions, we also found that we shared many speculative interests. By the end of the summer, we agreed that we had all found the working sessions so profitable that we ought to continue summer scholarly collaboration for the indefinite future.

Having committed ourselves for the long haul to create and nurture a scholarly community of shared philosophical and theological discourse, we groped for a patron after whom to name our research group. By the end of the summer of 1979, we knew that we wanted to develop a systematic theology in dialogue with the classical American philosophical tradition. As the first Catholic practitioner of creative philosophical and theological thinking in the Unites States, Orestes Brownson recommended himself to us as a possible patron. So did John Courtney Murray, who, as we have seen, had spent his theological career wrestling philosophically and theologically with "the American proposition." We found both candidates attractive; but, since at that point our little group contained only Jesuits, our brother Jesuit won the contest. We became The John Courtney Murray Group. I, for my part, saw the Murray Group as standing in the same historical tradition as the Transcendental Club and the Metaphysical Club.

Over the years, a number of interrelated factors have shaped and reshaped the Murray Group's identity and institutional structures. 1) Very early we decided that we needed to create support structures for fostering community among the members of the Murray Group over and above our working sessions and weekly recreation together. 2) The group projects we undertook generated other institutions within the Group. 3) Recruitment and publicity shaped and reshaped us. So did 4) hospitality and 5) the different ways in which we learned to recreate together.

During the summer of 1981, the five founding members of the Murray Group lived at the Weston School of Theology in Cambridge, Massachusetts. We all occupied 40 Kirkland Street with John Padberg, S.J. (MIS)[1], the then president of Weston. John loves good and substantive conversation and delighted both in hosting the Group and in our conversation at meals. The Weston maintenance crew was renovating 40 Kirkland that summer, with the result that we had to put up with lots of hammering and other noise during the day. Toward the end of the summer, John, who once said, "Too much of a good thing is just about enough," treated us to an elegant dinner at a private club in Boston to which he, as president of the Weston School, belonged. We sensed that he did so as a way of atoning for the inconvenience caused by the renovations. By the end of the summer, we knew that as long as John continued as president of Weston, the Murray Group could always count on a very warm welcome there. We looked forward to other summers with him.

During that summer in Cambridge, Frank Oppenheim, whose immersion in Royce sensitized him to the importance and difficulty to creating and sustaining communal life, suggested that, in addition to our working sessions and weekly recreation together, we ought to set aside time for each member of the group to share with the others how things had gone during the previous year and to discuss with the group any important decisions that the coming year would hold. The other members of the Murray Group supported Frank's suggestion enthusiastically. The addition of sharing sessions doubled the number of meetings we had in the course of the summer, since each member of the Group had both a working and a sharing session. As the group grew in size, we eventually consecrated the first half hour of each working session to personal sharing in order to shorten the number of hours we spent in meetings.

Moreover, during the summer of 1981, the fact that we lived together in one house, meant that we regularly did Eucharist together as a group. We found that both the faith sharing and regular prayer together as the Murray Group significantly enhanced the Group's quality of life over the course of the summer. Both experiences convinced us that the Murray Group should not make the mistake of narrow professionalism. We wanted and needed to continue collaborating professionally; but, after 1981 collaboration also meant creating a community of personal support in which the members of the Group both knew one another personally in some depth and stood ready to support one another personally, in faith, and in prayer.

Toward the end of the summer of 1981, Bill Spohn attended a meeting at Georgetown University. He described the Murray Group and its work to Walter Burghardt, S.J. (MAR), the then editor of *Theological Studies*. Walter in response graciously invited the Murray Group to consider doing a thematic issue of *Theological Studies*. The Jesuits at the Woodstock Center were also engaged in collaborative research and offered to host the Murray Group during the following summer.

When Bill returned to Weston with both offers, we decided to accept them. We agreed to go to Georgetown the following summer in order to write and edit the essays which we hoped would appear as a single issue of *Theological Studies*. We wanted the issue to announce the Murray Group to the scholarly community in the United States and to communicate to that community our strategy for doing inculturated theological thinking in an American context. We also decided to include in our working sessions those members of the Woodstock Center who desired to participate. Since Bill had made the initial contacts in Georgetown, the Group charged him with making housing arrangements there for the following summer.

When we convened in Georgetown during the summer of 1982, the Murray Group had acquired two new members: Andrew Christiansen, S.J. (MD) and Mike Mahon. Drew had just joined the JSTB faculty and provided a voice in theological ethics to dialogue with Bill Spohn. Mike was working on an essay about the ethical issues involved in nuclear deterrence which he eventually published in a *National Jesuit News Supplement*. The following year Mike's essay won a national award. Mike's project did not form a part of the *Theological Studies* project; but we did discuss his paper with members of the Woodstock center also participating. As we shall see, Mike's essay would influence in significant ways the Murray Group's sense of scholarly purpose.

For a variety of reasons, that summer proved one of the most taxing the Group ever experienced. First of all, Bill had not succeeded in getting us housing all in one place. Bill and I lived at the Woodstock Center. Johnny and Frank stayed with the Georgetown community. J.J. found himself in the O street community with Mike in K street and Drew in Jennifer Street. As a consequence, we found ourselves deprived of many of the personal and communal support structures which we had come to prize during the preceding summer. We missed keenly day-to-day social contact. This social vacuum within the Murray Group convinced us all the more of the importance of living together and of praying together regularly in the course of the summer. We all vowed never to settle again for separate living quarters.

Second, including the members of the Woodstock Center in our discussions proved a mixed blessing. We did get helpful input from them; but the tone of our discussions in the Murray Group had from the beginning taken a constructive rather than an aggressive, confrontational tone. We found more often than we would have preferred that the interventions from the Woodstock Center tended to follow the latter pattern. Just as the lack of common housing convinced the members of the Murray Group of the importance of maintaining over our future summers a constructive, communal support system, so too the academic style of the Woodstock Center convinced us all the more of the importance of maintaining a constructive, supportive tone in our professional working sessions.

Third, we had accepted with naive enthusiasm Walter Burghardt's offer to undertake a thematic issue of *Theological Studies*; but we had completely underestimated the amount of work involved in writing from scratch and editing seven essays in the course of a single summer. Walter, an old and seasoned hand at editing, probably foresaw that we had bitten off more than we

The Murray Group at Notre Dame University in 1988: from left to right: the author, Karl Starkloff, S.J., John Stacer, S.J., Andrew Christiansen, S.J., J.J. Mueller, S.J., Stephen Rowntree, S.J.

could chew and offered to publish whatever we came up with, either as a single issue or in separate issues of *Theological Studies*. Since the Murray Group had accepted Walter's offer in part as a way of announcing to the scholarly world our existence and aims as an ongoing research seminar in theological inculturation, we arrived in Georgetown with our hearts set collectively on a single issue. As a consequence, we found Walter's suggestion of sequential publication unexpected and initially off-putting. Unfortunately, as the summer wore on and our nerves got increasingly frazzled from stress and overwork, the idea of sequential publication eventually occasioned a minor misunderstanding between us and Walter, but one which we quickly patched up.

Fourth, although Drew had worked closely with Walter before that summer, the rest of us had not. We soon discovered that he maintained extremely high editorial standards indeed. As our summer labors sapped our limited human resources, we all came regretfully to realize that we would not succeed in producing a single thematic issue of *Theological Studies*. The enormity of the task of writing, discussing , revising, and editing seven major essays in the course of a single summer left us exhausted and dispirited. This experience too, however, gave decisive institutional shape to the Murray Group. We determined that we would never again attempt to complete a common project in a single summer.

Over the years, the Murray Group has discussed four common projects, completed two, and partially completed a third. We are currently finishing a fifth. After the summer at Georgetown, in every common project we have undertaken, we have allowed at least two summers to complete the work. During the first summer, we discuss the shape of the project and assign topics to individual members of the Group for scholarly development. During the intervening year, we write the projected essays. Then, during the second summer we discuss, edit, and revise the essays. Ordinarily, one or more members of the Group then takes responsibility for a final editing of the entire project and for seeing it into print.

Even though we did not succeed in producing a thematic issue of *Theological Studies*, all our essays did appear in successive issues of that journal. Bill Spohn also arranged with Georgetown University Press to bring all six essays out in a single volume which had something of the same effect as a theme issue of *Theological Studies*, even though the book enjoyed a smaller circulation than the theme issue would have had. Frank Oppenheim did the book's final editing. The first joint project of the Murray Group appeared under the title *The Reasoning Heart*.

Despite its pressure, wear, and tear, the summer of '82 defined the Murray Group in yet another and unexpected way. The collaborative attempt to give shape to what we hoped would become a single thematic issue of *Theological Studies* forced us to articulate for ourselves the scope and purpose of the Murray Group. We gave verbal expression to our enhanced, shared self-understanding as a scholarly community of inquiry in a never-published preface to the single thematic issue which never saw print. I cite here much of that preface because its statement of purpose has ever since functioned as a kind of charter of the John Courtney Murray Group.

The Purpose Of This Issue

The authors of this issue of *Theological Studies* all belong to the Murray Group, a post-doctoral seminar in philosophical theology. The Group takes its name from the late John Courtney Murray and honors his pioneering contribution to the formulation of an indigenous North American theology. Like Fr. Murray, the members of the Group that bears his name ambition an inculturated theology in dialogue both with contemporary religious thought and with the classical North American philosophical tradition. That ambition gives the present issue of *Theological Studies* both its theme and its method. We, the authors, have chosen as its theme the development of an inculturated theology for the United States and as its method the retrieval in a theological context of classical North American philosophy. Since both the theme and the method of this issue may strike some of the readers of *Theological Studies* as unusual, if not quixotic, both deserve explanation.

The term "inculturation" was coined in the wake of Vatican II. It connotes a certain ideal of evangelization, one which respects religious and cultural pluralism. Inculturated evangelization thrusts simultaneously in two directions. First, because it respects the right of people to incarnate the gospel in symbols derived from their particular cultural tradition, inculturated teaching adapts its idiom to those it addresses; but inculturated evangelization cannot rest content with superficial adaptation. In addition, therefore, it seeks to transform every culture from within in such a way that the Christian message unifies, animates, and directs the shared life of a people.

In order to accomplish this end, an inculturated proclamation of the gospel needs a sound theology of conversion articulated in categories derived from the culture it addresses. Classical American philosophy offers a rich source of the kind of categories we mean, a far richer one than the analytic philosophy currently in vogue in most American universities. Anglo-American thinkers from Jonathan Edwards in the eighteenth century to Alfred North Whitehead in the twentieth have probed the dynamic structure of human religious experience. Fascinated with the dynamics of conversion, with religious psychology, with the logic of faith, and with the sources and significance of religious insight, they have produced classic accounts of religious growth in David Tracy's sense of the term "classic." One discovers in their work both a surplus of meaning and an enduring relevance to contemporary religious problems.

The classical American philosophers have described, formed, and challenged cultural patterns in the United States. John Courtney Murray sensed this keenly

when he chose to wrestle with "the American proposition." His systematic theological retrieval of the insights of the founding fathers of our republic eventually gave rise to the most significant contribution of the North American church
to Vatican II: the decree on religious liberty. But other classic American thinkers
have redirected the life of this nation. They too have something still to say about
the meaning of "the American proposition." In the present issue of *Theological
Studies* we shall attempt to listen to their voices.

The next section of the statement of purpose introduced the thinkers
we proposed to consider in our aborted thematic issue of *Theological
Studies*. Having done so, our statement returned to a consideration of the
aims and goals both of the issue and of the Murray Group as a research
seminar.

Of the many advantages that would result from the systematic elaboration of an
indigenous North American theology, we ask the readers of *Theological Studies*
to ponder initially only three.

We live in an ecumenical age. The classical American philosophers who
have described and in some measure given direction to our culture emerged
by and large from a Protestant tradition. Sometimes they turned to philosophy because they did not find in the mainline Protestant churches intellectually satisfying answers to the religious questions they faced. Some of them
learned to speak in an almost Catholic idiom; but all of them shaped in some
significant way secular American culture. A theological retrieval of the classical American philosophers could as a consequence offer an interesting common ground for ecumenical discussion among American Catholics and
Protestants; for both religious groups have been shaped by secular culture
and they need to come to terms critically with its influence on their religious
beliefs and practice.

The systematic pursuit of an inculturated Anglo-American theology promises other benefits as well. Communities come to full consciousness as communities by re-appropriating the event that founds them and the heritage that
results from that event. Once we concede the legitimacy and importance of
cultural pluralism within Christianity, then the Church in different countries
faces a twofold challenge if it is to achieve full community consciousness.
Not only must it constantly re-appropriate the Christian heritage that inserts
it into the life of the world Church, but it must also retrieve its national and
religious heritage as well. Only through inculturated theological thinking can
American Christians reach a shared understanding of those gifts which a distinctively American incarnation of Christianity has to offer the rest of the
Christian world.

Finally, only through the pursuit of inculturated theology can Christians in
this country begin to deal systematically with the inauthenticity, hypocrisy, and
oppressive uses of power that mar "our American way of life." For inculturated

theology seeks not only to appropriate in faith the legitimate values incarnate in diverse cultures but also to summon both individuals and communities to repentant transformation in Christ.

That final paragraph in many ways reflects the contribution which editing Mike Mahon's essay on nuclear deterrence made to the Murray Group's self-understanding. Mike's essay grappled with a major issue of morality and justice in contemporary United States culture and did so masterfully. The original members of the Murray Group had agreed to develop a theology in dialogue with the classical North American tradition. Mike's essay helped us to realize that the work of the Murray Group would remain incomplete unless it addressed pressing issues in contemporary U.S. culture.

By the summer of 1985, the Murray Group had sufficiently recovered from its first joint project in order to ambition a second one, beginning with the summer of 1986. We had all read *Habits of the Heart* and had resonated with its trenchant critique of the individualism which corrupts and subverts the consciences of otherwise good, well-intentioned Americans, especially of the middle and upper classes. Moreover, the *Habits* team posed a challenge to students of the cultural tradition in the Unites States to which we members of the Murray Group felt we could make an initial and intelligent response. *Habits of the Heart* called for a retrieval of dimensions of the cultural tradition in this country which challenge the more dominant individualistic ethos and which provide a positive alternative to it. As a research seminar we had dedicated ourselves to just such a retrieval. We decided to spend the following summer discussing the issues raised by *Habits of the Heart* and deciding which issues among the many it raised we desired to address.

The summer of 1986 found the Murray Group at Lewis-Bremner House on the campus of Loyola University in Chicago. A member of the Chicago Province, Frank Oppenheim acted as our contact with the University. Our host community at Lewis-Bremner welcomed us warmly, although we fretted in the course of the summer about upsetting their normal communal routines with the now fairly standardized, working schedule of the Murray Group. That summer, Stephen Rowntree, S.J., (NOR), who taught philosophy at Loyola University in New Orleans, joined the Murray Group for the first time. Stephen and I had lived in the same community at Fordham while we both pursued doctorates in philosophy with a focus on American thought. Stephen had developed a keen interest in the implications of Whitehead's theory of education.

By the end of the summer, we had identified the themes from *Habits of the Heart* which each of us would develop. I, predictably, chose conversion; Stephen, the nature of marital love; Frank, Royce's contribution to an in-depth understanding of community; Drew, John XXIII's development of the Catholic understanding of the common good; Johnny, William Ernest Hocking's understanding of world citizenship.

Robert N. Bellah, who had headed the *Habits* team and had done the final rewrite of the text of that collaborative work, taught at UCB but worked regularly with GTU students. The prospect of working with GTU doctoral candidates had in part drawn Bob to UCB, and he told me on more than one occasion that it kept him in Berkeley. Bob found in GTU students outstanding, gifted doctoral candidates who exhibited more interest in values discourse than most of his colleagues and students in sociology. When Bob heard of our response to his book, he showed great interest in our project, sat in on one of our working sessions, and eventually wrote a response to our essays in an afterword to our volume, which appeared with Notre Dame University Press under the title: *Beyond Individualism: Toward a Retrieval of Moral Discourse in America* (1989). *Beyond Individualism* remained in print longer than any other joint project we attempted, largely, I suspect, because teachers, as we had hoped they would, used it as a companion text to *Habits of the Heart*. It represents, in my judgment, our most successful joint project to date.

During the summer of 1988, we decided to take on a third joint project; but it had mixed results. John Padberg, now the director of the Institute of Jesuit Sources at St. Louis University, had repeatedly offered to host the Murray Group at the Institute and to help us plan a volume on Jesuit spirituality. We took a while to accept John's oft repeated invitation, because we had genuine forebodings about spending a hot, humid summer in St. Louis.

No doubt the many summers the Murray Group had spent in Berkeley had spoiled us. During the summer, the northern part of San Francisco Bay may provide the only habitable place in the United States. The Golden Gate controls summer weather in the north Bay. It marks the only gap in the Coastal Range. As the summer sun heats up California's central valley, it sizzles in the high nineties. The hot air it generates rises and moves east across the Sierra Nevadas. There it cools and transforms itself into scattered thunder showers, ordinarily the only precipitation the Sierras know during the summer drought. As the air from the central valley rises, it draws in the cool sea air through the Golden Gate and with it the fog bank which sits off the California coast during the summer.

Berkeley sits directly opposite the Golden Gate. When the high fog comes in every day, as it typically does like clock-work at five o'clock in the afternoon, the temperatures drop twenty degrees and remain that way all night. Since the fog normally burns off at ten o'clock in the morning, temperatures in the north Bay tend to range from fifteen to twenty degrees cooler than anywhere else in entire Bay Area. This unusual weather pattern explains the oft-quoted aphorism attributed to Mark Twain: "The coldest winter I ever spent was a summer in San Francisco." In the west Bay, sometimes the fog never burns off. When that happens, people in San Francisco shiver. Many summer tourists know nothing about the fog and its gelid consequences. They step off the airplane at the San Francisco airport in shorts and tee shirts, turn blue, and buy warm clothes as quickly as they can. As a consequence, the sale of sweaters and sweat shirts during the summer provides a staple of the San Francisco tourist trade.

At any rate, the combination of JSTB hospitality, outstanding library facilities, and cool, dry summers made Berkeley the Murray Group's place of preference for summer research. The prospect of spending a month or more of slow roasting in St. Louis heat left its pampered members reluctant to accept John's invitations to join him for a summer's work in America's heartland, despite the warm and genuine affection we all felt for John from our summers with him in Weston. Finally, we decided to spend the summer of 1988 working with him and planning a volume on Jesuit spirituality. Since J.J. Mueller taught at St. Louis University, he took charge of setting up our living and working arrangements.

During the summer of 1989, the community at Jesuit Hall went out of its way to make us feel welcome. Barry McGannon, S.J., hosted the Murray Group at a dinner in Père Marquette State Park. During the excursion we viewed the locks in the Mississippi River north of St. Louis and visited the rocks on which Fr. Marquette had seen and subsequently described strange Indian hieroglyphs. On our regular days of rest, we made good use of the Jesuit villa in Green Hills, especially its swimming pool. Stephen's unabashed enthusiasm for professional baseball even got the Murray Group to a Cardinals game. At it I learned that professional baseball fans in St. Louis do not attend games in order to watch them. The Cardinal fans carried on conversations, drank beer, ate hot dogs, and did the wave; but nothing they did, including the wave, had anything to do with what was happening on the field.

Despite all the kindnesses and warm hospitality, the Murray Group never did feel quite at home in Jesuit Hall, which remains a hotel despite the Jesuit community's imaginative attempts to turn it into a residence. By the end of the summer, we all agreed, however, that the privilege of working closely with both John Padberg and Walter Ong, S.J. more than made up for the impersonality of spending one of our summers in a hotel at the heart of sweltering, muggy St. Louis.

Our brainstorming on the state of U.S. Jesuit spirituality at the end of the 1980s drew two broad conclusions: 1) We agreed that in the sixties and seventies, Jesuits in this country had groped for ways to humanize the impersonal, legalistic, canonical spirituality which pre-Vatican-II Jesuits had generally absorbed. Given the therapeutic caste of U.S. culture, we had often used psychological insights to impart a measure of personal warmth to the living of Jesuit life. We American Jesuits had not, however, sufficiently criticized the individualistic presuppositions which skew therapeutic thinking in the United States, or so the Murray Group felt. Our essays on Jesuit spirituality sought, therefore, to move beyond a therapeutic, psychological model for Jesuit spirituality to one more focused on the apostolate. 2) We also agreed in the course of our brainstorming that U.S. Jesuits needed strategies for sustaining their commitment to an apostolic spirituality under the often dispiriting restorationist papacy of John Paul II. This theme too our essays tried to develop.

Unfortunately, the revised essays never saw print as a single volume. When John Padberg got them in their final draft, his own high editorial standards led him to deem that they needed more work than his busy schedule allowed. He decided, therefore, that the Institute of Jesuit Sources would not publish our project. The attempt to find another publisher misfired. Most of the essays we had written on Jesuit spirituality did eventually find their way into print, but as separate pieces.

The summer of 1993 saw a faithful remnant of the Murray Group gathered in Berkeley. Johnny and Stephen spent a significant portion of that summer in Zimbabwe at a meeting to plan the new English-speaking collegiate program which they would subsequently help found in Harare. Johnny had already taught philosophy in Nigeria during the summer of 1992. Elizabeth Linehan, R.S.M., who had joined the Group in 1991 had to cancel at the last minuet. John Staudenmaier, S.J. (WIS), who had joined us in 1987, also did not attend. Nor did Mark Massa, S.J. (DET), who like Betsy had joined in 1991. Carl Starkloff, S.J. (MIS), who had joined in 1987, did attend. Carl, an old classmate, had spent most of his professional theological career teaching at our theologate in Toronto and studying the Church's mission to Native Americans. John Markey, O.P. a full member of the Murray Group since 1991, found himself plagued with major health problems but attended as many working sessions as he found physically possible.

Over the years, the number of the Murray Group remained from eight to twelve as old members fell away and new members joined. During the summer of '93 we recruited some important new members. Joe Tetlow had been longing for years to participate in the Murray Group; but his work during the summers as tertian instructor made that impossible. After he resigned as tertian instructor, he accepted a chair in spirituality at St. Louis University. In the summer of 1993, Joe joined the Murray Group for the first time. So did Si Hendry, one of the participants in the Lonergan seminar I had given during my final semester in New Orleans. Si was now pursuing a doctorate in spirituality at the GTU and would eventually write a major study of the spirituality of the Jesuit Volunteer Corps. Robert Lassalle-Klein, a GTU Inter-Area doctoral candidate, also participated for the first time. Bob would eventually put the philosophy and theology of Ignatio Ellacuria into dialogue with Peirce's pragmatism. Thomas Regan, S.J. (NEN) had done his dissertation on Whitehead and joined the Group briefly at the end of the summer in order to present a provocative paper on the post-modernism of James Madison. Despite the absence of old timers, then, the new members brought our total number up to eight.

Joe had anthologized his articles on *The Word* written during his years on the staff of *America* magazine as essays in lay spirituality. At the beginning of the summer of 1993, he persuaded several of the Murray Group to undertake a joint project on lay Catholic spirituality. We planned it more carefully than any other joint undertaking; but it never got off the ground. Joe provided most of the energy fueling the project. He spent the summer of 1994 preparing to attend our next General Congregation in Rome. The Missouri Province, who knew quality when they saw it, had elected Joe their province delegate, even though Joe continued to belong to the New Orleans Province at the same time that he held a chair at St. Louis University. By the summer of 1995, Joe had to drop out of the Murray Group because Fr. General Peter Hans Kolvenbach had appointed him to the General's Extended Council in charge of the apostolate of spirituality. In a sense, however, a popular volume in lay spirituality did eventually emerge from the Murray Group: not the volume we had planned but my own book, *The Conversion Experience*, which appeared in 1998 and which popularized my theology of conversion and of the sacraments with special attention to the RCIA. The text of *The Conversion Experience* expanded and completed a series of popular lectures I had agreed to give at Sogang University in Seoul, Korea but had never delivered.

Over the years, the Murray Group has used a variety of strategies to recruit new members. First of all, we invited interested individuals to function as satellite members of the Group. If they showed an interest in becoming permanent members, we asked them to participate for a second summer. After two summers of participation both the new candidate and the permanent members of the Group made a decision about permanent participation. We adopted this policy because we felt it important that the Group grow slowly and organically and that new members understand and endorse the aims and goals of the Group before joining it on a permanent basis.

Not all satellite members turned into permanent members; but a significant number did. Over the years, the personal interests of new members modulated discourse within the Murray Group. Betsy Linehan focused our attention on U.S. obsession with the death penalty. Carl Starkloff sensitized us to the dilemmas facing the Native American community. Robert Lassalle-Klein, Alejandro Garcia-Rivera, and Nancy Pineda taught us to value the distinctive contribution of Hispanic theology to thought in the United States. Gregory Zuschlag sought to involve Peirce's thought in the dialogue among eco-theologians. Daniel Groody, C.S.C. and Si Hendry alerted us to significant movements in popular lay spirituality. John Staudenmaier educated us to the values embodied in U.S. technology. Not all satellite members who became core members stayed on permanently. Many participated for several years and then severed connection with the Group: Mike Mahon (1988), J.J. Mueller, (1991), Drew Christiansen (1991), Johnny Stacer (1993), Stephen Rowntree (1993), Carl Starkloff (1993), John Staudenmaier (1996).

Besides the recruitment of satellite members, the Murray Group used other strategies to publicize itself. Like the Clavius Group we moved around during the summers. The Murray Group met in Cambridge, Massachusetts, in 1981, 1984, 1991, and 1995, at Georgetown in 1982, at Loyola University in Chicago in 1986, at Notre Dame University in 1988, at St. Louis University in 1989. In 1982 Bill Spohn published an article about the Murray Group in the *National Jesuit News*. In 1987, The Catholic Theological Society of America approved the Murray Group's sponsorship of a permanent seminar in American contextual theology. In 1989 Cornel West participated in that seminar which discussed his book, *Keeping Faith*. We have seen occasional references to the work of the Murray Group in scholarly journals. To date, the work of members of the Murray Group with doctoral candidates has proven the most effective way to recruit new members.

During the more than twenty-five years of its existence, the Murray Group has also used hospitality both to foster a sense of community among its members and to acquaint other members of the academic community with our existence and work. Richard Hocking, the son of William Ernest Hocking and a personal friend of both Johnny Stacer and Frank Oppenheim, visited the Murray Group in 1981. In 1998, Richard and Frank collaborated in editing *Metaphysics*, Josiah Royce's last lecture course on metaphysics. Richard's father had done the preliminary editing of Royce's lecture notes. Richard and Frank did a final re-editing and saw them into print. Frank had met William Ernest Hocking before he died; and Johnny had lived at the Hocking home while researching his dissertation on the elder Hocking's philosophy. During the same summer that Richard Hocking visited us, Lisa Cahill, the distinguished moral theologian from Boston College and personal friend of Bill Spohn spent an evening with us. During the summer of 1984, Cecil McGarry, S.J., the then

Frank Oppenheim, S.J. and John Markey, O.P. (right) flanking the owner of the site of Avon Farm, the house in which Josiah Royce grew up, during the Murray Group's excursion into California gold country in 1988.

dean of Hekima College in Nairobi, spent a week with the Murray Group in "Padberg's Palazzo" at 15 Hawthorne Street in Cambridge, a handsome, three-story residence for the Weston School of Theology and half a block from the apartment Al and Barbara had occupied on Acacia Street. During the Murray Group's summer at 2014 Delaware Street in Berkeley, Michael Buckley visited us frequently. In 1986, our summer at Loyola University in Chicago, Jon Nilson and Robert Harvenak, S.J. (CHI), who both participated in a group somewhat analogous to the Murray Group, had several interchanges with us. During our many summers in Berkeley, Al and Barbara regularly trekked from Stanford to Berkeley to dine with the Murray Group.

During the summer of 1984, when the Murray Group still had an all-Jesuit membership, John Padberg paid us a handsome complement. "I don't find it extraordinary," John said, "that a group of Jesuits should get together for a summer to collaborate professionally. I don't find it extraordinary that besides collaborating they would also take time to recreate together as you do; but, when on top of all of that, they all genuinely like one another–now, that's extraordinary!"

From the beginning, the Murray Group has consisted of a community of good friends and has remained that as we have welcomed more and more non-Jesuit members. The founding members of the Murray Group all enjoyed the outdoors and spent their day off hiking the abundant parks of the San Francisco Bay Area. Over the years, not all members enjoyed such strenuous relaxation; but the Group has maintained as a top priority spending quality time together in the course of the summer. The summer of 1988 at Notre Dame University we re- member as the year of the bicycle, as we took long cycling trips over the rolling hills of Indiana. During the summer of 1992, besides visiting Big Basin and other memorable California parks, we made a pilgrimage to Grass Valley, where we viewed the site of the Royce family's Avon farm, secured a map of the orig- inal farm in Nevada City, and dined on the way back to Berkeley at the Nan- tucket Seafood Company, a restaurant at the bottom of the bridge over the Car- quinez Straits. During the following summer, at the urging of Carl Starkloff, we swam a lot in the Del Valle Wilderness and once at Contra Loma State Park. Dur- ing the same summer, Bill Spohn, who had just joined the faculty of Santa Clara University, hosted the Murray Group at Ben Lomen, the Santa Clara community villa, where we spent most of the afternoon in the pool. As the Group has ac- quired family types as members, they have regularly hosted us in their homes. During the summer of 1999, Bob and Lyn Lassalle-Klein graciously hosted one of my many retirement parties.

Very early the Murray Group evolved into an organized effort to create community around one of the loneliest of the Jesuit apostolates: namely, the apostolate of research. That effort expressed our shared commitment to a philosophical belief enunciated by Peirce and systematically elaborated by Royce: namely, that the human mind functions best in a community of inquiry whose members live dedicated to collaborating with one another in the search for truth. Everyone who has participated in the Murray Group has expressed satisfaction at the benefits derived from its institutionalized repudiation of in- tellectual individualism. More than any other community to which I belong, the Murray Group has shaped the way I think.

I have profited not only from our group process each summer but also from suggestions made by individual members of the Group. Shortly after *Experi- encing God* saw print, for example, Bill Spohn urged me to make more of an effort to find my own theological voice. I took his advice to heart in writing *The Divine Mother*. I abandoned Whiteheadean jargon and with that work be- gan to construct a system.

Switching from technical philosophical language to ordinary language took some time. Like Whitehead, Peirce recognized that philosophy has no other tool than language and that ordinary language teems with vague and ambiguous terms. As a consequence, he too felt the need to coin technical philosophical terms which sound to non-philosophers like jargon but which endow Peirce's philosophical prose with technical precision. It took me, therefore some time to hit upon less technical terms for communicating as accurately as I could technical philosophical insights.

Peirce's technical terms make some important metaphysical points. His phenomenology, as we have seen, recognizes three generic kinds of descriptive categories: "quality," "fact," and "law." In transforming them from descriptive to metaphysical categories, he calls quality "Firstness," fact "Secondness," and law "Thirdness." Any concept would exemplify a quality. The term "Firstness" calls attention to the fact that concepts simply are what they are and in this sense enjoy a certain ontological simplicity. He calls fact, or efficacious action and re-action, "Secondness." This term calls attention to the dyadic character of factual exchanges. For Peirce, action and reaction constitute not two distinct events but a single event with a dual character. Habitual tendencies exemplify laws. In his metaphysics, Peirce calls habitual tendencies "Thirdness." This term calls attention to the fact that habit (law) mediates between Firstness and Secondness in the symbolic interpretation of experience.

Nevertheless, it seemed to me that if I were going to try to write philosophically about experience in ordinary language, terms like "Firstness," "Secondness," and "Thirdness" would not do. At first, I contented myself with Peirce's descriptive categories: quality, fact, and law; but eventually I abandoned them as well. I replaced "quality" with "evaluation," partly as a way of repudiating the Enlightenment myth of scientific objectivity. All thinking evaluates, and scientific theories have explanatory value. Calling cognition evaluation also seemed to me to connote intentionality more than did the term "quality."

I replaced "fact" with "decision." "Fact" connoted for me givenness, and environmental impact does force itself upon us whether we like it or not. "Decision," however, seemed to me to have more dynamic connotations and described better how facts function within experience. "Decision" also applied without qualification to what Peirce called "degenerate Secondness." Immanent activity exemplifies degenerate Secondness because it has the decisive character and concreteness of a fact but lacks a dyadic character since it provokes no corresponding reaction from another.

Finally, I replaced "law" with "tendency." The term "law" struck me as somewhat impersonal, whereas "tendency" seemed more open to a personal interpretation. I called autonomously functioning tendencies "selves" and self-conscious selves capable of conversion human persons.

I therefore came to define "experience" philosophically as a process composed of relational elements called feelings; and I discovered in the higher forms of experience three generic kinds of relations: evaluations, decisions, and tendencies. Evaluations exemplify conceptual, intentional relations; decisions environmental and social relationships, and tendencies a relationship to the future.

"Evaluations," "decisions," and "tendencies" designate three distinct but interrelated realities because they enjoy irreducible traits. In and of themselves, human evaluative responses like sensations, emotions, images, concepts, or ideals enjoy qualitative particularity. They become individual, general, or universal through predication. They themselves, however, exemplify particular possibilities. Decisions exemplify concrete actualities, not particular possibilities. Decisions make experience this rather than that. We deliberate about decisions which mutually exclude one another and eventually choose this one rather than that one. Tendencies exemplify real generality, not concrete actuality or particular possibility. Particular possibility differs from concrete actuality, and they both differ in character from generals which enjoy reality rather than possibility and actuality.

Nevertheless, the three variables which shape the higher forms of experience never exist in isolation. They constantly interplay in the development of experience. As both Peirce and Whitehead saw, human evaluative responses make us present to reality. We become conscious when we distinguish between our own bodies and their surrounding environment. When we can no longer distinguish between the two we faint, go to sleep, or succumb to total anesthesia. We grow in personal consciousness by making distinctions and by grasping relationships among the things we have distinguished from one another. In this context, I found Whitehead's term "presentational immediacy" a suggestive one and decided to endorse it. He used it to characterize how evaluative responses function within experience. In making us present to ourselves and to our world, they ground the experience of the present moment.

In Whitehead, every instance of presentational immediacy perishes in a fraction of a second. As a result, every occasion of experience experiences a past becoming present but perishes before it can experience a future. This manifest deficiency in Whitehead's system results from his failure to give an adequate account of temporal continuity.

Having endorsed Peirce's account of continuity within development, I therefore invoked the notion of presentational immediacy in order to explain the human experience of real as opposed to clock time. Real time coincides with the continuous development of selves and persons through their ongoing interaction. Clock time measures real time by some standard, like a stopwatch or a sundial.

We sense the decisive impact of our environments upon us. Sensations occur a fraction of a second after the physical stimulus which causes them. The physical stimulus provides us with an immediate past to which our sensations make us initially present. Sensations make us therefore initially but very vaguely present to reality and ground our initial experience of the present moment.

Close study of sensations reveals, moreover, that they also have emotional coloring. I endorsed Peirce's insight that we perceive more than we sense, because in addition to sensing the factual, decisive impact of our environments on our sense organs, we perceive the tendencies which ground and explain that impact. We do so emotionally, imaginatively, inferentially, and deliberatively. If we perceive tendencies with our emotions and if sensations have emotional coloring, then even our sensations yield an extremely vague perception of the tendencies operative in ourselves and our worlds. We sense, moreover, not only external objects but our own bodies. We call the latter "propriosensation."

As our emotional response to the realities around us develops, it yields a clearer insight into the tendencies operative in them. When, for example, I fear something, I perceive it as threatening and as stronger than myself. When I feel anger, I perceive something as threatening but as conquerable. Since we judge reality with our feelings, negative emotions like anger and fear function within intuitive thinking much the way in which the adverb "not" functions in rational thinking. By the same token, the sympathetic emotions–affection, friendship, romance, etc.–function in intuitive thinking much the way in which "yes" functions in rational thinking. As our emotional perception of tendency grows it begins to endow my experience of the present moment with a future because tendency orients experience to a predictable future. The clarification of emotional perceptions through memory and imagination endows our sense of possible unfolding futures with even greater clarity. I call cognitive perceptions mediated by image and affect "intuition."

I endorse Peirce's logic of inference and recognize three irreducible but interrelated forms of inferential thinking: abduction, deduction, and induction. With hints from Emerson, Peirce, and Dewey, I find strengths and limitations in both intuitive and inferential perceptions of reality. Inferential thinking endows my perception of things with rational precision and greater rational control but does so at the price of abstractness. Having adopted Whitehead's equation of reality with process, I endorsed as well his suggestion that history makes spatio-temporal realities what they eventually become. In the course of our personal history, we must decide from one moment to the next the kind of self we intend to exemplify. Peirce had defended a similar position, but his triadic metaphysics gave a much better account than Whitehead had of continuity within development. Peirce, as we have seen, called that account his doctrine of "synechism," from the Greek verb *synechô*, I hold together. I have already discussed the superiority of Peirce's synechism to Whitehead's conceptual nominalism in chapter four.

Abstract essences make us present to reality with greater precision and control than most imaginative thinking; but their abstractness causes them to conceal more than what they reveal. To understand any finite person or thing exhaustively, one would have to recapitulate its entire history; and no abstraction can do that. The abstract essences which make us present to reality disclose to us only limited facets of the real. William James did well, then, to rail against "vicious abstractionism." Vicious abstractionism confuses abstractions with reality itself and in the process commits the essence fallacy.

Intuitive thinking, on the other hand, as Emerson correctly saw, tends more to exhibit a synthetic, holistic character than does analytic, rational inference. It therefore yields a felt sense of the whole that compensates cognitively for everything that abstract, inferential perceptions leave out. People, therefore, tend to live their lives at a felt, intuitive level rather than at an abstract, inferential level, as Peirce correctly argued in 1898 in his lectures on *Vitally Important Topics*.

The enhanced clarity and precision of inferential perceptions of reality does, however, transform human time perception. Abductive reasoning re-categorizes a reality which one is trying to understand on the basis of an initially vague rational perception of the tendencies that explain its behavior. It therefore enhances one's experience of the present by presenting reality to us in sharpened conceptual focus. Through abductive reasoning, our sensed past becomes present to us in a new way with an enhanced, though abstract vividness. When, for example, a physician diagnoses the vague pain in my tummy as an ulcer rather than a cancer, I find myself better positioned to deal with it realistically. As deduction predicts both the operational consequences of sharpened abductive perceptions of the state of things as well as the conditions required for those predicted consequences to happen, my abductively clarified sense of present reality transforms itself into an inferential prediction of a specific future. When one verifies that predicted future inductively, my deductively anticipated future becomes a perceived present. When I act decisively on the basis of my perception of reality, the sensation of what I effect and propriosensation of my own activity create a new immediate factual past for sensation to make present.

Because evaluations make us present to reality they endow experience with its "how." The "what" of experience consists of acting persons and selves. Persons and selves act decisively upon one another and create social and environmental relationships. Living things act on themselves; and immanent activity endows them with the capacity to develop new habits, new tendencies. If each finite self and each finite, human person, as Peirce saw, exemplifies an evolving complex of continuously developing tendencies, then by the decisions we take we are determining constantly, both consciously and unconsciously, the kinds of selves and persons we will eventually become.

As a result, the subject of change and development does not underlie the change as classical substance philosophy supposed. Instead, each self, each person emerges from the conscious and unconscious evaluations and decisions which make up its history. If finite persons and selves emerge from change rather than underlie it, then their physical bodies provide the immediate environment from which they emerge. Indeed, the bodies of living things exemplify a life-support system which each emerging self and each human person has to create and maintain over the course of a lifetime. For the same reason, the body functions as a significant sign of the self. Moreover, near-death experiences provide experiential evidence that in dying, the personal self emerges completely from its body and enters into a new and different mode of vital existence in which one apparently enjoys a greater sense of wholeness as well as enhanced sensations and perceptions.

My triadic, relational, social construct of experience developed over time. Several circumstances influenced its development. Frank Oppenheim's suggestion that I situate my own philosophical thinking with respect to both Rahner and Lonergan caused me to clarify in my own mind how experience develops. When I wrote *Experiencing God* I had blended elements from both Peirce and Lonergan in my philosophical construct of experience. As I have already indicated, I sensed real agreement and convergence in their thought; but at that early stage in my own thinking, I had failed to realize that, if I was going to derive from Peirce a strictly relational construct of experience, then, I needed to abandon Lonergan's linear understanding of how human cognition grows and develops.

Lonergan endorses a "linear" construct of cognition in the sense that human knowing advances in four stages. A later stage in the cognitive process "sublates" the stage which precedes it. Thus, "experience," the first stage of cognition in Lonergan, functions much as Kant's sense manifold does and provides "understanding" with the raw materials of insight. When insight transforms experience into understanding, it sublates it. It transforms it into something different from the mere raw material of thought. Similarly, when judgment grasps the truth of an insight, it sublates mere insight into the judgmental grasp of the real. Decision then sublates judgment by turning it into concrete activity. While I find some truth in Lonergan's position, I have come to believe that it suffers from vagueness and that it fails to do justice to the relational character of the real. Lonergan's linear construct of cognition suffers from vagueness because Lonergan's category "understanding" fails to distinguish with Peirce's logical precision the difference between abduction and deduction. Similarly, Lonergan's "judgment" fails to grasp the leading principle of induction.[3]

The more I pondered the implications of understanding experience as a developing complex of relational realities, the more I realized that Whitehead's aesthetic model of finite, experiential growth fit Peirce's philosophical vision better than Lonergan's linear notion of sublation. In Whitehead, when one adds a new relational component to an emerging experience, one does not have the old experience plus the new component, one has a new kind of experience because one must understand all the other relational components of the experience both in their relationship to the new component and in their relationship to one another. One must also view the new component in its relationship to them.

I have experienced socially this kind of change every year I have lived in a religious community. When some people leave a community and new people join it, the community's self-perception shifts correspondingly. The way all the members of the community interact changes both because of the absence of the former members and because the way in which the new members relate socially causes everyone in the community to deal differently with one another. Something analogous happens as emerging selves and persons build into themselves new tendencies through conscious and unconscious evaluation and decision. I, for example, now possess the basic bodily control I developed as an infant, but I am not now the person I was at age two.

By replacing Lonergan's notion of sublation with a relational construct of change, I came to perceive that everything in a developing experience conditions everything else. Nothing functions independently of the relational whole to which it belongs. The introduction of new relational components into experience, whether of a conceptual, decisive, or habitual character changes the constitutive character of the experience viewed as a relational whole.

My construct of experience developed in other ways as well. I began to realize that in addition to distinguishing the relational variables which make up experience, I also needed to identify different realms of experience. Here tendency supplied the conceptual key. I define a realm of experience by the generic kinds of habitual tendencies which govern it. Intuitive thinking, for example, advances through creative fantasy, free association, synchronicity. Abductive reasoning begins intuitively but ends rationally in the formulation of an explanatory hypothesis. Deduction and induction derive their validity from the laws of logic which they follow. In other words, the creativity of intuitive thinking exemplifies and follows more spontaneous cognitive tendencies different from controlled inferential reasoning.

At first I recognized only two realms of human cognitive response: intuition and inference. I agreed with H. Richard Niebhur that judgments of feeling shape the human conscience. Since judgments of feeling characterize the intuitive mind, I viewed judgments of conscience as a form of intuitive thinking. Closer study of Dewey's logic caused me, however, to identify a third realm of human evaluative response.

Bill Spohn, Mike Buckley, and I resided together for many years in a faculty community located at 2536 Virginia Street, one of the Jesuit community's residences on Holy Hill. In a conversation one day, all three of us expressed an interest in a deeper reading of some of Dewey's major works. The following semester, therefore, we offered an advanced, team-taught seminar in Dewey's philosophy. Perhaps the make-up of our team intimidated students, for only one person signed up for the course. We therefore canceled it; but we decided to read through our syllabus on our own and to discuss Dewey's writings together. In a sense, we did the course but without students.

Among other works, we did a close reading of Dewey's *Logic: The Theory of Inquiry*. In the first part of that work, Dewey provided, in my judgment, his clearest articulation of what he meant by "instrumentalism," his peculiar brand of pragmatism. By instrumentalism, Dewey meant that the human mind thinks logically about indeterminate situations in order to render them controllable and determinate. Peirce would have correctly conceded that sometimes we do think with that kind of practicality; but he would also have correctly insisted that at other times we think, not in order to get something done, but simply for the sake of understanding some reality or complex of realities.

Moreover, on the whole, I found Dewey's logic less insightful than Peirce's. Like classical logicians, Dewey developed a propositional logic. Peirce had revolutionized the science of logic by replacing the analysis of propositions with the analysis of inference. Peirce regarded a proposition as linguistic shorthand for a more complex act of inferential reasoning. He also adopted and developed the logic of relations. Dewey knew of the logic of relations; but, of the two, Peirce, in my judgment, had seen more deeply into the workings of the reasoning mind.

As we have seen, Peirce divided science initially into sciences of discovery, sciences of review, and practical science. Peirce regarded sciences of discovery and sciences of review as theoretical. They do not seek to transform the world so much as to provide a sound speculative explanation of the nature of reality. Peirce, as we have also seen, included the philosophical sciences among the theoretical sciences and focused his philosophical reflections on the point where logic and metaphysics intersect. Peirce had little interest in the logic of practical science which studies systematically how to get something done. Dewey's instrumentalism, however, his insistence that reasoning seeks to render indeterminate situations determinate and controllable, in my judgment, provided a formal logic for the kind of thinking that interested Peirce the least: namely, practical science. If so, then Dewey's instrumentalism illumined how practical science works; but it had little to say about the theoretical sciences of discovery and of review.

I did, however, find Dewey's account of deliberative thinking sound. He depicted deliberation as disjunctive, either-or thinking about mutually exclusive decisions. His analysis of deliberation convinced me that it follows a logic different both from creative, intuitive thinking and from rational inferential thinking. If so, then the habits which ground human deliberation define a third realm of experience. Accordingly, I expanded my account of the realms of evaluative human thinking to include three: intuition, inference, and deliberation.

At the same time, I recognized that, while one deliberates about ethical decisions (i.e., about judgments of conscience) or about purely practical decisions (i.e., about getting something done which has no identifiable ethical significance), deliberation also functions within both intuitive and inferential forms of thinking. Artists, for example, can deliberate about the size and shape of a painting, about which medium to use: oils, acrylics, or water colors. Similarly, scientists can deliberate about which hypothesis to test first. The fact, however, that deliberation functions within intuitive and inferential thinking accorded well with the relational construct of experience I was developing, for in that construct every component of experience conditions every other.

My philosophical account of human experience took other new turns. As I have already indicated in reflecting on the operations which govern cross-disciplinary thinking, when one's philosophy interprets the verified results of the idioscopic sciences, those results amplify one's philosophical understanding of reality. In writing *Experiencing God*, I had verified my philosophical construct of experience in the results of developmental psychology. I argued that my philosophy could both critique and interpret the developmental theories of Jean Piaget, Eric Erickson, and Lawrence Kohlberg. Those theories amplified my construct of experience by suggesting plausible or even probable accounts of the stages of human cognitive, emotional, and ethical development.

When I wrote *Experiencing God*, I had already studied James Fowler's theory of the stages of faith; but I did not examine it in the text of *Experiencing God* because Fowler's theory deals exclusively with cognitive religious development. In other words, Fowler's theory examines the kinds of categories people invoke in talking about religious experience rather than faith itself. I preferred therefore to examine the developmental mysticism which Teresa of Avila outlines in her *Interior Castle*. Her discussion of the stages of faith and of prayer seemed to me to deal with human religious experience in greater depth than developmental psychology can ever do, even though I endorsed in general what Fowler had to say.

One cannot, of course, make Peirce's philosophical turn to community without taking into account the social, communal dimensions of human experience. In the first three foundational studies I attempted, however, I had contented myself with endorsing Josiah Royce's creative elaboration of this facet of Peirce's thought. As we have seen, in *The Problem of Christianity*, Royce articulates a philosophical account of the conditions necessary for the creation of shared, communal awareness. As we have also seen, Royce distinguishes individual and communal consciousness and grounds the latter in a community's social, dialogic self-interpretation through the sharing of memories, of hopes, and of lives. I endorsed Royce's analysis and built it into my philosophical account of the social dimensions of human experience.

As I reflected critically on my first three published studies in foundational theology, I realized, however, that the developmental psychologists I had utilized had all focused on individual psychological development. In developing a foundational Christology, I had to give an account of Jesus' humanity as a developing human experience. In doing so, I resolved to make up for my earlier failure to verify my philosophical construct of experience in the results of social psychology. Accordingly, in volume one of *The Firstborn of Many* I examined Daniel Stern's theory of the development of infantile social awareness. I also incorporated into my philosophical understanding of human experience Walter Ong's insightful analysis of how written language transforms the way the human mind works. In dealing with the social dimensions of human thought, I invoked the work of Lev Vigotsky, cross-cultural studies of social development in children, R.L. Selman's studies of the growth of human friendship, and, apropos of Jesus' humanity, studies of male development in the United States. Finally, I also invoked Fowler's theory in discussing plausible stages in Jesus' religious cognitive development.

In dealing with psychological studies of the social and religious dimensions of human experience, I verified in a preliminary way my philosophical construct of experience in the individual and social developmental theories I examined. I critiqued what appeared to me questionable philosophical assumptions made by developmental psychologists, and I contextualized their studies within my philosophical account of experience. In the process, I also amplified my own understanding of both the individual and the social dimensions of human experience.

Since in writing *The Firstborn of Many*, I had updated my examination of what personal and social psychology had to contribute to a philosophy of human experience, in *The Gracing of Human Experience,* like a contrite fallibilist, I revised and updated the theology of nature and grace I had initially formulated in *Experiencing God*. In that later work, I developed in much greater detail than I could in *Experiencing God* the philosophical and theological presuppositions of my theological anthropology. My argument in *The Gracing of Human Experience* identified fundamental philosophical fallacies which have distorted theological perceptions of humanity and of the human condition. I identified the fallacies in question as essentialism, dualism in all of its forms, extreme pessimism about the human condition, extreme optimism about the human condition, nominalism, and rationalism. I also invoked Peirce's triadic, social realism as an alternative way of conceiving the human which avoids those same fallacies. My argument in *The Gracing of Human Experience* elaborated in greater detail philosophical and theological themes I had touched upon in *The Firstborn of Many*. In that later work, I also amplified my philosophical account of experience with insights from George Herbert Mead's social psychology and from Peter Berger and Thomas Luckman's sociology of knowledge.

I did not, however, want to rest content with formulating a verifiable philosophical and theological anthropology. I wanted to develop a metaphysics of experience. In order to do that I needed a strategy for transforming my philosophy of experience from an epistemological and psychological construct into a metaphysical abduction universally applicable in intent. In this enterprise, I found considerable help in Stephen Pepper's *World Hypotheses*.

I found Pepper's work compatible with Peirce's logic. Both thinkers viewed philosophical hypotheses as fallible abductions. Pepper went beyond Peirce, however, in clarifying how models function in the formulation of metaphysical hypotheses. Pepper argued that every metaphysics offers a systematic rational elaboration of some root metaphor for reality. A root metaphor functions in metaphysical thinking as an imaginative model for reality. Plato and Aristotle compared reality to an idea and in the process formulated and handed on the fallacy of essentialism. Thomas Hobbes compared reality to a machine and in the process formulated and handed on the fallacy of mechanism. Other philosophers compared reality to an event. Whitehead compared reality to an organism. With hints from Whitehead's reformed subjectivist principle, I proposed to take experience as a root metaphor for reality.

I felt that most people would concede the legitimacy of extending the term experience to all forms of sensate life. Dogs, cats, elephants, and kangaroos do in some sense experience themselves and their world. Whitehead, however, had already attempted to extend the term to vegetable forms of life and even to inanimate realities. The question remained, however: does Whitehead's transformation of "experience" into a metaphysical term universally applicable in intent finally succeed?

It seemed to me that psychoanalytic theory and clinical practice had established the reality of unconscious human evaluative responses. We have evidence that some of the higher animals, like dogs, dream. That suggests that they too have an unconscious mind. Can one find evidence of unconscious evaluations in plants? Whitehead believed that we know with our bodies; and phototropisms in plants give some evidence of something akin to unconscious sensation in vegetable life.

As I pondered this question, it seemed to me that, by invoking a triadic construct of experience, I could leave it an open question whether plants experience something akin to unconscious knowing. I could also leave it an open question whether unconscious evaluations extend, as Whitehead thought they did, even to purely physical processes. Does hydrogen, for example, feel unconsciously the difference between oxygen and nitrogen, or do they just fit physically together? I decided that I could not rule out the first possibility *a priori*. Neither did I feel I had evidence to verify it. Nevertheless, even if neither plants nor inanimate realities have unconscious evaluations, they would still qualify as "experiences" in the sense in which I defined the term because they would exhibit two of the variables which lend dynamic shape to the higher forms of experience: namely, decisions and tendencies. I decided that I could responsibly leave it to the idioscopic sciences to determine whether the evidence warrants extending unconscious evaluations to plants and to inanimate objects.

Evolutionary theory offered further warranty for my metaphysical hypothesis. Given the extreme probability that living things evolved from non-living things and then further evolved into conscious living things and then into human persons with shared religious experiences, it seemed to me that the continuity within that development lent at least plausibility to extending my metaphysical definition of experience to non-living processes. If decisions and tendencies function as unconscious feelings in the higher forms of experience, might they not also so function in plants and minerals?

As we have seen, Peirce's logic requires one to verify one's metaphysical hypothesis in the results of the idioscopic sciences. To date, the metaphysics of experience I have derived in part from Peirce's triadic realism seems to me to interpret successfully the results of psychology and of the social sciences. In 1890, Peirce wrote an unpublished essay called "A Guess at the Riddle." In it he tried to show that his triadic metaphysical theory successfully interpreted the results of psychology, physiology, biology, and physics in those sciences' state of development at the end of the nineteenth century. His *Monist* articles, published between 1891 and 1893, argued that it could also make sense of evolutionary theory. Peirce scholarship has made a plausible case for the fact that his cosmology can take into account quantum theory; and it seems to me that his theory of tychism, which vindicates chance as an indispensable factor in an evolving universe, also makes room for chaos theory.

Having espoused a contrite Peircean fallibilism, however, I also knew that I would have to verify or falsify my philosophical God-talk in the historical and eschatological events which reveal the Christian God. That meant that I needed to demonstrate that my philosophical construct of experience could interpret the Incarnation and the Triune God which the Incarnation reveals; for with Rahner I discern three fundamental Christian mysteries: the Trinity and the two historical missions of the Son and of the Breath which reveal the Trinity. Moreover, before I could test my metaphysical God-talk, I needed to figure out how one goes about developing a theology of the Trinity and of the Incarnation within the context of foundational theological thinking.

Since I was thinking experientially, in developing a normative theology of conversion I decided to focus initially on those things we experience most immediately in faith: ourselves and the community of worship which nurtures, contextualizes, and sometimes corrupts our personal religious experience. The metaphysical implications of what I was attempting philosophically began to appear more explicitly in *The Divine Mother,* which made a plausible case, I believe, for extending the language of experience to the Triune God. I did not feel, however, that I could make formal metaphysical claims for my philosophy of experience until I had also demonstrated more systematically than I had in *The Divine Mother* that I could use the same philosophical language to interpret the hypostatic union.

As I began to use my philosophical construct of experience in order to engage in foundational theological thinking as such, I saw that I needed first of all to formulate a verifiable account of the different kinds of conversion. In *Method in Theology*, Lonergan argued for three forms of conversion: intellectual, moral, and religious. My immersion in classical American philosophy had alerted me to the fact that Lonergan's strong bias toward rational thinking had caused him to give short shrift to the intuitive, imaginative dimensions of experience. Early on, I realized, therefore, that I needed to add affective conversion to the three forms of conversion which Lonergan had correctly identified. Affective conversion, as we shall see in greater detail below, targets affective and imaginative forms of knowing.

Robert Doran, S.J. came quite independently to an analogous conclusion when he argued for the need to supplement intellectual, moral, and religious conversion with what he called "psychic conversion." If I understand him correctly, by psychic conversion he means the extension of the insights of intellectual conversion to psychic phenomena. While I do not rule out the contribution which intellectual conversion can make to an understanding of the human psyche, I hold that intuitive thinking grasps reality in its own right. I therefore tend to regard the operations which structure affective conversion as predominantly intuitive rather than as abstractly rational.

Bill Spohn prodded me into a more detailed elaboration of my construct of conversion when he suggested that besides distinguishing different kinds of conversion, I needed to explain how each form of conversion happens. In approaching affective conversion, I acknowledged that contemporary psychology has yet to formulate a unified theory of the emotions. Karl Menninger and his colleagues had, however, demonstrated to my satisfaction that humans find the negative emotions of shame, guilt, fear, and anger the most difficult to manage. Because we find them unpleasant, we tend to repress them. The more we repress them the more neurotic and psychotic we become. Moreover, in *The Vital Balance* Menninger and his colleagues had formulated a highly plausible account of stages of personality dysfunction.

I had already distinguished initial from ongoing conversion. Clearly, in converting affectively, one would have initially to deal with repressed and disordered emotions. Since I was attempting to give a normative account of conversion, I realized that I needed to identify the kinds of norms each form of conversion invokes in measuring the authenticity of human behavior. If in converting affectively one had to deal with disordered, repressed, negative affections, then psychological norms would govern authentic affective conversion as one grappled intuitively with ordering one's psyche and with cultivating emotional health.

Cultivating a balanced affectivity includes, however, more than the healing of pathology. In addition, one has to educate oneself to appreciate genuine excellence and beauty. More than any other person I have known C.J. had taught me how to do that. From him I learned that the appreciation of genuine excellence invokes esthetic norms. Artistic and literary criticism, the philosophy of art, and Peirce's normative science of esthetics would, I saw, all provide positive norms for cultivating an appreciation for genuine excellence and beauty. Moreover, as we have seen, Royce's philosophy of loyalty yields, in my opinion, a sound insight into how the human mind reasons about the proper object of Peirce's science of esthetics: namely, the *summum bonum*. If Royce has the right of it, then people wrestle with the question of the *summum bonum* when they decide which cause in life claims them with moral ultimacy and moral absoluteness. A cause claims me with moral ultimacy when I stand ready not only to live for it but, if necessary, to die for it. A cause claims me with moral absoluteness when it claims me in any circumstance.

I also agreed with Royce that loyalty to loyalty, the recognition of the legitimacy of causes other than one's own, helps keep commitment to a cause from degenerating into narrow selfishness and chauvinism. It also made sense that the clash of particular human causes forces the fallible human mind to look to an omniscient God to bring about the ultimate reconciliation of all legitimate causes. God, in other words, functions finally as the *summum bonum*, as the final arbiter of all attractive finite causes and therefore as the ultimately desireable good. Moreover, a Christian esthetics, which transvalues any natural esthetics in faith, finds the *summum bonum* eschatologically and historically revealed in the Son of God incarnate and in commitment to His cause: namely, to the establishment of God's just reign on earth as in heaven. Why? Because His human, religious vision gives us the best historical evidence we have of how a saving God relates to us finite sinners and of how God wants us to relate to one another and to the world. Jesus' religious vision enjoys supreme normativity because it exemplifies the human experience of being a divine person.

I suspect that no two humans convert in exactly the same way, since no two human lives unfold in exactly the same way. By the same token, if no two human experiences coincide perfectly, the analogy of experience would seem to imply the analogy of conversion. The analogy of conversion includes both the fact that conversion comes in more than one form as well as the fact that no two people convert in exactly the same way. The multiplicity of conversions also requires their analogous resemblance because, if different kinds of experience all qualify as conversions, they have something in common that justifies calling them all by the name "conversion" at the same time that their multiplicity means that they all differ from one another in some way.

With help from H. Richard Niebuhr, I decided that in every conversion one moves from irresponsibility to responsibility in some realm of human experience. Responsibility means accountability. Accountability to oneself requires the willingness to measure one's future behavior in some realm of experience by appropriate norms one has interiorized. Social accountability means the willingness to justify to others the motives and consequences of one's choices. Religious accountability makes us ultimately accountable to God. Accountability to God requires one to respond to God on God's terms, requires faith.

If all conversions exemplify the transition from irresponsible to responsible behavior in some realm of experience, then they differ from one another by the realm of experience they engage. They also differ from one another by the kinds of norms they invoke in measuring the authenticity of one's decisions in different realms of experience.

Affective conversion deals with intuitive thinking and engages psychological and esthetic norms. When, however, does one experience an initial affective conversion? As I reflected on my own life, it seemed to me, as I have already indicated, that I did not really experience an initial affective conversion until the mid-life crisis. While I would not rule out the possibility that one could convert affectively at an earlier age, Jungian psychology made me think that, if one had not converted affectively prior to the mid-life crisis, then its successful negotiation would almost force one either to take full responsibility for one's own psychic health or else to remain in bondage to one's psychic demons. In Jungian theory, in the process of consolidating a normal adult ego, every human psyche finds itself forced to repress painful or troublesome emotions. The mid-life crisis occurs when those repressed feelings reach such a pitch of dysfunction that one can no longer ignore them. Jung preferred to work with people experiencing the mid-life crisis because he believed that assisting a fully formed adult personality to deal with repressed and disordered emotions held great promise for healing and creativity.

I agreed with James Fowler that developmental psychology in its present incarnation has little to say about the experience of conversion as such because developmental psychology deals only with stages in human cognitive development. He argued, correctly in my estimate, that one can pass from one stage of religious cognitive development to another without converting and that one could convert without changing cognitive stages. I endorse both insights. Here, I believe, my theological approach to the psychological dimensions of conversion contrasts with that of Walter Conn, who seems to equate conversion with cognitive development.

If, however, developmental psychology does not deal with conversion as such, the insights it yields into the progress of human development into adulthood and beyond can tell one something about the kinds of cognitive growth experience which make a mature, adult conversion possible. Both Fowler and Kohlberg, for example, discern a conventional stage in human development. The transition from conventional to personalized faith and morality need not, however, coincide with either religious or moral conversion, since people can and do make that transition irresponsibly. Clearly, however, until one has moved beyond conventional morality, one cannot claim to have experienced an adult moral conversion. Why? Because in converting one decides to live responsibly and because conventional morality blends wisdom and folly, virtue and vice, oppression and genuine liberation. One who fails to distinguish personally between wisdom and folly, virtue and vice, oppression and liberty cannot judge reality with responsibility.

An honest appraisal of conventional religion needs to avow the same. Religious converts need to move responsibly beyond conventional religion, for conventional religion blends faith and unbelief, genuine piety as well as superstition and hypocrisy. Moreover, it seemed to me that one could make an analogous claim for the other forms of conversion as well. In order to convert intellectually, one would have to do more than parrot the beliefs of the society to which one belongs. One needs to take personal responsibility for deciding between the truth and falsity of particular beliefs, between the adequacy and inadequacy of inter- pretative frames of reference, and between the validity and invalidity of particu- lar inferences. To convert affectively, one would have to distance oneself from the way in which one's community has institutionalized neurosis and bigotry.

Affective conversion targets a particular realm of human evaluative re- sponse: namely, intuitive thinking. It measures intuitive responses by two sets of norms: psychological and aesthetic norms. In other words, the realm of ex- perience on which a conversion focuses plus the norms it invokes in measur- ing the authenticity of one's subsequent behavior in that realm of experience distinguishes it from the other forms of conversion.

Intellectual conversion focuses on beliefs. We fix our beliefs in two ways: namely, both intuitively and inferentially. Intellectual conversion, therefore, engages both the intuitive and inferential realms of experience. While affec- tive conversion concerns itself with the health and esthetic cultivation of one's intuitive responses, intellectual conversion in dealing with beliefs fixed by judgments of feeling concerns itself, not with their health or aesthetic cul- tivation, but with their truth and falsity and with the adequacy or inadequacy of the intuitive frames of reference in which one fixes one's beliefs. Paul Ri- coeur's *The Symbolism of Evil* provides, for example, a fine dialectical com- parison of the relative adequacy of different mythic frames of reference for imagining the origin of evil. Intellectual conversion also judges inferential thinking by the same norms. It assesses the truth or falsity of particular infer- ences. The intellectually converted also assess the relative adequacy of infer- ential frames of reference. An adequate frame of reference allows one to ask and answer any question relevant to the reality one is investigating. An inad- equate frame of reference does not. Finally, in evaluating normatively infer- ential thinking one judges the validity or invalidity of deductive and induc- tive inferences by their conformity to the laws of sound logic.

Logic, of course, cannot tell one how to come up with the right abduction; but it can, as Peirce saw, provide criteria for deciding which hypothesis to choose for testing. One should first of all focus on hypotheses which one has the actual means to test, for an untestable abduction, however interesting, re- mains speculatively trivial as long as one lacks the evidence to decide its truth or falsity. Second, one should prefer abductions which one can break down into several independently testable hypotheses, since one can that way assess with greater precision a complex theory's degree of truth. Third, one should prefer for testing that hypothesis which has the greatest number of consequences not only within its own discipline but for other disciplines as well, for it promises the greatest speculative fruitfulness. Finally, one ought to opt for the most attractive hypothesis, since the history of science shows that they tend to prove true.

This last criterion implicitly endorses Lonergan's repudiation of the fallacy of the empty head. That fallacy maintains that the less one knows about a subject the more objectively one can discourse about it. The exact opposite holds true. The educated mind that has studied something exhaustively can discourse about it most accurately. Peirce in preferring attractive hypotheses for testing presupposes that an educated, scientific mind is assessing the relative attractiveness of different possible abductions. Religious studies departments which hire atheists by preference (they have existed) because atheists can speak more objectively about religion than believers offer an excellent example of the fallacy of the empty head.

Intellectual conversion also requires one to advance beyond all forms of fundamentalism. Fundamentalists tend to objectify truth and in the process to endorse another fallacy, which Lonergan calls the fallacy of the already-out-there-now-real. Those who hold this fallacy view all truth as literal, objective, and unchanging. The human mind appropriates such truth by rote memorization. In fact, the acquisition of truth requires much more complex processes of creative and disciplined thinking. In the end, therefore, fundamentalists fail to recognize the fallible, relational, and developmental character of all finite, human knowing.

An example may clarify what I mean. I once had a student who had initially embraced religious fundamentalism but eventually abandoned it out of boredom. She told me that academicians commonly suppose that fundamentalism lacks intellectual content. In fact, she said, it has lots of content: namely, the content of the ready answer. One must anticipate possible objections to the literal truth of unchanging propositions so that one can memorize the correct unchanging response to it. With time she came to realize that, if the human mind never advances beyond the rote memory of unchanging, "objectively true" propositions, it lacks the ability to distinguish between truth and folly in received human wisdom and therefore lacks intellectual responsibility.

Moral conversion targets prudential deliberation about the ethically correct way to act. When I wrote *Experiencing God*, I assumed erroneously that people who converted morally would act responsibly both in dealing with other individual persons and in dealing with questions of public morality. Several circumstances led me to recognize, however, that personal moral conversion differs from what I would subsequently call "socio-political conversion."

When I came to JSTB, I did a fair amount of counseling work with students. As I tried to help people deal with questions of conscience, I found more than one who understood well the importance of respecting the rights and duties of other individuals but who, when confronted with questions of institutional injustice, simply blinked. They showed no hostility but seemed unable to recognize questions of public morality as either ethically important or personally engaging.

At first I attributed their moral obtuseness to the individualism which infects our culture; but the more I thought about the matter, the clearer I saw that personal and public morality constitute two distinct though related moral frames of reference. One needs different kinds of information to resolve problems in private and public morality. Often one can reach clarity in questions of personal morality by talking through the moral issues with the persons involved. Questions of public morality require the careful analysis of increasingly complex institutional arrangements. An institution consists of an identifiable group of people acting in socially sanctioned ways.

In addition, one invokes different moral norms in resolving questions of personal and of public morality. In dealing with personal morality, one tends to invoke personal rights and duties. In questions of public morality one invokes the common good. Lonergan correctly saw that the decision to convert creates a new interpretative frame of reference. Since personal and public morality define two distinct but related ethical frames of reference, then people have the capacity to convert morally in two different ways. If they can convert morally in two different ways, they may decide to convert morally one way and not the other.

The individualism which pervades U.S. culture of course makes it easier for Americans to close their eyes to issues of institutional injustice. Individualism persuades people to objectify institutions, to oppose them to individuals, and to perceive them as unrelated to their "private" lives. The majority of people in this country ordinarily do not vote and feel no responsibility for what politicians may or may not do in Washington. For the majority of Americans, the term "right" tends to connote personal immunity from institutional interference, not, as it ought, the legitimate claim which those who will fail to grow without one's assistance make upon one's conscience. As long as the government does not try to tell them what to do or think, innumerable Americans display little or no interest in what their government in fact does. The same people tend fallaciously to equate good government with as little government as possible. In fact, good government serves and insures the common good. For that reason, good government insists that rich and selfish classists stop using and oppressing other people and use their considerable means to promote actively the common good, not just their own good. Social and economic justice requires good government to enforce transfer payments from the rich to the poor through taxation.

Other influences caused me to regard the distinction between personal moral and political conversion as an important one. I grew fascinated with both Latin and Black liberation theology. The two, I saw, had at first developed quite independently of one another. Black liberation theology stretched its roots into the Civil Rights Movement of the sixties. The Black Power Movement resulted from a schism within the Civil Rights Movement. Black Power took shape when urban Blacks repudiated the non-violent methods of Martin Luther King's Southern Christian Leadership Conference. Black liberation theology represented in part an attempt to restore ministerial leadership to the radical, urban wing of the Black movement. Gustavo Gutierrez, of course, launched liberation theology in Latin America quite independently of religious and political developments in this country. Gutierrez responded to two initiatives mandated by Vatican II: the inculturation of theology and the Church's need to confront institutional injustice in secular society.

It seemed to me that liberation theology was, quite correctly, summoning both the Church and the academy to convert politically and in the process to deprivatize their message and their institutions. If so, then the basic method of liberation theology as articulated by Juan Luis Segundo–namely, closing the hermeneutical circle–offered sound operational procedures for exploring socio-political conversion. One completes the hermeneutical circle by analyzing a situation of institutional injustice, by deriving principles from the gospel which challenge the injustice, and then by transforming those principles into policies, strategies, and social action which rectify the injustice.

Unfortunately, however, in Latin liberation theology, closing the hermeneutical circle ordinarily requires one to choose orthopraxis over orthodoxy. As a result, the method of liberation theology often fails to deal adequately with the kinds of issues raised by the other personal forms of conversion: affective, intellectual, personal moral, and personal religious conversion. Closing the hermeneutical circle fails, then, to provide an adequate method for the entire enterprise of theology; for any adequate theological method must concern itself finally with both orthodoxy and orthopraxis and not force an artificial option between them. On this issue, Peirce's pragmatic logic has much to teach the practitioners of liberation theology; for it blurs any dualistic separation of theory from practice by insisting that the practical operational consequences of any hypothesis define its theoretical meaning. In 1994 I argued Peirce's potential contribution to liberation theology in greater detail in *The Turn to Experience in Contemporary Theology*.

The more I immersed myself in liberation theology the more uneasy I felt about the way some of my colleagues in the GTU approached its study. I found, for example, considerable academic interest in Latin liberation theology but practically none in Black liberation theology. Moreover, I suspected that an academic unwillingness to close the hermeneutical circle partly motivated that lack of interest. Academic study of a liberation theology imported from abroad failed, as far as I could see, to raise student consciousness of the manifest injustices in U.S. culture, injustices like racism, classism, a predatory capitalism, hunger, and militarism. Nor did it challenge one effectively to do anything about them. I suspected that the neglect of Black liberation theology in the U.S. academy stemmed at least in part from the challenge it posed to the largely lily-white academic establishment to face its own racism. I therefore began offering with some regularity a course called "Liberating the U.S.A." In it I applied the method of closing the hermeneutical circle to an analysis of institutions of oppression in U.S. culture.

In the GTU I did, however, find lots of practical interest in one complex of issues of gross injustice in both the United States and in the Church: namely, feminism. The GTU has a Center for Women and Religion, and most of the women who study at the GTU have a keen awareness of the oppression of women in both secular society and in the Church. In addition, my sister-in-law Barbara helped make feminists of both Al and me.

Barbara and Al came to Stanford after Al failed to get tenure at Harvard because only Stanford offered them anything like a joint appointment: full professorship for Al and a part-time lectureship for Barbara. Not until they had served at Stanford for several years did they learn that at the time of their appointment, the chair of the department wanted to give Barbara the same appointment as Al. At that time, she had the same academic credentials as he; but the English department voted down a full professorship for Barbara on the principle that faculty spouses (i.e., wives) don't belong on the tenure track. They get lectureships and then in fact wind up working full time for half pay. That discovery understandably made a feminist of Barbara; and she in turn helped make feminists of both Al and me. It would, however, take years for Al and Barbara to get the Stanford English department and the University administration to rectify the injustice they had done her. Confronting the issues raised by the feminist movement caused me to acknowledge and repent of my own sexism.

Not only did liberation theology help me recognize political conversion as a distinct form of conversion and provide a method for exploring it; but it also transformed the Society of Jesus and in the process transformed me. The

Thirty-First General Congregation of the Society of Jesus elected Pedro Arrupe, S.J. General of the order after the first session of Vatican II had adjourned. Arrupe ranks among the great and saintly Jesuit Generals. Until a stroke felled him and John Paul II dictatorially deposed him as General, he presided over the reform of Jesuit religious life mandated by Vatican II.

Richard Hill, who taught canon law for many years at JSTB, wrote an excellent article on the council's decree on religious life. Dick would regularly introduce his course on canon law by saying, "This is the bad part of the good news." In his article on religious life, he argued that, despite its rather tedious prose, the decree on the reform and updating of religious life had perhaps effected more changes in the Church than any other. The first Code of Canon Law had homogenized religious life on a monastic model. Vatican II challenged religious orders and congregations to re-diversify by rediscovering their community's original purpose and by adapting their rule and way of life to modern times.

A beloved and visionary leader, Arrupe led the Jesuit order in the wake of Vatican II to redefine its corporate existence. We did that in the course of the subsequent General Congregations over which Arrupe presided. In adapting to the contemporary situation, the Society of Jesus heard the voices of liberation theologians and made the fostering of faith in the service of justice the focus of all Jesuit apostolates. Before taking the vote on the document which would consecrate the entire Society to this end, Arrupe counseled the delegates to the Thirty-Second General Congregation to take time to pray over what they were about to do. He wanted them to realize that, if they dedicated Jesuits to promoting a faith in the service of justice, they would be asking many of their brothers to die for that cause. The delegates did pray and then voted to approve the document. As Arrupe predicted, many Jesuits have indeed since died as martyrs to that corporate commitment.

Four Generals of the Jesuit order have shaped and reshaped it in decisive ways. Ignatius, of course, defined the order's original corporate identity with his *Spiritual Exercises*, his *Constitutions* and his voluminous correspondence. Inspired by Ignatius, the first Jesuits went about their work with a high level of improvisational creativity. Claudio Aquaviva, S.J. during his generalate fended off an attempt to increase the authority of the local provincials at the expense of the General's authority. Aquaviva's insistence on preserving intact the original constitutions of the order gave rise to a period of flexible legalism which lasted until the order's suppression. Jan Philip Rothaan, S.J. presided over the institutional restoration of the Jesuits, which in some ways resembled the restoration of the temple in Jerusalem after the Babylonian exile. Both restorations created something that had not hitherto existed. The restored Society had a conservative, ultramontane spirit. Under Arrupe and in the wake of Vatican II, the Jesuits made a decisive shift to the left, which the present General, Peter Hans Kolvenbach, S.J., has consolidated institutionally.

Arrupe's generalate did for the Society of Jesus as a whole what the Province Assembly on racism had done for the New Orleans Province when I lived at Grand Coteau. Today as a result of the reforms over which Arrupe presided, every Jesuit wrestles with the question of how to make his apostolate better serve a faith that does justice. Having come to terms with my racism and sexism, I now found myself challenged by the Society of Jesus to commit myself in a new way to transforming institutional structures of injustice. Liberation theology taught Jesuits the importance of making a preferential option for the poor. It also alerted us to the importance of regular personal contact with poor people. In my own case, the attempt to live a preferential option for the poor made me realize that I had unconsciously interiorized all kinds of middle class values dubiously compatible with genuine gospel living. I realized the extent to which an individualistic ethos had corrupted my conscience. That realization intensified my teaching activism. I tried to integrate commitment to a faith in service of justice into everything I taught theologically.

At the same time, I began to feel dissatisfied with just teaching activism. I began groping for a way to become more politically active by collaborating with others in the struggle against structural injustice. Drew Christiansen joined the faculty of JSTB in 1981. Passionately concerned with social ethics, Drew first made me aware of the work of Bread for the World. While in Washington and before he came to JSTB, Drew had actively collaborated with Bread for the World in their work to pass legislation to reduce and eventually to end world hunger.

Two Jesuit theologians, William Verbryke, S.J. (CHI) and Michael Evans, S.J. (DET) organized at the GTU a weekend workshop on the work of Bread for the World. I not only attended it but joined Bread for the World and organized a local GTU chapter. In active involvement in a lobby like Bread for the World, I found a form of political activism compatible with all the other responsibilities I had as a graduate teacher in a very busy and demanding academic situation. Bread for the World asks its members to pray for the end of hunger, to educate themselves and others about the causes of world hunger, and to write regularly to their Senators and Representative in Washington, DC in order to encourage them to support legislation which seeks to eliminate hunger both in the United States and abroad.

As I reflected on my own gradual politicization, I began to realize that it had begun with my renunciation of my personal racism as a sophomore at Jesuit High School. Regency had transformed me into a teaching activist. The Civil Rights Movement and the anti-Vietnam-War protest had transformed me into a sporadic political activist. Not until I joined Bread for the World, however, had I committed myself for the long haul to a political cause which addressed institutional injustice in an effective and practical way. Moreover, as I reflected on that fact in the light of Royce's philosophy of loyalty, I came to realize that in a democratic country like ours one cannot legitimately claim to have converted socio-politically until one does the kind of thing that I had done in joining Bread for the World. One cannot claim to have converted at a socio-political level until one makes a commitment which dedicates one for the long haul to some just cause and joins one to others of similar commitment in an ongoing, collaborative political activism that seeks to eliminate the structural causes of injustice.

Moreover, the more I studied the causes of world hunger, the more I realized that all just causes finally converge if they seek to improve the lot of humanity as a whole. War and violence contribute to world hunger. So does racist and anti-feminist bigotry. So does a predatory, planetary, trans-national capitalism. So does environmental degradation. Anyone battling any of those institutionalizations of sin and injustice is also advancing the fight to end world hunger. My own tardy socio-political conversion gave me further personal evidence of its distinction from moral conversion.

In dealing with Christian conversion, I saw from the beginning that one could not give an adequate account of it without understanding the dynamics of conversion. By the dynamics of conversion I mean all the ways in which the different forms of conversion re-enforce one another positively. When the absence of conversion in one realm of experience undermines a conversion which has occurred in another realm of experience, I call that negative influence a counter-dynamic. My insight into the complexity of the dynamics and counterdynamics of conversion advanced, however, only gradually.

In formulating the dynamics of Christian conversion, I got initial help from the theology of Jonathan Edwards. He had not only experienced Christian conversion; but his defense of the First Great Awakening and of the conversions it effected expressed a remarkable clarity of insight into what does and does not constitute a genuine Christian conversion. His insightful discernment of authentic religious affections alerted me to the presence within the total process of conversion of what I now call conversion dynamics.

The relational construct of experience I had derived from Peirce's thought moved me in the same direction. If everything in a developing experience conditions everything else, then so must different forms of conversion condition one another.

I eventually came to believe that in *Religious Affections*, Edwards had accurately described the first dynamic of Christian conversion, even though he did not use the phrase "conversion dynamic" as such. The first dynamic of conversion requires that initial Christian conversion, mediate between affective and moral conversion by putting them into a new kind of relationship with one another. Initial Christian conversion has moral consequences. It dedicates one to the cause for which Jesus lived and died: namely, to establishing the just reign of God on earth as in heaven. While Christian conversion does indeed culminate in Christian practice, as Edwards also correctly insisted, it does not begin there. It begins affectively, as I have already indicated, with a confrontation of any emotional obstacle to committing one's life to Christ. Edwards's ten fallacious criteria for certifying a genuine religious affection, which he discusses in the first part of *Religious Affections*, dealt implicitly with this problem. The fallacious criteria identified false norms commonly invoked in the Great Awakening for certifying religious experiences as divinely inspired.

I had come to believe with Menninger that repressed negative affections tend to cause the greatest emotional dysfunction. They can also create problems in a religious context. One might fear the demands that living in Jesus' image makes upon one. Anger at the hypocrisy of nominal Christians or at sinful injustice in the institutional Church might inhibit religious commitment. Guilt over sinful attachments one feels loathe to renounce can also prevent initial Christian conversion. So can shame, which prevents one from believing than anyone can love one, including God.

Psychological studies of the authoritarian personality had taught me that the disordered repression of negative emotions inhibits esthetic sensitivity. It made sense, therefore, that as one brings disordered religious affections to conscious healing through repentance, the conversion process will yield enhanced sensitivity to religious excellence and beauty. Moreover, Pastor Edwards had seen clearly in the eighteenth century that the spontaneous attractiveness of the excellence incarnate in Jesus and in people whose lives resemble His motivates an initial conversion to Him in justifying faith. Since beauty perceives excellence, esthetic perception of the divine and human excellence incarnate in Jesus motivates the consent of justifying faith. Faith justifies us when it teaches us to espouse Jesus' cause in faithful and practical loyalty. Moreover, Edwards had seen that not only does Christian practice find its motive in the beauty which perceives the excellence embodied in God incarnate, but practical consent to that same incarnate divine excellence beautifies. Years ago, in St. Louis, Daddy Wade had at some level perceived that same truth.

Christian conversion mediates between affective and moral conversion in several ways. First of all, it transforms affective conversion into Christian repentance of all disordered religious affections. That repentance allows the positive emotions to play more freely in a religious context and yields en-

hanced sensitivity to the way in which divine excellence incarnate can enthrall the human heart and make one want to embody the same excellence in
one's own life as Jesus did. That desire commits one to Jesus' cause and to
actually living in His image. The commitment of justifying faith, therefore,
transforms the human conscience by committing it to live by revealed moral
ideals. Jesus lived the ideal of the kingdom and proclaimed it to others. The
anawim, the little folk, of Jesus' day felt the power of that lived vision. Nor
has the vision of the kingdom lost any of its power to enthrall the human
heart. Think, for example, of the spontaneous admiration Mother Teresa of
Calcutta evoked from anyone who knew of her Christlike compassion for the
destitute and suffering. Think of the prophetic power of Martin Luther King's
religious and social vision. Think of the healing power of Nelson Mandela's
capacity for atoning forgiveness.

My work in Karl Rahner's theology while studying at St. Marys had convinced me for several years of the truth of his doctrine of the supernatural existential. By the supernatural existential Rahner meant an *a priori* gracing of
the active spiritual intellect. That gracing allegedly transforms the active intellect from a natural desire for the beatific vision into a supernatural yearning for Christ. In Rahner's Thomistic anthropology the fact that the intellect
has Being as its formal object makes it virtually infinite and orients it naturally to God, who exemplifies infinite Being. The active intellect's natural
and dynamic orientation to God makes it into a natural cognitive thirst for the
immediate knowledge of God, for what medieval Latin theologians called the
beatific vision. Since Rahner found the idea of a natural desire for a supernatural reality too Pelagian, he invoked Kantian transcendental logic in order
to deduce *a priori* an *a priori* gracing of the agent intellect which falls short
of justifying faith but which transforms it into an unthematized, supernatural
yearning for Christ.

Three things caused me to abandon this theological abduction as demonstrably false. First of all, Peirce's logic had made me see that one can prove nothing by invoking Kantian transcendental logic, the logic which Rahner in fact
endorsed as his distinctive method for doing theology. In asserting the reality of
the supernatural existential, Rahner argued *a priori* and therefore invalidly. In
addition, Rahner's argument acquiesced in the presuppositions of Thomistic
Aristotelianism and therefore endorsed the essence fallacy.

Second, having recognized with Peirce the need to verify all philosophical
hypotheses in the idioscopic sciences, through study of individual and social
psychology I had grown in the conviction that one cannot in fact verify the virtual infinity of the agent intellect in the results of contemporary developmental
psychology. Those results suggest instead the radical finitude of the human

mind, not its virtual infinity. Unfortunately, however, belief in the virtual infinity of the agent intellect gives Rahner's doctrine of the supernatural existential its only speculative warranty. The doctrine therefore rests on a false and unverifiable set of philosophical presuppositions.

Third, in dealing with people in the Charismatic Renewal who had converted from unbelief to belief, I found that they did not talk about thematizing their *a priori* spiritual orientation to an infinite God and to Christ, as the doctrine of the supernatural existential required them to do. They talked in fact of a total sea change in their lives, of a radical transformation of their commitments and perceptions of reality. As I listened to the personal testimony of converts from unbelief to belief, I began to wonder exactly what would have happened if on the first Pentecost the apostles had burst from the upper room proclaiming not, "Repent and believe the good news about Jesus Christ" but, "Thematize the *a priori* spiritual orientation of your agent intellect to Christ." I thought that I knew what would have happened: only puzzled bewilderment, not conversion and religious commitment.

The more I reflected on the transforming power of a genuine Christian conversion, the more I realized that it holds the key to the second dynamic which Christian conversion contributes to the total process of conversion: namely, it transvalues in justifying faith the other forms of conversion, which when they occur in abstraction from the historical self-revelation and self-communication of God occur naturally. One transvalues something, when, having perceived it in one frame of reference, one sees it in a new light, in a different frame of reference. When, for example, justifying faith transvalues natural prudence, it transforms it into the gift of discernment by teaching natural prudence prayerful docility to the leading of Christ's Breath.

I came to see that the commitment of justifying faith which characterizes initial conversion engages every aspect of the human person. That insight led me to rethink the reality of the theological virtues. Aquinas had felt constrained to locate all three theological virtues–faith, hope, and love–in the spiritual intellect and in the spiritual will, the only powers of the soul which allegedly enjoy a natural, essential orientation to God. The spiritual character of these two powers, moreover, allegedly elevates them above human emotion. Roberto Unger and my own experience taught me, however, to discover in all three theological virtues a strong affective component.

In contrast to scholastic faculty psychology, I had also come to view emotions both as cognitive in their own right and not as merely conative. We know reality with our hearts as well as with our heads; and when our hearts, our emotions and imaginations, focus on the future, we hope. When hope prescinds from the historical self-revelation and self-communication of God, if not neurotic or wicked, it has a natural goodness. The eschatological character of Christian revelation, however, transvalues human hopes into the graced hope for total transformation in the Breath of God in the risen Jesus' image.

That graced hope seeks to heal, elevate, and perfect natural, sick, wicked, and sinful hopes. It heals in justifying faith their sickness, malice, and sinfulness by teaching one to long for the establishment of God's just reign on earth as in heaven. It elevates natural hope by giving it a revealed, supernatural object. It perfects human hope by universalizing it, by teaching the finite human heart something human nature does not, left to its own resources, tend to do: namely, to hope good for others with the universal love and forgiveness of the Son of God incarnate.

Intellectual conversion engages beliefs. Since we judge reality both with our feelings and inferentially, intellectual conversion takes responsibility for the fixation of both intuitive and inferential beliefs. The transvaluation of intellectual conversion in justifying faith infuses into the human mind the theological virtue of faith. The theological virtue of faith transvalues both intuitive and inferential beliefs. In the process theological faith also heals, perfects, and elevates human intelligence. It heals the mind of erroneous beliefs about God by grounding both intuitive and inferential beliefs about the deity in God's historical self-revelation and self-communication. It elevates the mind by focusing it on supernatural realities. It perfects the mind by endowing it with a graced desire for the beatific vision, for face-to-face knowledge of the triune God whom the Incarnation and Pentecost reveal partially and sacramentally. Faith, as the medievals correctly saw, bears fruit in the vision of God in the next life by teaching us to live in this life in the sinless image of His incarnate Son. Consent in faith to the vision of the kingdom makes theological faith practical.

Personal moral conversion deals with human interpersonal relationships. Its transvaluation in justifying faith infuses the theological virtue of charity. The vision of the kingdom defines the practical shape of Christian charity; and the love of charity heals, elevates, and perfects natural and sinful human loves. It heals natural love of any immoral or sinful disorder. It elevates natural love by grounding it in the love of God incarnate. It perfects human love by universalizing it. Left to ourselves we tend to love our own: our friends, some of our relatives, our benefactors; but we tend when left to ourselves to fear the alien and the stranger and to fear and hate our enemies. The vision of the kingdom, however, requires us to expand our love and forgiveness to include all people both in aspiration and in practice, even our enemies.

Socio-political conversion seeks to create a just social order and measures justice by the common good. Its transvaluation in justifying faith transforms it into the Christian search for a just social order in which the vision of the kingdom defines the meaning and the practical measure of justice in public morality.

The graced transvaluation of the natural forms of conversion in justifying faith coincides with ongoing conversion. It also defines the meaning of sanctification by teaching humans to live responsibly in the image of the sinless Son of God. As one matures in holiness, moreover, one's hope, faith, love, and commitment to Christian justice ought to mature into some form of charismatic ministry to others in the Church and in human society. The sharing of all the charisms in community creates the shared faith-awareness of the Church. Such an account of the practical transformative character of Christian conversion, in my judgment, better interprets Christian religious experience than Rahner's unverified and unverifiable theory of unthematized grace.

Christian conversion contributes, then, two dynamics to the total process of conversion: 1) it mediates between affective and moral conversion in the experience of initial conversion, which coincides with justifying faith. 2) Justifying faith requires the sanctification of the whole of human experience in ongoing conversion through the graced transformation of affective conversion into supernatural hope, of intellectual conversion into theological faith, of personal moral conversion into charity, and of socio-political conversion into the Christian search for a just social order. Sanctification, moreover, matures into charismatic ministry and service.

As I pondered the complexity of the conversion process, however, I gradually came to see that each kind of conversion contributes a dynamic to the total process of conversion. 3) Affective conversion animates the other forms of conversion by endowing them with emotional zest and enthusiasm, with imaginative flexibility, and with hope. 4) Intellectual conversion orders both itself and the other forms of conversion by yielding an insight into the normative shape of conversion, into its forms and dynamics. 5) The two forms of moral conversion help orient the other forms of conversion to ideals and realities which make morally absolute and ultimate claims. As we have seen, an ideal or reality claims one ultimately when one stands ready not only to live for it but, if necessary, to die for it. It claims one absolutely when it binds one in all circumstances. 6) Socio-political conversion deprivatizes the other forms of conversion by committing one to collaborate with other people of good will in creating a just social order, one which institutionalizes the common good. 7) The four forms of personal conversion–affective, intellectual, personal moral, and religious–authenticate socio-political conversion by enabling it to recognize and transform institutionalized neurosis or psychosis, institutionalized bigotry, institutionalized deception, and the institutional violation of human rights.

As I have already indicated, I also came to realize that the existence of seven dynamics within an integral five-fold conversion implies the possibility of seven corresponding counterdynamics as well. By a counterdynamic within conversion, I mean the way in which the absence of conversion in one realm of experience tends to undermine or even to subvert altogether a conversion which has in fact occurred in another realm of experience.

I discern the following seven counterdynamics in the total process of conversion: 1) The absence of affective conversion tends to suffuse the other forms of conversion with neurosis, psychosis, and bigotry. 2) The absence of intellectual conversion deprives all forms of conversion of conscious, normative ordering and leaves their development haphazard, chaotic, and vulnerable to fundamentalism. 3) The absence of both forms of moral conversion leaves the other kinds of conversion ethically disoriented and disordered. 4) The lack of socio-political conversion privatizes the personal forms of conversion and leaves them socially irresponsible. 5) The absence of the four forms of personal conversion leaves the socio-political convert bereft of the norms which they supply for dealing with institutional oppression. 6) The absence of initial Christian conversion leaves the other forms of conversion unaware of and uncommitted to the divine justice incarnate in Jesus Christ. 7) The absence of ongoing Christian conversion suffuses the other forms of conversion with religious hypocrisy, as one professes with one's lips a fidelity to God's just reign which one's affective, intellectual, moral, religious, and political behavior belies.

I had reached these insights into the forms, dynamics, and counterdynamics of conversion by the time I finished writing *The Divine Mother*; and, in *Grace as Transmuted Experience and Social Process*, these same insights transformed and deepened my metaphysics of experience. The insights I gleaned in writing that book deepened my insight into human freedom. I grounded human freedom, not in the virtual infinity of the human will, as Thomism had, but in the limited and flickering human ability to distinguish realistic choices from one another. In my construct of experience, the kinds of evaluative experience human choices terminate define their character. As a consequence, the more realistic possibilities about which one deliberates and from which one has to choose, the freer will one's decision prove. I call this kind of freedom "elementary human freedom" and hold that its conditioned character causes it to flicker. We find ourselves freer in some circumstances than in others. Our ability to distinguish options conceptually or to think in more than one frame of reference will also condition our freedom. So will the kinds of habits, skills, and satisfactions we cultivate.

Affective, intellectual, personal moral, and socio-political conversion all transform elementary human freedom into "liberty." We enjoy liberty when we experience the freedom to desire the beautiful, the true, and the good. Affective conversion schools the heart to appreciate genuine excellence and to love the beautiful. Intellectual conversion schools the human mind to seek the true. The two forms of moral conversion teach the conscience to treasure the good.

In addition, socio-political conversion also dedicates one to creating environments that foster liberty by institutionalizing the five forms and seven dynamics of conversion. Such environments liberate. In transvaluing socio-political conversion, Christian conversion seeks to replace natural and sinful environments with graced and gracing ones. The letters to the Colossians and to the Ephesians call this process the *plerôma*, or fullness, because it extends the saving consequences of the paschal mystery into one's surrounding world.

Christian conversion transvalues the other forms of conversion in justifying faith and by transvaluing them graces them, sanctifies them. Christian conversion thus enhances the natural human liberty which the secular forms of conversion inspire by healing, elevating, and perfecting it. Christian conversion heals natural and sinful disorder more effectively than mere natural conversion by opening one to the healing power of Christ's Breath. Christian therapists who integrate prayer for healing into the therapeutic process find, for example, that more healing occurs than with therapy alone. Christian conversion elevates the experience of natural conversion by focusing it on graced, supernatural realities, and it perfects the natural forms of conversion in the universal love and justice of Christ.

The preceding experiential theology of conversion summarizes some of the principal dimensions of the theological anthropology which I have been developing during my years in Berkeley; and it gives, I hope, some insight into how that anthropology evolved. My foundational theology of conversion, however, further evolved as I began to ask and answer different theological questions in a foundational context. I saw, moreover, that one could in fact ask and answer any theological question in that context. Thinking about theological issues normatively simply requires one to include an "ought" in any question one addresses. How, for example, ought one to understand the shared commitment of faith embodied in Christian sacramental ritual? How ought one to verify or falsify doctrinal affirmations about the God Christians worship? How ought one to grow in Christological knowing, i.e., in the knowledge of Jesus Christ which results from practical assimilation to Him in the power and illumination of His Breath? In the chapter which follows, I shall describe how I have been constructing a system on the foundation of my theological anthropology.

Colloquy:

In the beginning,
        confusion sired my word.
                I knew that You must lead,
                        knew better than to teach myself,
                        knew where to search
                and whom to follow;
                        and step by step
                                a path took shape.

I knew that those who scorned
        to lay thought's firm foundation
                would build on Mississippi ooze
                        and watch thought's tower
                                sink and disappear,
                                        drowned in the suffocating slime.

You made me build on turning from and to,
        root my words in what I knew first hand,
                take as the cornerstone on which to build
                                experience,
                live the truth I thought,
                        or try.

I grew in confidence
        by letting things,
        by letting You
                teach me.

I begged You for the gift to teach.
        In the end,
                I seemed to think for others
                        and watched You turn confusion's child
                                into presence,
                                into love.

NOTES

1. The Jesuit order has created its own version of institutional alphabet soup: standard abbreviations indicating the province of the Society to which any given Jesuit might belong. The abbreviations for the provinces of the American Assistancy go like

this: California (CFN), Chicago (CHG), Detroit (DET), Maryland (MAR), Missouri (MIS), New England (NEN), New Orleans (NOR), New York (NYK), Oregon (ORE), Wisconsin (WIS).

2. A "leading principle" enunciates the law that grounds a particular kind of inference. The leading principle of induction, for example, asserts that a verified induction concludes to a rule, not to a result or to a case.

Chapter Eight

Shaping A System

More than any other group of friends and colleagues, the Murray Group shaped the way I came to think theologically. One cannot, however, join a distinguished faculty and serve with them for some thirty years without incurring enormous intellectual debts of gratitude for their encouragement, support, and on occasion correction of one's oversights. Shortly after I joined the faculty of JSTB, we agreed to do a faculty faith-sharing weekend. We had a facilitator and followed the traditional format of such an exercise. In our first session, each member gave a family genealogy: a description of one's family and cultural roots. In our second session, we gave an account of significant faith experiences up to the experience of personal vocation. The third session recounted significant faith experiences from vocation up to the present. In the final exercise, we did the "Christ Seal." In the Christ Seal, each individual told each of the other members of the group how he or she found Christ reflected in that particular colleague's life.

The faith-sharing weekend bore fruit in two faculty institutions: a weekly faculty liturgy and the faculty colloquium. The weekly faculty liturgy eventually succumbed to, among other things, the complexity of scheduling at the GTU; but the faculty colloquium continues to this day. When I arrived at JSTB, John H. Wright, S.J., (ORE) presided over a monthly discussion of some theological article. At the faith sharing weekend, however, we decided to discuss during the faculty colloquium a draft of some research project a member of our own faculty was working on. In the course of the years, the faculty colloquia educated all the members of the faculty to their colleagues' interests and expertise. The work of Mary Ann Donovan, S.C. helped, for example, to ease me into the complex and fascinating world of the fathers of the Church; and I found the insights of Sandra Schneiders, I.H.M. into the fourth gospel always illuminating and on target.

From the beginning, I found universal support from the JSTB faculty for my attempt to create a novel, inculturated theological system; but initially none of the faculty showed an interest in adopting the method I had devised for inculturating North American theology: namely, immersion in the U.S. philosophical tradition as a critical point of entry into culture in the United States. That situation began to change when Bill Spohn joined the faculty in 1978. The fact that he functioned as one of the founding members of the Murray Group created even closer personal and professional bonds between us.

By the time Alejandro Garcia-Rivera and Robert Lassalle-Klein joined our faculty, Bill had departed for Santa Clara University. The presence of Alex and of Bob on our faculty made up for the vacuum that Bill's absence created. Both now belong to the Murray Group; and I count both among my dearest friends and colleagues.

Alex came to JSTB in 1993. Almost immediately after joining JSTB, he dropped a note in my box asking me if I knew anything about the philosophy of Charles Sanders Peirce. I responded by putting several volumes of the *Collected Papers* in Alex's mailbox. He read them and became a committed Peircean.

I never cease to feel astonishment at the scope and originality of Alex's mind. A Cuban exile who almost got a doctorate in physics, who was ordained a Lutheran pastor, who returned to the Catholic Church, and who got a doctorate in theology from the University of Chicago, Alex brings to theological thinking such a diversity of background–from physics, to philosophy, to theology, to the experience of a Cuban exile, to a period as the pastor of a Lutheran church, to his current active involvement in Catholic Hispanic theology and in grass-roots Hispanic piety–that he invariably sees issues differently from and more creatively than any other colleague I know. A leading Hispanic theologian, Alex's work shows a determination to bring Hispanic theology into dialogue with the rest of culture in the United States. He is currently developing a theological esthetic.

I had worked with Bob while he was a doctoral candidate at the GTU. Bob discovered Peirce in an advanced seminar I offered on the meaning of praxis. In the seminar, I tried to put liberation theology into dialogue with Peircean pragmatism. Bob resisted my efforts for half a semester; but eventually came around with enthusiasm. Bob joined the JSTB faculty in 1995. He has put the thought of Ignatio Ellacuria, S.J. into creative dialogue with Peirce's pragmatism and has formulated an ambitious program for developing an inculturated theology for the Church in the United States. His work has earned him respect and credibility among Hispanic theologians as well.

I also became very close to several of the faculty who in 1979 agreed to form a faculty community which resided at 2536 Virginia Street for eleven

The faculty community at the Jesuit School of Theology at Berkeley: from left to right: Michael Buckley, S.J., Edward Flaherty, S.J. (the then rector of the Jesuit community), John Boyle, S.J., Harry Corcoran, S.J., the author, Thomas Schubeck, S.J. and Thomas Leahy, S.J.

years. The following circumstances led to that community's formation. When the then Vice-Provincial for Formation, Charlie O'Neal, S.J. assigned me to JSTB, he stipulated that I should work there for three to five years or until the Institute for Spirituality and Worship, which I was going to help Jake Empereur to found, had become a successful and functioning program. By 1979, I had served on the JSTB faculty for six years, the ISW was flourishing, and I no longer had anything to do with it. Louis Lambert, S.J., had replaced Charlie as my major superior. I regard Lou not only as a close personal friend but as one of the finest superiors under whom I have served. We had lived together for a year of regency at Jesuit High School in New Orleans and had directed school plays together. In 1979 I wrote Lou asking him whether or not he, as my religious superior, wanted me to return to the province or to continue serving on the faculty in Berkeley. He responded that I should look over the situation in the province and at Berkeley and let him know where I could do my best work.

I looked over possibilities at Loyola but did not get a positive response from the then Academic Vice President about my returning to the faculty there. Moreover, when I discussed matters with the Dean of JSTB, it became clear that the faculty and administration very much wanted me to continue teaching in Berkeley. As I pondered my options, it made more sense to me to attempt to create an inculturated, systematic theology in a graduate, ecumenical context rather than in an undergraduate, exclusively Catholic context. I told Lou Lambert that I thought I could do my best work at Berkeley, and he assigned me to the faculty for the indefinite future.

Michael Buckley, S.J., after presiding as rector over the community's move from Alma to Berkeley, stepped down as rector and joined the faculty, where he taught systematic theology and spirituality. When he got wind of the possibility that I might leave JSTB, he closeted me and asked me what it would take to keep me on the faculty. I told him that I needed more peer support.

I had been living in scholastic communities since I had come to JSTB. I love and respect younger Jesuits and treasure gratefully their friendship; but I had experienced an obvious disadvantage as an older Jesuit living with scholastics studying theology. I kept getting older, while they remained the same age. As one ages, one's personal and emotional agenda changes; and as an aging member of the faculty, I had not in my first six years at JSTB experienced the kind of peer support I needed. Indeed, the younger men supported me generously in every way they could; but the older I got the harder it became for them even to understand the kind of support I needed. I do not blame them for the difficulty they experienced. If developmental psychology has it right, one can understand only the next cognitive stage beyond one's own. When Mike heard that I needed peer support, he went to work immediately and organized a faculty community which took up residence on Virginia Street. It lasted eleven years and finally died of retirement. We shopped and cooked for ourselves, and eventually such chores began take their toll on the community's older members.

Besides Mike and myself, our original community consisted of Thomas Schubeck, S.J., (DET), who taught moral theology and had a passionate interest in liberation theology, Harry Corcoran, our emeritus dean, and two New Testament professors, John Boyle, S.J. (CAL) and Thomas Leahy, S.J. (CAL). I learned from each of them an enormous amount. Harry taught me much about the history of the move from Alma to Berkeley and gave me a living example of how to age gracefully. Mike Buckley, like myself, had done his doctorate in philosophy but was teaching theology. We shared many intellectual interests and enjoyed innumerable philosophical and theological conversations over the years. Tom Schubeck eased my way into liberation theology and taught me to distinguish clearly between personal and institutional processes. Tom Leahy and Jack Boyle provided an ongoing education and update in New Testament exegesis. Jack especially taught me to understand both the strengths and limitations of different kinds of New Testament exegesis.

I have had three sabbaticals since joining the faculty of JSTB. I spent the first one in Berkeley and never made that mistake again. I got a lot of work done that year; but it may have borne its chief fruit in a resolution which I have since honored. I decided on my first sabbatical that, like my mother, I would resign as soon as I became eligible at the age of sixty-five. It seemed to me on the basis of that sabbatical's productivity that, if the Society of Jesus just kept the food coming and gave me a place to work, I could in retirement lead a very active and productive apostolic life. After the end of my first year of retirement, the full-time faculty assured me that during that year alone I had missed about a month and a half of committee meetings.

I spent my second sabbatical living in a mansion in Palo Alto built by the novelist Kathleen Norris. After her death, her home had become the Newman Center for the Catholic students at Stanford University. Fr. Timothy Kidney of the San Jose diocese could not have welcomed me more warmly. I had access to the Stanford libraries, to the library of the diocesan seminary, St. Patrick's, in Menlo Park, and, with a short train and bus ride, to the libraries in Berkeley.

During my second sabbatical I revised the tentative sacramental theology I had sketched in *Charism and Sacrament*. I had long known that I needed to revise and update that work and had immersed myself much more systematically in the New Testament foundations for sacramental worship, in the history of the development of each sacrament, and in the issues which had marked the theological understanding of each of the sacramental rituals. As a result, during my second sabbatical I found myself much better positioned to apply Lonergan's theory of functional specialization in theology more systematically to my understanding of sacramental worship. As my revised sacramental theology took shape, I continued the practice of testing my insights against God's people's *sensus fidei* both in the pulpit and in the RCIA program on the Stanford campus run by Nancy Greenfield.

In developing a normative theology of conversion, I had invoked Peirce's pragmatic logic. That logic requires one to clarify the theoretical meaning of any doctrine by spelling out deductively its lived, practical consequences; for in Peirce's logic those *practical* consequences define a doctrine's *theoretical* meaning. Indeed, as I got deeper into sacramental theology, it seemed to me that by regrounding foundational theology in Peirce's logic one could bring to resolution some of the most vexed questions in sacramental theology. I refer to issues like 1) the meaning of confirmation, 2) infant baptism, 3) the meaning of original sin and of concupiscence, 4) the goods of Christian marriage, 5) the correct understanding of Christian priesthood, 6) Christ's real presence in the Eucharist, and 7) the number of the sacraments. In what follows, I shall ponder briefly each set of issues in turn even though, in a personal autobiography like this one, I can treat each set of issues only impressionistically. For a more thorough treatment of the same questions, the reader will have to refer to *Committed Worship*. In each case, however, a normative insight into the kind of conversion experience which any given sacrament ritualizes allows one to distinguish between authentic and inauthentic developments in the rite's history as well as sound and unsound interpretations of what it ought to signify.

1) The Meaning of Confirmation: A foundational, experiential approach to sacramental theology requires one, for example, to understand adult initiation as a ritual which seals not only an initial Christian conversion (i.e., the commitment of justifying faith, which ought to occur before one enters the catechumenate proper) but also the first attempts of neophytes to advance in ongoing Christian conversion during the course of the catechumenate and mystagogy. Catechumens during the catechumenate and neophytes during the mystagogy need to make progress in all five forms of conversion as well as in an understanding and experience of the seven dynamics which structure an integral five-fold conversion. Moreover, during the catechumenate and especially during the mystagogy, new Christians need to open themselves to and to experience the Breath's charismatic empowerment, for Breath-filled service to others integrates the newly initiated into the ongoing life of the Church. As I pondered these practical pastoral insights, I came to realize that the fact that ongoing conversion ought to culminate in a Pentecostal moment of empowerment to serve others in the name and image of Christ clarifies the vexed debate about the significance and purpose of the rite of confirmation.

In the first four centuries of the Christian era, initiation advanced in two stages: first baptism and then Eucharist (first holy communion). A brief blessing rite invoking the Holy Breath marked the transition between stage one and stage two. The two stages constituted a single rite of initiation which sealed all three relationships which a converted Christian has with the Breath of Christ: 1) justifying faith, 2) sanctification, and 3) charismatic empowerment. Moreover, as we have seen, until the second half of the fourth century, the historical evidence informs us that in three different ritual traditions and in four different places in the Roman empire, the Christian community expected those initiated to manifest the charisms of the divine Breath during the rite of initiation itself: either during baptism or during first eucharistic communion.

When Pope Innocent I in the fifth century transformed the transitional blessing ritual between baptism and Eucharist into a solemn invocation of the

Holy Breath reserved to the bishop, he appealed, with questionable exegesis, to the Lukan tradition and by papal fiat created the rite of confirmation. That disciplinary fiat transformed confirmation in the Latin rite into the second stage of a three-stage sacramental initiation. The pope's action also changed the meaning of baptism in the Latin rite. After confirmation became the second stage of a three-state rite of initiation, baptism now sealed initial conversion and committed one to a lifetime of ongoing sanctification; but baptism no longer symbolized charismatic empowerment. Confirmation did. Confirmation now committed neophytes to life-long openness to the divine Breath's charismatic call to service and so symbolized, as the council of Florence would teach many centuries later, the Pentecost of each individual Christian.

In other words, after the fifth century in the Latin rite, baptism sealed a commitment of justifying faith and a life-long commitment to sanctifying growth in hope, faith, love, and a Christian search for a just social order while confirmation signified life-long commitment to respond to whatever charismatic call to service the Breath of Christ might choose to impart.

2) Infant Baptism: Reservation of confirmation to the bishop led to its dissociation from the rest of the rite of initiation. That created the false theological perception that baptism alone effects Christian initiation, whereas it only begins the process of initiation which confirmation and first holy communion complete. Re-conceiving sacramental initiation, not as three different sacraments (baptism, confirmation, and first communion) but, as the history of the ritual makes clear, as a single rite of initiation which advances in three stages throws new light on infant baptism. Infant baptism does not complete the initiation of a child into the Church. It only begins a process of sacramental initiation which confirmation and first holy communion eventually complete.

We have evidence that the baptism of infants goes back to apostolic times. It probably first occurred during the baptism of entire households. As the number of Christians increased, more and more parents presented their infants for baptism. The high infant mortality rate probably helped motivate the practice. Moreover, in the Latin Church, as the debate between Augustine of Hippo and the Pelagians heated up, Augustine's questionable doctrine of personal predestination consigned unbaptized babies to a less severe form of hellfire. Fear lest their children roast everlastingly in the next life probably helped motivate the numerical rise in infant baptisms, especially in the Latin Church.

The question of when to baptize babies continues to divide the churches. The more I pondered the issues, however, the more it seemed to me that contemporary theologians missed the point when they focused on the timing of infant baptism. Both in churches which forbid infant baptism and in churches which practice it, the timing of the ritual has far less importance in insuring its practical efficacy than does the quality of religious formation young people receive as they grow into Christian faith and practice. If, moreover, infant baptism only begins a three-stage rite of initiation, the real issue in dealing with the infant baptized comes to this: when ought one to complete the initiation which infant baptism only begins?

It seemed to me that the restored catechumenate suggests the correct answer to that question: the completion of the rite of initiation in the case of the infant baptized should not occur until they have reached the same degree of conversion one would expect of an adult catechumen. One ought to expect of an adult catechumen not only the commitment of justifying faith but initial progress in all five forms of conversion through growth in faith, in hope, in love, in a Christian passion for justice, and in openness to any charismatic gift the Breath of Christ may choose to give one. It would appear extremely unlikely that the infant baptized in this country can reach the necessary level of conversion to justify completing sacramental initiation until they reach young adulthood. One must, of course, judge each person individually; but in all likelihood most of the infant baptized in this country will not have reached the degree of conversion required to complete the rite of initiation until they reach college age. Confirmation should, moreover, occur before infant-baptized Christians have made a firm vocational option, since that decision ought to flow from a sense of the Breath's charismatic surprises. My call to the Jesuits exemplifies one such surprise.

3) Original Sin and Concupiscence: The Christianization of socio-political conversion allowed me to politicize the notion of original sin and concupiscence. Both terms derive from Augustine of Hippo, who gave them an individualistic, psycho-sexual interpretation. Augustine held that God had created the world good, but that original sin had so corrupted human nature that, left to itself, it could only sin. Parents supposedly communicated original sin to their children in the act of sexual intercourse. Moreover, concupiscence manifested itself both in disordered passions which contradict spiritual goods and in the refusal of the male sexual organ to submit to the dictates of the spiritual will.

I doubt that any competent theologian would today endorse a dualistic, Augustinian understanding of "original sin" and "concupiscence." The terms, however, continue to pose a contemporary problem because the conciliar tradition endorsed both of them but left them undefined until the council of Trent finally defined "concupiscence" but did so very differently from Augustine. Trent defined "concupiscence" as all those forces in the situation of the baptized other than personal sin which come from sin and lead to sin. In the Catholic tradition the two terms "concupiscence" and "original sin" mutually connote one another. The official transformation of concupiscence into a social, environmental reality suggests the possibility of approaching the idea of "original sin" under a similar theological rubric.

As we have seen, the Christian tradition distinguishes two kinds of sin: personal sin and original sin. Moreover, a sound insight into Christian religious experience suggests that one ought to understand original sin perspectivally. Personal sin means all the sins I myself commit. Original sin when viewed experientially consists, therefore, of the rest of experienced sin: everyone else's personal sins and the specific ways in which a given culture, era, or society has chosen to institutionalize sin. If we commit personal sin, we acquiesce in original sin by interiorizing more or less consciously the corrupt values of the societies which nurture us. I call such an understanding of original sin perspectival because no individual experiences original sin from exactly the same angle of vision, since we each have different histories and occupy different places in the spatio-temporal continuum.

One actively interiorizes original sin, of course, not through imitation, but through a process of cultural osmosis. For example, as a little white boy growing up in New Orleans in the 1930s and 40s, I more or less consciously acquiesced in a racist ethos. Social psychology insists that sinful environments corrupt human consciences not so much by direct imitation as by a kind of ethical absorption, by the more of less conscious appropriation of the ethos inculcated by particular social institutions. As a result, the more or less conscious appropriation of original sin, differs from personal sin in the same way in which acquiescing more or less consciously in a sinful ethos differs from deciding deliberately to act in a way which contradicts God's will. I, for example, interiorized a racist value system but never decided to lynch a Negro.

The Christianization of socio-political conversion requires, as the letters to the Colossians and Ephesians correctly insist, that Christians extend the saving consequences of the paschal mystery into the environment. Christians do that by replacing sinful institutions with graced, charismatic communities of mutual sanctification and service. The social analysis which enlightens socio-political conversion names sinful institutions as sinful and prepares the social, political, and economic reforms which will replace sinful institutions with liberating institutionalizations of a five-fold experience of conversion.

If original sin coincides with personally interiorized environmental sin, then Christian initiation takes away original sin by translating one from a corrupt and corrupting environment of sin to a graced environment. Christian initiation, then, takes away original sin by translating one from a corrupt and corrupting sinful environment into an environment of grace which educates one to name environmental sin as sin and which provides the supernatural means to resist its corrupting influence. Still, initiation into the Christian community does not cause environmental sin, whether secular or ecclesiastical, to disappear. After Christians convert and enter into the graced social life of the Church through the rite of initiation, they still experience the forces of evil which corrupted them prior to initiation. They experience environmental sin as different from their own personal sins but as coming from sin and leading to sin. After initiation, therefore, sacramentally initiated Christians experience as concupiscence the same environmental evil which prior to initiation corrupted them as original sin. That means that Christian initiation takes away original sin by changing it into concupiscence.

4) The Goods of Marriage: This perspective on original sin and concupiscence creates a context for rethinking the goods of marriage. Augustine's view of original sin and concupiscence colored his theology of marriage. He believed that, because intercourse even in marriage stimulates concupiscent lust, it probably exemplifies venial sin. This Augustinian doctrine helps explain why theologians in the Latin Church took so long to include marriage in the canon of the sacraments; for, if Augustine had it right, even Christian marriage puts one in a proximate occasion of regularly committing venial sin. It took the scholastics' replacement of Augustine's overly pessimistic vision of the human condition with a more optimistic one for theologians in the Latin tradition to take seriously the possibility that Christian marriage might have a sacramental character.

As we have seen, when one interprets Christian initiation in the light of a five-fold construct of conversion, then initiation commits one 1) to deepen in justifying faith through ongoing repentance and recommitment to gospel living, 2) to grow in sanctification by advancing in theological hope, faith, and love and by habitual practical dedication to establishing God's just reign on earth as in heaven, and 3) to live one's entire life in openness to whatever charismatic call to service the Breath of Christ might summon one. Paul the apostle includes marriage among the charisms of the Breath. In every human society, marriage has an institutional character. Hence, responding to the Breath's charismatic call to the ministry of marriage needs public ritual sanction in its own right.

Jesus did not create the institution of marriage. He held rather that God had done so in creating men and women. Jesus did, however, transform the institution of marriage in three important ways. First, He repudiated Mosaic divorce practices and held up to His followers the ideal of life-long marital fidelity. Second, He required of them a certain quality of love which conformed to the practical demands of life in the kingdom. Third, in the paschal mystery He transformed Christian marriage into a form of Christian charismatic ministry by sending the Pentecostal Breath into the Church.

Christian initiation (in the Latin rite, specifically the rite of confirmation) commits one to life-long openness to whatever charism the Breath of Christ gives one. One cannot, however, respond authentically to a charism of the Breath unless that response also incarnates justifying faith and ongoing sanctification. Hence, a thoroughly converted Christian cannot respond to Her charismatic call to the ministry of marriage without committing himself or herself to allow growth in ongoing justification and sanctification to transform the institution of marriage from within and to endow it with graced, saving significance.

The term "sacrament" in the broadest sense designates an event which both reveals and conceals the reality of God. The Incarnation exemplifies such an event. The Incarnation reveals to us the Son of God in human form; but it also conceals God because no finite human experience, not even the human experience we call Jesus of Nazareth, can reveal God exhaustively in space and time. The gracing of Christian marriage reveals God because it manifests visibly the action of the divine Breath in the lives of believers. The gracing of Christian marriage also conceals God because no finite human event can reveal an infinite God exhaustively. To the extent that the gracing of the natural human institution of marriage does in fact endow it with revelatory significance, it sacramentalizes it.

These insights into the graced significance of Christian marriage allow one to rethink Augustine's doctrine of the goods of marriage. Augustine discovered four goods in marriage: 1) offspring, 2) the mutual support of the spouses, 3) the alleviation of concupiscence, and 4) sacramentality. The 1917 Code of Canon law equated the supreme good of marriage with the creation of offspring. It viewed the mutual support of the spouses and the alleviation of concupiscence as secondary ends.

Prior to the second Vatican council, however, personalist theologians questioned whether making babies in fact constitutes the primary end of the institution of marriage. A personalist re-interpretation of marriage saw the mutual commitment of two persons to one another in faith-filled love as the most fundamental good of marriage. Indeed, only by making and sustaining such a commitment can married people create the kind of social context needed to rear children to adult Christian maturity.

Both Vatican II and Pope Paul VI endorsed this personalist interpretation of Christian marriage. Vatican II spoke of Christian marriage as "a community of love," as "an intimate partnership." The 1917 Code of Canon Law had depicted the marital commitment of Christian spouses as a legal "contract." Vatican II, quite correctly, replaced this shallow, legalistic reading of the commitment of Christian marriage with the Biblical term "covenant." Unfortunately, the new Code of Canon Law continues to describe the marital commitment with legalistic shallowness as a contract rather than as a covenant; but a conciliar document outranks in authority a mere code of law. One cannot reduce the graced, supernatural reality of Christian living to legal formulas.

Most people remember Paul VI's encyclical *Humanae vitae* for the single paragraph in which the pope condemned the use of contraceptives as sinful. The pope's stand on contraception in fact contradicted the majority opinion of the papal commission set up to study that very question. Unfortunately, the debate over contraception in the wake of *Humanae vitae* obscured the fact that the rest of the encyclical not only endorsed but developed a personalist reading of marriage in more detail than Vatican II. A contemporary theology of marriage should, then, look upon the mutual love and commitment of the spouses in mutual faith and love as the supreme good of marriage and as the indispensable context for the Christian nurture of children.

Problems, however, surround the phrase "the alleviation of concupiscence." For Augustine, who coined the term, it connoted the right to give vent to one's sexual lust within marriage. The social, perspectival understanding of concupiscence suggested above allows us, however, to rethink the meaning of this traditional phrase in a manner which better accords with the teaching of Trent. If one understands "concupiscence" with the Council of Trent as all those forces in the environment of the baptized, apart from their own personal sins, which come from sin and lead to sin, then Christian parents alleviate the impact of concupiscence on themselves and on their children by creating environments of grace which nurture both in themselves and in their offspring an integral, five-fold conversion.

While one needs to recognize the sacramentality of Christian marriage, as I have already indicated, theological reflection on sacramentality as a good of marriage has had a checkered history. The Orthodox Church endorsed Jesus' teaching on the indissolubility of marriage and correctly interpreted it as a moral ideal which one cannot violate without committing serious sin; but the Orthodox Church, while opposed to divorce, recognized both realistically and correctly that sometimes spouses do in fact destroy their marriage. When that happens, the Orthodox tradition looked to the rite of reconciliation to forgive the sinful spouses; but the Orthodox did not deny the fact that the offending spouses had in fact sinfully destroyed their marriage. Indeed, if they had not, then the rite of reconciliation would have had nothing to forgive. In addition, the Orthodox allowed and still allow divorced spouses to contract another marriage.

The Latin tradition, typically, developed in a more legalistic, rigoristic direction. Augustine taught that after Christian spouses separate, "something matrimonial (*quidquid matrimoniale*)" remains. Theologians debated what this "something matrimonial" might signify. As canon law in the Latin

Church took shape during the twelfth century, canon lawyers by arbitrary and questionable legal fiat equated "something matrimonial" with Augustine's fourth good of marriage: namely, with the sacrament. In other words, quite arbitrarily and on very questionable theological grounds, canon law in the west endowed sacramental marriage with something akin to metaphysical indissolubility. Only one thing could dissolve a sacramental marriage in the Latin tradition: the death of one or both of the spouses. Even Latin casuistry, however, eventually recognized the Petrine and Pauline privileges as exceptions to the law of indissolubility.

In this as in a number of other matters, the Latin Church needs, in my judgment, to aline its canonical treatment of indissolubility with the Orthodox tradition. Jesus' teaching on indissolubility holds up a moral ideal which makes marriage morally indissoluble. Marriage becomes morally indissoluble when one cannot destroy one's marriage without sinning seriously.

We need, however, to distinguish moral from metaphysical indissolubility. We also need to avoid interpreting moral indissolubility with narrow, legal rigorism. Jesus formulated a religious morality of ideals which contrasted with the legalism and rigorism of the Pharisees. Jesus, however, seems also to have believed that His religious vision expressed the true intent of the Torah. Jesus, in other words, taught that, in the new Israel He was beginning, spouses *ought not* to destroy their marriage. He did not teach that marriage is metaphysically indissoluble. Divorced Christians ought to bring to the rite of reconciliation any sinfulness which attends the culpable destruction of their marriage commitment to one another; but, after sacramental readmission into the communion of the Church, the Code of Canon Law ought, in my opinion, to allow them to remarry if they so desire. The idea that they could not did not emerge clearly until the twelfth century and then only in the Roman rite. The excommunication of the divorced without the possibility of readmission to the Church should they decide to remarry strikes me as precisely the kind of legalism and rigorism which Jesus censured in the Pharisees.

5) Christian Priesthood: The leadership structures in the Church which the rite of ordination sanctions have evolved over the centuries and will continue to evolve in all the churches. So have the rites which sanction Church leadership and Church order. The institutionalization of Church leadership tended to reflect *ad hoc*, common sense solutions to particular challenges and crises. Moreover, not all developments in the institutions of Church leadership have marked forward progress.

We find a growing consensus among questers for the historical Jesus that He headed a renewal movement in Palestinian Judaism rather than a Church, even though that renewal movement, in the wake of the paschal mystery, eventually transformed itself into the Christian Church. In other words, Christianity began as an enthusiastic religious renewal movement within first-century Judaism which gradually separated from the synagogue and began to develop its own institutions. Things that Jesus said and did helped give shape to those institutions; but, during His mortal ministry, Jesus did not create the institutions of the post-apostolic Church. Moreover, all Church institutions, including institutionalized leadership, can enjoy the sanction of God's Breath only if they fail to contradict "the mind of Christ," i.e. Jesus' vision of the God's reign.

One can trace the initial institutionalization of the Jesus movement back to Jesus Himself. He called the Twelve to function symbolically as peasant patriarchs of the new Israel which He was summoning into existence. The Twelve, moreover, functioned as leaders within an inner circle of disciples, which included both men and woman who traveled around with Jesus and collaborated actively with Him in proclaiming God's reign. The Twelve did not exhaust that inner circle of disciples, though they did belong to it and did help collectively to lead it.

The gospels give us evidence that Jesus did call some disciples to follow Him, often in a peremptory, prophetic manner. Moreover, the calls seem to have targeted especially disciples whom Jesus deemed suited for close discipleship. Close disciples joined Jesus' company, learned to know Him more intimately, and collaborated in His ministry of evangelization. Jesus seems to have demanded more of this inner circle of disciples than of others who believed in Him but who, like Martha, Mary, and Lazarus, continued living ordinary lives reshaped by Jesus' teaching and example. He required of close disciples, for example, that they renounce their possessions, give them to the poor, and travel about with a vagabond messiah, living on alms, and sharing what they had with the poor and needy. He also required close disciples to put commitment to the work of proclaiming God's reign before the most sacred family ties. The gospels also give us evidence that Jesus did not automatically admit into the circle of close disciples those who volunteered to join it on their own. He personally oversaw and directed the ministry of close disciples.

By making these special demands on close disciples who exercised collaborative leadership in His renewal movement, Jesus made a statement about the shape which leadership in the new Israel He was founding ought to take. Leaders must renounce the power of wealth and dedicate themselves actively to the service of the poorest and neediest. They must make the service of the gospel their top priority. In addition, Jesus made quite clear the kinds of role models religious leaders in the new Israel could and could not follow. The Twelve exercised a special leadership within the community of close disciples, and Jesus made it quite clear to the Twelve that they must never, ever take as a model for religious leadership the kings of the Gentiles, who abuse authority in order to make their power felt. Instead, religious leaders in the new Israel can take only one person as a role model for leadership: namely, Jesus Himself, the servant messiah who came not to be served but to serve and to lay down his life in service of the many. We also know that Jesus included both men and women among His movement's inner circle and therefore among its leaders.

If the leadership structures of the Church had always conformed to the ideals Jesus laid down, we would today be living in a very different Church and in a very different world from those we in fact inhabit. Leadership structures in the Church resulted from a gradual process of institutional sedimentation conditioned by economic and political circumstances and either imposed by secular authority or informed by questionable perceptions of the Christian tradition. That process spanned centuries of growth and decline, of legitimate development and of scandalous corruption.

The Breath of God began to transform Jesus' renewal movement into a Church on Pentecost by creating the Christian community through an outpouring of charismatic gifts and through empowering the Church's witness to Jesus as risen Lord and messiah. Those who saw the risen Lord and testified to their personal encounter with Him bore the title "apostle." We do not know the number of such apostles, but we do know that they included many more than the Twelve. In First Corinthians, Paul asserts that at one point Jesus appeared to over five hundred disciples simultaneously. Since Jesus, in contrast to other rabbis, had women disciples, the five hundred would almost certainly have included some women. Indeed, the New Testament informs us that Jesus appeared to both women and men. One can also make a plausible exegetical case for the fact that Mary Magdalene numbered among the apostolic witnesses to the risen Jesus. We also know that some women headed Pauline churches.

The apostles founded churches and claimed an authority in those churches rooted in their confrontation with the risen Jesus and in their possession, as a result of that confrontation, of a share in His Breath; for She endowed their ministry, as She had endowed Jesus' own, with charismatic authority. Apostles like Paul also claimed special authority in those communities which they themselves had founded and in virtue of having done so.

The apostles exercised a collective, collegial leadership within the Church of the first century; and either they or their successors seem to have established elders to preside over local churches. These elders, then, succeeded functionally to the apostles as Church leaders after the apostolic era ended. The New Testament asserts that the leadership exercised by the elders had charismatic grounding and therefore enjoyed charismatic authority confirmed by the laying on of hands.

Not until the second century, however, did the *monepiskopos*, or personal overseer of local churches, provide personal leadership to local communities. It would appear that a single executive bishop (the word means overseer) dealt more effectively with divisions in the community than a committee of elders. When the single overseer emerged as an institution, he functioned more like a parish priest than like the episcopal diocesan administrator into which he eventually evolved. The other elders advised him and probably co-presided with him at the Eucharist. With the rapid expansion of the Church in the fourth century, these elders, or presbyters, evolved into parish priests. They presided over Eucharists in communities where the bishop could not preside. At the same time, bishops began their evolution into diocesan administrators. The creation of episcopal dioceses imitated the division of the Roman empire into dioceses.

Constantine's Edict of Milan made Christianity one of the religions officially recognized by the Roman empire. Constantine believed that Christ had given him the victory at the Milvian Bridge which exalted him to sole imperial status. In gratitude, he began conferring special privileges on Church leaders, especially on bishops: tax exemptions as well as legally sanctioned authority to function as imperial judges and to serve on city councils. The bishops on the whole welcomed Constantine's attentions; and the systematic clericalization of the episcopacy resulted. As a result of imperial privilege, bishops found themselves increasingly transformed into a power elite. Clericalization corrupts Church leadership with the lust for power and privilege. Some saintly bishops during the patristic era resisted the corruption; but the record shows that not all bishops had reached the status of sainthood.

Other forms of clericalism also corrupted Church leaders in the Latin tradition. With the institutionalization of the Papal State in the thirteenth century, the papacy transformed itself into something Jesus, the Son of God incarnate, had forbidden absolutely to leaders in the new Israel He was founding. The creation of the Papal State transformed the pope into one of the kings of the Gentiles, something the incarnate Son of God explicitly forbade to leaders in the new Israel (Mk 10:35-40, Mt 20:20-23, Lk 22:24-27). To put the matter in legal, canonical language, the creation of the Papal State violated divine law. Bishops in the West were already desporting themselves like increasingly rich, aristocratic barons.

I will not attempt here to rehearse in detail the corruption of Church leadership which helped produce the alienation of the Orthodox from the Latin Church and which eventually bore fruit in the Protestant revolt. Here it suffices to note the fact that both events happened and that both resulted in no small measure from the sinful clericalization of the institutions of Church leadership.

Human communities tend to create institutions haphazardly, in response to concrete challenges, needs, and pressures. Once created, institutions grope for the means to rationalize their existence and claims to authority over subsequent generations. The same processes mark the growth of Church institutions, including sinfully corrupt Church institutions. At the same time, the Breath of God never abandons the Church and seeks to undo its personal and institutional sinfulness. Nevertheless, the speculative rationalization of sinfully corrupt Church institutions produces not theology, the word of God, but ideology and propaganda, a sinful human word. By ecclesiastical ideology and propaganda, I mean, then, the rationalization of sinful Church institutions as divinely ordained.

As I pondered the human rationalization of Church leadership structures, two theological portraits of ordained leadership seemed to me to qualify as ideology. The first developed in the fourth century and called itself "sacerdotalism." The second took speculative shape at the earliest in the fifth century but gained ecclesial significance in the historical consequences of the Gregorian reform of the Latin Church in the eleventh and twelfth centuries. It called itself "hierarchicalism." Let us consider briefly why both positions fail to qualify as authentic doctrine.

Sacerdotalism rationalized the growing clericalization of the episcopacy which accelerated during the fourth century. That clericalization resulted from imperial patronage, from clerical privilege, and from political jockeying for power among bishops. Sacerdotalism portrayed the ordained, especially bishops, as the high priests of the new covenant: in other words, as the Christian equivalent of Annas and Caiphas. Sacerdotalism thus rationalized the transformation of Christian priesthood into a spiritual power elite.

Nowhere does the New Testament depict Church leaders as the Christian equivalent of levitical priests. Jesus, the lay peasant prophet from Nazareth, had denounced the religious bankruptcy of the levitical temple priesthood of His day. In His confrontation with the priests, a lay prophet challenged an entrenched and powerful priestly hierarchy, an extremely poor peasant denounced the cupidity and greed of a rich, aristocratic priestly class, an eschatological prophet of the end time offered Israel and its religious leaders a once-only chance to hear and embrace the good news of God.

The gospels all portray the chief priests as those principally responsible for engineering Jesus' legalized murder on the cross. Should we wonder, then, that the first leaders of the Christian community never thought of modeling Christian Church leadership on the likes of Annas and Caiphas? Yet, by the fourth century, more than one Christian theologian was trying to justify modeling Christian Church leadership simultaneously on Jesus Christ and on the Jewish levitical priesthood.

Jesus, as we have seen, insisted that the leaders of the religious community He was summoning into being must never pattern their behavior on the kings of the Gentiles. Instead, they should take Jesus and Jesus only as their sole model for leadership in service. Jesus came to serve, not to be served, and to lay down his life for the ransom of sinners. Jesus' example of leadership gives, then, normative definition to the purpose and scope of all public leadership in the Christian community. The letter to the Hebrews calls Jesus the high priest of the new covenant. The same letter teaches that Jesus and the paschal mystery redefine the meaning of the priesthood and that Christian priesthood, thus divinely redefined, puts an end once and for all to the need for a levitical priesthood.

Moreover, Hebrews makes it clear that the Incarnation grounds the unique priestly function which Jesus and Jesus only performs. The levitical priests functioned as a religious elite, separate from the people, and, with the increasing politicization of the temple priesthood, as set over the people in a position of political power. Jesus, by contrast, exercised a priesthood of identification, the very opposite of a levitical priesthood of separation, when He became physically one with a sinful humanity through the Incarnation and when He identified with the dregs of humanity by dying as a criminal and a blasphemer. As the author of Hebrews saw clearly, not only can one never reconcile Jesus' priesthood with that of Annas and Caiphas; but the incarnation and paschal mystery together put an permanent end to the need for any future levitical priesthood.

In other words, when sacerdotalism portrayed bishops as levitical priests of the new covenant, it did not hand on authentically the New Testament witness as Christian tradition ought. Sacerdotalism replaced the New Testament witness with an ideological rationalization of a politically compromised ordained leadership, a rationalization irreconcilable with the New Testament witness.

In the fourth century, not only did calling bishops the levitical priests of the new covenant rationalize the transformation of the episcopacy from leadership in service in the image of Jesus into a position of institutionalized power and privilege, but it had anti-Semitic motives as well. In the first three centuries, Judaism numbered among the officially recognized religions within the Roman Empire. As the Church evolved into the only imperially established religion, sacerdotalists portrayed bishops not only as the levitical priests of the new covenant but as superior to the levitical priests of the old covenant. That superiority rationalized the promotion of Christianity to privileged imperial status and the concomitant legal demotion of Judaism within Greco-Roman society.

As Church structures evolved, the vision of the Church as hierarchical also degenerated into an ideology. A Syrian monk of the fifth or sixth century and quite possibly a monophysite heretic, who wrote under the pseudonym of Dionysus the Aeropagite, whom Paul the apostle converted in Athens, coined the term "hierarchy." A committed Neo-Platonist, Pseudo-Dionysus believed that visible reality must participate in and reproduce the order of purely spiritual reality. Pseudo-Dionysus imagined the angels, moreover, on the pattern of Greco-Roman imperial institutions. The *cursus honorum* in the Roman empire created a stratified, honorific political order in a rigidly hierarchical society. Pseudo-Dionysus imagined some kinds of angels as superior to others. He called every group of three kinds of angels a hierarchy and by an invalid, *a priori*, imaginative fiat proclaimed invalidly the order of all hierarchies eternal and immutable. Moreover, he required the action of divine grace to trickle down all nine hierarchies of angels from the higher to the lower, from the more perfect to the less perfect, before it could reach mere humans.

Since Pseudo-Dionysus believed that the Church on earth must imitate the order of heavenly things, he divided the Church into two hierarchies: the clerical and the lay. The clerical hierarchy consists of bishops, priests, deacons; the lay hierarchy of religious, laity, and catechumens. As in the case of the angels, divine grace must trickle down all the other ecclesiastical hierarchies before it can reach the laity and catechumens. By the time Pseudo-Dionysus wrote, the catechumenate had pretty well disappeared. As a result, most of the laity occupied in fact the final rung in the ecclesiastical, hierarchical ladder and in Church matters played a purely passive role in the Church's life. Here we find the origins of pray-pay-and-obey Catholicism. Vatican II explicitly repudiated this warped vision of the laity as well as a trickle-down, hierarchical understanding of ordained leadership.

It would appear that no one took the hierarchicalism of Pseudo-Dionysus very seriously until it took institutional shape in the wake of the Gregorian reform of the Church. Other popes before Gregory VII had recognized that the Dark Ages, which followed upon Charles the Great's "Holy" Roman Empire, had corrupted Church institutions. The Iron Age of the Papacy dates from the Dark Ages. During the Iron Age, the richest families of Rome transformed the papacy into a political football which they tossed around with a determination to win from it as much wealth and power as possible. The Cadaver Synod dates to this era. Pope Stephen had the corpse of his predecessor Pope Formosus exhumed. He summoned a synod of the bishops of Rome, sat the corpse on a throne, and made the bishops excommunicate it and declare all Formosus's ordinations invalid so that Stephen could ordain his own cronies to the most lucrative posts. This did not amuse those in power, so they threw Stephen into prison where they had him strangled.

Before becoming pope, Gregory VII had moved in the reform circles in Rome. A monk with scant theological education, Gregory had a formidable will and a passion for Church renewal. Before him Pope Leo the Great had begun to imagine the pope as something like the emperor of the Church. In other words, he too did what Jesus said Christian leaders must never do: he patterned the papacy on the Roman emperor. Pope Leo failed to get the rest of the Church to agree with them about papal jurisdictional primacy. Gregory VII, however, blended the idea of a papal monarchy with a hierarchical vision of the Church as a way of rationalizing Church reform. Apparently, Gregory's chief justification for institutionalizing a monarchical papacy expressed his conviction that Church reform would advance more efficiently if everyone simply did what he told them to do. In his encyclical *Ut unum sint*, Pope John Paul II has made it clear that in its present institutional expression, the papacy needs reform. One can trace that need all the way back to Gregory VII's ecclesiastical reforms.

The emergence of a monarchical papacy in the thirteenth century simply brought to a climax a process of institutional sedimentation and institutional rationalization begun in the fourth century. After recognizing Christianity as one of the approved religions of the Roman empire, Constantine engaged in the elaborate patronization of the Christian bishops and transformed them into something like the "senate" of the eastern empire. In the western empire, the emperor consulted the senate about important decisions. In the east, bishops became Constantine's advisors. As the Byzantine empire absorbed the Church into its political structures, Christians in both the east and west came to assume that God had providentially raised up the Roman empire shortly before the birth of Jesus so that Rome, by unifying the world, could facilitate the spread of Christianity and "Christianize" the empire itself. Increasingly, the imperial Church acquiesced in the ethos and structures of imperial Rome.

If neither sacerdotalism nor hierarchicalism offer correct interpretations of ordained ministry, can foundational theology yield a normative insight into the way in which ordained leaders ought to function within the Church? I think that it can. 1) Since the ordained have the responsibility of setting the example for the community in the matter of Christian living, all the ordained need to experience an integral, five-fold conversion and to cultivate their own ongoing conversion in ways that edify the communities they serve. 2) The ordained leaders of the Church have the responsibility of extending in space and time Jesus' own ministry of proclamation by proclaiming and embodying the just reign of God. 3) In virtue both of their call to ordained leadership and of the ritual confirmation of that call through ordination, Church leaders participate in the power to bind and loose, to admit into the Christian community and exclude from it. 4) The ordained have the collective responsibility of serving the Christian community collegially and of ensuring the common good of all. 5) Finally, as Vatican II made clear, the ordained have the responsibility to serve the Christian community in responsiveness to the Divine Mother's charismatic inspirations not just in their own lives but in the Church as a whole. It belongs to the evolving discipline of the Church to specify just how bishops, priests, and permanent deacons go about exercising these responsibilities common to all the ordained.

Can we find some truth in sacerdotalism and hierarchicalism? Yes, but both doctrines require radical reformulation before one can even dream of endorsing them. Sacerdotalism correctly saw that the priesthood of the ordained differs qualitatively from the priesthood of the baptized, but it erred in portraying that difference as a priesthood of separation, as membership in a power elite which stands over the Church and exercises power over it.

The New Testament makes it clear that the entire Christian community has a priestly character, for like Jesus it lives called to mediate God's saving Breath to a sinful world through converted living. Authentic Christian priesthood, however, must always pattern itself on Jesus and on Jesus only. It must, in other words, identify completely with a sinful humanity and serve it in His image, even to the point of sacrificing one's life if required. Each member of the Christian community participates in that priesthood of service differently in virtue of one's particular charismatic call and divine authorization to serve. The ordained, then, exercise a different priesthood from the baptized in virtue of their charismatic calling to public leadership of the Church. In other words, ordained priesthood differs qualitatively from the priesthood of the baptized because all the gifts differ qualitatively from one another.

Hierarchicalism perceived correctly that as the Church expands, it needs institutional structures which facilitate its shared life and which foster its union in mutual love and service. Hierarchicalism erred by patterning the institutions of the Church on the Roman empire. By patterning the papacy and the rest of the clergy on the kings of the Gentiles, institutionalized hierarchicalism explicitly violates divine law and rationalizes sin.

We need then to replace authoritarian, trickle down, totalitarian, hierarchical Church structures with genuine institutional subsidiarity. The Church works best from the bottom up, not from the top down. Genuine subsidiarity would, therefore, insure that as much as possible all decisions in the Church take place at a local level in response to the charismatic inspiration of God's Breath. Those decisions need to express the shared faith vision of the universal Church and, as much as possible, of those who know the local community's situation first hand. In that context, the college of bishops in solidarity with the patriarch of Rome has the ultimate collegial responsibility for insuring the Church's unity in diversity.

6) Real Eucharistic Presence: Latin scholasticism offered different interpretations of Christ's eucharistic presence, but the real presence of Christ in the Eucharist did not become a widely debated theological issue until the Protestant Reformation. Luther defended a doctrine of consubstantiation, which asserted that in the Eucharist the substantial reality of Christ existed along side of the substance of the consecrated bread and wine. Others during the middle ages had defended such a position. Calvin held that the Holy Spirit provided the key to Christ's real presence in the Eucharist. The radical reform denied the real presence of Christ in the Eucharist and reduced eucharistic worship to a mere act of recall.

The council of Trent defended the real presence of Christ in the Eucharist. In so doing, the council fathers intended to reassert the New Testament witness to Christ's real presence in the Eucharist, most notably in the fourth gospel's Bread-of-Life discourse. The council also vindicated the legitimacy of using the medieval term "transubstantiation" in order to speak about Christ's real eucharistic presence but left its meaning vague.

One found no philosophical unanimity at Trent. Those attending endorsed Augustinianism, some form of scholasticism, or an emerging Renaissance humanism. Accordingly, when Trent used the term "substance" in talking about Christ's real presence in the Eucharist, it did not give the term any technical philosophical definition but used it as more or less the equivalent of "reality."

Had Trent used "substance" as a technical philosophical term, its eucharistic theology would have contrasted the technical Aristotelian language of "substance" with the equally technical term "accident." In fact the Tridentine decree on the Eucharist did not use such terminology. When Trent talked about Christ's real eucharistic presence, it opposed to "substance," understood as "reality," the term "appearance." Trent asserted that after consecration, the bread and wine appear to be ordinary bread and wine but are in reality the whole Christ, "body, blood, soul, and divinity." In other words, Trent approached the doctrine of Christ's real eucharistic presence, not under the philosophical rubric of substance and accidents, but under the more colloquial rubric of reality and appearance.

I must confess that in formulating my own interpretation of Christ's real eucharistic presence I took wicked delight in using the thought of crusty, naturalistic John Dewey in order to build an ecumenical bridge between John Calvin and the Council of Trent. Dewey wrote a brilliant little essay in which he distinguished three different ways of understanding the terms "reality" and "appearance."

1) In the first understanding of these terms, the two coincide. The reality itself appears. The actor appears on the stage. The leaves appear on the trees.

2) In the second understanding, something appears in the first sense but what it discloses holds the key to a deeper reality whose appearance requires reflective understanding for the mind to grasp it. Such reflective understanding can legitimately invoke Peirce's distinction between sensation and perception since Peircean perception requires reflective understanding. Thus, the guilt or innocence of the accused appears in the testimony of legal witnesses. The solar system appears every morning in the rising of the sun, provided, that is, one understands what the appearance of the sun on the horizon signifies.

3) In the third understanding of reality and appearance, we speak of a "mere appearance." For example, we thrust a stick into water and observe, "Oh, look! The stick is bent." Then, we remove the stick from the water and say, "Oh, it wasn't really bent, it only appeared to be bent." In other words, we use the language of "mere appearance" when, in the course of trying to interpret some reality, we make a mistake but, instead of admitting that we have erred, we blame the thing we have incorrectly interpreted. In the case of the stick in water, we blame the stick for "only appearing" bent.

The council of Trent contrasted "reality" and "appearance" in teaching about Christ's real eucharistic presence, but the council failed to distinguish as clearly as Dewey did the preceding three senses of these two terms. In other words, as councils often do, Trent left the terms of its doctrinal statement about Christ's real presence in the Eucharist vague. From a logical standpoint, a term qualifies as vague when one can neither verify it nor falsify it until one clarifies it. When one invokes Dewey's clarification of the terms "reality" and "appearance" in interpreting Trent then one can verify in the faith-filled worship of eucharistic communities a clarified Tridentine doctrine concerning Christ's real eucharistic presence.

Before bread and wine undergo consecration in the shared act of eucharistic worship, what you see is what you get. The bread looks like bread and is bread. The wine looks like wine and is wine. Here we invoke the first sense of "reality" and "appearance."

After consecration, however, they only appear to be bread and wine. In other words, if you said that the consecrated bread and wine were no different from bread and wine on a shelf in Safeway, you would err. Here, we invoke the third notion of the "mere appearance."

Why would you err? Because the total reality which appears in faith-filled eucharistic worship and especially in the sacrament of eucharistic communion, if you understand its deep and true significance, is the risen Christ inspiring His Church to renew the covenant of grace it sealed in Christian initiation through the action and inspiration of His divine Breath. The community renews its covenant of initiation by repeating the last and only repeatable part of a three stage initiation: the Eucharist and holy communion. An appeal to the deep reality which appears in the visible act of faith-filled eucharistic worship invokes the second meaning of "reality" and "appearance."

The doctrine of the real presence gets its clearest formulation in the New Testament in the gospel of John because the Beloved Disciple wrote his gospel for a doctrinally divided community. The proto-Gnostics who eventually left the Johannine community refused to discover divine reality in anything material or physical. They denied the Incarnation, denied the efficacy of Jesus' physical death on Calvary, and denied that Christ could be really present in a physical act of eating and drinking.

The Beloved Disciple quite correctly asserted the opposite at considerable narrative length in his gospel. He also viewed the divine Breath whom Jesus sends as making Him present in the community of believers. In other words, linking real presence to Spirit makes good exegetical as well as experiential sense, as John Calvin saw, because in John's gospel, which insists on Christ's Eucharist presence, the Spirit functions as the experienced presence of the risen Christ. Viewing the Breath as the presence of the risen Christ also makes theological sense of Vatican II's assertion that we must find Christ present in all the sacraments, since the divine Breath inspires and empowers every authentic act of sacramental worship.

7) The Number of the Sacraments: When I wrote *Charism and Sacrament*, I dealt exclusively with contemporary issues in sacramental theology. When I revised that sacramental theology in *Committed Worship*, I invoked Lonergan's theory of functional theological specialties in a more systematic way. In dealing with each of the sacraments, I laid out the New Testament foundations for each ritual and so invoked the results of theological interpretation. I sketched the history of each sacrament; and then I dealt dialectically with the major disputed issues surrounding each ritual.

While ecumenical dialogue has muted many differences between Catholics and Protestants, major disagreement still divides the churches when it comes to sacramental theology. In *Baptism, Eucharist, and Ministry* the World Council of Churches summarized the principal areas of consensus in sacramental theology, although the churches of the radical reform take considerable exception to the document's main text.

In *Committed Worship* I proposed an ecumenical strategy for resolving the perduring debate over the number of the sacraments. Catholics, Protestants, and Orthodox all agree on the sacramentality of baptism and Eucharist. My ecumenical approach to sacramental worship attempts to derive from the shared experience of those two sacraments a descriptive definition of the theological term "sacrament." It then argues that we can legitimately call a sacrament any other Christian ritual which fits that definition when one understands Christian worship as the expression of an integral experience of conversion.

I find the following descriptive traits present in both baptism and the Eucharist:

1) It seems to me that the churches ought to find it easy enough to agree that both baptism and Eucharist exemplify symbolic, communal acts of communication. They both exemplify communal professions of shared, Christian faith.

2) Both baptism and Eucharist have a ritual character. By that I mean that they function as traditional acts of shared, institutionalized worship handed down from generation to generation in a religious community of faith. Because in both baptism and Eucharist the community as a community performs an official public act of worship, both require a celebrant authorized by the community.

3) Both rituals derive from Jesus and the paschal mystery. As for baptism, both Matthew's Great Commission and the apocryphal ending of Mark's gospel depict the risen Christ sending forth His disciples to baptize. Moreover, in the synoptic gospels, Jesus' own baptism serves as the prototype of Christian baptism. As for the Eucharist, Jesus instituted the Eucharist at the Last Supper. By that I mean that His eucharistic words and gestures at the Last Supper interpreted prophetically the significance of the paschal mystery, which therefore endows the Eucharist with its saving, revelatory meaning.

4) Because both baptism and Eucharist derive from the paschal mystery, they challenge worshipers prophetically to faith in the Lordship of Jesus, in the Father He proclaimed, and in the divine Breath whom He sends.

5) As a result, the sacraments effect the saving grace they signify to the extent that they come from faith and deepen the faith of believers.

If all the churches would agree that this descriptive definition of a sacrament correctly interprets the two official rites of the Church whose sacramentality all Christians acknowledge, we could conceivably also reach agreement concerning the number of sacramental rituals. The achievement of such a consensus would require all the churches, including the Roman Catholic Church, to rethink the significance of the sacraments in the light of their historical development. Indeed, most of the disputes about the sacraments at the time of the Reformation resulted in no small measure from complete ignorance of the history of the Church's rituals on the part of both Protestants and Catholics. One can only hope, then, that the rapid development of liturgical history might provide a new talking point among the churches in their search for consensus about the number of the sacraments.

Protestants generally reject the sacramentality of the rite of confirmation. Since the Church for four centuries celebrated a two-stage rite of initiation consisting only of baptism and first holy communion, I see no need why Catholics need insist that Protestants adopt a three-stage ritual, which developed only in the fifth century and only in the Latin church through a somewhat arbitrary papal disciplinary fiat. It would suffice, it seems to me, if the churches could first agree on the significance of Christian initiation: namely, that in adult initiation, the ritual seals all three dimensions of a convert's relationship to the Breath of Christ. By the three dimensions of a convert's relation to the Breath I mean 1) justifying faith, 2) a commitment to grow in sanctification, and 3) a commitment to lifelong openness to the Breath's charismatic call and empowerment. If and when the churches come to a consensus about the significance of adult conversion which Christian initiation ritualizes, then, in my opinion, ritual diversity in the Church could sanction Protestants continuing to initiate in a two-stage ritual (baptism and first holy communion) even though Roman Catholics continue to initiate in a three-stage ritual. In my opinion, that would suffice as consensus as long as the churches all agree that, whether celebrated in two stages or three, Christian initiation signifies the same thing.

The authentic exercise of any charism needs to express a commitment both of justifying faith and of ongoing sanctification. This principle also applies both to the charismatic call to ordained ministry and to the charismatic call to marriage. We seem to have reached a growing consensus in the churches that ordination seals and certifies a charism, and Paul the apostle certainly includes marriage among the Christian charisms.

Both ordination and marriage commit an initiated Christian to new responsibilities within the Christian community over and above those signified by the rite of initiation. One cannot, therefore, commit oneself ritually to either ordained ministry in the Church or to Christian marriage without simultaneously reaffirming the commitment one made in joining the Church. By that I mean that in both marriage and ordination, one accepts a particular charism of the Breath as one promised one would do in the rite of initiation. At the same time, one simultaneously commits oneself to exercise it in justifying faith and ongoing sanctification. If initiation counts as a sacrament, then the vocational sacraments must do so as well, since they reaffirm the commitment one made in the rite of initiation in the context of taking on entirely new charismatic responsibilities in the Christian community.

Both rituals also embody the definition of a sacrament derived above from reflection on the experience of baptism and Eucharist. Both rituals exemplify symbolic ritual acts of communication. The one who ordains functions as the ritual's minister. Husbands and wives minister the rite of marriage to one another. Both rituals derive from Jesus' ministry and from the paschal mystery. Christian marriage derives from Jesus' abolition of Mosaic divorce practices, from His teachings about loving others in His name and image, and from His mission in His resurrection of the charism-dispensing Breath. The sacrament of orders derives from Jesus' call of the Twelve and of other close disciples to assist Him in the work of evangelization, from His self-revelation to *all* the apostles (not just to the Twelve), and from His commissioning them to proclaim the paschal mystery with divine authority. Because both rituals have roots in the paschal mystery they challenge those who receive them to faith in the Lordship of Jesus, in the Father He proclaimed, and in the charism-dispensing Breath whom They send. Both rituals effect grace to the extent that they come from faith and lead to faith.

In writing *Charism and Sacrament*, I did not treat either the rite of reconciliation or the rite of anointing. Understood historically, the rite of reconciliation has as its principal purpose to readmit into the Church serious backsliders previously excommunicated from the community. The right to excommunicate roots itself in the authority of leaders to bind and loose, i.e., to admit people into the community or exclude them from it. Since the rite of reconciliation thus interpreted explicitly reaffirms the same commitment of faith as the rite of initiation, it too qualifies as a sacramental action. One must say the same of the optional, devotional use of the rite of reconciliation which extends the forgiveness of Christ to minor sins committed by believers and does so in the context of an official, public reaffirmation of one's covenant of initiation. The devotional use of the sacrament began in Irish monasteries but spread to Europe in the sixth century when Irish monks re-evangelized Europe in the wake of the barbarian invasions.

So understood, the rite of reconciliation also reproduces the same sacramental traits as baptism and Eucharist. The rite of reconciliation reaffirms the commitment of faith one made in the rite of initiation and readmits officially a serious backslider into the Christian community after a period of official excommunication. The practice of excommunicating and readmitting into the community dates back to Paul the apostle and to the ecclesial discourse in Matthew's gospel. The one who readmits into the Church needs authority to do so. Reconciliation roots itself in Jesus' proclamation of divine forgiveness and in His mission of the sin-forgiving Breath of God. Because it roots itself in the Incarnation and in the paschal mystery, reconciliation challenges the one reconciled to faith in the Lordship of Jesus, in the Father He proclaimed, and in the divine Breath whom He sends. As a public act of worship, reconciliation effects the grace it signifies to the extent that the ritual act of worship comes from faith and deepens it.

The devotional use of the rite of reconciliation holds the key to the sacramentality of the rite of anointing. Jesus in his ministry of faith healing linked healing to the forgiveness of sins, as, for example, in His healing of the paralytic (Mk 2:1-12; Mt 9:1-8; Lk 5:17-26); and the letter of James makes it clear that when the elders of a church prayed over and anointed those seriously ill, the ritual also prayed for the forgiveness of minor sins and peccadillos (Jam 5:14–15). The rite of healing differs, therefore, from a purely charismatic ministry of healing because the ritual publicly and officially absolves one from minor sins in the context of praying for physical healing. In other words, besides praying for healing, the rite of anointing, like the devotional use of reconciliation, publicly and officially reaffirms one's covenant of initiation. It too, therefore, enjoys the same sacramentality as the rite of initiation and exemplifies the same descriptive traits as baptism and Eucharist.

The discrimination between sound and unsound sacramental doctrine and practice evaluates Church rituals in the light of the five-fold conversion which they either seal initially, as in initiation, or reaffirm, as in the Eucharist. The vocational sacraments, reconciliation, and anointing all reaffirm one's covenant of initiation in the different faith contexts which each ritual addresses.

During my years on the JSTB faculty, I spent much of my time teaching, but my method of teaching I learned in the course of the four years I taught at Loyola University in New Orleans. During those years, Hacker Fagot and I, as I have already indicated, lived with our Jesuit scholastics in the same community on Freret Street. Hacker taught learning theory and assured me that we know the way adults normally learn. They do so in four steps. First, their instructor needs to prelect materials that they have in hand and which they will subsequently study. One prelects by giving an overview of the assigned materials and by highlighting their most important points. Step two requires the students to study and assimilate the assigned material on their own. In step three they discuss the materials read. Discussion speeds up the evaluation of the matter studied by confronting each student with viewpoints on the matter other than his or her own. In the final step, the students must use practically the materials discussed before proceeding to the next batch of matter.

Hacker also said that we have identified the most inefficient way to communicate information to adults: namely, discussion. Discussion produces genuine learning only if the discussants have all read and studied the same materials. We also know, he claimed, the second most inefficient way to communicate information: the lecture. Most people can summarize what they learned from a lecture in one or two sentences. If you just gave them those two sentences, you would have saved them an hour of largely wasted time.

From the beginning of my tenure at JSTB, I put Hacker's theories to the test in the classroom. I always requested one class a week which met for three consecutive hours. The first class never lasted that long. In it I explained the syllabus, gave an overview of the course, and prelected the matter for the following week. Thereafter, my students used the first hour to discuss the materials which I had prelected and which they had studied the preceding week. Their discussions generated questions which each discussion group posted on the blackboard. I took as much time as we needed to respond to all the students' questions. I concluded the third hour with a prelection of the next week's matter. We have institutionalized education on the Aristotelian fallacy that theory has nothing to do with practice. As a result, I never built effectively into my pedagogy the fourth step: use. I did, however, require students going on for ministry to design a catechesis based on the materials covered in class, a catechesis which targeted some group of people to whom they would likely minister. They had, in other words, to imagine how they would use the materials discussed.

Student evaluations of my classes told that Hacker had basically gotten things right. Moreover, like George Klubertanz, in my lecture courses I increasingly taught my own materials. As I explored grace, the sacraments, the Trinity, and Christology in the context of a normative theology of conversion, I began to see that foundational thinking allows one to reground traditional theological doctrines in the experiences which they seek to interpret.

Hacker taught me something else about education. He once told me that he defined an uneducated person as someone who had to learn from a teacher who knew more than the student. He defined an educated person as someone who could learn from those who knew less than oneself. If Hacker has it right, then, the longer I stayed in Berkeley, the more educated I became, because I found myself learning more and more from my students and from their questions.

When Judith Berling took over as dean of the GTU, she established a core doctoral faculty responsible for supervising the Union's doctoral programs. I resisted at first joining the core doctoral faculty, because membership multiplied the number of committees on which one could find oneself required to serve. Eventually, at her urging, I relented and did join. As a result, I have had the good fortune to work with a series of outstanding doctoral candidates. Moreover, I found a steady stream of people who came to the GTU to study with me. John Markey, O.P., a Southern Dominican, who had done his M. Div. degree at the Dominican School of Philosophy and Theology, after his ordination returned to the GTU to pursue his doctoral studies with me. As I have already indicated, I found John one of the most brilliant students I have ever worked with. A voracious reader, he kept whatever he read stored in his head and could hold forth indefinitely on almost any speculative issue one might raise. I directed Robert Lassalle-Klein in a GTU inter-area doctorate. Bob would develop into a fine thinker and scholar; and I took great pleasure in watching both him and John also develop into good friends and colleagues in the Murray Group.

I also welcomed Pentecostal doctoral directees. I supervised Daniel Albrecht as he researched and eventually published the first systematic study of Pentecostal ritual. Koo Yun, a Korean Pentecostal, did a dialectical study of different theological interpretations of Spirit-baptism which enjoyed a wide audience. Evan Howard, a charismatic Evangelical with a passion for U.S. philosophy and for spirituality wrote and published his dissertation on the meaning of discernment in which he put my own work into dialogue with cognitive psychology.

As I immersed myself in the daunting task of mastering the dialectical development of Christological doctrine through a series of advanced seminars, I drew enormous satisfaction from the fact that the trinitarian theology I had developed in *The Divine Mother* seemed to stand up to the critical reflection which a deepening insight into Christological issues engendered. I realized that the events which could verify or falsify any theological abduction about the triune God happened some two-thousand years ago. In chapter six, I argued that despite the distance of two millennia, the New Testament gives us sufficient access to those same events in order to permit falsifying at least one trinitarian doctrine: namely, the *a priori* identification of the second person of the Trinity with the mind of God. The challenge of formulating a logical, coherent, applicable, and adequate philosophical construct of one God subsisting in three divine persons ought, however, to strike a chill of apprehension in any theologian's heart. When I approached formulating a foundational account of the triune God, I felt that chill. I felt it again as I began work on a foundational Christology. I had no doubt even then that a foundational theology of the Trinity and of the Incarnation would either make or break the metaphysics of experience I had formulated.

My metaphysics of experience asserts that the realities we experience stand within experience and make it into the kind of experience it eventually becomes. Such a metaphysics requires the foundational theologian to give a normative account not only of how Christian converts respond to divine revelation but also of the revelatory realities to which they respond. That meant that I needed to reach a sound normative insight into how one ought to perceive in faith the Incarnation and the triune God which the Incarnation reveals.

A metaphysics of experience requires one to approach even the Trinity experientially. An experiential approach to Trinitarian thinking needs to focus on the Holy Breath because no one has seen the Father and because Jesus is not physically around any more. Our experienced access to the Triune God results from the empowering enlightenment of the justifying, sanctifying, charism-dispensing Breath.

Approaching the Trinity with a focus on the divine Breath also made systematic sense. An experiential approach to foundational thinking needs to begin with those realities which we experience most immediately in faith. I therefore began laying foundations for my system by developing a theological anthropology which dealt with fundamental issues of the relationship between nature and grace. As my thought developed, I kept refining that anthropology and finally brought it to mature formulation in *The Gracing of Human Experience*.

I discovered our next most immediate experience of faith in sacramental worship. My sacramental theology had culminated in a rethinking of the theology of real presence which linked the notion of Christ's presence in the Eucharist to the action of the divine Breath within eucharistic worship and indeed in all the sacraments. It made systematic sense to advance from reflection on the shared experience of sacramental worship to an examination of the God Christians encounter within sacramental worship. In other words, my sacramental theology led logically to the development of a trinitarian theology with a focus on the Holy Breath.

As I wrestled with the Biblical witness to the divine Breath, I found myself struck by the consistency of Breath-talk in the Bible, even though different Biblical authors undertake to depict Her activity in human hearts and even though the documents which make up the Old and New Testaments literally span centuries. The historical books of the Old Testament attribute a broad spectrum of experiences to the Breath's activity: ecstatic prophecy, visionary experience, practical wisdom, the creation of religious art, faith-filled leadership. A common element unites all these different experiences of the Breath: namely, an empowering divine enlightenment which comes from and leads to God. The historical books, therefore, distinguish the sanctifying action of God's Breath from the dark, disordered, destructive impulse of an evil breathing. The need to distinguish the Breath's life-giving impulses from destructive impulses which masquerade as religious requires a gift of discernment.

As George Montague's exegetical study of Biblical pneumatology demonstrates, Biblical pneumatology develops. The pre-exilic, writing prophets sought to distance themselves from ecstatic prophecy. They summoned Israel to an authentic living of the Torah which insured the repudiation of all false gods, single-hearted commitment to Yahweh, and justice for the poor and marginal. Since ecstatic prophets attributed their enlightenment to the Breath of God, the pre-exilic, writing prophets attributed their illumination to the Word of God, not to His Breath. The pre-exilic, writing prophets did however talk about the Breath's saving action in history. In the process, they developed the soteriological dimensions of Biblical pneumatology. The pre-exilic writing prophets attributed to the divine Breath saving enlightenment, purification, judgment, and obedience to the will of God enshrined in the Torah. Post-exilic prophecy ascribed prophetic illumination freely to the Breath of God; and when discoursing about Her divine activity, the post-exilic prophets also portrayed Her as the inspiration of God's creative activity and of God's providential guidance of human history. Wisdom literature depicted Her as the source of authentic religious wisdom and as the mind and wisdom of God.

The New Testament further developed Biblical pneumatology by describing the Breath's activity in Jesus and in the apostolic Church. In Jesus She inspired His messianic sense of mission, His *Abba* awareness, His religious vision, His proclamation of the divine reign, His miracles, and His exorcisms. The paschal mystery brought to a culmination Jesus' transformation in the Breath of God. Those who encountered the risen Christ experienced Him in Paul's phrase as a "life-giving Breath" (1 Cor 15:44-45): in other words, as so totally transformed in the divine Breath that He both shares with Her an identity of life and becomes Her efficacious source. Moreover, that eschatological fact–the risen Christ's efficacious sending of the Breath–reveals the divinity of the Son of God. Throughout the Old Testament, the divine Breath makes an invisible, transcendent God who defies depiction in graven images an immanent, present, dynamically active reality. In both the Old and New Testaments, the Breath of God *is* the saving presence of God, *is God*. If the risen Jesus functions as the Breath's efficacious source, then He too has to enjoy divinity, because only God can send God.

In Acts, the arrival of the divine Breath on Pentecost transformed the renewal movement which Jesus headed into the Church through the outpouring of the charisms which create the ecclesial community as a dynamic, functioning witness to Jesus' person and ministry, on the one hand, and to the paschal mystery, on the other. The arrival of the Pentecostal Breath also empowers that prophetic community of witness to embody Jesus' religious vision. That Breath-inspired community prolongs His testimony to God's reign by embodying that reign even as it proclaims it to others. The Church embodies God's reign when it shares the physical supports of life with others and especially with the poor and marginal, when it lives Jesus' egalitarian vision of the family of God, when it forgives with the same gratuity as God forgives us in Christ, when it allows mutual forgiveness and reconciliation to inspire its worship. Moreover, by thus proclaiming and embodying the kingdom, the Church prolongs in space and time Jesus' own mission and ministry.

The Pauline witness makes it abundantly clear that one cannot confine the empowering enlightenment of the Breath of Christ to charismatic inspiration. She does indeed dispense the charisms, and the sharing of the charisms creates each local church as well as the Church universal by teaching Christian communities to embody corporately the mind and religious vision of Christ. The Breath imparts the mind of Christ to the Church by inspiring ongoing justifying faith, progressive sanctification through growth in hope, in faith, in atoning, Christlike love, the Christian search for a just social order, and mutual charismatic ministry.

The preceding descriptive account of the divine Breath focuses on Her action in salvation history. It therefore exemplifies an aspect of the economic Trinity by narrating the eschatological events which reveal the triune God historically: namely, the historical missions of the Son and Breath.

In *The Divine Mother* I argued that one must verify or falsify all metaphysical God-talk in those missions. The mission of a divine person transforms human experience in God in such a way as to reveal sacramentally the divine person sent, the way that divine person relates to the divine person or persons efficaciously active in the sending, and the conditions necessary to experience the missioned divine person as such. So understood, the missions do in fact allow one to verify some metaphysical abductions about the Trinity and to falsify others.

I regard that fact as extremely important; for a science or scholarly endeavor which lacks the means both to verify and falsify hypotheses does not merit studying. Why? Because without the means to verify some hypotheses and falsify others, the affirmations of such a science or scholarly discipline, however interesting, remain speculatively trivial since we can never know whether or not they assert anything true.

As we have already seen, the preceding account of the missions of Son and Breath falsifies Justin Martyr's *Logos* Christology. That Christology equates the second person of the Trinity with the mind of God. Throughout the Bible, however, the Breath of God functions as the source of an empowering, divine enlightenment. The fact that She inspires authentic religious wisdom led Hebrew wisdom literature to equate the Breath of God with divine wisdom itself. As the wisdom of God, the Breath functions as the mind of God.

The New Testament, however, provides the historical evidence which decisively falsifies Justin's trinitarian abduction. The action of the Breath in Jesus during His mortal ministry inspires His awareness of relating to the Father as *Abba*. She also inspires Jesus' awareness that the Father has sent Him to proclaim and embody the divine reign and to bring Israel to such a level of religious conversion and commitment that it can serve as the Father's instrument for effecting a more universal salvation. In other words, in the Son's historical mission, the Breath functions as the cognitive link between Him and the Father and therefore as the mind of God. Jesus' mission by the Father reveals His distinction within the Godhead from the Father, just as Her mission by the Father through the Son reveals Her distinction within the Godhead from both of Them. Mission, therefore, reveals procession; and procession within the triune God grounds distinction among the persons.

The fact that the Breath stands historically and eschatologically revealed in the Incarnation and paschal mystery as the divine mind means that evaluations function within the Godhead with the Breath as their divine source. If, however, the Son of God does not function in either the economic or immanent Trinities as the divine mind, how, then, ought one to understand His relationship to the other divine persons?

Once again the missions provide the evidence for answering that question. Throughout the New Testament we find Jesus' relationship to the Father portrayed as obediential. Obedience involves decisive action, the decision to do what someone else wants one to do. If, then, we must find in the missions of the divine persons the evidence which tells us how They relate to one another within the Christian Godhead, that evidence forces us to say that the Son of God functions within the Trinity as a source of obediential efficacy. If, moreover, the Son knows His relationship to the Father and His mission by the Father through the illumination of the divine Breath, in obeying the Father, the Son simultaneously obeys the Breath who reveals to Him the Father's will.

Moreover, throughout the New Testament, the Father functions as the aboriginal, efficacious source of both the Son and the Breath. He sends the Son into the world to proclaim the divine reign and to summon Israel to repentance and to converted commitment to the vision of kingdom. In the paschal mystery, the Father sends the Breath through the efficacious mediation of the Son. As the efficacious source of Son and Breath, the Father stands revealed in the economic Trinity as the aboriginal source of creative efficacy within the Godhead.

The revelation of the Son's divinity in the paschal mystery through His efficacious mission of the divine Breath means that His obediential relationship to both the Father and the Breath in no way implies his subordination to Them in divine perfection. Instead, the Son's obediential relationship to the Father and Breath reveal Him as the one through whom They act upon all created reality whether to create it, to save it, or to judge it. Indeed, very quickly the New Testament deduces from the fact that the Father and Breath have acted through the Son in order to save us the further conclusions that They will act through the Son in judging the world and also that They acted through the Son in creating it.

Greek trinitarian theology recognized the presence within the Godhead of three particular, subsistent realities, which they designated by the Greek noun "*hypostasis.*" Reverence for the ineffable mystery of God, however, prevented the Greek fathers from even attempting a clear definition of the term "*hypostasis.*"

Matters developed differently in the Latin West. Tertullian's genius had formulated technical philosophical terms for talking about the unity and trinity of God long before the Arian crisis erupted in the Eastern Church. Tertullian used the term "*persona*" in order to designate the three members of the Trinity and the term "*substantia*" to designate the divinity they share in common. Accordingly, in the Latin Church, trinitarian theology learned very early to speak about the Triune God as three persons in one substance. By a person, Tertullian seems to have meant a "communicating subject." I find his definition of person true as far as it goes (persons do have the capacity to communicate with others of their kind) but in need of clarification and inductive verification.

In my metaphysics of experience, a person exemplifies a self-conscious, autonomously functioning tendency with vital continuity and the capacity to enter into responsible relations with entities like itself. If the Triune God contains three persons, then tendencies function within the Trinity. If, moreover, the Son proceeds efficaciously from the Father within the Trinity and if both send the Breath simultaneously and efficaciously, then decisions also function within the transcendent reality of the Trinity. Finally, if the Breath of God functions as the divine mind, then evaluations also function within the Trinity. I could, therefore, verify in the economic Trinity, in the events which reveal to us the Triune God, the presence in the immanent Trinity of the same three variables as function in the higher forms of created experience. In other words, the events that reveal to us the Triune God tell us that that God exemplifies a transcendent, divine experience.

The analogy of experience required me, however, to deny that a divine reality could exemplify experience in the same way as created, finite, spatiotemporal realities. I felt disinclined, however, to ground the analogy between divine and created experience in the actual infinity of God, as Aquinas did.

As I have already indicated, Anselm of Canterbury offers a perfectly orthodox alternative to the Thomistic doctrine of analogy and one better suited to the human experience of divine transcendence. Anselm understood God as supremely perfect, as that reality than which the mind can conceive none greater. *Deus semper major* (God is always more). God's supreme perfection lures finite minds to contemplate more and more facets of the divine reality in the assurance that human thought will never exhaust the divine plentitude. As the supreme exemplification of experience, God experiences the totality of everything experienceable: all possibility, all probability, all actuality, all reality. Since, moreover, in a metaphysics of experience, the reality experienced stands within experience, not outside of it, God as supremely perfect encompasses creation, which, as the Christian tradition has consistently held, therefore exists in God.

Panentheism, as we have also seen, differs from pantheism. Pantheism identifies God and creation. Panentheism insists on the distinction between God and creation, but holds that creation exists in God. "In Him we live, move, and have our being" (Acts 17:28). The fact that God encompasses all things and is encompassed by none makes God infinite in the sense in which Hilary of Poitiers, with complete orthodoxy, defines infinity. Hilary, as we have seen, defines infinity as the character of that reality which encompasses all others and is encompassed by none.

Moreover, as the supreme exemplification of experience, God would logically have to enjoy all the other attributes we traditionally attribute to the divine reality in its transcendence. As the supreme exemplification of experience God would have to enjoy unrivaled perfection, uniqueness, supreme desirability, self-existence, eternity, omniscience, omnipotence, and ontological priority to any created reality.

In other words, when I attempted to verify my metaphysical construct of experience in the historical and eschatological data of revelation, it gave initial evidence of interpreting the transcendent God revealed in the missions of the Son and of the Breath as the supreme exemplification of experience. I knew, however, that my metaphysics of experience could not prove its mettle unless it also allowed me to think simultaneously the unity and trinity of God without contradiction.

Here I faced an vipers' tangle of debated issues. Two major modern theologians, Karl Rahner and Karl Barth, had questioned the advisability of calling the three members of the divine triad "persons." For Barth, the term "person" in a modern context connoted "personality." The great Swiss theologian felt understandably loathe to attribute three different personalities to God. Rahner, on the other hand, had so absolutized the mystery of God as to make it impossible for him to discover anything in common between human persons and divine persons. Both theologians preferred therefore to speak of three modes in God, not three persons.

Neither felt any need to verify or falsify his suggestion in the events which reveal the triune God. Rahner, as we have seen, fallaciously believed that he could deduce *a priori* the conditions for the possibility for revelation happening. Whereas Barth, in banishing philosophers from his fideistic republic had apparently banished logicians as well. As a result, he seems never to have bothered thinking about the kinds of issues which correctly preoccupied Peirce.

As a committed Peircean, I had no such luxury. My method required me to verify or falsify any inference about the Christian God in the missions of the Son and Breath, i.e., in the events which those missions graced. When, however, I brought to those events Barth's and Rahner's suggestion that we call the three members of the divine triad "modes" instead of "persons," in my judgment those events falsified their suggestion. Jesus' experience of God as *Abba* had all the characteristics of a deep interpersonal relationship. It made no sense to me whatever to call it a deep "intermodal" relationship, whatever that might mean. The fact that those who saw the risen Christ experienced Him as the efficacious source of the divine Breath revealed eschatologically His divinity. Once that happened, then the interpersonal character of the Son's relation to the Father during His mortal ministry revealed something important about the immanent Trinity. If in his humanity, the Son experienced an interpersonal relationship with the Father, then, the revelation of the Son's divinity required one to assert interpersonal relations within the Christian Godhead. Moreover, if Jesus and the Father clearly enjoyed an interpersonal relationship with one another, the co-equality of the divine persons required one to conceive all of them as enjoying something analogous to human interpersonal relations.

The need to think the Christian God as tri-personal further entailed that one come up with an understanding of "person" analogously predicable of both divine and human persons. My metaphysics of experience defined a person as "a dynamic relational reality endowed with the autonomous capacity to initiate its own activity, with the capacity for responsible self-understanding and for making decisions which flow from that responsible self-understanding, and therefore with the ability to enter into responsible social relationships with entities like itself."

Clearly, if one applied the term "person" so defined to both divine and human persons the key terms in the definition could not apply univocally to both. They could only apply analogously. Divine persons could not exemplify personal existence in exactly the same way humans do. For one thing, Christian monotheism required one to assert that the three divine persons exist in the unity of one divine reality. They therefore had to enjoy a social communion whose unity transcended any human social communion. They, not we, exemplify the supreme perfection of interpersonal existence. That meant that, in order to understand how divine persons differ from human persons, one had to come up with a noncontradictory way of thinking the unity and trinity of the Christian God.

As I surveyed the history of trinitarian theology, I could discern six ways in which theologians had tried to understand the unity of the Trinity. Two of them clearly qualified as heretical and deserved rejection: modalism and tritheism.

Modalism sacrificed the divine Trinity to the divine unity. Modalism discovered only one person in God and looked on the Son and Breath as different manners or "modes" in which the one Father had manifested Himself in human history.

Tritheism committed the opposite blunder. It sacrificed unity to Trinity. Tritheism could find no difference between a human community and the transcendent communion of the Trinity. Tritheism spoke of three fully constituted gods. The Fourth Lateran Council condemned the tritheism of Joachim of Flora, a Franciscan monk with a mystical bent. Joachim thought of the three divine persons as substances with only a similar resemblance to one another. Instead of constituting one God, they exemplified a collectivity, i.e., enjoyed the same kind of social communion as human persons.

The events of Christian revelation rule out both positions. The missions of Son and Breath falsify modalism by revealing historically the distinction of the Father from the Son whom He sends and of the Father and Son from the Breath, since the Father sends the Breath through the mediation of the glorified and risen Son. Moreover, in the encounter with the risen Christ, Paul the apostle experienced Son and Breath as sharing an identity of divine life, since anyone who participates in the Breath of the risen Jesus shares here and now in the divine life of the risen one. Three divine persons who share an identity of life exemplify one God.

Augustinian theology dominated the middle ages. Most medieval treatises on the Trinity play variations on the argument of Augustine's *De Trinitate*. Two aspects of that argument left me disinclined to endorse it: its *a priori* reasoning and the fact that it logically implies the quaternity rather than the trinity of the Christian God.

Augustine argues *a priori* because he begins the doctrinal argument of the *de Trinitate* with a meditation on the divine substance which allegedly unifies the Trinity. He portrays that substance as wholly spiritual, i.e., immaterial, and as possessed of two conceptually distinct powers of operation, a spiritual intellect and a spiritual will. Augustine's psychological construct of the Trinity appeals to the distinction of the divine intellect from the divine will in order to explain the distinction of the Son's procession from the Spirit's. Augustine fallaciously endorsed Justin's hypothesis that the Son of God represents the mind of God. He therefore had the Son proceed from the divine intellect. He also had the Spirit proceed from the divine will and described the third person of the Trinity as the bond of love uniting Father and Son.

Had Augustine reasoned *a posteriori* rather than *a priori*, he would have recognized that trinitarian theology must begin with the events which reveal to us the triune God. That means that trinitarian abductions must result from reflection on the missions of Son and Breath rather than from an *a priori* metaphysical construct of the divine substance, because apart from those missions we know nothing about the Trinity. Had Augustine begun his trinitarian theology with an examination of the missions, he might also have recognized that they falsify his and Justin' hypothesis that the Son exemplifies the mind of God, since the missions disclose the Breath as the cognitive link between Father and Son and therefore as the divine mind, as Paul the apostle clearly saw. Paul equated the third member of the divine triad with the mind of God and of Christ (1 Cor 2:10-16, Rom 8:27, Phil 2:1-11). In any *a posteriori* trinitarian theology, the missions ground the distinction of the divine persons from one another, not the postulation of a purely conceptual[1] distinction between the divine spiritual intellect and the divine spiritual will. In other words, despite the popularity of Augustinian trinitarian theology among medieval theologians, Augustine's argument in the *De Trinitate* by reasoning *a priori* fails the test of logical validity. In also fails to interpret correctly the events which reveal to us the triune God. Hence, those events falsify important aspects of Augustine's trinitarian doctrine.

Moreover, as I reflected on the development of the Augustinian trinitarian tradition during the middle ages, I saw that it logically implies quaternity, not trinity, in the Christian God. The single substance that allegedly unifies the Trinity has to enjoy a reality other than the three distinct divine persons, since it supplies the divine unity while the persons supply divine diversity. A substance other than the persons which subsists in itself and not in anything else and which possesses a spiritual intellect and a spiritual will sounds exactly like a person in its own right. That, however, puts four persons in God, not three. Augustine himself did not assert quaternity in God; but the specter of quaternity haunted the Augustinian tradition because it flows logically and deductively from Augustine's abductive construct of the Trinity.

Once again, the events which reveal the Triune God falsified such an hypothesis, since no other person proceeds from the third member of the divine triad. As I reflected on the issues raised by Augustin's theology of the Trinity, I realized that, not only did I need to come up with a better explanation of the divine unity than Augustine had; but I also had to explain why no other person proceeds from the third member of the divine triad.

I found three other possible explanations of the unity of the Trinity in the orthodox tradition: 1) reduction to mystery, 2) *perichoresis*, or the existence of the divine persons in one another, and 3) vital identity. I found all three explanations both Biblically grounded and speculatively plausible. I shall consider each explanation in turn.

1) Reduction to Mystery: Conceiving the divine reality as the supreme exemplification of experience, as that experience than which we can conceive
none greater, entailed the mystery of God, since no finite mind can know a
supremely perfect God exhaustively and comprehensively. Moreover, as we
have seen, supremacy provided a much more plausible explanation of the divine mystery than Rahner, who had grounded the human experience of mystery in the essential orientation of the human agent intellect to actually infinite Being. Not only did his explanation commit the essence fallacy by
endowing the human intellect with a fixed and unchanging essence; but the
evidence of contemporary psychology, as we have also seen, tended to falsify
his hypothesis. Psychological evidence tends to support instead the radical
finitude of human minds, not their virtual infinity. Moreover, as we have seen,
Rahner so stressed the absoluteness of the divine mystery that, in the end, he
transformed analogy into paradox.

It also seemed to me that the finitude of the human mind offered a much
more plausible explanation of the human experience of mystery than the virtual infinity of the agent intellect. We experience things as mysterious when
we reach the limits of what we can know about them. As the supreme exemplification of experience, God completely comprehends all reality, actuality,
probability, and possibility and can be comprehended by no other reality. We
experience God as mysterious because our finite, peanut brains find the reality of God ultimately incomprehensible at the same time that a supremely perfect God exemplifies supreme intelligibility. From the standpoint of finite, developing human minds, *Deus semper major* (God is always more) and
therefore remains mysteriously unfathomable.

2) Perichoresis, *or the Existence of the Divine Persons in One Another:*
John of Damascus invoked *perichoresis*, or the existence of the divine persons in one another in order to explain the unity of the Trinity. John got that
idea from the fourth gospel, which appeals to the mutual indwelling of the divine persons as a way of uniting the Father, the Son, and the Paraclete in a
single divine reality. Moreover, the Beloved Disciple derived that idea from
the Christian community's experience of the divine Breath. In His last discourse, Jesus assures His disciples that when He sends them the Paraclete,
they will understand how He can dwell in the Father and the Father in Him
because through the indwelling of the Breath they will experience Him
dwelling in them and them in Him (Jn 14:15-21).

All well and good, but how ought one to understand the image of mutual
indwelling inferentially and rationally? Here neither the New Testament nor
John of Damascus offered any help. The Beloved Disciple offered an image
of divine unity grounded in the Christian community's experience of the indwelling of the Breath of Christ, but not a rational explanation of the divine

unity; and John of Damascus did no better. He explained the meaning of *perichoresis* rhetorically by metaphors, not by inferential argument. He compared the mutual inexistence of the divine persons, for example, to the way heat interpenetrates metal without becoming the metal. So too, the divine persons enjoy unity because in the Godhead They interpenetrate one another while remaining distinct from one another. I saw that, if I wanted to invoke the notion of *perichoresis* in explaining the unity of the divine persons, I would have to come up with a way of thinking it rationally.

3) Vital Identity: Finally, Gaius Marius Victorinus, a fourth century father who converted to Christianity late in life and who immediately involved himself in the refutation of Arianism, argued that the three divine persons remain one because they share an identity of life. I saw that in John's gospel the mutual indwelling of the divine persons also produces an identity of life. If, then, I could come up with a way of thinking divine mutual indwelling philosophically, perhaps my metaphysical categories would make vital identity also thinkable.

In a metaphysics of substance, one finds it impossible to conceive of two substances existing in one another without contradicting oneself, because substance metaphysics defines a substance as that which exists in itself and not in another as in a subject of inhesion. My relational metaphysics of experience, however, made mutual inexistence a trait of every exemplification of experience. It portrayed experienced reality as standing inside experience and helping to make it the kind of experience it eventually chooses to become. Two spatio-temporal experiences exist in one another to the extent that they experience one another. They nevertheless remain distinct from one another because, as Whitehead had seen, they have different histories and therefore remain qualitatively different. In Whitehead's thought, as we have seen, quality explains individual existence, not quantity. The latter individuates Aristotelian substances.

As I wrestled with the question of thinking the unity and Trinity of God in the context of a relational metaphysics of experience, however, I realized that history could not explain the distinction of the divine persons from one another because the immanent Trinity transcends space and time and therefore enjoys eternal reality, not historical development. Moreover, qualitative distinction could not explain a trinity of persons, because qualitatively distinct persons could not enjoy the perfect equality which divinity requires.

The more I thought about the matter, the more convinced I felt that having different histories does not adequately explain why even spatio-temporal realities differ from one another. Spatio-temporal realities enjoy different histories because they enjoy autonomy. By autonomy I mean the capacity to initiate one's own activity. Autonomy endows selves and persons with the capacity to decide eventually what they will become. You and I differ as personal selves because I cannot do your growing for you, nor can you do my growing for me. I cannot think or decide for you, nor can you think or decide for me. That makes the autonomy we both possess incommunicable. In the Latin tradition, incommunicability also helps define what it means to be a person.

I saw the necessity to distinguish autonomy from freedom. Elementary human freedom, as we have seen, results from the ability to distinguish realistic alternatives for choice. It has a more-or-less character depending on the circumstances, on my conceptual versatility, on my ability to see things in more than one frame of reference, on the kinds of habits and satisfactions I choose to cultivate. Ultimately, then, the character of my conscious, evaluative response makes me more or less free; but, while freedom has an flickering, more-or-less character, autonomy does not. It has a clear either-or character. Either you said and did this or that, or I did. We cannot initiate identically the same activity. While freedom describes a modality of one's evaluative response which a decision terminates, autonomy describes the modality of a tendency. In other words, freedom and autonomy inhabit different realms of experience and exemplify adverbs. By that I mean that freedom describes *how* we decide consciously. Autonomy describes *one way* in which tendencies function.

Charles Peirce seems to have felt a divine call to rethink the foundations of logic and metaphysics. His discovery of a logic of relations caused him to reconceive of all reality creatively in relational, functional terms. His relational, functional metaphysics avoided the essentialism of classical philosophy by restricting essences to the how of experience and by excluding them from the what of experience. As we have seen, we construct an essence when we abstract the way we sense or perceive something from the object sensed or perceived and from our minds which do the sensing and perceiving. Having created essences through abstraction, we then arrange them alphabetically in dictionaries.

As I reflected in more depth on the nature of individuality in a relational, functional universe, I realized that I had to rethink individuality in relational, functional terms. It seemed to me that the notion of autonomy as the incommunicable ability to initiate one's own activity offered a relational, functional notion of individuality which lived, human, social experience verifies. Moreover, it suggested a way of conceiving the individuality of the divine persons on an analogue with finite individuals. The presence of three autonomously functioning centers of activity in the Godhead would require one to think of the divine persons as entities distinct from one another.

Rahner, I knew, resisted attributing autonomy to the divine persons because he feared that it led logically to tritheism. Rahner, however, remained stuck in an essentialistic metaphysics of substance. In a relational, functional metaphysics of experience, need the presence of three autonomous centers of activity in God lead to tritheism? I began to think that the answer to that question depended on how one chose to explain philosophically the unity of the Trinity.

If one approaches the Trinity with *a posteriori* reasoning, as Peirce's logic correctly requires, then the events which reveal to us the triune God force us to acknowledge that Father, Son, and Breath do in fact initiate Their own activity. In sending the Son into the world, the Father acts autonomously. In freely choosing to fulfill the mission entrusted to Him by the Father, the Son acts autonomously. In illumining and empowering the missions of both the Son and of the Church the divine Breath, whom the Father and Son both send, functions autonomously.

I found a hint of how to think the unity of the Trinity in relational, functional, experiential terms in an offhand remark which I read in Albert the Great's discussion of relationship within the Trinity. Albert observed that relationships do not only explain distinction; they also unite. Albert had got it right; but the same relations which explain distinction cannot explain unity. Other relations have to do that.

In the Augustinian tradition, theologians during the middle ages tended to speak of the substance which allegedly unifies the Trinity as essentially simple. They defended the essential simplicity of the divine substance in order to explain why each of the divine persons possesses it totally. Simplicity precluded dividing up the divine essence into pieces with each person having only a limited share of the same essence; for a person who partially shared the divine essence would qualify as only partly divine and therefore not fully God.

My relational, functional metaphysics neither sanctioned nor invoked the Aristotelian concept of substance. Even had it done so, however, I still would have had serious difficulties with explaining the unity of the Trinity by identifying the three persons with something essentially simple. Why? Because essential simplicity precludes all multiplicity. In the Plotinian universe the One, the hypostasis from which all things emanate does possess essential simplicity. I remembered a class in the history of philosophy in the Fuse Box taught us by Linus Thro, in which a frustrated scholastic found difficulty in wrapping his mind around the notion of essential simplicity. As he groped for greater clarity, he asked Linus, "Well, what exactly does the One do?" "Well," Linus replied thoughtfully, "I guess you would have to say that it ones." I doubt if the answer gave the questioner much help; but Linus had it right. An essentially simple reality can only be itself and can have no internal complexity whatever. To portray the deity as essentially simple made the presence of multiplicity within the Godhead metaphysically impossible. In other words, it did not explain the Trinity; it explained the Trinity away and made it logically unthinkable. The fact, then, that the historical missions of the Son and Breath reveal three autonomously functioning realities in God falsified the hypothesis of essential simplicity in God.

How, then, explain the unity of a complex reality? By recognizing with Albert the Great that relations not only ground distinction, they also unite. The unity of the Trinity could become thinkable in a relational universe if, in addition to the negative relations of distinction which ground the multiplicity of persons in God, one could discover within the Triune God other kinds of relations which so unite the divine persons that they share an identity, not just a similarity of life.

How do divine persons relate to one another? Our only evidence lies in the historical missions of the Son and Breath. Moreover, of the two missions, the Incarnation gives us the clearest historical evidence of how divine persons relate. The full historical and eschatological revelation of the Incarnation comes with the paschal mystery. The paschal mystery includes Jesus' death, resurrection, and mission of the divine Breath. The eucharistic words of Jesus give us our clearest historical evidence of how He experienced His passion and death. Those words and symbolic gestures make it clear that Jesus viewed His impending death as the total gift of Himself in atoning love to His disciples and to the Father who required of Him fidelity to His mission even unto death. "Take, eat, this is My body. Take, drink, this is My blood of the covenant." If the relation of mutual self-donation in love accurately depicts the way in which divine persons relate to one another, then, in addition to the processions within the immanent Trinity, which ground the distinction of the divine persons from one another, one needs to recognize unitive relations of vital identity. How, then, ought one to characterize those unitive relations within the Trinity? If one takes Jesus as the norm, the events which reveal the Trinity, most especially the paschal mystery, teach us that divine persons give themselves to one another totally and absolutely.

In addition, the paschal mystery also reveals that the divine persons do indeed share an identity of divine life which the gift of the Breath communicates to those who receive Her into their hearts through faith. Those who possess the Breath of the risen Christ share the unquenchable life of the Risen One who now lives so totally transformed in the Breath of God that He has the power to mediate Her to all who believe in Him.

This last piece of revelatory evidence suggested the possibility of conceiving the unity of the Trinity on an analogy with the human social experience of mutual self-donation in love. When two human persons give themselves to one another in love, they blend their lives by existing lovingly in one another as experiences. The embodied character of finite human existence, however, precludes human persons ever sharing an identity of life. The historical blending of human lives in love can yield at best only an analogous similarity of life. Nevertheless, even finite human beings do become part of one another through their mutual self-gift in love. We experience that fact most poignantly in the death of one we deeply love.

Because the divine persons transcend space and time, they also transcend corporeal existence. That means that their mutual self-gift to one another in love suffers from none of the limitations of embodied, human love. If God exemplifies the supreme perfection of experience, then the divine persons ought to have the capacity to give Themselves to one another with a supreme perfection of love which creates in Them, not just the similarity of life which human persons enjoy, but an identity of divine life.

Such a conception of the unity of the Trinity requires a revision of a medieval doctrine of notional predicates in the Trinity. Medieval trinitarian theology argued that the Son's eternal generation by the Father and the Father and Son's eternal co-spiration of the divine Breath within the Godhead give rise to five relational predicates applicable to the Trinity. Scholastic theology called these relational predicates "notions." A sound trinitarian theology must assert: 1) that the Father generates the Son, 2) that the Son is generated by the Father, 3) that Father and Son together co-spirate the divine Breath, and that 4) She is co-spirated by Them. Since Father proceeds from no one, He in addition enjoys the negative relational predicate of 5) innascibility, of self-existence, of the inability to be originated.

I found all this true, as far as it went; but, if in addition to negative relations of distinction within the Godhead, we need to include positive, unitive relations of mutual self-donation which ground an identity and not just a similarity of divine life, then we need to expand the number of relational predicates one can make of the Triune God to eight. In addition to the five notions of which the medievals speak, we need also to discover within the Triune God the three positive relations of total self-donation in love which create the identity of life which unites the divine persons into one God.

Not long ago, after one of the seminars at the Catholic Theological Society of America in which I made a presentation, a colleague who spoke on the same panel as I told me that one day he would like to talk to me about crypto-tritheism. He said no more, and left abruptly before I could reply; but I assumed that he was referring to my relational, experiential construct of the Trinity. Had he given me the opportunity to respond, I would have said

"Crypto-shmipto!" The construct which I have developed explicitly rules out the possibility of tritheism. Tritheism discovers in the Trinity three complete and distinct gods. The construct I have developed rules that possibility out by arguing that the evidence of revelation forces us to understand each of the divine persons as contributing something distinctive to the shared life of the Trinity in such a way that, without the mutual self-donation of the divine persons, none of them would qualify either as fully personal or as fully divine.

As we have seen, the New Testament witness perceives the Father as the source of creative efficacy within the Godhead, the Breath as the source of divine omniscience, and the Son as a principle of obediential efficacy which in no way compromises his co-equality with the Father and the Breath but which transforms Him into the one through whom the Father and Breath act whenever they act on anything outside the Godhead. In other words, without the Father's total self-gift to the Son and the Breath, They would lack the divine power to create. Without the Son's total self-gift to the Father and the Breath, They would lack the divine ability to act on anything outside the Godhead. Without the divine Breath's total self-gift to the Father and the Son, They would lack personalizing, omniscient self- awareness. The self-donation of the Breath to the Father and the Son, in other words, transforms Her into the ultimate personalizing principle within the Godhead since personal existence requires responsible self-consciousness. We humans experience Her full personalizing power in a Christian conversion which perceives the divine reality ultimately revealed in the paschal mystery and which perfects our humanity by empowering us both to love with the universal, forgiving, atoning love of Christ and to live for ultimate divine Beauty, Truth, and Goodness.

My construct of the Trinity also offers an explanation of why no fourth divine person proceeds from the divine Breath. The Father and Son can give rise to another divine person because they both function within the triune God as the eternal source of two kinds of efficacy: one creative, the other obediential. The Breath, as Paul the apostle insisted, functions as the mind of God. Cognition makes one present to reality and can lure decision; but it effects nothing efficaciously, including another divine person. Moreover, the term "Breath" translates fairly well the meaning of the Hebrew term for the divine Spirit, *ruah*, which means wind in motion, breathing, life breath.

My relational, functional construct of the Trinity also made rational, inferential sense of a pun in the trinitarian theology of Gaius Marius Victorinus. As the mind of God, Victorinus argued, the divine Breath conceives the Word which the Father speaks in sending us His Son. The Son, therefore, confronts us as the spoken Word of God. Since, moreover, the New Testament tells us that Mary also conceived the Son in His humanity through the power of the

Breath, the third person of the Trinity confronts us, according to Victorinus, as the Mother of the Son both on earth as in heaven.

In *The Divine Mother* I gave this suggestion psychological plausibility by arguing that the archetype of the feminine in its function as a positive symbol of divine, transcendent reality connotes all the images which the Bible traditionally associates with the third person of the Trinity. Imagining the third member of the divine triad as the divine Mother also supplies a sore lack in Christian iconography; for while speculative theology has come to perceive Her as a person, as yet we lack the ability to imagine Her as a person. My construct of experience requires that we coordinate affective and inferential perceptions of reality. To imagine the third person of the Trinity as a pigeon or as water has no personal connotations; but imagining Her as the Mother of the Son does and completes the familial image of God which Jesus' renaming the Creator *Abba* originally began.

Moreover, the conception of the Son by the divine Mother in no way connotes His procession from Her. Her historical mission by the Father through the Son reveals that She proceeds efficaciously from Them. Her conception of the divine Word in the Trinity expresses not an efficacious relation of distinction but the unitive relation of divine illumination with omniscient wisdom. Moreover, if the Breath functions in the Trinity as an eternal source of evaluation rather than of decision, that fact explains why no person proceeds efficaciously from Her.

My decision to designate the third person of the Trinity as "Breath" rather than the more traditional word "Spirit" may seem to some quirkish and needlessly idiosyncratic; but it has strictly speculative motives. I have adopted Peirce's triadic, relational metaphysics because it seems to me to avoid all the major philosophical fallacies of both classical and Enlightenment philosophy. Few philosophical fallacies have led Christian speculation down the primrose path to self-contradiction and unintelligibility as the fallacy of dualism in its many speculative permutations. I have argued this point at some length in *The Gracing of Human Experience*. As a technical theological term, "spirit" connotes spirit-matter dualism, mind-body dualism, operational dualism, and cosmic dualism. As a result, I ordinarily avoid it whenever I engage in technical theological discourse because it connotes serious philosophical errors which I repudiate. In other words, those who believe that Christianity must embrace some form of spirit-matter dualism err seriously. A systematic study of Peirce's logic and metaphysics would cure their theological minds of that fallacious assumption.

By the time I had completed writing *The Divine Mother*, I had proven to my own satisfaction at least, that my relational metaphysics of experience had the capacity to interpret both the unity and trinity of the Christian God. The presence of three autonomous centers of activity in the Christian God does not, as Rahner feared, imply tritheism. It grounds personal distinction within the Trinity, but it does not divide the Trinity into three gods subsisting as complete persons and complete gods in their own right, as tritheism asserts. Why? Because the divine persons use Their autonomy in order to give themselves to one another in such a way that They share the identity of life which makes them both fully personal and fully divine. As fully personal and fully divine, the three persons in the trinity exemplify a single living reality, one God. Moreover, the supreme perfection of Their mutual self-gift makes Them, not us, supremely personal.

At the same time, my construct of the Trinity respected, I believe, the incomprehensible mystery of the triune God. No human construct of the Trinity can ever comprehend the Godhead in its infinite perfection. Trinitarian theologians must rest content if they can offer a non-contradictory metaphysical account of the partial, sacramental revelation of the Trinity which we have in fact received. As far as I could see, most attempts at systematic trinitarian speculation had not succeeded in formulating a consistent metaphysical language for talking about the triune God because they lay mired in the fallacies of classical logic and metaphysics. The switch from an essentialistic metaphysics of substance to a relational, triadic metaphysics of experience seemed to me to allow one to succeed where others had failed. It seemed to me on reflection that I had indeed successfully formulated a fallible, non-contradictory, working metaphysical account of the immanent Trinity which successfully interprets the economic Trinity.

As a matter of fact, Peirce suspected that one could use his metaphysics to rethink trinitarian theology, even though he himself never, to the best of my knowledge, attempted systematic theological thinking. Needless to say, it gave me no little satisfaction to prove his hunch correct.

My construct of the Trinity also allowed one to conceive of God as an eternal process without falling into the errors of Whitehead's philosophical theism. I rejected Whitehead's suggestion that the world creates God at the same time that God creates the world. In fact, nothing in space and time can in any way effect the eternal processions and mutual self-donation of the divine persons which constitute the eternal reality of the triune God. Nevertheless, a relational, triadic metaphysics of experience does allow one to conceive the Trinity as an eternal process. Within the Trinity the divine persons proceed eternally from one another and give themselves eternally and totally to one another.

By so understanding the Trinity, one also avoids Plato's identification of eternity with unchanging and unchangeable spirit. In classical thought, the eternal immutability of God made divine intervention in space and time difficult, if not impossible, to think consistently. If, however, the spatio-temporal process transpires in an eternal, divine process, the saving, self-revelation of the triune God in space and time seemed to me thinkable without contradiction.

When I wrote *The Divine Mother*, I recognized that any systematic account of Christian religious experience needs to coordinate one's theological understanding of the Trinity with one's theological understanding of the Incarnation. The Incarnation includes the Son of God's human conception by the Breath, His birth, His life, His mortal ministry, His passion, His resurrection, and His historical, eschatological mission of the Breath. Her mission in space and time reveals not only His divinity finally and fully but also the reality of three persons in one God. In other words, the Incarnation reveals the Trinity at the same time that the Trinity contextualizes the Incarnation.

Accordingly, in *The Divine Mother*, I sketched an experiential construct of the Incarnation which seemed to me coordinate with the experiential construct of the Trinity I had developed and which I hoped would prove verifiable. I did not in that work, however, claim to have demonstrated the truth of my experiential construct of the hypostatic union. I proposed it rather as an interesting, fallible abduction which needed systematic testing against the data of revelation and against the Christian tradition. Until I did that, I could not claim to have formulated a working experiential construct of the hypostatic union.

Theologians have called the third person of the Trinity both "the forgotten God" and "the God about whom no one writes." The literature about pneumatology looks puny by comparison with the mountains of books and articles which treat of Christology. In order to verify my Christological hypothesis I would have to deal dialectically with virtually all of the New Testament as well as with two thousand years of Christological speculation. I had the right to feel daunted. In the end, my Christological research took me over twenty years.

I decided to begin research with contemporary Christology and to work backwards. The Christomonism which characterizes so much of contemporary theology causes scholars to grind out one Christological treatise after another usually without a mention of the Trinity. If I could get on top of contemporary Christology and stay there while I worked my way backwards through the history of Christological speculation, at least I would have a finite, though still dauntingly massive amount of historical evidence with which to deal. If I began at the beginning and worked forward, I feared that the growing number of contemporary Christologies would so dishearten me that I would eventually give up the project of writing a Christology in utter despair.

I postponed my third sabbatical so that I could complete my research into the dialectical development of Christological thinking. That way I could devote my entire sabbatical to writing the first draft of the foundational Christology which I ambitioned. I spent this sabbatical too in the Kathleen Norris mansion in Palo Alto; and by the end of my stay there I had virtually completed the first draft of *The Firstborn of Many*.

After my first sabbatical I had determined to spend a significant amount of time traveling abroad. During my second sabbatical, I had visited Hekima College, our theologate in Nairobi, Kenya, in the hope of laying foundations for collaboration between it and JSTB. I had also explored possibilities of teaching theology there and in Zambia. I made three tries to teach a semester at Hekima College but never brought it off. With time, however, a growing number of African students came to JSTB as candidates for the papal licentiate and papal doctorate which we as an ecclesiastical faculty award. As a result, I did not need to go to Africa in order to test my theology in a different cultural context from the U.S. Africa came to me.

During my second sabbatical, I spent Holy Week in Lusaka and with Charlie Searson, S.J., an Irish Jesuit who had studied at JSTB. Charlie and I paid a call on many of the mission stations in Zambia. Our trip culminated in a visit to Victoria Falls in the spring, with the Zambezi River in full spate. Natives called the falls "The Smoke that Roars"; and as I stared gape-mouthed for the first time at the spectacle of its plunging waters, an American nearby noticed my dumbfounded state, ambled over and said with a smile, "It makes Niagra look like a trickle, doesn't it?" I could only nod in wordless agreement.

During my third sabbatical, I had secured a grant from the Luce Foundation to visit three Asian countries and to interview people there about the question of inculturation: namely, how Christianity interfaces with the local Asian culture. I spent eight days in Korea, two weeks in Japan, and eight days in Taiwan. Our school was acquiring a growing number of Asian students; and I wanted a first-hand experience of Asian culture. My Asian jaunt kept me from finishing the first draft of *The Firstborn of Many* while in Palo Alto; but I successfully completed it during the summer before the academic year began.

In Tokyo, I met Mark Koo, S.J., a Korean Jesuit who would work with me at JSTB on a papal S.T.D. As I watched Mark's dissertation take creative and original shape, I felt great satisfaction in his conviction that the theology of conversion I had been developing spoke to important needs in Korean culture. He currently teaches theology at Sophia University in Tokyo where he has been introducing Koreans and Japanese to my work.

As I immersed myself more and more in contemporary Christology and in an analysis of the issues it raised, I felt increasingly alarmed at what seemed to me a confused drift back into a degenerate form of Arianism. The drift resulted in no small measure from the bewildering pluralism which characterizes post-Vatican-II theological thinking. As long as Catholic systematic theologians felt some constraint to adopt Thomism as a metaphysical frame of reference, Catholic theology prior to Vatican II enjoyed something like an artificial, canonically induced illusion of consensus. Once Vatican II dethroned Thomism and allowed greater philosophical pluralism in speculative theological thinking, theologians went scurrying off in all directions, if indeed they made any attempt at all to think with systematic philosophical rigor.

Christology offers a more or less systematic account of the unity of divinity and humanity in the person we call Jesus Christ. As consensus about the meaning of divinity, of humanity, of unity, of person, and of the historical Jesus disintegrated into an increasingly vague babble, overreaction to the so called "high" Christologies of the middle ages, which stressed Jesus' divinity at the expense of His humanity, led a growing number of contemporary Christologists, to stress, in my judgment, Jesus' humanity at the expense of His divinity. I found a significant number of Christologists portraying Jesus of Nazareth as just a human person like the rest of us. Sometimes they even confused Christology with traditional Mariology by portraying Jesus as the most perfectly graced human person who had ever lived. Even the Arians would have felt shock at that degree of "lowness" in one's account of Jesus Christ. They at least regarded Jesus as a super-creature, as a kind of Platonic demiurge.

Most of the systematic theologians I read had no apparent interest in logic and had not even heard of Peirce. As a result, too often they had not learned from Peirce to advance beyond the fallacies of modernity. They seemed to me far too inclined to fix their theological beliefs by what Peirce called the method of taste. They seemed to assume that the personal attractiveness of an idea offers a good substitute for verifying or falsifying it in historical and eschatological evidence. The more contemporary Christology I read, the more convinced I felt that that kind of logical perversity offered a very effective formula in doctrinal matters for a muddled rather than malicious drift into heterodoxy.

Grounding doctrines in the events which reveal the triune God clarifies their authentic meaning. As I advanced in my understanding of how that regrounding clarifies the authentic meaning of Christological doctrines, I began to name with greater clarity the operations of the functional theological specialty called "doctrines." The functional theological specialty of doctrines, as we have seen, seeks to differentiate between authentic, true doctrines and inauthentic, false ones.

The Christology I eventually formulated in *The Firstborn of Many* at least attempted on a number of issues to break new Christological ground. It made the first attempt, for example, to formulate a cross-disciplinary portrait of Jesus' humanity. My purely rational portrait of the man Jesus had a philosophical component, a psychological component, and an historical component.

In formulating a systematic, foundational Christology, I wanted to test the ability of my developing metaphysics of experience to interpret the hypostatic union. I decided to confront the easiest part of Christology first. I began with an attempt to clarify how I understood human nature rationally and inferentially. I saw clearly what too many contemporary "low" Christologists fail to see: namely, that offering a purely rational account of Jesus' humanity produces a Jesusology, not a Christology, for the simple reason that it prescinds from the paschal mystery which reveals Jesus' divinity historically and eschatologically through His sending of the Breath.

Moreover, Peirce's logic made sense out of Lonergan's suggestion that a foundational theology must advance as an exercise in cross-disciplinary thinking. As we have seen, Peirce's logic requires the verification or falsification of fallible metaphysical hypotheses both in lived, human, social experience as lived and in the verified results of the idioscopic sciences. In discussing Jesus' humanity philosophically, I presented it as a finite, developing human experience. In my purely philosophical argument, I proved to my own satisfaction at least, that my triadic, relational construct of experience could successfully interpret lived human experience as lived.

As I have already indicated, in verifying that same philosophical construct in the results of contemporary psychology, I decided to spread my nets wider than I had in writing *Experiencing God*. I therefore tested the ability of my philosophical construct of experience to interpret the results of both individual and social psychology. I also took into account James Fowler's developmental construct of religious, cognitive growth. I invoked the normative sciences to critique questionable presuppositions of some developmental psychiatrists. Piaget's intellectualist bias and Kohlberg's rationalism and individualism exemplify the kinds of questionable presuppositions I mean. I concluded that my philosophical construct of experience could interpret as philosophically defined the provisionally verified results of both personal and social psychology. In *The Gracing of Human Experience*, I would also argue that that same construct could interpret the results of the sociology of knowledge.

The fact that I, following Peirce, was attempting to think through Christological issues while using a scientifically verified philosophical hypothesis seemed to me to mark another Christological breakthrough. No one else in the history of Christology, as far as I could see, had ever even attempted to do that. As my reflections on foundational method had taught me, I also argued that the verification of my philosophical construct of experience in the results of contemporary individual and social developmental psychology amplified my construct of the human. It allowed me to flesh out, at least with some degree of plausibility, the kinds of human growth experiences Jesus of Nazareth would have experienced during the hidden life in Nazareth.

I claimed no more than plausibility for my psychological portrait of Jesus. I did not on the whole claim probability, and I certainly did not claim certainty; and that for two reasons. First of all, developmental psychology really began with the work of Jean Piaget and remains still a very young science. The research done since Piaget did his has caused a number of qualifications of his original account of human cognitive development. A contrite fallibilist like Peirce, I anticipated that as developmental psychology continues to unfold, it would require further qualifications both of his work and of that of subsequent developmentalists.

I had a second reason for claiming only plausibility for my psychological portrait of Jesus' human experience: namely, the difficulty which attends the attempt to project onto a first-century peasant living in a largely oral, agrarian culture, the psychological results of studies of people living in contemporary, literate, technological culture.

I used my own personal assessment of the results of the new quests for the historical Jesus in order to complete my cross-disciplinary account of Jesus as human. Moreover, in dealing with the results of the new quests, I invoked a principle suggested by E.P. Sanders and one which more questers for the historical Jesus would do well to own. Sanders has suggested that we characterize the results of the new quests with something like logical "notes." Accordingly, in dealing with the results of the new quests, I spoke of some facts about Jesus as either certain or uncertain, of others as plausible or implausible, of others as probable or improbable, and of others still as possible or impossible. If more new questers used either the same or some better set of logical notes to qualify the results of their rational investigations into what we can say historically about Jesus of Nazareth, they might succeed better than they have to date in reaching a scholarly consensus.

I further argued that my philosophical construct of experience could successfully interpret the results of the new quests. I therefore also concluded, as my method taught me, that those same results amplified my philosophical construct of Jesus' humanity as a finite developing human experience by endowing it with historical concreteness. When logically qualified as I have suggested, the results of invoking the criteria which new questers use for authenticating the historicity of what we know of Jesus' mortal ministry and death on a cross provide us with a fairly detailed account of the kind of human experience Jesus of Nazareth in fact chose to develop.

My insistence on the distinction between Jesusology and Christology also struck me as an important and neglected Christological distinction. It claimed the middle ground between the fideism of Neo-orthodoxy and the Enlightenment rationalism of Paul Tillich. Against Neo-orthodoxy I argued for the legitimacy of invoking metaphysical categories in order to describe Jesus' humanity as long as one recognizes their fallibility and the need to verify them in an ongoing way both in lived human experience as lived and in the verified results both of the idioscopic sciences and of scholarly disciplines relevant to theological reflection. Against Tillich I refused to use my particular set of metaphysical categories with the kind of rationalistic reductionism with which he used his particular version of existentialism.

The distinction between Jesusology and Christology also called into question the legitimacy of the faddish distinction between "high" and "low" Christologies. Too many contemporary Christologists seem to assume it a matter of taste whether one will develop one or the other. In *The Firstborn* I argued that we would eliminate the considerable confusion spawned by the vague distinction between "high" and "low" Christology if we would replace it with a distinction between "good" and "bad" Christology. Good Christology takes into account all the evidence we have concerning Jesus' mortal ministry *and* the evidence supplied by the events of the paschal mystery to which the New Testament gives us contemporary scholarly access. Bad Christology fails to take into account all of the same evidence. Good Christology formulates a logically valid, adequate, and verifiable account of Jesus' humanity, divinity, and the relationship between them. Bad Christology does not. I fear that unless we replace the distinction between "high" and "low" Christology with the distinction between "good" and "bad" Christology, logically confused Christologists will continue to confound their personal Christological preferences with gospel truth.

As I turned to the challenge of formulating a foundational Christology, I saw that I would have to allow my construct of conversion to structure the argument. A foundational Christology seeks to understand how a fully converted Christian ought to relate in faith to Jesus Christ. When one poses the Christological question in the context of a normative theology of conversion, then the second dynamic which Christian conversion contributes to the total process of conversion acquires considerable methodological and speculative significance. As we have seen, the second dynamic of Christian conversion requires the commitment of justifying faith made in an initial Christian conversion to transvalue the other four forms of conversion. That means that the foundational Christological question as I formulated it asks, "How ought commitment to Jesus Christ in justifying faith to transform affective conversion, intellectual conversion, personal moral conversion, and socio-political conversion?" Even to pose the Christological question in the context of a normative theology of conversion marked another important Christological advance.

As we have seen, justifying faith transforms and transvalues affective conversion by suffusing it with Christian hope. Since we grasp reality first of all in judgments of feeling illumined by remembered and constructed images, I decided to explore first the way in which commitment to Jesus Christ in justifying faith transforms affective conversion into the theological virtue of hope in Jesus Christ. Here I found both Pauline Christology and the Christology of the book of Revelation invaluable for reaching a normative insight into the meaning of Christological hope.

Paul developed a kerygmatic Christology which focused primarily on the paschal mystery. In his surviving letters, the apostle says little about Jesus' mortal ministry. The paschal mystery reveals the divinity of Jesus by disclosing Him as the Breath-baptizer, i.e., as the efficacious source of a divine reality and therefore as divine.[2] As a consequence, a discussion of a Pauline Christology of hope established initially the context I needed to make a successful transition from Jesusology to Christology. Christology goes beyond Jesusology by offering an account of how the paschal mystery and the apostolic encounters with the risen Jesus transformed human perceptions of His person and mortal ministry.

I believed that I could legitimately characterize Pauline Christology as a Christology of hope precisely because the apostle's focus on the paschal mystery endowed his Christology with a strong eschatological character. For Paul, one enters the eschaton, the last age of salvation, by opening one's heart to the gift of the Breath of the risen Christ. That gift transforms the way believing Christians experience the future. Apart from the gift of Christ's Breath, we experience the future as a concatenation of more or less attractive, more or less threatening possibilities. The risen Christ's mission of God's sanctifying Breath makes the reality of God into the future coming at us, as the Breath of the risen Lord begins to conform us, even in this life, to His risen image by teaching us to put on His mind, to embrace His religious vision, to live our lives as He would have lived them in our circumstances, and therefore to embark down the same experiential religious path which culminated in His resurrection.

Jesus therefore rises differently from everybody else. Only his resurrection effects resurrection in others through the gift of the divine Breath who imparts to repentant mortals a share in His risen life. That same gift, as we have seen, reveals historically and eschatologically Jesus' divinity. It also makes Jesus unique among the founders of world religions. In every other founder of a world religion we encounter a converted, human sinner who left behind a doctrine and a community of religious faith. Only Jesus died, rose, and in His risen glory sends continuously and efficaciously into the world the divine Breath who conforms sinful humans to His sinless example and so prepares in them a share in His risen glory.

It seemed to me as I worked my way through all the Christological texts in the Pauline corpus that his assertion in 1 Cor 15:45 that "the first man, Adam, became a living soul, but the last Adam became a life-giving Breath" summed up succinctly half of what Paul asserted about the paschal mystery as a saving event. I found virtually every word in that sentence pregnant with important Christological meaning.

Jesus "became" a life-giving Breath. Paul here speaks dispensationally about the economic Trinity. By that I mean that he is describing how the disciples' experience of Jesus in religious faith evolved. During His mortal ministry, they did not experience Him as a life-giving Breath; but those who saw the risen Christ did so experience Him. By that I mean that they experienced Him as the efficacious source of the divine reality of God's Breath and therefore as divine.

The fact that Jesus efficaciously gives or sends the Breath establishes their distinction from one another. The sender remains distinct from the one sent. At the same time, if one omits the phrase "life-giving," Paul is saying that the risen Christ "became the Breath." That kind of talk gives the willies to theologians who live on the other side from Paul of the trinitarian controversies of the fourth century. To say that Christ became the Breath identifies Them; and, if one identifies Them, how can one maintain that they exemplify distinct persons in a triune God? Paul knew nothing of the trinitarian controversies of the fourth century. Moreover, the apostle did not think like a contemporary systematic theologian. He thought more like a first-century rabbi. Moreover, in saying that the risen Christ became the Breath the apostle had every intention to assert Their identity with one another. Identifying the risen Christ with the Breath provided Paul with one of his standard rhetorical gambits for locating the risen Lord in the realm of the divine and therefore for asserting His divinity. By qualifying the clause that "the last Adam became the Breath" with the adjective "life-giving," Paul had also already implicitly asserted Their distinction from one another, since mission reveals distinction. In other words, without using the technical language of the fourth-century creeds, Paul affirmed that the risen Christ and the divine Breath are both one and distinct, just as those later creeds would insist more abstractly. The apostle was portraying the risen Lord and the Breath of God as equally divine despite their real distinction from one another within the Godhead.

Paul does not say that the second Adam became a life-giving Breath but that "the last Adam" did so. First and last endow his assertion with a certain absoluteness. One cannot get beyond the first Adam in the order of creation; and one cannot get beyond the last Adam in the order of salvation. Now that Jesus has died, risen, and sent the Breath, humanity has everything it needs to attain salvation. If, then, the phrase "the last Adam (ὁ ἔσχατος Ἀδαμ)" suggests to one the eschaton, the last age of salvation which the paschal mystery inaugurates, the apostle intended that it would.

Whenever Paul used Adamic imagery, it had universal connotations. As the last Adam, Jesus mediates a salvation which God intends for all sinful humans. Paul's ongoing battle in the apostolic Church to insure that his Gentile converts stood within the Christian community on a completely equal footing with Jewish Christians helped motivate the universalist strain in his Christology; but one finds a similar universalism in other parts of the New Testament.

Adamic imagery recalls, of course, the creation of humanity in Genesis. It therefore also connotes the new creation which Jesus begins. By His sinlessness, Jesus reconstitutes human nature in its original sinless state. Moreover, His gift of the divine Breath empowers a sinful but repentant humanity to live in His sinless image. Such sinless living motivates the Christian hope that those who so live in Jesus' image in this life will also find themselves transformed in His risen image in the next life.

Paul's proclamation of the risen Jesus as a life-giving Breath deals, however, with only one half of the paschal mystery. Jesus' passion and death constitutes the other half. It characterizes a Pauline understanding of Jesus' death, moreover, to portray it, not simply as something He suffered, but as a moral act, as something He did, because He freely chose to suffer it. Paul characterizes Jesus' death as "death to sin." In other words, at the precise moment when the chief priests joined forces with the principalities and powers of this world in order to murder Jesus legally as a blasphemer and an insurrectionist, His death embodied the ultimate expression of His sinless accomplishment of the saving mission the Father had given him. This understanding of Calvary also colors Paul's theology of baptism. In baptism, Christians die with Christ to sin by welcoming into their hearts the empowering enlightenment of His Breath who comes to teach them to put on His mind collectively and personally by living from day to day in His sinless image.

The rest of Paul's Christology spells out the saving consequences of what happened in the paschal mystery. Not only does it mediate a salvation universal in its scope, but it also transforms the entire body person in the image of the crucified and risen Christ. Though Paul never mentions the empty tomb as such, he does insist on the mysterious, transformed physicality of the risen Jesus who embodies what Christians hope to become.

The Breath's outpouring of the charisms endows salvation with a spatial dimension by transforming churches into the Body of Christ on earth, living environments of graced, mutual service. The letters to the Colossians and Ephesians further develop this metaphor in their theology of the pleroma. The pleroma, or fullness, extends out into the world the salvation incarnate in its personal fullness in Jesus. These letters extend the metaphor of Christ's body to the Church universal. They also portray Christ as head of His body and that same body as His instrument for extending the consequences of the paschal mystery into the physical world by replacing sinful environments with graced ones. Ephesians especially looks to the Breath's charisms to create such environments.

Pauline apocalyptic endows the salvation Jesus brings with a temporal di mension. It teaches Pauline Christians to look forward with hope and longing to their final vindication and perfect union with God which the second coming of Christ will effect. Paul deals most explicitly with this dimension of salvation in Christ in his earliest letters to the church at Thessalonika. These letters, however, yield only a partial glimpse into Pauline apocalyptic.

The book of Revelation comes from another tradition in the apostolic Church; but it develops an important theme in Paul's apocalyptic: namely, the ultimate victory of Jesus over the principalities and powers of this world. In *The Firstborn of Many*, I chiefly used the book of Revelation in order to politicize Christian hope. Throughout the New Testament one finds it proclaimed that commitment to Christ pits believers in unrelenting opposition to the principalities and powers of this world. Revelation, however, written probably in anticipation of the persecution of the Church under the Emperor Domitian, insists with greater narrative emphasis than any other book of the New Testament that violent and oppressive institutions like the Roman empire incarnate the Satanic Anti-Christ and can have nothing in common with authentic gospel living. On the contrary, Christians must maintain nonviolent, prophetic opposition to all forms of faithless institutional violence and oppression, including those of an emerging United States empire.

Justifying faith not only transforms affective conversion into Christian hope; but it also suffuses intellectual conversion with the theological virtue of faith. Intellectual conversion deals with beliefs; and, as we have seen, the construct of experience which grounds my approach to conversion insists that the human mind fixes its beliefs with two kinds of judgment: with imaginative and intuitive judgments of feeling and with abstract inductive inferences.

Any attempt to understand how commitment to Jesus Christ in justifying faith transforms intellectual conversion needs to deal with both kinds of beliefs about Jesus.

The narrative Christology enshrined in the gospels illumines the intuitive dimensions of Christological faith. The human mind first perceives reality imaginatively and intuitively and only subsequently reflects on the same reality abstractly and inferentially. Any adequate account of theological faith must take care to coordinate abstract, inferential judgments of faith with more basic judgments of feeling, which also perceive the saving significance of revelatory events. One needs, in a word, to make sure that the human head says the same things as the human heart about the revelation of God made to us in Jesus Christ; for both heart and head perceive and judge the same saving reality.

I decided that, unfortunately, theologians had yet to develop an adequate method for dealing with the narrative statement made about Jesus in the gospels precisely as narratives. Historical-critical method has made remarkable contributions to our understanding of the gospels by situating them in the historical context which gave rise to them and helped shape them. It seemed to me, however, that the strongly analytic character of historical-critical method prevents it from dealing with gospel narrative precisely as a continuous, unified narrative. Historical-critical method chops the gospels up into chunks of text it calls "pericopes" and then undertakes a minute and detailed historical contextualization of each chunk.

One finds other methods in contemporary exegesis for reading the gospels, including attempts to read them as literature. The attempts at a literary reading of the gospel which I perused did not, however, in my judgment altogether succeed, chiefly because they continued to use historical critical method as their principal approach to the gospel text and only supplemented it with periodic lapses into literary analysis.

I had immersed myself in narrative theology as a preparation for my Christological reading of the gospels. I found in narrative theology impassioned appeals for theology to take seriously the insights of the intuitive, imaginative mind. I did not, however, find there a technique for reading each of the gospels as a narrative whole. Moreover, I had convinced myself that one needed to read any gospel precisely as a narrative whole in order to understand the kind of narrative statement it was making about Jesus of Nazareth. I decided therefore to develop a method of my own for doing that.

My method takes into account the results of historical critical method; but it proposes a specific technique for reading gospel narrative as narrative. Moreover, if applied systematically to each of the gospels, the method I developed allows one to do a dialectical comparison of the narrative

Christological statement each of the gospels makes about Jesus. That dialectical comparison highlights where they agree, where they converge, where they complement one another; and, if they disagree, it allows one to clarify the terms of disagreement. In fact, I found in the synoptic gospels mostly agreement, convergence, and complementarity.

In order to understand how gospel narrative works, I tried to situate it within the spectrum of different kinds of narrative. I therefore turned to literary theory in order to understand exactly how narrative works. Literary theory distinguishes typical kinds of narrative: oral and written narrative, scholarly history, and different kinds of fictional narrative: the epic, slice-of-life fiction, romantic fiction, allegory, fable, fairy tale, myth, parable.

In *The Firstborn of Many* I argued that the gospels do not fit any of the standard literary classifications of narrative. They lie somewhere between oral and written narrative. Though written, they stitch together into a unified gospel narrative anecdotes about Jesus handed down orally in the apostolic Church. They talk about historical figures but they do not exemplify scholarly history as we currently practice it. Myths tell adult communities stories which create the world of reality and value in which those communities live. Narrative parables subvert the familiar world in which people live in order to open them up to new and better possibilities. In other words, myth and parable typically serve contrary narrative ends. Paradoxically, however, the gospels function simultaneously as both myth and parable. The gospels function as myth because the story of Jesus–His life, ministry, death, resurrection, and mission of the divine Breath–creates the world of reality and value in which Christian communities live. The gospels, however, also function as parable because the story of Jesus subverts the familiar world in which people ordinarily live and challenges those who read them to a conversion which puts them at serious odds with the world of the unconverted.

I concluded that any literary reading of the gospels has to respect the uniqueness of gospel narrative. Mark probably created the gospel as a literary form of narrative. While Mark writes fractured Greek, one should not underestimate the extraordinary character of his artistic achievement in creating gospel as literary form. As an evangelist, Mark had to figure out from scratch how to transform a bunch of miscellaneous anecdotes about Jesus into a coherent narrative; and he succeeded.

The method I employed in *The Firstborn of Many* to read the gospels as narrative wholes I called linkage analysis. By a gospel linkage I meant a literary technique for stitching together into a single narrative different anecdotes about Jesus which originally had no narrative relationship to one another. I argued that all the evangelists use the same narrative linkages as Mark created in writing the first gospel: dramatic linkages, thematic linkages, and allusive linkages.

By a dramatic linkage, I mean the way in which Jesus, the hero of all gospel narrative, relates to the different persons and constituencies who confront Him. Moreover, having read and studied Walter Ong's *Orality and Literacy*, I realized that oral narrative holds the key to understanding the gospels' dramatic linkages.

The gospels reproduce many of the traits of oral narrative. It typifies oral narrative, for example, to start *in medias res*, although both Matthew and Luke try to mute the abruptness with which Mark begins his gospel by starting with an infancy narrative. Having described Jesus' birth, however, both Matthew and Luke start the story of Jesus' ministry abruptly, *in medias res*, even though Luke does narrate one incident from Jesus' adolescence—the finding in the temple—as a very short bridge between his infancy narrative and his account of Jesus' public ministry. As in oral narrative, each of the evangelists adapts the story of Jesus to the needs of the particular community he addresses. It also characterizes oral narrative to have one-dimensional characters. Subtle psychological portraiture does not develop until written language fixes narrative to a page. In oral narrative, if a character has a distinguishing trait, he or she rarely has more than one. Think of impetuous Peter, of Judas the traitor, or Pilate the vacillator. Although the evangelists depict the person of Jesus in greatest detail, none of the gospels gives us a detailed portrait of how His human psyche worked.

Given the one-dimensionality of most of the characters in the gospel, I divided Jesus' constituencies into good guys, bad guys, and wishy-washy people. John the Baptizer, the Father, and the divine Breath exemplify the good guys. Satan and his demons, the scribes and Pharisees, Herod, the chief priests, and Pilate and the Roman empire exemplify the bad guys. The disciples and the crowds represent the wishy-washy people. Jesus always relates positively to the wishy-washy crowds and disciples; but in the course of the gospel narrative, they cannot figure out how exactly to relate to Jesus. Finally, the wishy-washy people find themselves forced to take a stand for or against Jesus in the face of the paschal mystery. The Jerusalem crowds turn against Jesus and demand His crucifixion; and the disciples relate to him in a variety of ways which typify attitudes which Jesus' disciples might in principle adopt toward Him. Judas betrays Jesus and despairs. Peter denies Him, repents, and gets rehabilitated. The women function as faithful witnesses to Jesus' death and to the empty tomb of the risen one, and in Matthew they actually see the risen Christ and testify to the encounter to the other disciples. Simon of Cyrene finds himself forced to carry the cross after Jesus as an ironic type of the true disciple. Joseph and the women bury Jesus.

All the evangelists handle two of Mark's thematic linkages: Jesus' teachings and His deeds of power: his miraculous healings and, in the synoptics, His exorcisms; but the evangelists all handle Jesus' teachings and miracles very differently. Mark created the literary convention of the gospel discourse which connects different thematically related saying of Jesus in something like an oration. Mark, however, made much less use of this literary device than either Matthew or Luke. Mark reproduces Jesus' vision of the kingdom but mostly in pronouncement stories scattered throughout his gospel; for the first evangelist looks more to events than to words in order to reveal the deep mystery which Jesus incarnates. Matthew tells Jesus' story as Christian Torah and collects most of Jesus' teachings in five discourses which correspond to the five books of the original Torah. Luke's gospel has five short discourses, but Luke collects most of Jesus' teachings in his journey discourse. The synoptic Jesus rarely talks about Himself; the Johannine Jesus does practically nothing else. The Jesus of the fourth gospel never tires of lecturing unbelieving "Jews" about His pre-existence with the Father.

The evangelists also have distinctive ways of handling Jesus' miracles. Matthew, for example, collects most of Jesus' miracles in the narrative section which follows the sermon on the mount as a way of dramatizing that the good news Jesus proclaims heals and transforms those who accept it. John uses the miracles in order to develop his theology of "signs." Mark's and Luke's accounts of particular miracles often function as pronouncement stories in which Jesus clarifies by some short teaching the revelatory significance of the mighty act He has just performed.

In addition to Jesus' teachings and miracles, each evangelists develops pet theological themes as Jesus' story unfolds. Mark, for example, develops the theme of the messianic secret; Matthew, the theme of fulfillment; Luke, the theme of the journey as the Christian exodus, which began with Jesus' final journey to Jerusalem, continues with the spread of the gospel, and will last until the second coming. The Beloved Disciple develops across Jesus' discourses many of the theological themes in his gospel's hymnic prologue.

Finally, each of the evangelists uses literary allusion in order to tie together his narrative. By literary allusion, I mean the use of the same narrative detail in more than one story in order to indicate that the two anecdotes cast light on one another. For example, in Mark's gospel Jesus three times takes someone by the hand and raises the person up. Each time the verb for raising up connotes resurrection. Each story calls attention to different consequences of sharing in the risen life of Christ. When Jesus raises up Peter's mother-in-law, she serves Him and his disciples (Mk 1:29-31). Clearly, those who share in the risen life of Christ will serve Him and others faithfully in His image. After driving a deaf and dumb demon from the epileptic demoniac boy, Jesus also takes him by the hand and raises him up (Mk 9:14-27). Clearly, those with whom Jesus shares risen life, He delivers from the power of Satan and empowers to hear and to speak, to hear the gospel in faith and to proclaim it. After Jesus takes the hand of the dead daughter of Jairus and raises her up, He says, "Give her something to eat" (Mk 5:41-43). Jesus will say the same thing to the disciples in the multiplication of the loaves and fish (Mk 6:37). The multiplication miracles foreshadow the Eucharist because in them Jesus performs the eucharistic actions of taking, blessing, breaking, and giving (Mk 6:41, 8:6). Clearly, those with whom Jesus shares risen life He also nourishes on the eucharistic bread of wisdom.

Each evangelist, however, uses literary allusion differently. Mark constructs an elaborate network of literary allusions which focus his gospel on the two miracles of the loaves. Matthew's editing of Mark shatters the latter's rete of literary allusions. Matthew, however, uses the story of the Great Commission which closes his gospel to tie together his narrative allusively. Luke typically uses literary allusion in order to link together both volumes of his two-volume study of Christian origins and in order to portray Peter and Paul in Acts as other Christs who conduct parallel apostolic ministries. The Beloved Disciple typically uses literary allusion in order to develop theological ideas incrementally over Jesus' discourses as a way of dramatizing the waxing of revelatory, divine light.

In the second volume of *The Firstborn of Many*, I argued that a comparative, dialectical, linkage analysis of the three synoptic gospels not only enables one to compare and contrast the kind of narrative statement each evangelists makes about Jesus, but it also clarifies exactly how Christians come to know Jesus Christ in intuitive, narrative faith. In dealing with Paul's Christology of hope, I had argued that for Paul we come to know Jesus through what I called "Christological knowing." By Christological knowing I mean the grasp of Jesus' reality which results from practical assimilation to Him in the power of His Breath. This kind of knowing differs from common sense, from scholarship, from any form of theoretical understanding. It consists practically, in Paul's phrase, in putting on the mind of Christ, in learning to perceive reality through His eyes and to choose as He would have chosen had He found Himself in our circumstances. For Paul, putting on the mind of Christ has in the first instance a communal, ecclesial character. The Christian community learns to put on the mind of Christ through mutual charismatic ministry in His name and image. Individuals learn to put on the mind of Christ by active participation in a converted, charismatic community of mutual service transformed by justifying faith. In other words, one puts on the mind of Christ by allowing His Breath to teach one how to live in His image.

Although neither Paul nor the synoptics use the term"Christological know-ing," they both deal with the reality. The Pauline letters leave the concrete na-ture of Christological knowing somewhat vague. The synoptics, however, tell the story of Jesus primarily in order to challenge communities of believers to come to terms with any ambivalence which may yet survive in their relation-ship to their risen Lord. At the heart of all three synoptic gospels lies Jesus' question to His disciples, "Who do you say that I am?"

The synoptic evangelists also use narrative in order to make doctrinal af-firmations. They all, for example, use narrative strategies in order to assert the divinity of Jesus, especially Jesus' cosmological miracles in which He does what only God can do: calm a storm with a simple command, walk on water, and invoke the divine name I AM. The synoptic evangelists, however, do not make doctrine the central focus of their gospels. They focus their narratives rather on the practical demands of discipleship, on living the ideal of God's reign which Jesus embodied and proclaimed and on doing so as Breath-baptized Christians who participate in a eucharistic community of faith which collectively confesses Jesus' divinity and which repents of any behavior which contradicts the gospel.

In the second volume of *The Firstborn of Many*, I argued that one can use a dialectical comparison of synoptic gospel linkages in order to clarify the meaning of Christological knowing by naming the practical demands it makes on the converted Christian conscience. When one does that, one rec-ognizes the inherently practical character of Christian faith. One cannot truly believe *in* Jesus unless one allows His Breath to teach one to live and pro-claim in His sinless image the gospel which He lived and proclaimed. A more traditional theology called such practical faith "living faith."

The negative dramatic linkages dramatize all those sinful attitudes of which Christians must repent. The negative linkages also identify the Satanic powers to which the followers of Jesus must remain inexorably and prophet-ically opposed. The positive dramatic linkages dramatize the fundamental re-alistic and moral demands of Christian conversion as a condition for advanc-ing in Christological knowing. John the Baptist teaches Christians to look, not to him, but to Jesus as the only Breath baptizer. Those whom Jesus baptizes in His Breath, He draws into His relation to God as *Abba*. In all the synop-tics, Jesus relates to the Father in three fundamental ways: in unwavering obe-dience to His mission from the Father to embody and proclaim God's reign, in all-consuming love of the Father, and in unconditioned trust in the Father. The teachings of Jesus give these fundamental religious attitudes practical meaning by revealing in detail the moral demands of life in God's reign. The miracles of Jesus dramatize the saving consequences of Christological know-ing (recall, for example, the three raisings by the hand which Mark narrates), while the cosmological miracles dramatize the depth of the mystery which Jesus incarnates in human form.

A comparative linkage analysis of the synoptic gospels enabled me to accomplish three things. First of all, it gave much more systematic grounding to the understanding of the practical demands of gospel living to which I had prayed my way as a graduate student in the Bronx. Second, it allowed me to describe in theological detail the kind of knowledge of Jesus which one seeks in the second, third, and forth weeks of the *Spiritual Exercises*. Third, a dialectical comparison of gospel linkages prepared a normative insight into how the Christian conscience works. That insight built upon Bill Spohn's analysis of moral decision making in faith. This third insight needs more explanation.

Jesus transformed Jewish religion from a religion of laws and rules into a religion of ideals in which the ideal of the kingdom not only summarized the true intent of the Torah but made more demands than the Law did, not less. Matthew calls that transformation "fulfilling the Law and the prophets." Matthew shows how fulfillment works in the second part of the sermon on the mount, often described as Jesus' proclamation of a new morality. In it Jesus cites some negative precept of the Torah or of popular Jewish piety and then replaces it with a positive ideal which makes far more demands on the conscience than the negative precept ever could. In order to form one's conscience as a Christian, therefore, one needs first to come to clarity about the ideals of God's reign which bind Christian conduct. One must never water down those ideals and the practical demands they make. Nor must one replace them with anything else, like natural law theory or the ten commandments. Having understood clearly the practical demands of life in God's reign, one must next devise a method for relating those ideals to the sinful situation in which one finds oneself. In order to deal realistically with that situation, one must first learn to appreciate the good it embodies. One will not successfully do that until one comes to terms with whatever in the situation one finds threatening. Facing what threatens one in any situation one confronts requires ongoing repentance. Once one has appreciated the goodness in one's situation, one must next regret whatever in it falls short of the ideal of the kingdom. In order to bridge the gap between the ideal of the kingdom and the sinfulness of one's world in creative and transforming ways, one must derive from the vision of the kingdom principles relevant to one's moral situation. One must next derive from the those principles policies which promise to ameliorate the situation and move it the next possible step toward the ideal of the kingdom. One finally needs to devise corporate strategies for making the ameliorating policies realities.

In writing *Economic Justice for All*, the American bishops exemplified this process in an admirable way. They began by appreciating good things about the U.S. economy. One may argue that the bishops failed to critique sufficiently the evils of an aggressive, capitalistic economy; but they did name glaring economic problems and injustices which mar the way the U.S. does business. Next they recalled the ideal of the kingdom and from it derived principles relevant to the problems they had named: principles like preferential option for the poor and respect for the dignity before God of every human person. From those principles they devised economic policies which, in their judgment, promised to solve the problems or ameliorate the injustices. They left it to the faithful to improve, if possible, on their analysis and their proposed policies and then to translate the suggested policies into concrete strategies for moving the U.S. economy the next possible step toward the ideal of the kingdom.

In the third volume of *The Firstborn of Many*, I dealt with doctrinal and practical Christology. In it I treated the gospel of John as marking the transition within the New Testament from narrative to doctrinal Christology. Like the synoptic evangelists, the Beloved Disciple recognized that one comes finally to know who Jesus is by living in His image. The fourth evangelist, however, gave a much abbreviated account of the practical demands of discipleship in Jesus' last discourse. That Jesus would have waited until the night of His betrayal to begin to teach His followers the practical meaning of discipleship has no historical verisimilitude; but the Beloved Disciple puts the bulk of Jesus' teachings on discipleship in the Book of Glory (Chs 13-20) because he grounds discipleship in the paschal mystery which the Book of Glory narrates. For John, the paschal mystery establishes God's reign and defines the moral demands of discipleship. In the last discourse, John's Jesus reduces discipleship to three commands: serve one another as I have served you, love one another as I have loved you, and believe in the Father, the Son, and the Holy Breath. "As I have loved and served you" means "as I have loved and served you in the paschal mystery, i.e., even unto death." The paschal mystery also reveals the mystery of the trinity which the third commandment requires one to believe. Finally, Jesus summarizes these three commands in the omnibus commandment: "If you love Me, keep my commandments."

The fourth evangelist reverses the narrative emphases one finds in the synoptic versions of Jesus and His ministry. The Jesus of the synoptics shows great reticence when it comes to talking about Himself. The Johannine Jesus does practically nothing else. Moreover, the Jesus of the fourth gospel tends to speak from an atemporal point of view as he expounds at great length about the doctrinal differences which divided the members of the Johannine community among themselves and from the synagogue. The Johannine dissidents, probably proto-Gnostics, denied the incarnation, denied that physical death can have saving significance, and denied that Jesus could be really present in a physical act of eating and drinking. Accordingly, John's Jesus reflects at great length about His own divinity and pre-existence with the Father and about His real presence in the Eucharist. Moreover, the Beloved Disciple tells the story of Jesus' passion as the beginning of His glorification and as a saving act which both reveals Jesus as the divine Bridegroom incarnate and begins the new creation.

In the third volume of *The Firstborn of Many*, I argued that the fourth evangelist brought narrative theology as far as it could go and probably further than it ought to have gone. I in no way wanted to understate the extent of the fourth evangelist's theological achievement. All the gospels use narrative strategies to assert Jesus' divinity. The Beloved Disciple, however, found biblical terms for talking about the unity and trinity of the Christian God and about the incarnation of only one member of the divine triad. In addition, he coordinated both these theological firsts with a Biblical language for talking about the gracing of human experience. No small theological achievement that.

Nevertheless, in order to accomplish that impressive theological feat, the fourth evangelist throughout his gospel portrayed Jesus during His mortal ministry discoursing at great length about the doctrinal issues which divided the Johannine community, issues which did not arise until decades after Jesus had died, risen, and sent the sin-forgiving Breath. Those manifest anachronisms deprive the fourth gospel of a lot of historical verisimilitude. I find it unlikely, for example, that Jesus would have harangued Galilean peasants at great length concerning His real presence in a Eucharist He had not even instituted. Because the fourth gospel stretched narrative Christology about as far as it could go and probably further than it ought to have gone, it made historically inevitable the patristic turn to inferential forms of thinking in order to articulate Christological doctrine.

I invoked Lonergan's theory of functional specialties in order to formulate a foundational Christology in part because I wanted to test his claim that a normative insight into the kind of conversion which grounds Christian belief provides the criteria one needs in order to discriminate between sound and unsound doctrine. When I began to deal with the authentication of Christological doctrines, I recognized the importance of first retrieving the kinds of religious experiences on which doctrinal Christology reflects. I accomplished that retrieval through a normative insight into the practical shape of Christological hope and of narrative Christological faith. Until one makes that retrieval, one has no clear sense of the kinds of religious experiences which Christological doctrines attempt to bring to inferential expression.

Threading my way dialectically through the thicket of diverse and often contradictory contemporary accounts of the person and ministry of Jesus forced me to name the kinds of criteria which an integral, five-fold conversion provides for discriminating between sound and unsound doctrine. In the construct of conversion I had developed, affective conversion, intellectual conversion, personal moral conversion, and socio-political conversion can all occur naturally. In my metaphysics of experience, the kind of decision one makes derives its character from the kind of evaluative process it terminates, and different kinds of decisions create different kinds of habits or tendencies. After all, practice makes perfect. If, however, one's evaluative response defines the character of the decision which terminates it and which transforms it from possibility into concrete actuality, one decides naturally whenever one's motives and perceptions prescind from the historical self-revelation and self-communication of God: when, in other words, one decides simply on the basis of perceived created goods. I call all such decisions natural, not graced, not supernatural, because they lack justifying faith; and they build into the human person who makes them tendencies to react and respond only to created goods and therefore in a purely natural manner.

I concluded therefore that a natural conversion in and of itself can only provide negative criteria for calling Christological doctrines into question because as natural it has nothing whatever to say about the actual content of Christian doctrinal beliefs. One ought, therefore, to question any doctrine tinged with serious neurosis, with psychosis, or with human bigotry until one can find some other way to authenticate it. Similarly, one ought to call into question contradictory doctrines, doctrines formulated in manifestly inadequate frames of reference, or doctrines based on invalid, fallacious reasoning until one can find a methodologically sound way to authenticate them. Finally, one ought to call into question any doctrine which, either in what it asserts or in its consequences, justifies personal and public immorality.

Christian conversion, I also saw, provides two interrelated positive criteria for authenticating doctrines or for rejecting them. I called the first positive criterion historical and eschatological because it consists of those events which reveal the Christian God historically: namely, the historical missions of the Son and of the Breath. Both sets of events have an historical character because they happen in space and time; but they also have an eschatological character because in them God acts graciously in space and time in order to undo the effects of human sinfulness and to reorient history to life after death in God with the glorified Jesus. That intervention creates the eschaton, the final age of salvation. Events make doctrines true. The New Testament gives us access to the events which verify or falsify Christological doctrines. If any given Christological doctrine correctly interprets those events, it counts as true. If any given Christological doctrine fails to interpret those events, it counts as false.

The second positive criterion for authenticating doctrines has an ethical character; for the events which reveal the Christian God come with an initial self-interpretation. Jesus had a distinctive religious vision which gave practical expression to what it means to live as a child of God in His image. He called that religious vision the reign of God. Any Christological doctrine which either in what it asserts or in its consequences causes one to live in a way which contradicts the reign of God counts as false.

Even though the natural forms of conversion in and of themselves yield only negative criteria for calling doctrines into question, once transvalued in justifying faith, they can begin to provide positive criteria for authenticating doctrines or calling them into question. When transvalued in faith, for example, affective conversion can yield a normative insight into Christian esthetics by enabling us to name in faith the Christian *summum bonum*, that divine reality ultimately worth living for and, if necessary, worth dying for. When transvalued in faith, intellectual conversion can yield sound normative insights into what constitutes sound and unsound theological method. When transvalued in faith, personal moral conversion and socio-political conversion can give rise to Christian moral theology.

When I brought to bear on Chalcedonian Christology the first positive criterion for authenticating doctrine which Christian conversion grounds, it became obvious that the council of Chalcedon had basically got things right. The New Testament makes it clear that Jesus' disciples first experienced Him as human, as an extraordinary human being, to be sure, as a person of great attractiveness, magnetism, and approachability who could work miracles and expel demons with a simple command, as someone who knew God as *Abba* and who proclaimed a vision of an ideal religious community which He called the reign of God. Then in the paschal mystery, those who saw the risen Christ experienced Him as a life-giving Breath, as the efficacious source of a divine reality and therefore as divine. In both experiences, however, they encountered the same person. Hence, as Chalcedon insisted, in the person named Jesus we encounter only a single subsisting reality which is both human and divine without the two blending into some third reality neither fully divine nor fully human.

Those err, then, who fault Chalcedon with getting Christology wrong. I reject as erroneous any "low" Christology which substitutes Jesusology for Christology. Chalcedon spoke the truth about the Incarnation. The difficulty with Chalcedonian Christology lies not in its error but in its vagueness. In effect, Chalcedon contented itself with setting correct linguistic parameters for talking about the Incarnation; but the council failed to give any clear definition to all of its key Christological terms. The council did not say what it meant by "subsisting reality," by "divine," by "human," and by "the union of the two in a single divine reality." Any post-Chalcedonian Christologist faces the double challenge of clarifying these key Christological terms and then of coming up with a logical, consistent, applicable, and adequate construct of the Incarnation verifiable in the events of Christian revelation.

In the third volume of *The Firstborn of Many*, I argued that, if one replaces classical substance metaphysics with the social, relational, functional, realistic metaphysics of experience which I had derived from Peirce's philosophy, it provides one with a way of thinking the hypostatic union in logical, consistent, applicable, and adequate categories. I argued that when one reads the monothelite controversy in the light of such a metaphysics, the insistence of Maximus the Confessor on the synergy of the divine will and the human will in the Incarnation, the fact that the divine will rules the human will in all of its decisions, held the metaphysical key to formulating a non-contradictory construct of the hypostatic union.

Formulating an experiential construct of the Trinity had caused me to distinguish clearly between autonomy and freedom. Elementary human freedom consists in the ability to distinguish among realistic options. The higher forms of freedom exemplify the liberty to live for beauty, truth, goodness, and God. Liberty results from an integral, five-fold conversion, and it includes dedication to creating a social order which institutionalizes such a conversion. Liberty, therefore, presupposes and builds upon elementary human freedom. Evaluation ultimately grounds and explains a flickering human freedom; for humans remain more or less free to the extent that they succeed in distinguishing as many realistic ways as possible for dealing with any situation they confront. Freedom designates, not a thing, but an adverb. It names the modality of a decision, and that modality results from the kind of evaluation it terminates. I decide freely when I maximize my possible, realistic options before choosing. Freedom, then, ultimately roots itself in evaluation.

As we have seen, freedom has a more-or-less character. Autonomy has an either-or character. Autonomy means the capacity to initiate activity, either evaluations or decisions. Either I thought something true or did not. Either I said or did something, or I did not. Either Shakespeare wrote the dramas attributed to him or someone else did. One cannot reduce autonomy to freedom because they modify different realms of experience and possess irreducible traits, even though without the capacity to initiate my own activity I could not act freely because I could not do anything at all. Autonomy provides, then, a necessary but insufficient ground for free choice, since in order to choose freely I need in addition to use my head to maximize my options before choosing. Autonomy also differs from freedom because it modulates a different realm of experience, the realm of tendency, whereas elementary human freedom ultimately modulates the evaluation which specifies a decision.

My trinitarian theology discerned in the person of the Son an eternal source of obediential efficacy in the Triune God. If, as I had argued in volume one of *The Firstborn*, one can legitimately understand Jesus' humanity as a finite, developing, human experience, then that experience would have had to have been transformed in a divine principle of obediential efficacy. In other words, every conscious and unconscious finite decision which helped create that human experience we call Jesus of Nazareth had to be ruled efficaciously by the Son of God in a way which expressed perfect obedience to the will of the Father and to the empowering illumination of the divine Breath. That human experience remained, however, both finite and fully human and therefore distinct from the infinite divine experience.

When tendencies cease to function autonomously, the person or self they help constitute owns them, experiences them as part of oneself. When, for example, I digest food, I break it down into chemicals and incorporate those chemicals efficaciously into my body. I thereafter experience those same chemicals as part of me because they no longer function autonomously but as integral parts of me as a result of their efficacious incorporation into my body. If they start to function autonomously, they turn into a tumor or a cancer.

If the Son of God ruled His entire human experience obedientially and efficaciously, something analogous happened. By ruling efficaciously the conscious and unconscious decisions which defined the human experience called Jesus of Nazareth, the second person of the Trinity owned it, made it His own, experienced that particular human experience and no other as My finite, developing, human experience, as My growth, My human sensations, emotions, memories, fantasies, ideas, deliberations, pain. In other words, the perfect synergy of divine and human decisions in the hypostatic union transformed the human experience we call Jesus of Nazareth into the finite human experience of being a divine person. At the same time, the human experience we call Jesus of Nazareth remained humanly free to the extent that given its limitations and the limitations of the circumstances it confronted it could at any given moment maximize its human options before choosing.

The reader will find these ideas developed in much more detail in *The Firstborn of Many*. It gave me considerable satisfaction to realize, however, that by changing from a classical metaphysics of substantial essences to a functional, relational, realistic, triadic metaphysics of experience, I had found a way of understanding "person" in a logically consistent way which applied analogously to human persons, to divine persons, and to a divine person who has a human experience. That too struck me as an important theological achievement.

Having formulated an experiential construct of the hypostatic union, my logic and method required me to clarify what that construct meant by specifying deductively its practical operational consequences; for Peircean logic insists that the practical, operational consequences of any genuine insight clarifies its theoretical meaning. This logical insight allowed me to resolve a disputed point in contemporary Christology: namely, the relationship between Christology and soteriology. Does one derive Christology from soteriology as Edward Schillebeeckx suggests; or soteriology from Christology as Wolfhard Pannenberg holds; or does one see Christology as inherently soteriological, as Walter Kasper opines? Peircean logic forced me to cast my lot with Kasper. One cannot understand the full *theoretical* meaning of the hypostatic union until one understands its *practical*, saving consequences.

Dealing with the soteriological consequences of the hypostatic union, however, forced me to face the question of the doctrinal authenticity of medieval atonement Christology in all of its different historical permutations. Anselm of Canterbury created atonement Christology in the twelfth century as a way of arguing for the necessity of the Incarnation. In the process, he replaced a Biblical understanding of atonement with something completely different. In the New Testament, atonement means at-one-ment, the reestablishment of the life-giving relationship with God which sin ruptures and destroys. By atonement Anselm meant substitution, not at-one-ment. Jesus had proclaimed that God forgives us unconditionally. In order to claim God's forgiveness, we need only acknowledge our sinfulness, repent of it, and accept the divine offer to forgive. That offer remains always there for the claiming. Anselm, by contrast, believed that God could not forgive sin until He had first punished the sinner vindictively. Vindictive punishment does not seek to improve the one punished, only to make the person suffer. Anselm's Jesus atones for sin by becoming human and suffering the vindictive punishment which we sinners deserve but which in our case remains insufficient to reestablish the right order in the universe which sin shatters.

As this tradition developed it got more and more sinister. If one measured the enormity of a sin by the dignity of the one offended, as John of la Rochelle, a thirteenth-century commentator on Anselm suggested, then the infinity of God would seem to make human sin require infinite punishment. Duns Scotus explicitly rejected the idea that any finite human could suffer and therefore atone infinitely; and by the end of the middle ages Anselmian atonement theory had gone into something of an eclipse. Martin Luther and John Calvin resurrected it, however, and embellished it with an Augustinian theory of total human depravity. In classical Protestant Christology, sin so corrupts human nature that God can only relate to it in an attitude of undiluted hatred. The Father first vents that hatred on His innocent, crucified Son, even requiring Him to suffer the tortures of the damned so that the Father can thereafter deal mercifully with the rest of us. As I pondered this final development in medieval atonement Christology, I could not help but sympathize with Enlightenment *philosophes* who objected quite correctly that such a God manifests not only a peculiar but an immoral sense of justice.

When I measured medieval atonement Christology by the two criteria supplied by Christian conversion for authenticating doctrines, it failed both tests. It did not interpret correctly the events which the New Testament narrates. Jesus atoned for sin by suffering the worst a sinful humanity could do to Him while sustaining the Father's offer of unconditioned forgiveness and by rising and sending His sanctifying Breath to teach and empower sinful humans to live in His sinless image. Medieval atonement theory also failed the moral test by projecting sinful human vindictiveness into God. It therefore implicitly gave blasphemous divine sanction to immoral behavior.

How, then, does God save us in Jesus? 1) By living a sinless life, the incarnate Son of God recreated humanity in its original state of innocence. 2) By proclaiming the reign of God, He taught humanity the ideals which produce sinless living in all those who embrace them actively and practically. 3) In His passion He began to reestablish the life-giving relationship with God which sin had ruptured, by continuing to sustain His Father's offer of unconditioned forgiveness despite the worst a sinful humanity could do to God incarnate. 4) By rising, He completed the new covenant and fully reestablished a life-giving relationship between a sinful humanity and God because in His risen glory He efficaciously communicates to us the divine Breath who empowers us to accept God's unconditioned offer of forgiveness and to live sinlessly in the image of the incarnate Son of God. I also argued in *The Firstborn of Many* that the traditional titles attributed to Jesus–prophet, priest, king, and judge–all call attention to different aspects of the way He saves us provided we allow the paschal mystery to define what those titles mean and do not apply them to Jesus as we ordinarily understand them. I argued as well that Jesus' sinlessness made Him more perfectly human than us since, when we sin, we fail to achieve the perfection of humanity we might have achieved had we not sinned. Sin diminishes human perfection. It does not exemplify it.

By practical Christology, I mean the way in which commitment to Jesus Christ in justifying faith transforms personal moral and socio-political conversion. In discussing how the transvaluation of personal moral conversion in justifying faith transforms it into Christian charity, with hints from Roberto Unger, I insisted that all the theological virtues–hope, faith, and love–instead of qualifying the purely spiritual powers of intellect and will, as Thomism with its unfortunate operational dualism suggests, actually all have an affective, passionate dimension. In discussing the transvaluation in faith of socio-political conversion I invoked the methods of liberation theology to do an analysis of original sin American-style and to begin to suggest a strategy for conscientizing individualistic Americans to recognize the ways in which our culture institutionalizes sin and Anti-Christ and to begin to take an active stand against U.S. oppression both at home and abroad.

I have tried in this chapter to sketch how my theological system evolved into its present state of development. I do not regard that system as finished; and, if I remain a contrite, Peircean fallibilist, as I fully intend to do, I never shall. I will soon send off to a publisher a one-volume textbook version of my Christology. I am currently at work on a major study of ecclesiastical doctrines. Given the amount of confusion, ambiguity, abuse, and corruption in all the churches (along side of saving grace), it seems to me that one can honestly approach ecclesiology in a contemporary context only by invoking the theological specialty which Lonergan calls "doctrines." Accordingly, I am currently testing whether or not the norms I have derived for discriminating between sound and unsound doctrines and sound and unsound institutional practices have the ability to distinguish between ecclesiology and ecclesiastical ideology,[3] between sound and unsound Church discipline, between authentic and sinful Church institutions. By "ideology" I mean the rationalization of a system of injustice which lyingly palms itself off as self-evident truth. I would anticipate that completing the ecclesiology will take at least eight more years of research in addition to the eight I have already spent on this project. Of course, scholarly projects often take longer than we anticipate.

I also expect that, having completed that study, I will probably want to qualify and update my pneumatology. In addition, I would like to develop at greater length the foundational theology of Christian humanistic education which I sketched in an article in *Horizons*. I also have in my head the outlines of a book on the nominalistic tradition in American philosophy. In it I would like to show that in every generation of American philosophical thinkers, one finds at least one major thinker who acquiesces in the follies of nominalism and at least one other major thinker who offers a viable alternative to that particular philosophical dead end. Such a study would advance the dialectical analysis of U.S. culture through the lens of its philosophical tradition which

I began in *Varieties of Transcendental Experience*. I also have dreams of developing in more philosophical detail the metaphysics of experience which has begun to emerge from attempting a cross-disciplinary approach to theological thinking.

In 2001, I celebrated my golden jubilee as a Jesuit. I returned to New Orleans for a typically New Orleanian wing-ding: four solid days of parties. On the Saturday before St. Ignatius Day, we had a class reunion which included former Jesuit classmates. Al and Barbara managed to arrive in time for the tail end of that party. On Sunday, we had a public Eucharist followed by a reception in the hotel across from our church on Baronne Street. Both the Gelpis and the Delaups showed up en masse. My Aunt Coco also came, Daddy's last surviving sibling. One of the waiters at the reception complimented us on being the biggest and loudest table in the hall. On Monday, having promised the Gelpis that we would return for a Gelpi family reunion in October, we had the Delaup family get together. By the end of three days of partying, Al remarked, "These jubilees are a lot of fun, but they are exhausting." Finally, we had the in-house Jesuit celebration at Loyola University, a Eucharist on the feast of St. Ignatius, followed by what during my training as a Jesuit we used to call a first-class feast.

When the Jesuit community reassembled in Berkeley for the following academic year, our rector, Charlie Moutenot, S.J., told me that we would be celebrating my jubilee together with the anniversaries of other members of the community later that year. Ever the good friend of our school, Bishop John Cummins graciously attended; and Charlie asked me to preside at the Eucharist which preceded the community dinner.

In my homily, as I looked back over fifty years of Jesuit life, I saw an abundance of blessings which won my deepest gratitude: the gift of vocation itself, whose precious value I had had to live in order to appreciate; Jesuit spirituality and all that it implied; my brother Jesuits; the myriad friends I had made inside the Society and outside; the gift of family; my personal Pentecost in the charismatic renewal and the abundance of graces that flowed from it; the privilege of spending most of my professional life assimilating and teaching the word of God; the opportunity to live and work in one of the major ecumenical centers in the world; the community of scholarship and of faith that became the Murray Group; the sublimity of the natural beauty I had shared with wonderful, wonderful friends; the special privilege of having many, many younger Jesuits honor me with the gift of their friendship; the teachers, mentors, and colleagues who had nurtured me to maturity; the joy of art and of the humanities; the gift of life itself and of my mind. The list seemed endless.

With Bishop John Cummins at the Berkeley celebration of my fiftieth jubilee as a Jesuit.

As I looked back on the scholarly work I had done, it seemed to me that I first turned to theology as a way of trying to put order into my chaos. I am still working on that particular project; but gradually over the years my attitude toward doing theology has changed. In the beginning, I prayed my way with a pencil to a new religious identity and felt surprised when what I wrote helped other people as well. Now, having thought and prayed my way to something like an inculturated, theological system, I see myself primarily as someone called by God to think for, with, and in the Church. I have long since renounced any attempt to measure the consequences that the things I write have for other people. I have tried to write what I felt the Lords calling me to write. What it may accomplish lies in Their capable hands.

Colloquy:

I sought You in the tangle of my mind
 to give You back the gift You gave to me,
  at first from need,
   to mend a world You shattered.
    It shackled me,
     and You would have me free.

I knew I did not know,
>*surveyed the risk,*
>>*the brittle fragility of thought,*
>>*the labyrinth of human folly leading nowhere.*

I trusted You to lead
>*and thought I felt Your nudge,*
>>*Your whispering,*
>>*Your presence.*

I followed step by step
>*and saw a mystery unfold*
>>*as You converted thought to love*
>>*until I had no words.*

NOTES

1. In Augustine, the intellect and will enjoy only conceptual distinction and not a real distinction because of the essential simplicity of the divine substance.

2. The term "baptism in the Spirit" derives from the synoptic tradition and does not occur in Paul's letters, even though the apostle talks in his own terms about the reality of "Spirit-baptism."

3. As I have already indicated, by an ideology I mean the rationalization of a situation of injustice which lyingly palms itself off as self-evident truth.

Envoi

At the age of eighty-nine, my mother died of kidney failure at 6:06 P.M. on Thursday, March 21, 1996. She had slowly declined but remained quite active until months before her death. Finally, her doctor told us that she had only weeks or possibly a few more months to live.

On the Sunday of the weekend which opened our spring break, I anointed her in her apartment on the ground floor of Al and Barbara's house. She had spent a few days in the hospital but asked to die at home. In her final years, she had grown increasingly deaf but resisted wearing a hearing aid. Before I anointed her, I told her, "Mother, I am anointing you because the doctor says this is your last illness." "My last what?" she said. "Your last illness," I repeated louder. She nodded. She knew she was dying. I remember thinking as I administered the anointing, "What am I doing? This is supposed to be a rite of healing, and my mother will certainly die." I did not realize at the time that I would get a clear answer to my question.

I had to return to Berkeley that Sunday night to take care of some loose ends at school; but I returned the next day, prepared to stay until Mother died and not knowing how long that would prove. It did not take long.

The following Wednesday, I went down to Mother's apartment after breakfast to see how she was doing. When I asked her, she replied, "I didn't think it would happen so soon." I went back upstairs and told Al and Barbara that Mother said that she was dying. As soon as we had assembled around her bed, she led us in the rosary, which she said daily. When we finished, she said, "Good bye. I am dying. Thank you for everything. I love you very much. You keep praying for me and I will keep praying for you."

At that moment the phone rang. My niece Adrienne was calling Al about her car insurance. Al went upstairs; and, when they had concluded insurance-matters, he told Adrienne that Mother was dying. Al asked her if she wanted to talk to Mother, if Mother felt up to it. Of course, Adrienne did. Al came back downstairs, told Mother that Adrienne was on the phone, and asked her if she felt up to talking. "Oh, yes," she replied; and, when we handed her the receiver, she said, "Good bye, Adrienne. I guess it's time for me to go see God."

When she hung up, Al asked her if she would like us to call my nephew Christopher. Again she answered with a firm "Yes." Christopher lived with his wife Janet and their son Mitchell in Chapel Hill. He was teaching political science at Duke University. Al dialed his home. Janet answered and said that Christopher was working in his office at Duke. Mother, however, also wanted to say good bye to Janet. When she got on the phone, she said, "Good bye, Janet. I love you all. Make sure that you raise Mitchell in the right way; and make sure he knows who I am, because I won't be around when he grows up." We called Christopher in his office; and he too said good bye. Janet got her family a flight to San Francisco at the last minute; and the three of them arrived by the middle of the following day. By that time Mother could not see, but she could hear. They again made their farewells. Adrienne was due to arrive that evening.

On the previous afternoon I spent several hours with Mother, reminiscing about some of the happy times we had enjoyed as a family. I asked her forgiveness for any hurt I had ever caused her. I told her everything I wanted or needed to say to her; a gift for which I feel deeply grateful. At one point I told her, "You know, Mother, when you get to heaven a lot of people who love you very much will be waiting to welcome you."

"I know that," she replied, "That's the good part."

The nurse had instructed us to sedate Mother if she became restless. Late in the afternoon of the day when Christopher and his family arrived, Mother became agitated. The sedation had no effect. Al realized what was happening. Mother felt that she was about to die and was trying to stay alive until Adrienne arrived that night. Al said, "If you have to leave us now, Mother, it's all right. Adrienne loves you very much and will understand if you are not here when she comes." Mother relaxed immediately.

At that moment, David and Sou Riggs, Al and Barbara's friends and neighbors, came to say good bye to Mother. So did Manny and Libby Martinez, a young Hispanic couple who used to stay with Mother when Al and Barbara went away on trips. Al too started reminiscing about our days in New Orleans. He told the story of my father hitting Memere Delaup in the face with a watermelon rind. Laughter filled the room, and Al noticed the sides of Mother's mouth turn up in a little smile. The visitors left. I stayed holding

The Gelpi family at my Mother's eightieth birthday celebration at JSTB: from left to right: Adrienne, Christopher, Barbara, the author, Mother, Albert.

Mother's hand. While Al and Barbara saw the callers to the door, she quietly stopped breathing.

After tears, I realized that the Lord had indeed heard our prayer for healing. We all felt Mother's passing as a singular season of grace.

Losing both one's parents gives one a heightened sense of mortality. So does turning sixty. As I contemplated old age, the call to a new kind of discipline recurred anew in prayer. I had not heard it for about a decade. I recognized that the first call to a new discipline had tided me over the mid-life crisis. I anticipated that the new call would ease me through old age.

As the new call unfolded, I began to perceive more clearly the purpose of old age. It offers one an opportunity to complete this life's work and to prepare oneself for the next life. I have been trying to do both ever since. Completing this life's work seemed to mean bringing off as much as I could of the theological project in which I have been engaged since coming to the People's Republic. I do not know how many of the books in my head I will complete; but I intend to keep working at the project in the years that remain to me.

In that context a word gift came to me during one of my retreats and became the focus of prayer during the next two retreats as well. The word went like this: "Trust Me with your life and final days. I have been and will

continue to be with you in love. Trust My love and never doubt it, for I
have surrounded you with love and will continue to teach you and to lead
you. Abide with Me and follow me." As I have pondered these words again
and again in prayer, I cannot help but hear in them an echo of that old New
Orleans hymn:

> Just a closer walk with Thee,
> Grant it, Jesus, is my plea.
> Daily walking close to Thee,
> Let it be, dear Lord, let it be.
>
> I am weak but Thou art strong.
> Jesus, keep me from all wrong.
> I'll be satisfied as long
> As I walk, let me walk, close to Thee.
>
> When my feeble life is o'er,
> Times for me won't be no more.
> Guide me gently, safely o'er
> To Thy kingdom's shore, to Thy shore.

Bibliography Of Publications

BOOKS

Life and Light: A Guide to the Theology of Karl Rahner (Sheed and Ward, 1966).

Functional Asceticism: A Guideline for American Religious (Sheed and Ward, 1969).

Discerning the Spirit: Foundations and Futures of Religious Life (Sheed and Ward, 1970).

Pentecostalism: A Theological Viewpoint (Paulist, 1971).

Pentecostal Piety (Paulist, 1972).

Charism and Sacrament: A Theology of Christian Conversion (Paulist, 1976).

Experiencing God: A Theology of Human Emergence (Paulist, 1978).

The Divine Mother: A Trinitarian Theology of the Holy Spirit (University Press of America, 1984).

Grace as Transmuted Experience and Social Process (University Press of America, 1988).

Inculturating North American Theology: An Experiment in Foundational Method (Scholars Press, 1988).

Edited: *Beyond Individualism: Toward a Retrieval of Moral Discourse in America* (University of Notre Dame Press, 1989).

Endless Seeker: The Religious Quest of Ralph Waldo Emerson (University Press of America, 1991).

Committed Worship: A Sacramental Theology for Converting Christians (2 vols.; The Liturgical Press, 1993).

The Turn to Experience in Contemporary Theology (Paulist, 1994).

The Conversion Experience: A Reflective Process for RCIA Participants and Others (Paulist, 1998).

Varieties of Transcendental Experience: A Study in Constructive Post-Modernism (The Liturgical Press, 2000).

The Firstborn of Many: A Christology for Converting Christians (3 vols.; Marquette University Press, 2001).

The Gracing of Human Experience (The Liturgical Press, 2001).
Peirce and Theology: Essays in the Authentication of Doctrines (University Press of America, 2001).

IN PROCESS

Encountering Jesus Christ: Rethinking Christological Faith and Commitment.
As We are One: A Study of Church Doctrines.

ARTICLES

"Artistic and Prudential Judgment," *The Modern Schoolman* (March, 1959) 36:163–177.
"The Plotinian *Logos* Doctrine," *The Modern Schoolman* (May 1960) 37:310–315.
"Art and Communism," *Thought* (Spring, 1965) 38:39–55.
"Rahner's Theology of Sacred Heart Devotion," *Woodstock Letters* (Fall, 1966) 95:405–417.
"Understanding Spirit Baptism," *America* (May 17, 1970) 122:520–521.
"Religion in the Age of Aquarius,"*America* (November 13, 1971) 124:292–295.
"Pneuma 72: A Personal Theological Reflection," *New Covenant* (April 1973) 3:27–28.
"Charismatic Renewal: Problems, Possibilities," *The National Catholic Reporter* (August 3, 1973) 9:7.
"Development and Commitment: A Theological Viewpoint," *Seminary Newsletter Supplement No. 3* (November, 1973) 12:11–16.
"Pentecostalism," *New Catholic Encyclopedia Supplement* (November/December, 1974).
"Die amerikanische Pfistbewegung," *Concilium* (November, 1973) 652–657.
"Can You Institutionalize the Spirit?" *New Catholic World* (November/December, 1974).
"Preface" to *The Catholic Cult of the Paraclete* by Joseph H. Fichter, S.J. (Sheed and Ward, 1975) vi–xv.
"A New Look at Confirmation," *The Catholic Charismatic* (March/April, 1976) 1:32–35.
"The New Rite of Reconciliation," *The Catholic Charismatic* (December/January, 1980) 4:4–8.
"Pentecostal Theology: A Roman Catholic Viewpoint" in *Perspectives on the New Pentecostalism*, edited by Russell Spittler (Baker, 1976) 86–103.
"Lent, Repentance: A Parable," *America* (March 12, 1977) 136:223–224.
"Hanging Loose in the Spirit," *The Catholic Charismatic* (December/January, 1980)4:4–8.

"Conversion: The Challenge of Contemporary Charismatic Piety," *Theological Studies* (December/January, 1980) 43:606–628.

"Naming the Spirit," *Proceedings of the Catholic Theological Society of America* (1982) 159–162.

"Two Spiritual Paths: Thematic Grace vs. Transmuting Grace, I & II," *Spirituality Today* (Fall, 1983) 35:241–255; (Winter, 1983) 35: 341–357.

"Breath Baptism in the Synoptics" in *Studies on Pentecostal/Charismatic Experiences in History* (Hendrickson, 1984).

"The Charismatic Church and the Sacramental Church," *Church* (1987) 25–30.

"The Converting Jesuit," *Studies in the Spirituality of Jesuits*, XXIX (May 1985) 49–84.

"Theological Reflections on the Priestly Character of Jesuit Vocation," *Studies in the Spirituality of Jesuits*, XXIX (May, 1987) 49–84.

"Religious Conversion: A New Way of Being" in *The Human Experience of Conversion: Persons and Structures in Transformation*, edited by Francis A. Eigo, O.S.A. (Villanova University Press, 1987) 175–202.

"Le catéchumen en course de conversion," *Lumen Vitae* XLII (1987) 159–171.

"Priesthood" in *Dictionary of Liturgical Theology*, edited by Peter Fink, S.J. (The Liturgical Press, 1990) 1013–1018.

"Emerson's Sense of Ultimate Meaning and Reality," *The Journal of Ultimate Meaning and Reality* (1991).

"Celibacy" in *A New Handbook of Christian Theology*, edited by D.W. Mussner and J.L. Price (Abingdon, 1992).

"Creating the Human: Theological Foundations for a Christian Humanistic Education," *Horizons* (Spring, 1997) 24:50–72.

"The Foundational Phoenix: Regrounding Theology in a Postmodern Age" in *Community and Plurality in Catholic Theology*, edited by Anthony J. Cernera (Sacred Heart University Press, 1998) 35–72.

"Incarnate Excellence: Toward an American Theological Aesthetic," *Religion and the Arts* (Winter, 1999) 2:243–266.

"The Authentication of Doctrines: Hints from C.S. Peirce," *Theological Studies* (1999) 60:261–293.

"A Peircean Approach to Trinity as Community: A Response to Some Responses," *Horizons* 27(Spring, 2000) 114–130.

"Discerning the Spirit among Catholic Charismatics," *Dialog: A Journal of Theology* (Spring, 2002) 41:26–34.

"Finding Christ in the *Spiritual Exercises*," *Review of Ignatian Spirituality* 102(2003) 34:32–68.

Index

Catholic Philosophical Association, 156

Catholic Theological Society of
America, 270, 349

Catholic University of America, 95

Catholic Youth Organization (CYO), 18,
33n4

The Catholic University Review, 96

Catholic Worker Movement, 200

The Catholic World, 96

cause, 118, 124, 141–43, 285–86,
295–96; lost cause, 124

celibacy, 101, 106

Central Intelligence Agency, 94

certain, 251, 357

Chalcedon, council of, 373–74

chance, 231, 284

change, 112, 115, 277–78, 352

Channing, William Ellery, 148

character, vi, 68, 89, 100–102, 107,
152–53, 244, 246, 252, 273, 276–77,
298–301, 314, 329, 340, 359, 367,
373

Chardin, S.J., Pierre Teilhard de, 118

charism (gift), 40, 42, 46, 122, 156,
165–67, 169–74, 176, 184, 191–93,
195–97, 199–204, 222, 225, 298,
300, 310–11, 313–15, 320, 325,
330–32, 334–35, 337, 362, 367

Charism and Sacrament, 197, 222–23,
226, 309, 328, 331

charity, 102, 106, 144, 299–378

Charles the Great, 323

Cheerful Charlies, 158, 179–80

Child, Julia, 123, 125

Christiansen, S.J., Andrew, 190, 294

chief priests, 361, 365

choice, 40, 43–44, 46–47, 108, 111,
141–42, 188, 286, 301, 346–47, 367,
374–76

Christian (Christianity), vii, 10, 41, 56,
97–98, 100–102, 104, 106–7, 126,
142–43, 145, 147, 149, 155, 157,
163, 167, 172, 174, 182, 188,
194,196, 199, 203, 222–23, 225, 228,
234–35, 243–44, 249–51, 255–56,

263–64, 284, 296, 299–300, 302,
309–11, 314–16, 318–22, 324–25,
329–31, 335, 337, 340–42, 344,
351–52, 354, 359, 361, 366, 368,
371–74, 378; anonymous
Christianity, 84; Christian practice,
142, 296; petrine Christianity, 234;
Christian conversion (*see*
conversion)

Christiansen, S.J., Andrew (Drew), 260,
262, 266, 270

christology, iii, viii, 41, 62, 83, 141–42,
145, 185, 224–25, 333–34, 353,
355–78; atonement christology, 41;
christological knowing, 46–47, 186,
367–70; christological question, 359;
doctrinal christology, 370–78;
foundational christology, 253, 281,
358, 371; "high" christology, 358;
kerygmatic christology, 359; *Logos*
christology, 337; "low" christology,
355, 358, 373; narrative christology,
47, 362–64, 371; christology of
hope, 359, 367; Pauline christology,
359–62; practical christology,
377–78; Protestant christology, 41

christomonism, 353

church, v–vi, 10, 18, 32, 54, 62, 70, 89,
94–97, 105, 143, 145, 155, 157, 166,
169–71, 193, 195–97, 200–204, 209,
233–34, 250, 264, 291, 296, 300,
306, 310–11, 314, 317–27, 329–32,
336–37, 339, 361–62, 378, 380;
apostolic church, 170; Orthodox
church, 316–17, 320, 328; Lutheran
church, 306; Unitarian church, 145;
Universalist church, 148

Civil Rights Movement, 19, 93, 95, 291,
294–95

Civil War, 95, 149

The Clangbirds, 126

classic, 263

classism, 291–92

clarity (clarify), 119, 124, 143, 153,
236, 239, 241, 252, 275–76